OUR
MARVELOUS
NATIVE TONGUE

BOOKS BY ROBERT CLAIBORNE

OUR
MARVELOUS
NATIVE TONGUE

The Life and Times
of the English Language

Robert Claiborne

Times
BOOKS

Published by TIMES BOOKS, a division of
The New York Times Book Co., Inc.
Three Park Avenue, New York, N.Y. 10016

Published simultaneously in Canada by
Fitzhenry & Whiteside, Ltd., Toronto

Library of Congress Cataloging in Publication Data

Claiborne, Robert.
  Our marvelous native tongue.

  Includes indexes.
  1. English language—History.   I. Title.
PE1075.C47   1983   420'.9   82-40363
ISBN 0-8129-1038-9

Book design by Susan Windheim

Manufactured in the United States of America

PREFACE

THE seed of this book was planted, I think, when I was ten and studying French with my mother. To help me remember the meaning of French *siège* (seat) she pointed out that it was obviously related to English "siege," in which an army *sits* down around a town and waits for it to surrender. This incident, and doubtless many similar ones now forgotten, began my lifelong fascination with words: where they came from, why they mean what they do and how different words are related.

Under other circumstances, this fascination might have led me to embrace the scholarly field of linguistics. Things being as they were, and I the kind of person I am, I ended up a professional writer and editor, using the English language as an everyday tool of my trade. And it is with languages as it is with people: to really appreciate them, you have to live with them. It was my long professional intimacy with English, extending over twenty-five years, that begot my appreciation of its almost infinite variety of words and expressions—the enormous vocabulary that (as I've explained in the first chapter of this book) makes it the most remarkable and expressive tongue in the world.

In one sense, then, this book is a long love letter to the English language; in another, it is a tribute to the civilization that developed that language. During my lifetime, there have been many harsh things said about English and especially about American society; I've said many of them myself. But in criticizing my native country, America, and my ancestral one, Great Britain, I have always assumed that there was something there worth criticizing, and preserving. I love both America and England not because, like some vocal "patriots," I choose to believe they are without faults, but because of the virtues they share amid the faults. And having spoken out against the faults, I feel the more obligated to speak up for the virtues.

High among the things I love about Britain and America are the marvelous tongue they share—not always amicably—and the fundamental philosophy that underlies their rather different forms of government. As we shall see, moreover, the tongue and the philosophy are not unrelated: both reflect the ingrained Anglo-American distrust of unlimited authority, whether in language or in life. As long as the Americans and the English continue to distrust unchecked power, public or private, and retain the courage and determination to move against those who have or seek it, Anglo-American civilization will, for me, remain worth loving, whatever mistakes or even crimes its leaders may commit.

I hope readers will enjoy reading this book; I have certainly enjoyed writing it. I also hope that reading it will encourage them to appreciate and value their own linguistic and political heritage and will fortify their resolve to preserve it.

Any specialists in linguistics who may get hold of this work should be warned in advance that I have not tried to write a scientific treatise on their rather forbidding subject. I have neither the qualifications nor the desire to write for specialists; I have sought to keep technical terms and concepts at an absolute minimum, and where (as has occasionally happened) I have had to choose between academic precision and readability, I have unhesitatingly picked the latter.

In recounting the life story of the English language I have, of course, respected the facts, as far as they are known—which is sometimes not nearly as far as one would like. Where the facts were ambiguous, I have picked whatever interpretation seemed to me most plausible, and where, as occurred in a few places, they were missing I have frankly resorted to conjecture. As readers will discover, however, the best anecdotes in this book—and often the least believable—are not my, or anyone's, conjectures, but stark fact; I wouldn't have had the nerve to invent them.

I have also kept in mind the rather obvious fact that English, throughout its history, has not been spoken merely, or even predominantly, from church pulpits and other outposts of propriety; it was (and is) spoken also in barnyards, ships' forecastles, ironworks, barracks, taverns and whorehouses. Moreover, my own reading of English history and literature strongly suggests that most English-speakers, at most periods, have been a fairly uninhibited lot. Which is to say that a few of the English words discussed in this book are what some people would call vulgar. I haven't emphasized this aspect of English, but neither have I tried to pretend that it doesn't exist, much as some people might prefer it not to.

To those who may feel that I should have sanitized the English language more thoroughly than I have done, I would say two things. First, the words in question—there are only a handful of them—have been used by some of our greatest writers, including the two greatest, Chaucer and Shakespeare. Second, I would be prepared to bet that not one of them will be unfamiliar to any twelve-year-old kid of normal intelligence. They are not words I would use myself in every sort of social situation, nor do I recommend such indiscriminate use to anyone else. But they *are* part of the English vocabulary—for some groups, notably soldiers and sailors, almost a predominant part! Therefore I deem them worthy of at least brief notice.

The facts on which this book is based were drawn almost entirely from standard sources, most of which I have listed in the appendix. However, I want to note here my gratitude to Calvert Watkins of Harvard, for information on Indo-European and the Indo-Europeans; to James B. Anderson of the University of Louisville, for some useful pointers on the early relations between English and Norman-French; to Lionel Casson of New York University, for some facts on the evolution of Latin; to J. L. Dillard of Northwestern State University (Louisiana), for clarifying some points on Black English and other American dialects; to Mervyn Jones, for information on English dialects; to Eve Merriam, for drawing my attention to some recent publications on Strine by Prof. Afferbeck Lauder; to Drs. Marian and Don Melish of Honolulu, for drawing my attention to da kine; to my daughter Amanda, for supplying me with some recondite terms in legalese; to Rudolf Flesch, for up-to-date information on illiteracy in America; and to my sister, Clara Claiborne Park, and her husband, David, both of Williams College, for information respectively on the current state of English teaching and on Pidjin English. None of these helpful people, of course, is responsible for any errors I may have made in recounting the facts they supplied, let alone my interpretations of the facts. My wife, as always, made a number of suggestions for improving the text, most of which I have gratefully accepted.

Further appreciation is due my agent, Peter Skolnik, and my editor, Jonathan Segal, for negotiating the contract that enabled me to write the book. Jon also showed exemplary patience in awaiting the completion of a manuscript that, for reasons beyond my control or his, took a good deal longer than either of us had expected. However, I find it hard to forgive him for insisting that I eliminate a number of fascinating digressions, on the ground that they would distract the reader; even more unforgivably, he was right.

ROBERT CLAIBORNE
New York and Truro, 1978–82

CONTENTS

OUR
MARVELOUS
NATIVE TONGUE

. . . We leave their marvelous native tongue
To Englishmen . . .
—W. H. AUDEN AND
LOUIS MACNEICE

1. THE IMPORTANCE OF SPEAKING ENGLISH

A Most Extraordinary Language

☙

The miracle of our land's speech—so known
And long received, none marvel when 'tis shown!

— KIPLING

You English words, I know you:
You are light as dreams, tough as oak,
Precious as gold, as poppies and corn,
Or an old cloak . . .

— EDWARD THOMAS

BY any standard, English is a remarkable language. It is, to begin with, the native tongue of some 300,000,000 people—the largest speech community in the world except for Mandarin Chinese. Even more remarkable is its geographic spread, in which it is second to none: its speakers range from Point Barrow, Alaska, to the Falkland Islands near Cape Horn; from the Shetland Islands north of Scotland to Capetown at the southern tip of Africa; from Hong Kong to Australia's island state of Tasmania. It is the predominant language in two of the six inhabited continents (North America and Australia), and possesses a large block of speakers in a third (Europe) and a sizable one in a fourth (Africa).

English is also by far the most important "second language" in the world. It is spoken by tens of millions of educated Europeans and Japanese, is the most widely studied foreign tongue in both the U.S.S.R. and China, and serves as an "official" language in more than a dozen other countries whose populations total more than a billion—a medium of communication in political and intellectual life for peoples speaking different tongues under the same flag. Of these, only a small fraction speak it with any fluency—but even 2 percent of a billion adds up; a recent survey estimated that those using English as a second language considerably outnumber its native speakers. English is the lingua franca of scientists, of air pilots and traffic controllers around the world, of students hitchhiking around Europe, and of dropouts meditating in India or

3

Nepal. There has never been a "world language," nor is there likely to be, but English is the nearest thing to it that has ever existed.

The expansion of English around the world has been matched by the infiltration of English words into the vocabularies of dozens of other countries. Japanese sports fans talk knowledgeably of *beisuboru* and *garafu* (golf) over glasses of *koka-kora;* Spanish speakers, sometimes stimulated by too many *cocteles,* wax frenetic over *futbol*, while their newspaper *columnistas* deplore the spread of *gangsterismo.* West German newspapers run *Reporten* of legislative *Hearings* on *das Fallout* and *die Recession,* and cover *Press Konferenzen* complete with *no Komment* and *off die Rekord;* in France, *teenagers* (pronounced "teenah*zhair*") wearing blue *djins* buy *hot dogues* from street vendors.

The size of this linguistic infiltration—some would say invasion—has never been measured; one French savant has claimed, with considerable exaggeration, that some five thousand common English words, plus tens of thousands of technical terms, passed into French between 1953 and 1963 alone. Predictably, the influx has evoked denunciations from self-appointed guardians of linguistic "purity" in several countries. A few years ago, for example, a Soviet journalist, one Vladimir V. Vasilyev, deplored Russian adoption of such English terms as *referi, offis, servis, boss* and *plantatsiya* (plantation), and urged a declaration of war on "the torture of the Russian tongue"; similar viewings-with-alarm have come from Germany, Spain and Greece. Most violent of all has been the reaction of some French intellectuals. In 1963, Prof. René Etiemble, denouncing *"franglais"*—*français* contaminated with *anglais*—declared that unless something was done, "in forty years' time the French language will have ceased to exist." Soon after, the Académie Française—which has a strong claim to being the world's stuffiest academic body—set about preparing a list of linguistic no-no's *impropres à la langue.*

The truth is that if borrowing foreign words could destroy a language, English would be dead (borrowed from Old Norse), deceased (from French), defunct (from Latin) and kaput (from German). When it comes to borrowing, English excels (from Latin), surpasses (from French) and eclipses (from Greek) any other tongue, past or present. Well over *half* our total vocabulary is foreign; of the five English words cited by Tovarish Vasilyev as "torturers" of the Russian tongue, not one is "pure" English ("boss" comes from Dutch, "plantation" from Latin and "referee," "office" and "service" from French). Likewise, of the thousand or two recently borrowed English words that are allegedly destroying French, I'd give long odds that a large proportion were not only borrowed earlier into English, but borrowed from French. Nor is there anything new about this: earlier words that crossed the Channel from France to England and back again include *le rosbif* of Old England, *le sport,* and the useful verb *parquer,* as in *"Parquez l'auto!"*

For centuries, the English-speaking peoples have plundered the world for words, even as their military and industrial empire builders have plundered it for more tangible goods. And linguistic larceny has this major advantage over more conventional types of theft: it enriches the perpetrator without impoverishing the victim. Nor have these centuries of linguistic peculation left English "faceless and clichéd"; on the contrary, they have given us the largest, most variegated and most expressive vocabulary in the world.

The total number of English words lies somewhere between 400,000 —the number of current entries in the largest English dictionaries—and 600,000—the largest figure that any expert is willing to be quoted on. By comparison, the biggest French dictionaries have only about 150,000 entries, the biggest Russian ones a mere 130,000.

Our uncertainty over the size of the English vocabulary arises in part out of a longtime propensity among English speakers for making the same "word" serve several different functions. Thus "love" means something we feel, but also something we do—not to mention a zero score in tennis; do we count it as one word, or two, or three? Then, do slang words count, or dialect terms? If we include scientific and technical terms, most of them used by only a small percentage of English speakers, what about the special jargons and lingoes of various trades and subcultures: the newspaperman's "sidebar" (a subsidiary story running alongside the main story), the printer's "ems" (type spaces the width of a capital M) or the physician's "i.v." (intravenous) injection?

But no matter how one reckons up the numbers, the total is enormous. Of course, bigger isn't necessarily better; often it is a good deal worse. Words, on the other hand, are a kind of natural resource; it is impossible to have too many of them. Not, indeed, that any one of us will ever get around to using more than a fraction of our enormous thesaurus ("treasury"—from Greek) of words, not least because tens of thousands of them are intelligible only to specialists. But even the fraction in general use endows us with a uniquely rich assortment of synonyms on almost any subject under the sun: words that mean more or less the same thing, yet each of which possesses its own special qualities of sound and rhythm and shade of meaning. A couple of paragraphs back, I managed with no effort to include four different words referring to robbery in just three sentences: "plunder," "larceny," "peculation" and "theft" (all but the last are borrowed!). Had I cared to tax my ingenuity and the reader's patience, I could have injected as many again.

Consider merely one category of our words, verbs, and one subdivision of those: the verbs that deal with the everyday activities of eating, sleeping, working and playing. At table, we may eat, devour, consume, munch, nibble or gulp our food; if we then feel overstuffed, we may doze, nap, snooze, sleep, slumber or nod off. In factory or office or down on the farm, we work, labor, toil, drudge or slave at our appointed tasks—though we may sometimes loaf, laze, dog it or goof off. When the whistle blows, we play, sport, revel, make merry or amuse ourselves, some of us with drinking, tippling, boozing, carousing, wetting our whistles, bending an elbow or tying one on. And if, perchance, we find the strain of all this activity, linguistic and otherwise, too much to take, we may go crazy, mad or insane; wax lunatic; crack up; go berserk or run amok—not to speak of flipping out, going bananas or suffering a nervous breakdown.

Like the wandering minstrel in *The Mikado,* with songs for any and every occasion, English has the right word for it—whatever "it" may be. We have tough, blunt words that ram their way into the guts; caviling, quibbling words to bemuse the listener or reader with sophistical fallacies. We have sublime words to frame our most exalted sentiments or to lend a specious nobility to the tritest truisms; crude words spat out to pick a fight or just to let off steam. Our words can glide with the supple grace of a ballerina or lumber at the lumpish pace of a pedant; they can embellish our utterances with elegant arabesques of sound and sense or obfuscate them with meretricious and sesquipedalian rhetoric. They can scorch like the desert sun, caress like a summer's breeze, sting like winter sleet; they can say anything—or nothing.

It is the enormous and variegated lexicon of English, far more than the mere numbers and geographical spread of its speakers, that truly makes our native tongue marvelous—makes it, in fact, a medium for the precise, vivid and subtle expression of thought and emotion that has no equal, past or present.

At this point, some readers will suspect me of exaggeration if not outright cultural chauvinism. Can I really be claiming that English is not merely a great language but the greatest? Yes, that is exactly what I'm saying—and I don't consider myself any sort of chauvinist.

Whether any culture can be shown to be "better" overall than any other is doubtful. But it is a matter of historical record that certain cultures have been better *at certain things* than others. For example, be-

tween 1814 and 1914, England and America produced some able painters—yet would anyone seriously compare them with French artists of the
same period, not to mention the great Dutchmen of the seventeenth
century, or the great Italians of the fourteenth to sixteenth centuries?
Between 1650 and 1900, the German-speaking peoples produced half a
dozen top-rank composers and as many second-rank ones, while England
has not had a major composer since Handel (d. 1759)—and *he* was a
German! Anyone with even a modest knowledge of cultural history could
easily cite a dozen more examples.

If all these peoples have made their own remarkable, even unique
cultural contributions, it doesn't seem to me chauvinistic to credit the
English-speaking peoples with their own unique achievements. And one
of these, surely, is our English tongue, along with the rich heritage of
prose, poetry and drama it has helped create.

Another such achievement—not, I think, unconnected with our linguistic and literary ones—is our rooted distrust of arbitrary, unlimited power,
a distrust that we have successfully incorporated into our political institutions and kept there for more than three centuries. Nearly all native
English-speakers have an almost automatic dislike of people who arbitrarily tell them what to do, what to say—or how to say it. There has never
been, thank God, an English or American equivalent of the Académie
Française, and any English prime minister or American president who
proposed to "purify" the language (as did a recent French president)
would be laughed out of office.

Like any other language, English ultimately reflects the imagination
and creativity of those who speak and write it, from poets and scholars
to crooks and beggars. And though Anglo-American linguistic creativity
is doubtless no more vigorous than that of many other peoples, it has
operated with almost no inhibitions, while in other places it has too often
been checked (though never blocked absolutely) by the upraised finger
of official or scholarly authority.

The unchecked flood of linguistic invention and borrowing that has
made English what it is has, like any flood, carried with it quantities of junk:
clichés, ephemeral "in" words, words that are self-consciously learnèd or
self-consciously cute. But sooner or later, the junk decays, leaving behind
a rich sediment of new and useful words whose accumulations over the
centuries have nourished British and American speech and writing.

The story of the life and times of English, from perhaps eight thousand
years ago to the present, is both a long and a fascinating one. To make

any sense of that story, however, we need first to understand some basic facts about language in general.

To begin with, language is a system of communication. I make this rather obvious point because to some people nowadays it isn't obvious: they see language as above all a means of "self-expression." Of course, language *is* one way that we express our personal feelings and thoughts —but so, if it comes to that, are dancing, cooking and making music. Language does much more: it enables us to convey to *others* what we think, feel and want. Language-as-communication is the prime means for organizing the cooperative activities that enable us to accomplish as groups things we could not possibly do as individuals. Some other species also engage in cooperative activities, but these are either quite simple (as among baboons and wolves) or exceedingly stereotyped (as among bees, ants and termites). Not surprisingly, the communicative systems used by these animals are also simple or stereotyped. Language, our uniquely flexible and intricate system of communication, makes possible our equally flexible and intricate ways of coping with the world around us: in a very real sense, it is what makes us human.

Language is no less important as a means of communicating not with others but with ourselves: of thinking. Nearly all of us do our thinking in words, which symbolize objects and events (real or imagined) and the relationships among them. Mostly we don't "think out loud"—but we still "hear" the words in our minds. And if we choose, and know how, we can manipulate these silent words to symbolize *new* relationships among the objects and events they symbolize—new ideas, in fact. In this way, language has become not merely a system of communication but the most important medium of innovation—of devising new (and perhaps better) ways of coping with our environment and our fellows.

Any language is constructed in accordance with certain rules, which collectively we call its grammar. Ignorant or careless writers sometimes assert that such-and-such a language (usually spoken by some "primitive" people) has "no grammar" or "not much grammar." Taken literally, these people are talking nonsense. Every language possesses its own set of rules, because without the regularities of sound and structure that the rules specify, nobody could learn it. Some languages, indeed, have relatively *simple* grammars, employing a limited number of broad rules with few exceptions. But the simplicity has no relationship to the simplicity or complexity of the society that uses such a language. Both English and Chinese, spoken in complex and long-established societies, have relatively simple grammars, while Navaho grammar is so complicated it is virtually impossible to master unless you learn it in childhood.

Languages (apart from a handful of sign languages) are composed of sounds; grammar tells you how to deploy those sounds to say what you want to say. Like Caesar's Gaul, it is divided into three parts. *Phonetics* specifies which of the hundreds of sounds that the human vocal apparatus can produce are "permitted" in the language under discussion; it also specifies which combinations of sounds are permitted and which not. *Vocabulary* (or *semantics*) specifies which, among all the "possible" combinations specified by phonetics, actually mean something, and what they mean. *Syntax*, finally, specifies how meaningful combinations of sounds —loosely, words—can be combined into meaningful utterances. From one standpoint, then, any grammar is a system of progressive limitations: not all sounds or sound groupings are "possible," not all possible groupings are meaningful, and not all sequences of meaningful groupings make sense.

A fundamental point about any grammar is that every one of its rules (and also every exception to the rules) is arbitrary, the product not of logic but of consensus and custom: languages exist because the peoples who speak them have "agreed" that they must be constructed according to certain patterns. The agreement is quite unconscious—few of us could, even if pressed, list the rules that shape our everyday speech—but the rules are no less real and binding for all that. Moreover, as we shall see many times in later chapters, the customs that collectively make up a grammar are, like all customs, subject to change over time, meaning, of course, that the language itself changes.

A quick survey of English grammar can give us some perspective on how our tongue stacks up against some other major languages. At the same time, we can absorb some terms and concepts that we will need to talk intelligibly about its history and evolution.

In phonetics, English is more diversified than most languages; that is, it employs more different sounds than average. Nobody has ever enumerated the total number of distinguishable sounds that human beings can make, not least because "distinguishable" depends heavily on who is doing the distinguishing. English, for instance, does not distinguish between the rather explosive P-sound of "pit" and the softer one of "tip," but some Native American ("Indian") tongues do. What is certain is that collectively the world's languages include some hundreds of different sounds, but none of them uses more than a fraction of this total. The present record is held by Chipewyan, a native language of western Canada, with forty-five different sounds (one language of the Caucasus is reported to use seventy-five, but this has not been verified). At the other end of the scale is Hawaiian, which makes do with only twelve. World-wide, the average is somewhere between twenty-five and thirty, which puts English, with over forty, well above average.

The relatively high number of English sounds is a plus from the stand-point of English prose and poetry, since it adds variety and richness to their sound patterns. For the foreigner trying to learn English, however, it is a clear minus, since he or she will most likely find some of our sounds unfamiliar and therefore hard to pronounce. As children, all of us auto-matically pick up the phonetics of any language we may be exposed to, but this becomes increasingly difficult as we grow older.

Further problems for the foreigner arise out of the relatively intricate phonetic combinations found in English. As we've already noted, phonet-ics specifies not just which individual sounds are possible but which combinations of those sounds can be used to make words or syllables, and also (in some cases) where in a word or syllable they can be used.

The simplest phonetic structures are found in Hawaiian and other Polynesian tongues, in which a syllable can consist only of a single conso-nant followed by a vowel, or of a vowel alone. (Japanese phonetic patterns are only a little more complicated.) I don't know what language holds the record for syllabic complexity (perhaps Russian), but English must cer-tainly be a contender. Though many of our syllables are of the two simple "Polynesian" types, many others sandwich a vowel between two or three or, in at least one case, no less than seven consonants: the word "strengths" begins with a cluster of three consonants and ends—if it is pre-cise-ly ar-tic-u-la-ted—with four: /ng/, /k/, /th/ and /s/. (Letters enclosed by slashes refer to sounds; words thus enclosed from here on in will be spelled phonetically.)

The intricate clusters of consonants that English sometimes uses, like the number of individual English sounds, makes for phonetic and rhyth-mic variety in our tongue. However, the variations are still quite strin-gently limited. To say, for instance, that English words can and do begin with one, two or three consonants is not to say that they can begin with *any* consonant or combination of consonants. For single consonants, the limitations are barely noticeable: an English word can begin with any consonant sound but two: /ng/ (as in "siNG") and the /zh/ found in the middle of "pleaSure." But when it comes to *two* consonants at the begin-ning of a word, we use only fifty of the possible five hundred or so combinations (thus /sn/ is possible, but not /bn/, /dn/, /fn/ or most other pairs of similar pattern). And when it comes to groups of three consonants, though in theory there are over thirteen thousand possibilities, English actually employs only eight—and two of these very rarely.

Turning to vocabulary, we find, as noted above, that just as only a small proportion of the ways in which English sounds can be combined is phonetically "possible," so a still smaller proportion of these combinations is meaningful. The distinction can be seen when we compare the combinations "bnick," "blick" and "brick." The first cannot possibly be an English word; indeed, many English-speakers would call it unpronounceable, though any member of B'nai Brith knows better. The second *could* be an English word, as "block" is (that is, it doesn't violate the rules of English phonetics)—only it isn't. The third not only could be a word but is.

Vocabulary—the list of meaningful sound combinations in a language —is always the hardest aspect of a language to master, because it has virtually no rules at all. The phonetic rules of a language may be complicated, as are those of English, but once you have mastered them you can say pretty certainly that such-and-such a group of sounds *might be* a word. However, neither these nor any other rules will give you much help in deciding whether it really *is* a word. If your ear or the dictionary tells you that people use it as a word, then it is one; if not, not.

I emphasize this point because some grammarians and authorities on English usage have been heard to say that this or that combination of sounds, though widely used by native English speakers, is "not a word." This is nonsense: if enough people use any combination of sounds as a word, then by God it is a word, all the authorities in the world to the contrary. What these well-meaning folk are probably trying to say is that they don't like the word and don't think it should be used—which is as may be, but has nothing to do with the actual "wordness" of the sounds in question. ("Wordness," by the way, really isn't a word, since I just invented it—but if enough people ever start to use it, it will be.)

Syntax—the rules for putting words and other linguistic elements together to make meaningful statements—is by all odds the most complicated part of linguistics, far too complicated for even a summary treatment here. I shall therefore concentrate on a few aspects of English syntax which have changed markedly over the past couple of thousand years. A useful way of doing this is to contrast English with Latin. I have picked that language not because (as some Latinists would have it) its syntax represents some sort of linguistic ideal (it doesn't) but rather because Latin syntax is not unlike English syntax some twelve hundred years ago, and is even more like the syntax of the "proto-English" (usually called West Germanic) spoken around the beginning of the Christian era. Latin has also contributed heavily to the *vocabulary* of modern English, but that is a story for later.

English and Latin (and, as far as I know, all other languages) indicate syntactic relationships in three ways. *Inflection* involves changing the word in some way—in English and Latin by changing the ending (love/loving), or in English by changing a vowel within the word (sing/sang/sung), a process technically called ablaut. Some English inflections show relationships indirectly, by indicating the syntactic category of the word in question, at least to a degree. Thus "love" is either a noun or a verb; if preceded by a noun or pronoun ("I love you"), it must be a verb; if followed by a verb ("Love is blind"), it's a noun. "Loving," on the other hand, must take the role of a noun ("Loving is part of living") or of an adjective ("a loving husband"); again, the context will determine which. A few English inflections indicate relationships directly, as in "the farmer's daughter," in which the "'s" added to "farmer" shows his relationship to the young woman. Finally, some inflections change the meaning rather than the syntactic category of the word; thus "sing" and "sang" are both verbs, but mean somewhat different things.

The second method of showing syntactic relationships I choose to call *addition:* adding something to the sentence that defines the relationship between two (or sometimes more) other words. Two common categories of these "additives" in English are prepositions and conjunctions. Thus the additive prepositional phrase "the daughter of the farmer" shows the same relationship as the inflectional phrase "the farmer's daughter."

The third method of showing syntactic relationships is by *position,* which is almost self-explanatory. The headlines in the old story, DOG BITES MAN and MAN BITES DOG, manage, without the aid of either inflections or additives, to distinguish between the biter and the bitten.

Latin syntax relied heavily on inflection, less heavily on addition, and relatively little on position, while modern English, with few inflections, must rely more heavily on addition and (especially) position. The Latin versions of the two headlines above could be written CANIS MORDIT HOMINEM and CANEM MORDIT HOMO, in which the inflections of the two nouns, with no additives or change in position, show unambiguously who did what to whom.

Latin nouns were inflected in five (occasionally, six or seven) different "cases." The case inflection (e.g., *canis* vs. *canem*) showed whether the noun was the subject, the direct object or the indirect object of the verb, indicated possession and similar relationships, or had one of certain other functions in the sentence. Moreover, the inflections were different for singular and plural, giving a total, in theory, of ten different inflections for each noun (in practice, certain inflections were identical in two or more different cases). Even worse, the inflections differed from one noun to another, according to which of several categories, called declensions, it fell into. Most English nouns, by contrast, have only two inflections, singular and plural, and none has more than four—three of which sound alike, though they are spelled differently (farmer/farmer's/farmers/farmers'). The only exceptions are a few "irregular" plural forms (ox/oxen; deer/deer)—the vestiges of a declensional system resembling that of Latin.

Another major difference between Latin and modern English is that the former employed "grammatical gender"—that is, nouns were classified as masculine, feminine or neuter, and pretty arbitrarily. Thus *miles,* soldier (whence "military"), was masculine, while the equally male *nauta,* sailor (whence "nautical"), was feminine. The soldier's sword, *gladius* (whence the gladiolus with its sword-shaped leaf), was masculine, but his other weapon, the javelin or *pilum* (whence the pile that supports a wharf), was neuter. And so on.

So far as the nouns themselves were concerned, grammatical gender had no significance. Grammarians have speculated that it may once have had some special semantic or syntactic function, but those days, if they ever existed, were long gone in Roman times; the three noun genders had become signposts to linguistic ghost towns. They were distinctly important, however, in dealing with adjectives, since these had to be inflected so as to "agree" with the noun they referred to in gender, case and number, and with pronouns, since these had to agree with their nouns in gender and number and be in the correct case for their function in the sentence. Since there were three genders, five cases and two numbers (singular and plural), this meant $3 \times 5 \times 2$ or 30 inflectional forms for every adjective and pronoun.

Given the quite flexible word order of the Latin sentence, all these inflections were useful, since they showed which pronoun or adjective referred to which noun. Moreover, they enabled the Roman writer or orator to juggle the word order in various ways for the sake of emphasis, euphony or simply showing off, without muddying his meaning. From the standpoint of a foreigner trying to learn Latin, however—as millions of Roman subjects had to do—the multiplied inflections were inevitably confusing. (How they dealt with this problem we shall see later.) In the English sentence, by contrast, the word order is far less flexible, because position rather than inflection rules; for variety, euphony and other rhetorical effects we must rely mainly on our immense vocabulary.

Since word order is so central to English syntax, let's take a closer look at how it works. The earlier example involving DOG BITES MAN is the simplest case, but because of its simplicity it does not use any syntactic "markers"—certain types of words (prepositions, conjunctions and a few verbs) and some inflections—which play a very important role in defining the syntactic categories of the words adjacent to them in an English sentence.

As an example of how our marker-positional system works, we can do no better than study a famous English verse, in which I have emphasized the markers.

> 'Twas *brillig,* and the *slithy tove*s
> Did *gyre* and *gimble* in the *wabe;*
> All *mims*y were the *borogroves,*
> And the *mome rath*s *outgrabe.*

Now unless you happen to be extraordinarily well up on *Through the Looking Glass,* you can have only the dimmest notion of what's going on here. Yet you know more than you think. The toves were obviously gyring as well as gimbling; the raths, while engaged in outgrabing (or perhaps outgribing), were in some way related to mome, or had the quality of momeness, and so on. In fact, the markers enable you to place every nonsense word but two in its proper syntactic category.

> 'Twas *(noun or adjective),* and the *(adjective) (noun)*s
> Did *(verb)* and *(verb)* in the *(noun);*
> All *(adjective)* were the *(noun)*s,
> And the *(adjective or attributive noun) (noun)*s *(verb).*

How do we make these deductions—as we do, quite unconsciously, every time we hear or read an English sentence? Well, " 'Twas" must be followed by either a noun (" 'Twas midnight") or an adjective (" 'Twas cloudy"), but without additional knowledge we can't be sure which is meant here. On the other hand, "and the" must be followed by either a noun or an adjective+noun phrase; since there are two words following it, they must be a phrase, with the adjective—as nearly always in English —preceding the noun. In the second line, the auxiliary verb "did" tells us a verb is coming up, while "and" signals that a second verb is on the way. The rest you can work out for yourself.

The reduction of the number of inflections to simplify syntax has occurred in all western European languages over time, but to a lesser degree than in English. In particular, all of them cling to the quite unnecessary complication of grammatical gender, though most of them now use only two genders, not three. Like English, their syntax relies mainly on additives and word order, though the order differs somewhat from one to another. Thus adjectives normally precede nouns in grammatical (adj.) English (n.) but follow them in *français grammatical.* By contrast, in both English and French the verb normally follows its subject as closely as possible, whereas in German they often at opposite ends of the sentence fall. But any word order is as "logical" as any other, once you're used to it.

The simplicity of English syntax, I must emphasize, does not make it any clearer or more eloquent; what it does is ease the task of the foreigner who wishes to learn it—thereby compensating somewhat for the difficulty posed by English phonetics. Picking up a language as an adult is largely a matter of memory, and the more different inflectional forms, evidently, the more there is to memorize.

Yet our syntax, though relatively simple, is not as simple as it looks, especially in the case of some of our short, everyday verbs such as "make," "put," "get" and "go." When any one of these verbs cohabits with any of several equally everyday adverbs, such as "up," "on," "off" and "away," the offspring often have little resemblance to either parent —or to one another.

Consider, for example, an imaginary printer somewhere in these United States whose job is to *make up* pages for the press. Having missed a day on the job, he *makes up* the lost pay by working overtime. On payday, some of his good buddies *make up* a five-man poker game; he sits in, wins $40, and gets home in the small hours. Understandably, he tries to *make up* a story that will pacify his wife; it doesn't. Next day, he seeks to *make up* for his misbehavior by suggesting an evening out; after some hesitation, his wife *makes up* her mind to forgive him, *makes up* her face, and off they go.

A foreigner confronted with such goings on is likely to feel rather like the drunk in the old vaudeville sketch who keeps wandering on and off stage where two other actors are making with the jokes. At last he gazes blearily at them and inquires, "Shay, are you guysh in *all* the roomsh?"

As the foreigner progresses further with English, he will discover to his further confusion that nearly all the slippery adverbs that have been giving him trouble also double as adjectives or prepositions—sometimes both. We go *in* (adv.) the house, at which point we are *in* (prep.) it, though if unwelcome visitors call we may pretend to be not *in* (adj.). Indeed, this protean little word can even turn into a noun; who doesn't enjoy having an *in* with the powers that be?

Such shifts from one syntactic category to another are almost routine in English. As we noted earlier, "love" (like many other verbs) can double as a noun ("for the love of Mike"); indeed, it can even serve as an adjective ("love story"). Adjectives turn into verbs, as when we *slow* our steps, or into nouns, as any *black* can testify. This syntactic plasticity, which is so notable a feature of English, is in part a consequence of its loss of inflectional endings, which once told you fairly unambiguously whether a word was a noun, a verb or whatever.

Just as English syntax has changed over the centuries, so have English phonetics and English vocabulary. Thus the sound we write as "ch" appeared in English only about fifteen hundred years back, while the guttural sound /kh/ disappeared about five centuries ago, except in Scotland, (where it is spelled "ch," as in "It's a braw, bricht moonlicht nicht"). "Know" and "gnaw" were once pronounced as spelled, though today most of us would consider the combinations /kn/ and /gn/ unpronounceable.

As syntax and phonetics go, so goes vocabulary. New words come in, old ones drop out or change their meaning. Less than four hundred years ago, Shakespeare could write of "rats and mice and such small deer" without trying to be cute. Rather, he was using "deer" in its original sense: animal (of any sort), which is what its German counterpart, *Tier*, still means (the Berlin Tiergarten is an "animal garden"—a zoo). "Nice" once meant "stupid," "shape" meant, among other things, "sex organs," and "soluble"—I'm not making this up—originally meant "not subject to constipation."

The ever-changing, ever-growing vocabulary of English is, finally, its most remarkable feature. Where did all these words come from?

Many words, in English or any other language, don't "come from" anywhere, in the sense that they have been in the language, in one form or another, for as far back as we can trace. "Father" and "mother" are two out of several thousand examples: they have been English words for as long as there has been an English tongue, and for thousands of years before that, though their pronunciation has changed considerably.

New words come above all from new situations and experiences. As societies evolve and become more complex, their members are exposed to more varied experiences and things, and also feel moved to say more intricate and subtle things about their experiences; if their existing vocabulary doesn't provide the tools, they will invent or borrow new words. Sometimes, too, old words for quite mysterious reasons fall out of favor and are replaced by a new term for a familiar thing, as "animal" replaced "deer"—though the latter of course remained in English to denote a particular family of animals. People are also prone to play with words, and the playful, slangy metaphors, puns and nonsense words that they devise may (though they usually do not) become permanent parts of the national vocabulary. A generation ago, Stephen Potter invented "gamesmanship" and "one-upmanship"; both are now tolerably familiar words, and the latter has even begotten, by the linguistic process called "back formation," the verb "to one-up" somebody. Further back, Lewis Carroll, in the poem whose first verse we've already analyzed, invented "chortle," apparently by fusing "chuckle" and "snort"; it's still English a century later.

"Gamesmanship," though it was an "invented" word, also illustrates a very common way of making new words: by combining old words, or other linguistic elements, in new ways. Thus "father," which has "always" been in English, has over the centuries begotten "fatherly," "fatherhood," "grandfather," "godfather," "fatherland" and, most recently, "fathering," in the sense of the skill or art of being a father. To the great majority of these words, we can assign no specific author, as we can for "gamesmanship" and "chortle"—if, indeed, there *was* such an author; many of them may well have been contrived independently by many people.

Some words seem to have been made up out of whole cloth—almost invariably by a person or persons unknown. "Dog," for example, appeared in English (as *docga* or *dogga*) something over a thousand years ago, apparently out of thin air; it bears no resemblance to any word of even vaguely similar meaning in English or any other tongue of the period. Other such words, which appear in our dictionaries with the notation "o.o.o." (of obscure origin), include such everyday terms as "jaw," "kick," "pour," "job" and "put." Presumably somebody coined these words, either deliberately or accidentally (i.e., through a slip of the tongue); other people liked the sound of them and used them. As we continue to do.

Some of these words may, for all we can tell, have originated by a process still very active in English: naming something after a person or place associated with it. For "o.o.o." words, this is impossible to prove, since the person or place—if there was such—is long gone and forgotten. But once in a while, the identity of an ancient eponym—a proper noun converted to a common one—crops up unexpectedly. Some years ago, for example, Eric Partridge, that indefatigable collector of slang and other types of unconventional English, ran across "dover," a bit of hotel waiter's slang, apparently dating from the mid-nineteenth century, meaning a reheated dish. He guessed that it represented a sort of condensation of "do over," which seemed reasonable. Something about the word struck me as familiar, however, and sent me back to my copy of *The Canterbury Tales.* At one point the Host, needling the Cook, remarks (with the English modernized), "Full many a Jack of Dover hast thou sold/That hath been heated twice and twice grown cold." Here, I am convinced, is the true source of Partridge's "dover"—evidently the proprietor of some inn or cookshop better known for economy than for quality.

Who Jack of Dover was, and where he sold his loathsomely reheated dishes, we will probably never know. The source of many other eponymous terms, however, is a matter of history: they celebrate the hasty eating habits of the Earl of Sandwich, the sartorial tastes of Lord Cardigan and Mrs. Amelia Bloomer, the hard-wearing pants sold by Levi Strauss, the nuts that ripen around St. Filbert's day, the abrupt legal procedures of Judge Thomas Lynch, the curious amusements of the Marquis de Sade, and the useful little invention of one Dr. Condom.

Places, too, have given their names to English and to other tongues, usually as terms for commodities made in or imported from the place in question. Scallions came originally from Askalon in ancient Palestine, suede from Sweden, gauze from Gaza, and wine from such towns or regions as Bordeaux, Burgundy, Champagne and Chianti, not to mention the Spanish town of Jerez, whose name was once spelled Xerez and pronounced /sherres/. Other English words recall, to those who know their ancient history, the terse speech of the Greek Laconians, or, to those who know their Bible, the unspeakable vices of the Palestinian Sodomites.

The borrowing of foreign place names into English is, of course, merely a special case of word-borrowing in general, which for nearly a thousand years has been our main source of new words. Whenever two peoples speaking different tongues maintain prolonged contact, whether through trade, conquest or migration, they almost inevitably borrow words from one another. But who borrows what, and how often, depends very much on the nature of the contact, and of the peoples.

Borrowing is almost inevitable in situations where one people knows something the other doesn't. If a foreigner shows you something you've never seen before, you almost automatically ask, "What's that?"—and thereafter call it by whatever name he gives you. "Ivory" and "ebony"— the words as well as the commodities—were traded by the ancient Egyptians to the Greeks and from them to the Romans, whence they passed into most modern European tongues. Arab traders borrowed the originals of "sugar" and "candy" from some language of India (where sugar cane was first grown) and passed them on to western Europe. Technical terms like "alcohol," "alkali," "caliber" and "zenith" remind us of the brief period when the Moslem world knew a lot about science that Christian Europe didn't, while such later borrowings as "mousse," "sauté" and "hors d'oeuvre" commemorate France's superior knowledge of cookery.

Just as people borrow foreign words when they import exotic goods, so do they when they "export" themselves to exotic lands, meeting new birds, beasts and other things. English-speaking settlers in North America picked up Native American terms for the raccoon and skunk, the hickory and pecan trees, and native culinary specialities like hominy and succotash. British migrants to Australia learned about kangaroos and wallabies, as empire builders in India discovered teak, curry and mongooses.

Commonest of all among these immigrant borrowings are names on the land itself, especially its rivers, which continue to flow when towns along their banks have crumbled to dust. The native tribes who named the Kennebec, Merrimack, Connecticut, Susquehanna and Potomac, not to mention Canada's Ottawa and Saskatchewan, are long gone, but the rivers remain, under their old names.

Exposure to new things and new places is an obvious reason for borrowing new words. Not so obvious is why some languages—notably English—borrow words that duplicate (and sometimes replace) words they already possess. To some extent, the reason is merely humanity's perennial enjoyment of novelty, in words as well as clothes and other things. But when this sort of borrowing occurs on a large scale, as in English, we must seek other explanations: in particular, situations where two peoples have come to occupy the same territory (whether through peaceful infiltration or conquest) and, through intermarriage, merge into one. Children of linguistically "mixed" marriages are likely to learn the tongues of both their parents; according to a tradition in my own family, one of my great-grandmothers "never spoke a word of English to her [New Orleans French] mother or a word of French to her [Anglo-American] father" (the legend does not explain how Mom and Pop communicated). Even without intermarriage, children speaking different languages who play together borrow words as naturally as they borrow games and toys.

In these "bilingual" situations, words are bound to be borrowed, but how many depends on circumstances. The extreme case is when one group eventually "borrows" the entire language of the other, losing its own—which usually happens in the long run. But there seems no way of predicting beforehand which language will survive and which will vanish. Numbers must have something to do with it: other things being equal, the majority group in the population is likely to retain its own language, while the minority becomes linguistically assimilated. But other things often aren't equal: the minority may be politically and socially dominant, and may also be literate while the majority is not—and both situations make the minority language more likely to survive. Still, there is no certainty about it; the most we can say is that the more things a language has going for it, the better its chances for survival—or, if it does not survive, for contributing heavily to the vocabulary of the survivor.

Whatever the circumstance under which words are borrowed, the process is seldom as simple as borrowing a hammer or a lawnmower from one's neighbor. Languages, as we've seen, are systems of sounds organized according to certain rules, and a borrowed word, if it is to be any use, must fit—or, usually, be fitted to—its new linguistic habitat.

To begin with, it may well be hard or even "impossible" to pronounce, because it includes sounds or sound combinations not found in the borrower's tongue. It must then undergo phonetic assimilation, in which its outlandish sounds are transformed into "pronounceable" ones. The Japanese play *beisuboru* because "baseball" violates their phonetic conventions. First, they have no true L-sound, and therefore substitute their nearest indigenous sound, /r/, which in Japanese sounds a little like /l/ (as in the catch-phrase "Rotsa ruck!"). The substitution yields *beis-bor*, which still won't do, because Japanese syllables can't end in /s/ or /r/. The solution was to drop in two extra vowels, turning two "unpronounceable" syllables into four "pronounceable" ones: *bei-su-bo-ru*.

The same process, of course, operates in reverse: thus Japanese *karate* (/ka-ra-teh/) is likely to end up as /kurrotty/ in American mouths. Always the unfamiliar is replaced by the familiar. Spanish nouns often end in /o/ or /ah/, English nouns almost never; thus Spanish-American *el lagarto* ("the lizard") picked up a final /r/ to become English "alligator," and Spanish *cucuracha* (yes, the same one as in the song) dropped its final /ah/ to become "cockroach." Both these words show another aspect of phonetic assimilation: accent shift. The Spanish originals are accented on the next-to-last syllable, as most Spanish words are; the English versions accent the first syllable, as most English words do. Nearly all borrowings from French have been thus altered, with the accent shifted from the end of the word (its normal place in that tongue) to the beginning; thus "honor" came into English as /on-*noor* but has evolved into /*on*ner/.

Phonetic assimilation, like other linguistic processes, doesn't happen overnight. "Honor" and other words borrowed from French during the Middle Ages have shifted their accents, but more recent borrowings still retain something like their original sounds—at least in America, where (for example) "ballet" is pronounced /bal-*lay*/. But the English go to the /bally/, and the wogs begin at /Cally/ or /Callis/, rather than /Cal-*lay*/ in Franco-American style. In "garage," another recent borrowing, we can see different stages of assimilation at work simultaneously. Educated Americans usually say /guh-*rozh*/, which is close to the French; less educated ones, /guh-*rodj*/, thereby getting rid of the "unpronounceable" final /zh/. The educated Englishman shifts the accent to make /*ga*-rozh/, while his less educated compatriot has evolved the completely English-sounding word /garridge/, to rhyme with "carriage"—which was itself assimilated earlier from /car-*yazh*/.

Even after their outlandish sounds have been assimilated into respectable native syllables, borrowed words often remain hard to remember because they are so unlike native words. Frequently, therefore, they are further assimilated into the semblance of a familiar word or words; thus "cockroach" combines the English words for a rooster and a small fish. Neither is exactly relevant to an insect, but the word sticks in the memory better than its earlier version, "cockarotch."

Occasionally, this further step in assimilation manages to come up with native words that actually make sense. Thus Native American *muskwessu* was first assimilated to "musquash," but ended up as "muskrat"—and indeed the animal resembles a large rat and emits a musky odor. Through this process, called "folk etymology," the foreign word not only becomes easier to remember but is also given a plausible, though fictitious, native pedigree.

Among the most energetic and inventive assimilators of foreign words have been the British soldier and sailor. The Italian port of Ligorno (now Livorno) was long ago twisted into Leghorn—and gave its name to a breed of chicken and a kind of straw hat. Somewhat later, the jolly tars who manned H.M.S. *Bellerophon*, no experts in Greek mythology, christened her the *Bully Ruffian*. And World War II Tommies transformed the

Sicilian town of Fiumefreddo ("Cold River") into "Fuming Freddie," and its inhabitants into "Eye-ties."

Whatever other assimilations, humorous or merely practical, a borrowed word undergoes, it must at times undergo syntactic assimilation, acquiring whatever inflections it needs to function in its new home. This process is relatively uncommon in English, since our inflections are so few, but is still worth brief notice. A universal example is the suffix "-ing," whereby a verb, imported or domestic, is transformed into the adjective-like or noun-like present participle (honor/honoring; murder/murdering). Equally universal in imported verbs is the inflection "-ed" that turns present to past (a few native verbs are inflected differently).

For most English nouns, the only "live" inflection is the plural which in nearly all imported nouns conforms to English rules. Thus if you are ordering several cheese-and-tomato pies, you don't ask for *pizze*, as an Italian would do, but for pizzas. Often the process operates in reverse: confronted by a singular foreign noun that *sounds* plural, we "singularize" it. Thus "sherris" (Xerez) wine became "sherry," and Latin *pisa* became first "pease" but later "pea." In the old nursery rhyme, the man burned his mouth on cold *pease* porridge, but today we eat *pea* soup.

Language, the foundation of human communities, must change as the community itself changes—seeing and doing new things, encountering new peoples, traveling or migrating to new places. Often, too, it changes for the same mysterious reasons that peoples change their habits of eating, drinking and dressing: they just feel like it. Yet the "new" language is never really new: like every changing human institution, it is a blend of old and new, a compromise between innovation and habit.

Languages vary over space as well as over time. As long as the community remains small, unified and compact, the language too will remain unified. But if part of the community becomes separated from the rest, whether for social reasons (the formation of classes or castes) or, more often, by mere geography (i.e., expansion and migration), the languages of the separated portions will change in different ways, producing two dialects of the original language.

English, because of its enormous geographical spread, probably includes more dialects than any other tongue on earth: for proof, simply tune in on the broadcast of a UN session and listen to the Indian, Nigerian, Australian and West Indian speakers, not to mention the British and Americans. The latter two, indeed, differ to the point where comprehension is sometimes hindered, despite the influence of the printed (and, more recently, broadcast) materials shared by both peoples. American and British English also encompass regional dialects or subdialects, such as Down East, "Brooklynese" and Texas west of the Atlantic, and Scots, Yorkshire and Cockney east of it. *Class* dialects can cut across regional lines, as do "Public School English" in Britain and Black English in America. And in any country, different subcultures and occupational groups possess their own bewildering variety of cants, jargons and lingoes.

Clearly, then, anything we choose to say about our native tongue can be wholly true only for a particular time and place and social group. And some of what we say will not even be "true" in this limited sense, but merely educated guesswork. For example, the actual sounds of English have been recorded for less than a hundred years; we have no tapes of the premiere of *Hamlet* in 1603, let alone a bard reciting the epic of Beowulf at the court of Alfred the Great. We do, to be sure, have written records of these works, but these give us merely the words people used, not how they sounded. Figuring out what a tenth-century scribe "heard" when he was writing down a poem involves a lot of intricate inference and guesswork. Many of these guesses are doubtless accurate (though there is no way we can ever know for sure), but there are enough differences among the experts to make clear that we are dealing with something less than hard, provable scientific fact.

English, like all languages, is a sign of the times—present or past. It is also a record of the invention and imagination, the poetic or playful fantasies, the sly or sardonic humor, of the known and unknown people who have shaped it. For instance, the small nephew of the American mathematician Edward Kastner who, asked by his uncle to suggest a name for the enormous number 10^{100} (1 followed by 100 zeros), came up with "googol." The word, like the number, is seldom used, but is still in the dictionaries. Or the anonymous fourteenth-century laborer who first spotted the resemblance between the rising and dipping arm of a builder's hoist and the neck of a feeding crane—and gave the apparatus a name we still use. Or, still further back, the anonymous Roman who noted the mouselike motion of a muscle rippling beneath the skin and called it *musculus*—"little mouse."

A simple word like "escape," properly understood, can conjure up a vivid human encounter of centuries ago. It derives from Latin *excappare*, to get out of one's cloak; one imagines a traveler on a dark road, feeling the grasp of a robber or assassin on his shoulder, slipping out of his cloak and—escaping.

Something over a century ago, a French naturalist was investigating the animals of Madagascar in company with a native guide. The latter, spotting one of the lemurs for which that island is famous, cried out in his own tongue, "Indry!"—meaning simply "Look!" The Frenchman, however, assumed that his guide was pronouncing the animal's name—and "indri" it has been, in French and English, ever since.

Language is people: the human comedy and tragedy. The history of English, then, is also a panorama of the living, loving, joking, cursing, arguing, poetizing, working and playing people who, in their tens and hundreds of millions, in a score of lands and across fourscore centuries, have shaped and reshaped our native tongue into what it is.

2. THE COMMON SOURCE

Indo-European and Its Speakers

━━━━━━━━━━━━━━━━━━━━━━━━━━━━━

∾

What song the sirens sang, and what name Achilles assumed when he
hid himself among women, though puzzling matters, are not beyond
conjecture.

—Sir Thomas Browne

. . . all . . . sprung from some common source which, perhaps, no
longer exists.

—Sir William Jones

The history of the English tongue is conventionally dated from around
430 A.D., when the people inaccurately called the Anglo-Saxons began
migrating into Britain. The date is clearly arbitrary. If these immigrants
were speaking English when they landed, they must have been speaking
it when they embarked somewhere along the eastern shore of the North
Sea. And that ancient English, in turn, must have been much like the
language spoken by their grandparents, which in turn resembled that
spoken by *their* grandparents, as far back as one can trace the pedigree.

The ultimate roots of English, like those of every other language, lie
deep, deep in the past, perhaps as much as a million years ago. It was
about then—give or take a few hundred thousand years—that our still
rather apelike ancestors began engaging in activities requiring some degree of cooperation and foresight: the organized hunting of large animals, and the controlled use of fire. And from everything we know about
our species and its close relatives, activities of this sort required some
system of communication employing vocal symbols—a language, in fact.

These first human languages must surely have been far simpler than
any modern tongue. Their phonetics were limited by the anatomy of the
primitive human vocal tract, which could produce fewer distinguishable
sounds than our own. Their vocabularies were doubtless equally limited,
with only a few hundred or even a few dozen words, and their syntax was
surely of the simplest, with typical "sentences" including only two or
three words, like the first sentences of young children today.

But that is all we can ever know or guess about humanity's first languages, unless somebody invents a time machine. A century ago, some scholars believed that somewhere on earth there must exist primitive languages resembling those spoken by our remote ancestors. Missionaries and explorers claimed to have encountered tribes possessing only a few hundred words, while the German philologist Max Müller alleged that even European peasants had similarly restricted vocabularies. There is no evidence, however, that Müller was closely acquainted with peasants. Subsequently, some Swedish philologists took the trouble to record the different words used by one of their rural countrymen over a period of several weeks; the total was around twenty-three thousand. Still later, a Japanese group found that a workman in their country used no less than fifteen thousand different words in a single day. Time and the facts have been equally unkind to the obviously racist theory that primitive languages can be found in "darkest Africa" or some equally remote region: every human language that has been studied has a vocabulary in excess of twenty thousand words—about the number Shakespeare used, and far more than we find in the Bible.

Languages of this degree of complexity may have originated nearly fifty thousand years ago. It is from this period that prehistorians have dug up skulls with fully modern vocal tracts, capable of producing the full range of sounds found in today's tongues. Since these people, as far as we can tell, also had fully modern brains, the odds are that they possessed, or soon developed, fully modern languages—one of which must be the ultimate ancestor of our own. But that, too, is lost beyond recall.

The first identifiable ancestor of English dates from no more than about eight thousand years ago. We owe its discovery to the labors of Sir William Jones, a British judge in India who around 1780 set out to learn the ancient Sanskrit tongue. Jones' original intention was merely to familiarize himself with native Indian law codes, some of which were written in Sanskrit, though it had long been extinct as a spoken language. However, like other educated Englishmen of his day, he had studied Latin and Greek in school, and to his surprise began encountering Sanskrit words that clearly resembled words of identical or similar meanings in the classical tongues. The Sanskrit for "three," transliterated from the exotic alphabets in which the language was recorded, came out *trayas*, close to Latin *tres* and Greek *trias*. Sanskrit *panca*, five, resembled Greek *pente*, while the numbers from seven to nine, *sapta, ashta* and *nava*, equally resembled Latin *septem, octo* and *novem*. Sanskrit *sarpa*, snake, was surely kin to Latin *serpens; rajan,* king, was close to Latin *regem;* and *devas,* god, resembled Latin *divus,* divine.

Jones was not the first European to note such resemblances, but he was the first to study them systematically and to draw the logical conclusion, which he presented in an address to the Asiatick Society in Calcutta on February 2, 1786. The Sanskrit language, he declared, bears to both Greek and Latin "a stronger affinity . . . than could possibly have been produced by accident; so strong, indeed, that no philologer could examine them all three without believing them to have sprung from some common source which, perhaps, no longer exists." Similar affinities, he added, suggested a link with the Celtic and Germanic tongues as well.

Jones' brilliant deduction has been fully confirmed by nearly two centuries of research. We now know, in fact, that the linguistic descendants of his "common source" include not only Sanskrit (ancestor of the majority of tongues currently spoken in India, Pakistan and Bangladesh), Greek, Latin and its descendants (French, Spanish, Italian, etc.), and the Celtic and Germanic tongues, but also the Baltic and Slavonic languages, the Iranian tongues of western Asia, and various minor languages, both current and extinct, including Armenian, Albanian and ancient Hittite. Collectively, they are the native tongues of about half the human race. The common source itself is now called Parent Indo-European, Common Indo-European, or simply Indo-European.

This Indo-European language was evidently spoken at some time in the past by an Indo-European people. English, now used around the world, began as merely the language spoken in the eastern districts of Great Britain; Latin, whose linguistic descendants are almost as widespread as our own tongue, began as merely the language of Latium (modern Lazio), the district of Italy south of Rome. Indo-European, then, must once have been spoken by some tribe or group of tribes inhabiting an equally limited area, whence their multiplying descendants eventually carried their language, in scores of variations, around the world.

Just who were these linguistic founding fathers—and mothers—and where and when did they live? Finding answers to these questions involves putting together clues from a whole range of scholarly fields— linguistics, physical geography, ecology and archaeology—and seeing whether they can be maneuvered into any kind of plausible fit. Through linguistics, scholars have reconstructed much of the Indo-European vocabulary, including words referring to the natural environment and way of life of its speakers. Geography and ecology enable us to delimit regions which correspond to that environment; archaeology, finally, allows us—

perhaps—to identify some known human culture whose location, life-style and subsequent spread matches what we have already deduced about the Indo-Europeans. But "perhaps" is the operative word: the Indo-Europeans left no written records, and archaeological relics cannot speak. The time and place where our remotest linguistic forebears lived, though not beyond conjecture, will never be known for sure.

Before going further, I should emphasize that "Indo-European" refers to a people and a culture only in the remote past. Today, it is a purely linguistic term, with no racial implications whatever, despite the "science" of the Nazis and the similar balderdash currently being emitted by some French rightists. Though we can reconstruct hundreds of Indo-European words, there is not one Indo-European gene that anyone can identify.

The Indo-European family tree, like any other tree, divides and subdivides into limbs, branches and twigs. English can be described as the largest and most vigorous twig growing from the West Germanic branch of the Germanic limb. It is by this route that we have inherited the words that have "always" been in English. But our modern vocabulary also includes some thousands of words borrowed from other branches of the same limb, notably Old Norse (ancestor of the modern Scandinavian tongues), Dutch and Low German.

The great majority of English borrowings, however, come from another limb, the Italic. Only one branch of Italic survives, but an enormous one: the Romance languages, descended from the Latin of ancient Rome. French alone has contributed some fifteen thousand words to English, while smaller but significant additions have come from Spanish and Italian. Latin itself remained the scholarly and ecclesiastical language of Europe until a few centuries ago, and as such contributed additional thousands of words to English (as well as several hundred borrowed at earlier periods). Another copious source of borrowing has been the non-Italic Greek tongue, which has contributed thousands of words to English, either directly or via Latin, whose vocabulary was heavily indebted to Greek as Roman culture was indebted to Greek culture. Latin and Greek between them have, for example, supplied virtually all our scientific and medical vocabulary.

The Celtic limb of Indo-European was once enormous, stretching from Ireland to Asia Minor; today it is almost dead: the Celtic tongues Welsh, Erse (Irish), Gaelic and Breton are spoken by only a few hundred thousand people on the northwestern fringes of Europe. Their contributions to English have been equally meager: a couple of dozen words borrowed at various times between the sixth century and the present. The Balto-

Slavonic limb, though vigorous, has made even fewer contributions to our vocabulary, and these are almost all words denoting things peculiar to, or originating in, those lands, "vodka" being a notable example.

The other great limb of Indo-European, the Indo-Iranian, dominates the speech of the Indian peninsula, as well as of Afghanistan and, of course, Iran. Like Balto-Slavonic, it has given us mainly words for exotic things and concepts, though a handful of Indian words have passed into general English usage. The contributions of the remaining branches of Indo-European to English are essentially nil.

English borrowings from other Indo-European tongues come from the modern or relatively modern members of the family. The philologist seeking to reconstruct their common source, however, is much more interested in the oldest recorded members, which, being much closer in time to ancestral Indo-European, naturally resemble it more closely: since languages change with time, the less time elapsed, the less change. The earliest Indo-European inscriptions, dating from around 1700 B.C., are in Hittite, written in a cuneiform script borrowed from neighboring Mesopotamia. Inscriptions in Mycenean Greek date from around 1400 B.C., while Sanskrit documents, though themselves comparatively recent, record pretty accurately the language spoken in northern India at about the same date, since it was preserved virtually intact for cultural and religious reasons. Later but still useful contributions come from documents or inscriptions in Old Persian and Old Latin (c. 600 B.C.); Old Armenian and Gothic—the oldest recorded Germanic tongue (c. 300 A.D.); and Old English, Old Church Slavonic, Old High German, Old Irish, Old Norse and Tocharian (two extinct tongues of Central Asia), from a few centuries later.

To reconstruct the common parent of the Indo-European languages, the philologist consults dictionaries of these venerable tongues and draws up lists of correspondences—words from different languages having roughly similar sounds and meanings. Sometimes the similarities are tenuous, but they are usually clear enough so that the researcher can assume he is dealing with cognates—words descended from the same linguistic ancestor. His problem then is to reconstruct the ancestor from its varied descendants; his basic method is that of letting the majority rule.

Sometimes the vote is unanimous. For instance, the word for "mother" begins with /m/ in all the older Indo-European tongues (as it does in nearly all the modern ones), meaning that their Indo-European original must have begun with the same sound. The same is true of other words beginning with /m/, as well as those beginning with /n/ and (with one exception) those beginning with /r/ and /l/ (in Sanskrit, initial /r/ has in some cases been replaced by /l/, and vice versa).

For other sounds, the vote, though not unanimous, amounts to a landslide. The word for "father," for instance, begins with /p/ in all the older Indo-European tongues (e.g., Latin *pater,* whence "paternal"), except for Gothic and the other Germanic tongues, where /f/ occurs instead, and Old Irish, where the initial consonant has simply disappeared ("mother" is *mathair,* but "father" is simply *athair*). The same rule holds for other words beginning with /p/—e.g., Latin *piscis* is cognate with Gothic *fisks* and English "fish."

When the philologist seeking to reconstruct Indo-European words finds that no majority rules, he falls back on other clues and inferences, but he will always be aided by a basic principle of historical linguistics: phonetic changes do not occur at random, but in patterns. That is, if a particular sound in a particular phonetic context (say, at the beginning of a word) changes in a given tongue, the change will affect not just some words but all or nearly all words including that sound. The shift from Indo-European /p/ to Germanic /f/ affected not only "father" and "fish" but all other words beginning with /p/, including the ancestors of English "fire," "fight," "fart" and hundreds more. Our tongue does, indeed, contain scores of apparent exceptions to this rule: words that have retained their original /p/. But these are invariably not native Germanic words; rather, they were borrowed from other tongues (e.g., Latin and French) in which this phonetic shift did not take place.

Nobody really knows why phonetic changes should follow these systematic patterns, but the principle has proved out in tens of thousands of cases. With it, the philologist can establish connections between words that would otherwise seem wholly unrelated. For instance, there is no obvious phonetic connection between "foot" and the learned (originally Greek) term "pedology" (the science of soils), and only a tenuous connection in meaning (the soil is what the foot walks on). The laws of phonetic change tell us, however, that "foot" must derive from an earlier **pod-,* whose connection with the "pedo-" of "pedology" is clear enough.*

Patterns of phonetic change in non-initial consonants, those which

---

*Words and word roots preceded by an asterisk, like **pod-,* are "reconstructed"—i.e., they are not attested in written documents but are inferred from later cognates. This typographical convention emphasizes the distinction, important in linguistics, between what we know for sure and what we merely guess, however plausibly.

appear other than at the beginning of a word, are rather more intricate than those governing initial consonants. Patterns of vowel changes are more intricate still—in part because for some reason vowels are less "stable" than consonants over time. (English vowels have undergone three or four major shifts over the past five thousand years or so; its consonants, only one.)

Phonetically, Indo-European differed considerably from English, lacking half a dozen consonants that we use, and including at least three that we do not—notably, the "aspirated" consonants usually written b^h, d^h and g^h (these were apparently pronounced like B, D and G followed by a puff of breath). As for syntax, nouns were inflected in no less than eight different cases (as against five for most Latin nouns, six or seven for a few), and were inflected differently not only for the singular and plural but also for the "dual," whose special set of endings denoted two of the things under discussion. Verb inflections were even more elaborate, showing person (I, you, he, etc.), and number (singular, plural, dual) but also voice (active, passive), tense, "mood" and various other refinements of meaning.

As an example of Indo-European wordmaking in operation, consider *kerwom*, stag (whence the much altered and now archaic "hart"). It was formed from the root *ker-*, horn (one of its English descendants, as is another kind of horn, the cornet). To this was added a suffix, *-wo-*, making it into "the horned thing," while the inflectional ending *-m* showed that this particular stag was the object of a verb ("I killed the stag"); had it been the subject ("The stag got away"), it would have been *kerwos*.

This aspect of Indo-European syntax is obviously pretty remote from our own; another, however, remains very much alive in English and most other modern Indo-European tongues: the formation of new words by combining two old ones. Some modern examples are "stripteaser," "tape-recorder," "spaceman" and "radio-telescope," with "telescope" itself an earlier compound, from Greek roots meaning "far-look." Double-barreled words of this sort were specially common in Indo-European poetry, and a few have been reconstructed by comparing ancient Greek and Sanskrit epics. *Klewos ngwzhitom*, imperishable fame, crops up in both Homer and the *Rig Veda*, and the poet himself was *wekwom texos*, word-weaver (as you have probably guessed, the root *tex-* is the source of "textile").

Similar compounds were often used for Indo-European personal names, and continued to be in many of its linguistic descendants, such as the Persian Xerxes ("men's ruler"), the Greek Sophocles ("wisdom-famed"), the Gaulish chieftain Vercingetorix ("warrior king") and the good Slavonic King Wenceslas ("greater glory"). The same process has given us such English writers as "shake-spear," "gold-smith" and "long-fellow," as well as—via other Indo-European tongues—U.S. presidents "iron-beater" (*Eisenhauer* in German) and "hideous head" (*kennedy* in Irish).

These aspects of Indo-European are both interesting in themselves and also bear on the later history of our own tongue. But they bring us no closer to solving the mystery of who the Indo-Europeans were. For this, we must concentrate not on their syntax but on their vocabulary: if you know the things a people talked about, you are bound to know a lot about the things they saw and did, which in turn will reflect where they lived and how they got a living.

Reconstructing the meaning of a prehistoric vocabulary is a lot trickier than reconstructing its sounds, since meanings often change more frequently, more radically—and much less predictably. Thus *ker-* has given us not only "horn," "cornet" and other obviously related words, but also "carrot" and "ginger" (from their horn- or antler-shaped roots) and even such improbable derivatives as "cranium" and "runt." Likewise, the single Indo-European root *g^hosti-* has yielded, through various linguistic channels, such diverse words as "host," "guest," "hospital" and "hostile"—the last, presumably, because a guest might be a stranger, and therefore a possible enemy. About all we can say of the original meaning is that it had something to do with the host-guest relationship.

Nonetheless, when we find that the word for "plow" is *arðr* in Icelandic (the Icelandic letter ð sounds like TH in "this"), *ëar* in medieval English, *aratron* in Greek, *aratrum* in Latin, *arathar* in Irish, *arklas* in Lithuanian and *araur* in Armenian, it's a safe bet that the Indo-Europeans had plows of some sort (their word for it has been reconstructed as *arətrom*, with the letter ə pronounced like the A in "Cuba"). The obvious inference, that they were farmers, is confirmed by such reconstructions as *grno-*, grain (also "corn," which in England means the same thing), *mel-*, grind (whence "mill") and *yeug-*, yoke.

Yokes mean domesticated cattle—*uksen-* (whence "oxen") and *gwou-* (whence "cow"). Other Indo-European livestock were sheep (*awi-*, whence "ewe"), with a different word, *agwhno*, for "lamb"; swine (*su-*) and their piglets (*porko-*); and goats (*g^haido*). The horse (*ekwo-*, whence "equestrian") was known, but not necessarily domesticated; perhaps significantly, we can reconstruct no Indo-European word for "foal" as we can for "lamb" and "piglet." Along with their domestic animals, the Indo-Europeans also endured domestic pests, including the *mus*- and *lus*-, whose modern English equivalents still rhyme.

The Indo-Europeans lived in houses (*domo*-, whence "domestic"), walled with mud-plastered wattle, probably roofed with thatch, and with some sort of door (*d^hwer*-)—though this may originally have meant the gate of the fenced compound where the family (*gen*-, whence both "genetics" and "kin") and its animals lived. Gathered around the domestic fire (*pur*-), the kinfolk dined on cakes and porridge made of meal (*mel*-) from their *grno*-, including both wheat and barley (*b^hares*-); they also seem to have known, though not necessarily cultivated, rye (*wrugyo*-). Vegetable dishes included broad or fava (*b^hab^ha*-) beans, plus, presumably, whatever greens were in season.

Meat came mostly from the family's calves, lambs and porkers; the adult animals would have made tough eating, and were also more useful for breeding, milk (*melg*-) or pulling the *aratrom*. On occasion, the menu included fish (*pisk*-), including the *laksos*, usually interpreted as "salmon" (whence "lox"), perhaps venison from a *kerwos*, and wild duck and goose (*g^hans*-) in season. The "dessert" course may have included wild apples (*abel*-)—rather sour, but perhaps sweetened with honey (*melit*-, whence ultimately "molasses") from wild bees (*b^hei*-). Certainly the honey was sometimes fermented into mead (*med^hu*-) for celebratory or ceremonial tippling.

Clothing was made of wool (*wel*-) and perhaps the fibers of flax (*lin*-, whence "linen"), spun (*spen*-) into thread (*tretu*-), woven (*web^h*-) into cloth, which was sewn (*syu*-) into garments. In the colder months, at least, people must have worn some sort of footgear, made of *letrom* (leather); straps of the same material would have served to hitch the yoked *uksen* to the *aratrom*. Tools must have been made of wood, bone and stone (*stoino*-). Though the Indo-Europeans had a word for "copper" (just possibly, it may have meant "bronze"), this was apparently a rare, imported material, too precious for everyday use. But they unquestionably made pottery, which they may have called *keramo*- (whence "ceramic").

The Indo-Europeans, in short, were farmer-herders, living in relatively permanent settlements; their culture was thus typical of what archaeologists call the Neolithic stage of human societies. Where was that culture located—and when?

Since they had no word for "palm-tree," "lion," "tiger" or "camel," we can rule out the tropics—a deduction confirmed by their familiarity with snow (**sneigw-*) and freezing cold (**gel-*, whence also "congeal"). They also had no words for "olive," "vine," "laurel" or "ass" (the animal you ride on; the ass or arse you sit on was **ors-*), nor for "island" or— probably—"sea," which would rule out the subtropical lands along the Mediterranean. On the other hand, their lack of words for "spruce," "fir," "lemming" and "grouse" equally rules out the northerly parts of Europe and Asia.

Having deduced where the Indo-Europeans did *not* live, what can we infer from their vocabulary about where they *did* live? The animal life of their homeland included the (wild?) horse, the wolf (**wlkwo-*), bear, beaver (**bʰibru-*) and otter; trees included the birch (**bʰerag-*), ash (**as-*), beech (**bʰago-*), oak, willow, maple, elm (**elmo-*) and alder. Not all these names have been reconstructed with equal certainty, but collectively they provide a clear picture of the Indo-Europeans' natural environment: deciduous forest or open woodland, of the sort that stretches in a broad belt between the lands bordering on the Mediterranean and Black seas and those bordering on the Baltic, from the Atlantic east to the Urals. A much smaller area lies between the grassy Russian steppes and the Caucasus mountains to the south. (This description, of course, refers to the *original* vegetation of these regions, which today has mostly been replaced by cropland, pasture, or plantations of fast-growing evergreens such as pines.)

At one time, scholars believed they could further localize the Indo-Europeans with the single word **laksos*. If this meant the Atlantic salmon, then the Indo-Europeans must have lived toward the north of the deciduous forest belt, where streams drain into the Atlantic or Baltic (the fish is unknown in the Mediterranean or Black Sea drainage basins). However, modern studies show that these latter regions contain plenty of salmon-*like* fish: the brown trout and salmon-trout, both of which reach salmon size under favorable conditions, and the *huchen* of the Danube and Dneister, which looks very like a slim-built salmon. Any one of these could have been the original **laksos*, whose name was then transferred to the Atlantic salmon by such Indo-Europeans as subsequently encountered it, as the English long afterward transferred "robin" to an American bird with little resemblance, apart from its reddish breast, to the European robin. In short, the Indo-European "salmon" has turned out to be —well, a red herring.

To further localize the Indo-European culture within the European deciduous forest belt, we must focus on time rather than place. Archaeology tells us that farming-herding societies did not appear anywhere in this region much before 6000 B.C., meaning that the Indo-European culture as we have reconstructed it can have flourished no earlier than that date. Setting a "latest possible" date for their dispersal is more problematical, in part because we are not talking about a single event. At one time, indeed, Indo-European migrations from their ancestral homeland were seen in terms of what later scholars sardonically called the "campfire theory." Our linguistic forebears, that is, were imagined as seated around the tribal campfire and then, at a signal, standing up, gathering their household goods and setting off in all directions. People don't really behave like that, of course; the actual dispersal must have stretched over centuries. All we can hope to determine is when this protracted process began.

The most useful evidence on when the Indo-Europeans began moving out—though it is far from precise—is the degree of difference, in phonetics, grammar and syntax, among the most ancient recorded Indo-European tongues. As we noted earlier, languages change with time, and the more time elapsed, the more change. And when two groups speaking the same tongue become separated by migration, their languages change independently, in different ways; if this process goes on long enough, the two groups end up speaking different languages.

An early stage in this process of linguistic "splitting" is represented by American and British English, whose speakers became physically separated only a few centuries ago (and have remained in loose contact ever since); their languages are still more or less intelligible, and are therefore classified as dialects of English rather than two distinct tongues.

A later stage of linguistic splitting is seen in the Romance tongues, all of which stem from the Latin spread across Europe by Roman legionaries, officials and merchants. This widespread tongue had developed local dialects as early as the second century A.D.; we know this from Latin inscriptions in Spain that are "misspelled" in ways foreshadowing the phonetics of modern Spanish. Thus Latin *amatus*, loved (whence modern Italian *amato*), was sometimes spelled *amadus*, (whence modern Spanish *amado*).

Today, of course, the differences between the local Latin dialects have expanded to the point where we are talking about distinct languages— though anyone who has studied any two of them has surely noticed that they are still much more like one another than either is like English. Since the Romance tongues began splitting apart some 1,800 years ago, an obvious inference is that the Germanic and Italic branches of Indo-European must have begun *their* split much earlier—which, indeed, is confirmed by history.

Thus the differences between two related languages will reflect the amount of time that their speakers have been physically separated—but how accurately is uncertain. With these reservations, just how different *are* the earliest known Indo-European tongues—which, we may recall, are Hittite, Sanskrit and Mycenean Greek, all dating from around 1500 B.C.? Briefly, they are very different—much more so than today's Romance tongues. Almost certainly, then, their speakers had by that date been separated for a good deal longer than eighteen hundred years. The absolute minimum would seem to be twenty-five hundred years, which would put the beginning of the Indo-European dispersion around 4000 B.C., and some Indo-Europeanists, such as Calvert Watkins of Harvard, believe that double the Romance figure, or thirty-six hundred years, is none too much, putting the date back another thousand years or so, to before 5000 B.C.

There is one possible snag in putting the beginning of Indo-European dispersal even as late as 4000 B.C.. That is the existence in several branches of Indo-European of related words for "wheel," including that word itself and the Greek *kyklos* (whence "cycle" and "bicycle"). Indo-European also included a word meaning "transport in a vehicle," *weg^h*- (whence both "vehicle" and "wagon"). Now wheeled vehicles were invented, somewhere in the Near East, around 3500 B.C. or a little earlier, but there is no evidence that they were known anywhere within the Indo-European "environmental zone" much before 3000 B.C.—much too late for even the latest of the dates we have been talking about.

The conflict in evidence is probably spurious, however. The basic Indo-European root of "wheel," *kwel*-, meant merely "to turn" (various of its descendants, including "collar," refer not to vehicles but to the neck —"what the head turns on"). The actual source of "wheel" is Indo-European *kwekwlo*-, which originally meant merely "circle." As for the Indo-Europeans' vehicles, though to us a vehicle implies wheels, the wheeled cart or wagon was historically preceded by the sledge—actually, more efficient for heavy hauling over boggy or snow-covered ground. On the linguistic evidence, then, we need credit the Indo-Europeans with no vehicle more sophisticated than a sledge.

Summing up the linguistic, environmental and archaeological evidence, then, the Indo-Europeans' characteristic culture can have begun not much earlier than 6000 B.C., and its breakup, through migration, no later than 5000 or just possibly 4000 B.C. Can we now identify any archaeologically known culture that existed at the right place at the right time, as we have already defined these terms? There are in fact two leading contenders for the title of "the One-and-Only Original Indo-Europeans": the so-called Kurgan culture of the Russian steppes, and certain earlier farming-herding cultures of the Danube Valley.

The claims of the Kurgan people have been pressed most eloquently by Prof. Marija Gimbutas of UCLA. According to her account, this group —named for the kurgans, or burial mounds, they left behind—first becomes identifiable around 4500 B.C., in the area between the lower Volga and Don rivers. The region is a flat grassland, with trees growing mainly along watercourses, and the Kurganians, as Gimbutas describes them, were "predominantly pastoral," herding cattle, sheep and horses and keeping pigs. Horses were by far the most important food animal; in some Kurganian diggings their remains account for up to 80 percent of the animal bones present. Agriculture, by contrast, was "not highly developed": it is attested by only a few sickles and grinding stones—which might, indeed, have been used to harvest and grind the seeds of wild grasses. Gimbutas also claims that the Kurganians must have ridden as well as herded horses, since she finds the notion of controlling the animals on foot "inconceivable."

Between 4500 and 4000 B.C., as she tells it, some Kurganians expanded westward, "searching for pastureland," and therefore favored "flat grasslands" for settlement. As they expanded, they overcame and absorbed several more sedentary agricultural societies in what is now the southern Ukraine. A decisive element in their conquests, she believes, was the mobility given by their riding horses and by "war carts"—ox-drawn wagons with solid wooden wheels. Both the riding horses and the war carts, however, are hypothetical: there is no actual evidence of either.

By around 4000 B.C., says Gimbutas, the growing "hordes of pastoralists" were expanding into the Danube Basin, whence they moved into central Europe and eventually into northern, western and southern Europe as well. Rather later, around 2,500 B.C., another wave of Kurganians pushed south from the steppes, to become the Anatolian (Hittite) and Indo-Iranian-speaking peoples.

Gimbutas' theories just barely fit the time frame of the Indo-European migrations defined above. In many other respects, however, they go far beyond the linguistic and archaeological facts, and indeed contradict some of them. She claims, for instance, that the Kurganians "must have been seafarers" on the Black Sea; there is no "must" about it. Her only evidence is that the Indo-Europeans (to her, the Kurganians) had words for "boat" (**nau*-, whence both "nautical" and "navy") and one for "oar" (**ere*-, whence "row"); to expand a rowboat into a seagoing ship says more for Gimbutas' imagination than for her science. Moreover, the Indo-Europeans probably did *not* have a word for "sea," Black or otherwise, nor any terms for purely marine animals.

There is no archaeological evidence for horsemanship or carts, on the Russian steppes or anywhere else in the world, as early as 4500 B.C. And in any case, oxcarts moving at a walking pace could hardly have played any important role in warfare, comparable to that played much later by the light horse-drawn chariot.

The Indo-European **arətrom* drawn by yoked **uksen*- doesn't fit Gimbutas' "not highly developed" agricultural technology; really primitive agricultural societies have invariably used hoes and man- or woman-power, not plows and ox-power. Nor do swine and porkers fit the Kurganians' pastoral steppe life-style. The wild ancestor of our domestic swine was a forest animal, not a grassland one (as it still is in the few places it survives); it depended heavily on the fall crop of beechnuts and acorns for subsistence. Nor is the animal easy to herd over any distance; the nursery tale of the old lady whose pig wouldn't jump over the stile is only one of many folktales making the same point. Finally, if the Kurganians were, as she says, "searching for pastureland" in "flat grasslands," one wonders what on earth they were searching for in the densely forested, often hilly terrain of central and western Europe.

There is another and even more powerful argument against the Kurganians being the original Indo-Europeans, but it is a fairly complicated one which we must take step by step. To begin with, whenever the Kurganian expansion began (Gimbutas says 4500 B.C.; most other archaeologists say later), it occurred at a time when Europe was already inhabited by farming peoples. Agricultural societies were flourishing in the Danube Valley before 6000 B.C., and by 4500 B.C. had spread, by one route or another, to most of the rest of Europe. Moreover—and this is crucial— over much of this area (from the Netherlands to the Ukraine, but excluding Scandinavia) the first farming cultures were offshoots of the earlier Danubian cultures—the archaeological evidence is quite clear on this point—meaning that they almost certainly spoke dialects of the same language, which for the moment we may call Danubian.

Which is to say that from the beginning the westward-expanding, pastoral Kurganians would have been considerably outnumbered by the farming-herding Danubians. This is a matter of elementary ecology:

grain-raising yields far more usable calories per acre than stock-raising, and is thus able to support a much denser population. Gimbutas accounts for this disparity in numbers by describing her Kurganians as "Indo-European-speaking warriors who subsequently formed a superstratum on conquered lands." This could have happened: roving warrior bands have conquered more numerous peoples many times in history. They could even have imposed their language on the conquered, as later Indo-European invaders did in many places. But what they could not have done, given their modest numbers, was obliterate the conquered, "Danubian" language without a trace.

As noted earlier, the most favorable circumstance for one people's borrowing words from another is where the two come to occupy the same territory—which on Gimbutas' theory, the Kurganians and Danubians certainly did. Borrowing is even more likely when the lenders outnumber the borrowers—which on ecological grounds they must have done. And it is more likely still when the lenders know something the borrowers don't, which was very probably the case: the Danubians knew a good deal about agriculture that the Kurganians seemingly didn't.

Under the circumstances, it is just not conceivable that the Kurganians would not have incorporated a sizable number of Danubian words into their own allegedly Indo-European tongue. We should find traces of this common "exotic" vocabulary in all the places where the further expansion of the Danube Valley Kurganians carried that tongue—in northern, western and southern Europe. But there are no such traces. All these Indo-European tongues contain exotic words borrowed from non-Indo-European sources—but they are different words, borrowed from different sources. The Danubian language, on the evidence, must have been totally obliterated—and there is simply no example in history where this has happened, given the disparity in numbers already referred to.

We do not even find those seemingly ineradicable traces of lost languages: the names of rivers. Central and eastern Europe have no "Danubian" river names; from the Rhine and Rhone (based on Indo-European *sreu-*, flow) to the Danube and Don (from *danu-*, river), every one of them derives from some recognizable *Indo-European* root.

The implication seems inescapable: the people who named those rivers must have been the original inhabitants—and must have been Indo-Europeans. The archaeological remains of the Danubian farmers, who lived in semipermanent settlements, grew grain, kept cattle, sheep, goats and pigs, and used copper sparsely (they did not smelt it), fit the linguistic "remains" of the Indo-Europeans to a T—which is more than can be said for the archaeological traces of the Kurganians. The Kurganians were later arrivals, very likely speaking an Indo-European dialect, but they were an easterly offshoot of the original, Danubian farmers. Subsequently, the Kurganians may have turned westward again to conquer other Indo-European-speaking peoples. But the conquest, assuming it occurred, would have affected the language of the conquered people little if at all: at the time we are talking about, there would have been few differences between Kurganian and other Indo-European dialects.

To explain the Danubian expansion we need not hypothesize hordes of horsemen, "war carts" or any other secret weapon. The Danubians were able to expand—indeed, were compelled to—because of their expanding population, nourished by the more copious food supplies produced by the new technologies of farming and herding. And they could expand the more easily because over much of Europe *there was almost nobody to oppose them*—a fact attested to by both ecology and archaeology.

Ecology tells us that dense forests, such as then covered most of central, northern and western Europe, are a poor habitat for large animals, including human beings. Trees offer little subsistence to man or beast, while at the same time their shade keeps down much of the low-growing vegetation on which game animals (and therefore their hunters) depend. Archaeology tells us that in fact much of Europe was virtually uninhabited between the end of the Ice Age, when the grassy tundra south of the glaciers became tree-covered, and the arrival of farming cultures that did not have to rely on wild foods, but rather cut down the trees to clear fields for their crops and pastures for their beasts.

The Danubians, whose expansion was, by the standards of prehistory, virtually unprecedented in its speed and scope, may have had something else going for them besides no opposition: a new energy source. To us, "energy" is a strictly modern problem, but its role in human history didn't begin with the oil embargo—or even with the discovery of the steam engine. Something like a million years ago, the controlled use of fire enabled our ancestors to move out of their original tropical habitat into the chillier climates of Europe and eastern Asia; much, much later, the systematic use of water and wind power in parts of Europe made possible a spectacular growth in wealth and population during the late Middle Ages. The Danubians may have discovered animal power. They unquestionably had domestic cattle, which supplied them with meat, milk and hides; there is no reason to think that they had not also made—or learned of—the momentous discovery that castrating a male calf would produce not the ferocious bull but the docile ox, useful for hauling plows and other things. An ox, or pair of oxen, yoked to even the crudest plow, can till far more land than a man or woman wielding only a spade or digging stick.

Be that as it may, the Danubian expansion, attested by archaeology, parallels the Indo-European expansion, attested by linguistics. As Colin Renfrew of the University of Southampton (England) has pointed out, archaeologically speaking there was only one "really basic and wide-spread cultural and economic change in Europe" between the end of the Ice Age and the beginning of the Bronze Age (c. 3000 B.C.): the spread of farming. Linguistically, the spread of the Indo-European tongues was no less "basic and widespread." The simplest and most obvious explanation is that these radical changes were two sides of the same coin.

(To keep the record straight, I should note that Renfrew himself carries his theory even further: he puts the original Indo-European homeland in Greece or Asia Minor, where farming societies had existed for at least a thousand years before they spread to the Danube. I think this is too much of a good thing. To accept his idea, we would have to throw out most of the linguistic evidence concerning the Indo-Europeans' natural environment—can one imagine a people on either side of the Aegean with no word for "sea" or "island"? We would also have to throw out an enormous amount of evidence in the shape of Hittite documents, and Greek history and legend—not to mention place names such as Athens and Corinth, neither of them Indo-European—all of which adds up to the fact that when the Indo-European Greeks and Hittites arrived in Greece and Asia Minor, these regions were already inhabited by non-Indo-European farmers, known to us as the Minoans and Hatti respectively.)

The Danubian theory puts the beginning of the Indo-European expansion between 6000 and 5000 B.C., our "most likely" time frame. It explains why there is a lack of non-Indo-European river names between the Rhine in Germany and the Don in Russia: either the rivers were named by the "original" inhabitants—Indo-Europeans—or the indigenous population was, as archaeology tells us, so sparse and scattered that it, and its river names, vanished without a trace.

The same theory, looked at from another angle, also explains why river names and other traces of *non*-Indo-European peoples are found in parts of western Europe: specifically, west of the Rhine and Rhone, and in some coastal lands to the northwest. Unlike central Europe, these regions had relatively dense populations c. 4500 B.C., for technological and/or ecological reasons.

The Danube was not the only source of farming technology in western

Europe. Even as one wave of farmers was pushing north and west from that region, another more southern wave—of farmers or of agricultural know-how—was moving west along both shores of the Mediterranean; the two met somewhere in France around 4500 B.C. We find evidence of this "southern wave" in Roman references to the Iberians of Spain, whose name survives in the name of the Spanish-Portuguese peninsula. As late as a few centuries before the Christian Era, this people occupied much of Spain and is thought to have earlier dominated much of France as well. A few Iberian inscriptions have survived, too few to allow us to understand much of their tongue, but enough to make clear that it was not Indo-European.

The Iberians are thought to have originated in North Africa, meaning that their language may well have been akin to such known North African tongues as Berber and ancient Egyptian. It is therefore not without interest that the grammar of the Celtic tongues shows what appear to be North African influences, found in no other Indo-European language. These might well reflect the fact that the Celts conquered and absorbed Iberian or related populations in France and parts of Spain; at the same time they could have absorbed certain features of Iberian syntax.

It is in this same part of Europe that we find western Europe's only existing non-Indo-European people: the Basques. Nobody knows where *they* came from, if indeed they "came from" anywhere: they may well have been there since the Ice Age. They themselves are quite certain that they have been around a long, long time: according to one of their legends, when God made the first man, He used the bones of a Basque.

Other non-Indo-European linguistic traces are found along the northern and northwestern coasts of Europe—which are also places where the advancing Danubians would have found tolerably dense populations. Some seem to have already learned about farming, from southern rather than eastern Europe, but all had the advantage of living along the shores of the sea, or of the lakes and marshes that still dot many parts of the area. In such places, the forests would have been more open, providing more forage for deer and other game, while marsh, lake and sea would have supplied additional food resources: fish, shellfish, waterfowl and marine animals such as seal and whale (rock carvings in Scandinavia suggest that the natives may have been hunting whales as early as 4000 B.C.).

Archaeology confirms ecology: even before the coming of agriculture, the population in many of these areas was fairly dense—much denser than that of pre-Danubian central Europe. And linguistics meshes with archaeology: it is in these same coastal areas that we find exotic, non-Indo-European geographical and tribal names, including those of the Belgians, Frisians, Swedes, Goths, Jutes, Britons and Irish. The "Scandi-" in Scandinavia is also non-Indo-European, though the "-avia" comes from an Indo-European root meaning "island" or "peninsula."

To sum up, we find no traces of non-Indo-European tongues, in place names or otherwise, in areas where the pre-Danubian population was sparse. We do find such traces where the pre-Danubian population was denser. Which is precisely what we would expect if the Danubians were in fact the Indo-Europeans. The "Danubian theory" has not been proved beyond a reasonable doubt, and probably never will be. But it does account for all, or nearly all, the known facts, with a minimum of unnecessary or improbable assumptions—which is the best one can expect of any theory about prehistory.

Can we perhaps trace the roots of English back beyond even the Danube, linking Indo-European to some other linguistic family in a linguistic "extended family" or superfamily? Perhaps—and perhaps not. Scholars have long noted resemblances between Indo-European and the languages of the Afro-Asian family, the tongues that have dominated North Africa and western Asia for over five thousand years (they include the ancient Egyptian of the hieroglyphs and the almost equally ancient Akkadian of the cuneiform inscriptions, as well as modern Arabic, Hebrew and Berber).

In ancient Egyptian, for example, "six" was something like *sisw*, "seven" was *sefekh*, "bee" was *bit*—and "mother" was *mwt*. Egyptian inflections, like those of Indo-European, also distinguished the dual from the singular and plural, and all the Afro-Asian tongues are or were heavily inflected, using both inflectional endings and especially ablaut (vowel change). Some scholars are currently at work trying to reconstruct "Parent Afro-Asian," by methods like those used to reconstruct Indo-European; if and when they succeed, we may be able to say with more certainty whether the two families are kin. Similar possible relationships to Indo-European have been suggested for Finno-Ugric, a family whose modern representatives include Finnish, Hungarian and Lappish, and even for Chinese, in which one scholar recently claimed to have found "striking similarities" to Indo-European. Whether these will prove striking enough to exclude coincidence remains to be seen.

We should not, however, expect too much from such efforts. Knowing what we do about how languages change with time, we can be certain that, given enough time, even closely related tongues will diverge so radically that their relationship cannot be proved by the most sophisticated analysis. For now, and perhaps forever, the Indo-European of around 6000 B.C. is as deep as we can go in tracing the roots of English. It is time now to see what grew from those roots.

3. THE FIRST CONQUEST

From the Danube to the Baltic

☙

Faithfulness to the truth of history involves far more than a research, however patient and scrupulous, into special facts. . . . The narrator must seek to imbue himself with the life and spirit of the time.

—FRANCIS PARKMAN

If a man could say nothing . . . but what he could prove, history could not be written.

—SAMUEL JOHNSON

CENTURY by century and tribe by tribe, the Indo-Europeans pressed outward from their Danubian homeland—east into the Russian steppes and deep into central Asia, southeast as far as India, south into Greece and Italy, west to the Atlantic, and north to the Baltic. Our concern, at this point, is only with the last-mentioned migration, which gave rise to the Germanic branch of Indo-European.

The modern Germanic tongues include, along with English, standard or "High" German (the native language of most Germans and Austrians and a majority of Swiss) and its close relative, Yiddish; Low German (*Plattdeutsch*), spoken by a minority of Germans (most of whom also speak standard German), and *its* relatives—Dutch-Flemish (virtually a single language) and its Afrikaans offshoot, and the Frisian spoken by some 300,000 people in northern Holland. To the north lies another related group of Germanic tongues: Danish, Swedish and Norwegian and, far out in the Atlantic, Faroese and Icelandic.

All these languages show marked resemblances in phonetics, vocabulary and syntax. To take just one example, where we say "sing, sang, sung" the German says *singen, sang, gesungen,* the Hollander *zingen, zong, gezongen* and the Swede *sjunga, sjöng, sjungit.* As one would expect, resemblances among the older Germanic tongues—Gothic, recorded as early as the fourth century A.D., Old English, from the seventh century, and Old High German, from the ninth—are even more marked. From these similarities, it is clear that all the Germanic languages derive from a common source, called Common Germanic (or Primitive Germanic), just as the Romance tongues all derive from Latin, and Latin and Common Germanic from Indo-European. Like its ancestor, Common Germanic was never written down, but can be reconstructed by the same techniques. The job is a good deal easier, in fact, since the time span involved is much smaller: less than a thousand years.

Easily the most striking trait distinguishing Common Germanic from the other Indo-European tongues is phonetic: systematic changes in no less than nine of the original Indo-European consonants. These changes, often called the Great Consonant Shift, were summarized a century and a half ago by the German philologist Jakob Grimm (who with his brother also wrote *Grimms' Fairy Tales*).

According to Grimm's Law (as it is now called), the first step in the evolution of Common Germanic from Indo-European was the use of /f/ for Indo-European /p/ (a change already discussed in the previous chapter), of /th/ for Indo-European /t/, and of /h/ for /k/. We can illustrate these changes rather neatly in English by comparing "native" (i.e., Germanic) words, in which these changes took place, with borrowed ones from Latin and its descendants, in which they did not. Thus the shift from /p/ to /f/ is reflected in Germanic "FaTHerly" versus Latin "PaTernal"; the shift from /t/ to /th/ by "THRee" versus "TRiple"; and the shift from /k/ to /h/ by "HoRN" versus "CoRNet." Such pairs of words, coming from a common source but reaching a language through different routes, are called doublets. Note that /r/ and /n/ remained unchanged in both languages, thereby helping to point up the relationships.

Having gained three new consonants by losing three old ones, Common Germanic recouped the loss by making a "new" /p/ out of Indo-European /b/, a /t/ out of /d/, and a /k/ out of /g/. We see these changes in such doublets as Germanic "PeG" versus Latin "BaCillus" (a peg- or rod-shaped microbe, whose C was originally pronounced "hard," as /k/), Germanic "Ten" versus Latin "Decimal" and "CoRN" versus "GRaiN."

Again Common Germanic had "lost" three Indo-European consonants, while gaining (or regaining) three others. The final step was to form the lost /b/, /d/ and /g/ out of the Indo-European aspirated consonants, /bʰ/, /dʰ/ and /gʰ/. Here, unfortunately, there are no convenient doublets to illustrate the change, since the aspirates also vanished in Latin.

This game of phonetic musical chairs, though it did not radically alter the overall phonetic repertory of Common Germanic compared with Indo-European (three consonants gained, three lost), had the effect of changing the pronunciation of a *majority* of words in the vocabulary. These changes, as compared with those in Latin and most other Indo-European tongues, were unusually extensive, and also remarkably consistent. They affected initial consonants almost without exception, and most of the time also affected consonants occurring within words. Notable exceptions were the combinations /sp/, /st/ and /sk/, which did *not* shift to /sf/, /sth/ and /skh/ (as one would expect from Grimm's Law), perhaps because the Primitive Germans found these combinations hard to pronounce, as we ourselves certainly would. Since the same combinations also remained unchanged in Latin, we have such Germanic-Latinate doublets as "SPiLL" and "SPoiL" (if you spill something, you also spoil it, and often the carpet as well), "STaR" and "STellar," and "SCaB" and "SCaBies."

Nobody has any plausible explanation of why these extensive changes occurred in Common Germanic, nor is there any way of telling *when* they occurred, apart from the fact that the whole process must have occupied some centuries at least. It was probably complete by about 500 B.C., but when it started is anybody's guess. For simplicity, I will in the balance of this chapter use the "definitive" Common Germanic forms of words—i.e., those whose sounds reflect *all* the changes of the Great Consonant Shift, even though at times I may be writing about periods before the shift was complete or even before it started.

As Indo-European had its homeland—most likely, as we have seen, in the Danube Valley—Common Germanic evolved in *its* homeland: north-western Continental Europe, an area in which its speakers lived long enough, and in sufficient isolation from other Indo-European groups, for their language to develop its distinctive characteristics. It is in that area —roughly, modern north Germany, Denmark and the southern Scandinavian peninsula—that the ancestral Germans make their first dim appearance in history, through the writings of a few Greek and Roman authors; we have every reason to believe they had been there for centuries. How they got there, and how their lives changed during and after this great migration, is naturally reflected in their vocabulary, with other clues coming from ecology and archaeology.

When those Indo-Europeans who would one day become the Germans —or at any rate a major component of the Primitive Germanic population —began moving north from the Danube Valley, they were passing from a region of mixed woodland and grassland into one of dense deciduous forest. As we've already noted, this environment was ill suited to the needs of hunting cultures, because it yielded little game. It was also not much of a bargain to primitive farmers. The lowland areas were often boggy (the climate around 5500 B.C. was both moister and warmer than at present), while the uplands had thin and often rocky soil. And almost everywhere, clearing cropland meant felling virgin oaks and beeches up to four feet across—no easy job with stone axes.

Not surprisingly, then, archaeologists have found that the earliest Danubian migrants in northern Europe typically settled only in especially favorable sites: the so-called loess plateaus found along the sides of many river valleys in the area. Loess—soil laid down during the Ice Age by the cold, dry winds blowing off the glaciers—is free from rocks, and loose (which is what the word means in German), hence is well drained, rather thinly wooded, and relatively easy to cultivate.

By around 5300 B.C., according to the archaeological record, farming cultures with clear links to the earlier Danubians were scattered over the loess areas of northern Europe, between the mountains of modern Czechoslovakia and southern Germany and the sandy plains bordering the Baltic. Somewhere among them, presumably, were the ancestral Germans, but nobody knows where. My own guess would be among the most easterly of these groups, whose traces have been unearthed in central and southern Poland. My reason is the evidence of long-term contact between the Germanic peoples and the Finns, who were certainly living around the eastern Baltic at the beginning of the Christian Era, and had probably been there a good long time even then.

This evidence is the words borrowed from the Germanic tongues into Finnish. That language, for unknown reasons, is phonetically very conservative: its pronunciation has apparently changed little for at least two thousand years. Throughout this period, the Finns have borrowed words from their Germanic neighbors and preserved many of them virtually unaltered. Some sound like words in medieval Swedish; others are evidently earlier borrowings, from Old Norse. Still others are neither Swedish nor Norse but rather resemble reconstructed words from the vocabulary of Common Germanic.

Most of these words have undergone phonetic change, but usually little more than was needed to assimilate them to the phonetic rules of Finnish, as we know, a normal process in word borrowing. For instance, Common Germanic *kuningaz, king, became Finnish kuningas, because Finnish has no /z/; the same process assimilated Common Germanic *lambaz, lamb, into Finnish lammas—/b/, like /z/, being a foreign sound in Finnish. But Common Germanic *airo, oar, was perfectly consistent with Finnish phonetics and is still pronounced the same way, /eye-ro/, by today's Finns.

None of these borrowings need date much before the beginning of the Christian Era, but others hark back to some earlier period before the Great Consonant Shift was complete—specifically, when the primitive Germans were still using the aspirated consonants that they later converted into /b/, /d/ and /g/. There is no good reason why Common Germanic *sandam, sand, should have become Finnish santa, since /d/ is perfectly acceptable in Finnish, but the change makes sense if the borrowed word was pronounced *sand^{h}am, since /d^h/ was probably as strange to Finnish tongues as it is to our own. (The final /m/ was dropped "normally": Finnish words cannot end with that sound.) Similar reasoning would derive Finnish kulta, gold, not from Common Germanic *gultham but from the earlier *g^{h}ultam.

Finnish onki, fishhook, may take us back even further, to Indo-European *onki-, hook, rather than its Germanic offspring, *angul (whence both "angle" and "angler"); likewise, Finnish orpo, orphan, must come from Indo-European *orb^{h}o-, a word that apparently dropped out of the Common Germanic vocabulary ("orphan" came into English from Greek via Latin). Finnish sisar, sister, is closer to Indo-European *swesor than to Common Germanic *swestr-, and Finnish pelto, field, is surely from Indo-European *pelto-, not Common Germanic *felthu-.

We can therefore visualize the primitive Germans as moving north or northwesterly along the edge of the Finnish lands (wherever that may have been) over a period of many centuries, until they reached the Baltic coast. At some point, they must have encountered some other people who also knew the Finns, since Common Germanic *finnar, Finn, is not Indo-European, nor is it anything like what the Finns call themselves, hence was presumably borrowed from some third party. (In much the same way, our term "Eskimo" was not borrowed from that people, who call themselves Inuit, but from some native third party.)

Who this "third party" was, and where the Germans encountered them, we have no way of knowing. What we do know is that when they reached their eventual homeland, they encountered a people who already had some knowledge of agriculture and stockraising. The most likely candidate for this role is the "Ertbölle people," whose archaeological traces, dating from around 4300 B.C., have been unearthed in Denmark and adjacent areas. The "Ertbölleans" were the first farmers in that region, but were not themselves Indo-Europeans. Their tools, pottery and other cultural traits resembled those of western rather than eastern Europe, and they, were, moreover, only part-time farmers, relying heavily on hunting, fishing and the collection of shellfish and wild plants. By contrast, the Danubian-related (i.e., presumably Indo-European) cultures of southern Poland were already getting the *bulk* of their subsistence from crops and domestic animals a thousand years earlier.

The actual Germanic settlement in southern Scandinavia and northern Germany ought to show up in the archaeological record as a culture with resemblances to both the indigenous Ertbölle culture and the Danubian cultures to the southeast. We find just such archaeological relics dating from around 3800 B.C.—those of the so-called TRB culture (the initials stand for a distinctive type of pottery), which succeeded the Ertbölle culture in and around the Danish peninsula. Some of its artifacts were Ertböllean in style, others Danubian; moreover, it relied much more heavily than the Ertbölleans on food production, though hunting and fishing still supplemented the produce of crops and herds. Finally, the extent of the TRB settlements shows that its people were considerably more numerous than their predecessors, no doubt because their food supplies were more copious. This relatively dense population makes it unlikely that any later migrations could have imposed a new language on the area. Which is to say that the TRB people, or at least the majority of them, spoke Common Germanic, or a language directly ancestral to it— basically, Indo-European modified by whichever of the characteristic Germanic phonetic changes had occurred in the two thousand years or so between their departure from the Danube and their arrival in Denmark.

There can be little doubt, however, that that language also included by this time a number of exotic words that the Germans had acquired along the way from whatever aboriginal groups they encountered—in particular, along the Baltic coast, where the Germans must have run into some remarkable new experiences of the sort that, as we've seen, make for the borrowing of new words. In any individual case, to be sure, we can't be certain whether an exotic word in the Germanic vocabulary was borrowed or simply invented, as "dog" was invented by the early English. But when we find a whole group of exotic words, all relating to a particular new area of experience, the odds are heavy that they were borrowed, not made up in a body.

Surely the most striking new experience that the Germans encountered during their long migration was the first sight of the great expanse of salt-to-brackish water that we call the Baltic. Compared with the Atlantic or Pacific, the Baltic is not much of an ocean, but it must have been impressive enough to people who had never seen *any* ocean, as the Germans certainly had not and their Danubian ancestors probably had not. Not surprisingly, then, we find that the Germanic term for such great expanses of water was exotic, not Indo-European: *saiwaz (whence Dutch *zee*, German *see* and our "sea"). We find with it a whole series of exotic words for marine or coastal animals—*maiwa, mew (a kind of gull); *selkhaz, seal; *sturyon, sturgeon; and *haringaz, a fish still consumed by the barrel, in smoked, pickled or salted form, in every nation bordering the Baltic. Two other probably exotic maritime words are *ethi-, eider, and *alki-, auk.

Nonetheless, the Germans did not neglect their own linguistic resources in finding names for some new maritime creatures. *Swanuz originally meant something like "singer" (it comes from the same root as "sound"), but was applied to what must have been the whooper swan, European counterpart of the American trumpeter swan. Significantly, the whooper, unlike its notoriously silent relative the common swan, is seldom found far from salt water. From their word for "goose," *gans, the Germans coined *ganitaz for a bird almost as famous for its silliness at sea as the goose is on land (several species of gannet are called "boobies"). A Germanic root meaning "scratch" supplied a name for that scratchy sea creature the *krabb-; another, meaning "flat," begot the *flunthryo, while a related root produced the *flok-, whose flat descendants, the flounder and fluke, are still with us.

Along with new birds and beasts along the Baltic shore, the Germans found new technologies. Like their ancestors along the Danube, they had boats, though by this time they were calling them not *nau- but *bait-. The ultimate root of this latter word means "split," and suggests that these craft were dugout canoes (or, just possibly, made of split planks). The *bait- was propelled by some sort of oar or paddle, *ret-. But while a *bait- and a *ret- will carry you safely across a *straumaz (stream) or a *mari- (mere—a lake or pond), they aren't much use on the Baltic or any other *saiwaz—at least if you care about getting back to *landam.

The maritime tribes that the Germans found living along the Baltic evidently possessed a larger and more seaworthy craft that they called *skipam—or at least that's how the Germans pronounced it—whence "ship." It was powered by longer and narrower paddles whose aboriginal name, in German mouths, came out *airo (oar), and perhaps also by a *seglam (sail) hoisted on a *masta. (This last word, however, was coined by the Germans themselves, from a root meaning "pole.") The *skipam, too big to be carved from a single log, must have been built up piece by piece, starting with a strong *kelaz, probably with *rebya- (ribs) attached, and planked with split *bordaz. From both archaeological and historical evidence, we can guess that the vessel was a smaller version of later Germanic and Scandinavian craft, having (in the words of the Roman historian Tacitus) "a prow at each end . . . always ready for running into shore." (Tacitus also claimed that these ships lacked sails, which may or may not be true. He had never seen one, but based his description on travelers' tales and what we would call "military intelligence"—even less reliable then than now.)

Though the technology of shipbuilding was new to the Germans, most of its materials were not; thus *kelaz* is an exotic term, but *bordaz* comes from Indo-European *b^herd^h-*, cut. Equally familiar were the materials used for sewing the planks together (nails were unknown), a method still used well into the Christian era: *senawo-* (sinew) or tough *wrot-* (roots). Since sewing was an old story to the Germans, they called the junction between two *borda-* by their old word for the join between two pieces of cloth or leather: *saumaz* (seam). To caulk the *saumaz* they would have used still other familiar materials: hanks of *wullo* or twisted *heram* (hair), soaked in *terw-* (tar—i.e., pine pitch; the word comes from the same root as "tree").

The Germans' paddle or short oar (*ret-*) was not much good for propulsion compared with the new *airo*, but proved useful for *stiuringe* the *skipam*. Phonetically transmuted into *rothra*, it became a steering paddle—mounted, of course on the ship's *stiurbordaz* side. Much later, it would be permanently fixed to the stern ("steering place"), as the rudder.

With *skipam*, *airo* and perhaps a *seglam*, the Germans could now emulate the aborigines in exploiting the Baltic's food resources, catching the *flunthryo-* and *heringaz* with *angul* and *neti-*, and *huntjinge selkhaz* and even *smalaz hwaliz* with a *langaz speru*. (If you haven't yet got the knack of translating Common Germanic into English, this means "hunting seal and small whale with a long spear." This last may well have been a harpoon, a device known since the Ice Age, but the word itself is a much later borrowing into English.)

The Germans' northward migration brought them new technologies and food resources, but also a new problem: colder weather. This was the more true in that the climate itself was changing; the relatively mild temperatures of around 5000 B.C. had dropped to near present-day levels a couple of thousand years later. All of which raised the elementary problem of keeping *warmaz*.

At a plausible guess, the Indo-Europeans along the Danube wore some sort of tunic (linen in summer, wool in winter) over a loincloth; at the height of summer, the men, at least, probably dispensed with the tunic. In winter, these garments would have been supplemented by fur or sheepskin cloaks, with sandals or moccasinlike footgear.

But by the time the Germans had reached their new—and chillier—homeland, they had pretty certainly invented *galofo-* for winter wear (the word comes from an Indo-European root meaning "palm"). They also found the aborigines using a different type of hand-warmer (mittens?), called *wantuz* (whence, after unusually extensive phonetic alteration, "gauntlet"), and a new kind of footgear, whose name the Germans borrowed as *skohaz* (whence "shoe"). These may have been ankle- or calf-length boots, waterproofed with *talgaz* (tallow), which would have been equally useful aboard a *skipam* or traveling across the widespread *mariska landam* (marsh land) of Denmark and parts adjacent. An even more useful winter garment was the fitted, sewn trousers called *broks* (whence "breeches"), another exotic word. (It was borrowed independently by the Celts, presumably from an aboriginal group of similar speech.) These would have been made of *klath-*, *lethram* or perhaps *feltaz*—the last apparently a German invention, since it comes from an Indo-European root meaning "beat" (felt is formed by beating wool into thin layers).

The cooler climate forced agricultural as well as sartorial changes. Along the Danube, wheat and barley had been the main food crops, and archaeological evidence—impressions of grain on pottery, and sometimes the carbonized grains themselves—shows that they remained so in the Danubian settlements of southern Poland around 5000 B.C.; rye shows up so rarely as to suggest it was merely a weed in the fields. Along the Baltic, however, the cooler, shorter summers would have reduced the yield of the traditional grains so that the hardier rye could come into its own as a prime food crop, as it still is on both sides of the Baltic. It may well be at this time that wheat acquired its distinctive Germanic name of *hwaitaz,* referring to its white flour in contrast with the darker rye meal.

The Baltic aboriginals made their own contribution to the food supply, in the shape of a grain called *hafur.* This exotic word survives in English only in the borrowed word "haversack"—originally, the sack in which a cavalryman carried oats for his horse. ("Oats" itself came into English about the same time as "dog," and equally mysteriously.) The grain had been domesticated earlier, probably in northwestern Europe, to whose cool, damp climate it is well adapted.

The Germans brought domesticated sheep with them from the Danube, but almost certainly found the aborigines herding them too.

One exotic word for the animal might be coincidence, but three—
*ramma, *lambaz and *skaepa (sheep)—can hardly come from anything
but borrowing. The aborigines may also have kept goats; though that
word is Indo-European, *kidhyu- is not (it is now, of course, applied more
often to young humans than to young goats). Another domestic animal
was surely the dog, whose aboriginal name may be reflected in Common
Germanic *bekyon (whence "bitch"), and which doubtless rapidly inter-
bred with the Germans own *hunda- (whence "hound").

Just possibly the aborigines contributed something to Germanic agricultural technology more valuable than oats or new breeds of *skaepa: the
technique of fertilizing the fields with what they called—or the Germans
pronounced—*dunga. The Indo-Europeans had a word for this stuff,
*gwou-, which they also used to express annoyance (it is the ultimate root
of "bother"), presumably in an expression equivalent to "Oh, dung!"
But there is no evidence that they used it as fertilizer. Rather, they practiced "slash and burn" agriculture, cutting the trees on a patch of land,
letting them dry and then, after removing whatever timber was needed
for fuel and construction, setting fire to the remains. The ashes sweetened the rather acid forest soil, and added valuable minerals—which,
however, would last for only a few seasons, after which the whole process
had to be repeated on another patch of forest. And once all the nearby
land was used up, the tribe would have to pull up stakes and move to a
new location—as, on the archaeological evidence, the Danubian migrants
into northern Europe often did.

Slash-and-burn agriculture worked well enough as long as land was
plentiful. In Denmark, however, farmers had reached a sort of last frontier: to east and west lay the *saiwaz, while to the north lay still colder and
less fertile lands (even today, only 8 percent of Sweden and even less of
Norway is cultivated). Yet farming cultures persisted in the region from
4500 B.C. to the present, strongly suggesting that they had devised a way
of maintaining soil fertility: taking *dunga from the sheds where animals
were kept in winter and spreading it across the *felthuz (field) with a
wooden *skubilon (shovel).

Tacitus describes how the Germans of around 100 A.D. piled up dung
over caches of food, both to discourage thieves and to keep the food from
freezing (as many home gardeners know, a compost heap can generate
quite high temperatures within and beneath it). The historian does not
mention the use of dung as fertilizer, but probably took that for granted.
We have no proof that the Germans acquired this technique from the
aborigines, but their ancestral word for manure certainly dropped out of

use ("bother" is a borrowed word, from Irish) and was replaced by a borrowed (or invented) one.

Perhaps the most revolutionary discovery relating to agriculture concerned not food but drink—and it seems to have been a purely Germanic invention. Like their Indo-European ancestors, the Germans drank *medu*- fermented from *hunagam* (honey)—but not very often: wild bees' nests are not all that easy to find (or harvest!). Even after the Germans learned to domesticate *biona* in a *hufi*- (hive), the honey output still cannot have been copious: in Germanic mythology, mead is the drink of gods and heroes, not common folk.

What democratized alcohol in northern Europe was the discovery that if grain was allowed to sprout into *maltaz* and then fermented with a mash of ground barley, it would produce what Tacitus fastidiously described as "a liquor for drinking [with] a certain resemblance to wine." The Germans christened the new, cheap tipple *aluth*- (from the same ancestral root that produced "hallucination"), and evidently consumed it with abandon: Tacitus tells us that in Germany "to pass an entire day and night in drinking disgraces no one." The Germans and their linguistic relatives, from Berlin to Melbourne, have been drinking ale and its close relative, beer, ever since.

Fermentation was also put to more mundane uses. The primitive varieties of wheat that the Germans had cultivated since Danubian times would not rise well when converted into dough, and the same was true of barley and rye (modern risen "rye" bread is actually made from mixed wheat and rye flour). By around 2000 B.C., however, a new variety of wheat had made its way into northwestern Europe, one containing enough gluten so that when *yest*- was added to the dough it would rise into a light, puffy *hlaibaz* (loaf). This word, which originally meant (risen?) "bread," is exotic, perhaps borrowed from the unknown people who introduced the Germans to bread wheat. But the latter also coined their own word for the loaves, *braudam*, from the same root that produced "brew"—presumably because *yest*- was an essential ingredient in making both bread and ale.

Yet another product of fermentation was *yustaz*, a word that in most modern Germanic tongues has been replaced by "cheese" and similar terms, surviving only in the Scandinavian *ost*. The probable connection between *yustaz* and the Indo-European root of "juice" indicates that the stuff was moist and soft like modern cottage cheese—in fact, the "curds" that Tacitus cites as a prime ingredient in the German diet.

These three products of fermentation—bread, cheese and ale—remained central to the everyday Germanic (and English) diet right through the Middle Ages. Even today, they are served up as a "ploughman's lunch" at many English country inns.

Another possible aboriginal contribution to Germanic life is suggested by the exotic word *thwahan, bathe (whence, ultimately, "towel"). Doubtless the Indo-Europeans of the Danube washed themselves—at least occasionally—in the local lakes and streams, but in northern Europe this practice did not recommend itself except in midsummer. Yet Tacitus tells us that the Germans enjoyed hot baths; in fact, the Common Germanic *batham comes from the same Indo-European root as "bake." And thereby hangs a small linguistic detective story.

When I first encountered this linguistic and historical evidence of Germanic hot baths, I naturally wondered what they bathed *in.* Hot springs, like those that would later give the English town of Bath its name, existed in only a few places; metal tubs would surely have left archaeological traces. Barrel-like wooden tubs, then? Perhaps, though Tacitus doesn't mention them. An outside possibility was a sauna, but this seemed highly unlikely: the word is a modern borrowing into the Germanic tongues from Finnish.

A few weeks later, however, I happened to be looking up the derivation of "stove." Rather surprisingly, I found its ancestor, *stofa,* in a dictionary of Old English, where, however, it was translated not as "stove" (a much later invention) but as "bathing room." (Its modern German equivalent, *Stube,* means simply "room.") And the same dictionary gave the combination *stof-bath,* vapor bath—a sauna, in fact. It seems likely, then, that this Old English sauna had a long history in the Germanic lands, though in today's English-speaking world it is a new and trendy discovery. As Tacitus noted, hot baths "suit a country where winter is the longest of the seasons"—and the sauna is unquestionably the simplest kind of hot bath, requiring neither tub nor kettle but merely a small hut, a pile of heated rocks and a bucket of water. It was, in fact, used all over North America before Columbus, by peoples of about the same cultural level as the ancestral Germans. Indeed, its invention may go back to Ice Age times, when winters were even longer. European archaeologists have dug up collections of stones showing traces of having been repeatedly heated and then abruptly cooled. The usual explanation is that they were used in cooking, being dropped into a water-filled hide container, but their use in a *stof-bath* would have produced similar traces.

Thus far, we have discussed exotic words in the vocabulary of Common Germanic as they related to new animals and technologies—things that the natives knew and the Germans didn't. But many more such words are everyday terms, taken into Common Germanic in such numbers as to imply not merely contact between the two peoples but a true intermixture of populations in the Germanic homeland of northern Germany and southern Scandinavia. Particularly striking in this connection are terms relating to the sexes and to family relationships.

"Family" words are normally among the most stable words in any tongue—for example, "father" and "mother" in English and their equivalents in most other Indo-European tongues. In Common Germanic, however, we have a whole group of such terms in which an indigenous Germanic word, derived from Indo-European, is paired with an exotic synonym. Thus the Germanic *weraz, man (from the same root as Latin-derived "virile") pairs with exotic *karlaz. (Both terms have changed radically; *karlaz has undergone what the philologists call pejorative change, to yield the rude, grasping "churl," while *weraz has vanished completely from English except in the compound "werewolf" —man-wolf.) Likewise, Germanic *kwenon, woman (whence both "queen" and "quean"), pairs with the exotic *wif, which as late as the Middle Ages could mean any woman, married or unmarried. (Our "woman" comes from the Old English *wyfman*, female person.) Along with these are other exotic "sexual" terms like *brudhiz, bride, and *wamba, womb.

Marriages between a Germanic *weraz and an aboriginal *wif, or a Germanic *kwenon and an aboriginal *karlaz, naturally produced children —aboriginal *kiltha or Germanic *barna (whence Scottish "bairn"). These were, of course, either girls (Germanic *magadi-, whence "maiden") or boys (aboriginal *knapon—which, like *karlaz, has undergone pejorative change to yield "knave," though its modern German equivalent, *Knabe*, retains the original sense).

Further evidence of the intimate, relaxed relationships between the two groups shows up in a host of other commonplace exotic words: *husam, house (which replaced Indo-European *domo-); *tou-, make (whence the tools we make things with); *risan, rise; *hlaupan, leap; *lagjiz, leg; *handuz, hand; *skuldar, shoulder; *bainam, bone; *seukaz, sick; *hairsaz, hoarse; not to mention *newhiz, near; *lik-, like; *ibnaz, even; and *allaz, all. *Kak-, round object, eventually gave us, through various channels, "cake," "cookie" and "quiche," while an apparently aboriginal root *ker- or *kr- begot over the centuries a whole family of words related to bending: modern English members include "crooked" (in both senses— in English slang, a criminal is "bent"), "cripple" ("bent over"), "creek" (originally, and still in England, a crooked inlet from the sea), and "la-crosse"—played, of course, with a net attached to a bent stick. (The resemblance between aboriginal *ker- and Indo-European *ker-, horn, is purely coincidental: the Indo-European term, by Grimm's law, became *hor- in Germanic.)

What else can we deduce about these mysterious aborigines whose tongue survives only in the linguistic fossils it left in English and the other Germanic tongues? They were certainly pioneering farmers in that part of the world—their words for "sheep" and "oats" make that clear. But some of them, at least, may have been descended from the pre-agricul-tural inhabitants of the region, aborigines in the most literal sense. That is, they would have derived from the reindeer hunters who moved north into Scandinavia as the glaciers melted. This is a guess—but based on some striking features of Germanic mythology.

The Germanic myths naturally resemble those of the other Indo-European peoples in many respects. Most of their gods, for example, can be equated fairly easily with Greek and Roman deities—sometimes with different names, sometimes with the same name modified by phonetic changes: thus Germanic Tiw equals Greek Zeus equals Roman Jove—all from Indo-European *deiw-. But some Germanic myths are unique, meaning that they were probably borrowed from the aborigines. A nota-ble feature is the prominent role played by frost and ice; thus the Ger-manic *halyo (hell) was seen as freezing cold, not burning hot—as one would expect from people who had lived for thousands of years in the climate of Scandinavia.

Even more striking is the German creation myth. The world, it de-clared, consisted originally of a bottomless deep filled with ice; life began when the ice was melted by a warm wind from the south. This sounds remarkably like the actual end of the Ice Age as it might have been described by people who had witnessed it. At the height of the glacial retreat, the "warm winds" were pushing back the ice sheets at the rate of a mile or more a year; within the lifetime of a single person, this process would have "created" a fifty-mile strip of land in which life could begin. Equally, the Germanic version of the end of the world, Ragnarok, marked by "six years with no summer," may have been inspired by one of the sudden, temporary readvances of ice that marked the latter stages of the Ice Age, which to people dwelling near the glaciers might indeed have seemed the end of everything.

Other features of the aboriginal culture can be guessed at from other exotic words in the Germanic vocabulary. Doubtless they had tribal chiefs of some sort, whose title may be reflected in the exotic *erilaz* (whence "earl"), perhaps the counterpart of the Germanic *kuningaz* ("one of the royal kin," from whose ranks the historic Germans seem to have elected their kings). At the opposite end of the social scale we have *knihtaz*, servant, and *skalkaz*, slave, though we cannot be sure whether these terms reflect the pre-German aboriginal social structure, or the darker side of the Germanic conquest, in which some of the conquered aborigines may well have become servants or outright slaves. Interestingly, both words later underwent "ameliorative" change; unlike "knave" and "churl," they figuratively rose in the social scale to produce "knight" and "marshal," originally *markhazskalkaz*—a "horse slave," or stable hand.

The aboriginals, like other peoples civilized and otherwise, undoubtedly marked the year with religious-magical ceremonies. Perhaps the most important of these came in midwinter when the days, after shortening to some six or seven hours, began lengthening once more—surely worth a celebration in chilly Scandinavia. In fact, it seems to have been marked by a full twelve days of feasting (later, no doubt, including copious *aluth-drinkunge*) to mark the festival of *yehwla* (Yule)—the origin of our Twelve Days of Christmas.

We can even make a guess at what these people called themselves: the same thing that scores of other primitive people call or called themselves —"The People" (which is the meaning, for instance, of "Bantu," "Navaho" and "Inuit"). The Germans' own ancestral word for "people" was *manni*—which shows up in historical tribal names such as Alemanni ("all-the-people", whence the French word for Germany, *Allemagne*) and Marcomanni ("border people"—the "mark" being a landmark or boundary). But the Germans somewhere acquired an exotic term for "people," *folkam*, which quite possibly represents the tribal name of the indigenous Scandinavians they met and merged with. Eventually, of course, the Indo-European elements in the language prevailed, whether because the Germans dominated the natives as conquerors or simply because they outnumbered them, or both. The aboriginal, "Folkish" element survived only in bits and pieces in the merged vocabulary.

Additions to and changes in the Germanic vocabulary naturally didn't end with their absorption of the "Folk." Thereafter, however, the new words reflect mainly the arrival of new ideas and inventions from southern and eastern Europe. An important one was the *hwehulaz*, a circular slab of wood rotating on an *akhso* (axle). These primitive wheels, some of which have been dug up in Danish bogs, were carved from a single oak board—flat, but with a thicker ring in the center surrounding the *akhso-*

hulaz. This central portion was called the **nabo* (nave), akin to **nabulon* (navel)—which is about what it looked like. The **hwehulaz* reached Scandinavia around 2500 B.C.

In sets of two or four, the **hwehulaz* was used to mount a **wagnaz*— originally, no doubt, much like the sledges the Germans and their ancestors had been using for centuries, but with wheels substituted for runners, making the wagon much more efficient than its predecessor so long as the ground was reasonably firm. A thousand years or so later, the solid slab wheel began to be replaced by a much lighter version made with **spaiko* (spokes): a rock engraving from Sweden, dating from before 1000 B.C., shows a man riding in just such a light, spoke-wheeled chariot.

Significantly, this vehicle is not drawn by **okhson*, as were the heavy, solid-wheeled carts, but by what are clearly two **horsa-*. This word is usually classified as "o.o.o."—presumably borrowed from whoever supplied the Germans with their first domesticated horses (the animal was not native to northern Europe). The English word expert Eric Partridge, however, has suggested that it derives (through Grimm's Law) from Indo-European **kers-*, run (whence, via Latin, a host of words, including the "course" on which modern **horsa-* run races). The suggestion makes sense both phonetically and semantically: the outstanding trait of the new draft animals was that they *could* run, while the best the **okhson* could achieve was a shambling trot.

Whether indigenous or borrowed, the new word probably marks the introduction of the domesticated horse to what we may as well call Germania—the Germanic homeland as defined above (not to be confused with the Latin geographical term, which meant anywhere between the Rhine and the Danube). Common Germanic had inherited two perfectly good terms for the horse, **markhas* (whence "mare") and **ehwa* (whence Old English *eoh*, now extinct, and probably archaic even then, since it is found only in poetry). The **horsam* was doubtless also used for **ridunge*, which then or later brought other inventions: the **sadaluz* (originally no more than a cloth across the animal's back), the **spuron* and the **stigraipaz*, or mounting rope—a loop of rope tossed across the horse's back and held by the "horse slave," allowing the rider to mount more easily; much later it was applied to a new invention, the stirrup.

Even before the coming of the **horsam*, another new technology had reached Germania: the working of **aiz* (copper, and later bronze). The latter is of course an alloy of **aiz* (an old Indo-European word) and **tinam*, an exotic term as tin was certainly an exotic metal in Germania. Both the word and the metal must have come from or through some aboriginal group to the south—probably the same people from whom the Celts borrowed *their* term for tin, *stanom,* the source of Latin *stannum* and hence of our chemical symbol for the metal, Sn.

Metalworking brought the *smithaz* and his specialized tools—not just the *hamaraz* (versions of which had been used for other purposes since the Old Stone Age) but also the *tanguz* for holding the hot metal steady on the *anfilt* ("on-beaten"). Mastery of these tools, not to mention such recondite skills as casting and tempering, must have involved a long apprenticeship, which is to say that the *smithaz* was probably the first full-time "specialist" in Germania, as he was in many other primitive societies. (Initially, he may have been a man with physical handicaps barring him from more active pursuits: dwarfed, like the metalworkers of German mythology, or lame, like the Roman Vulcan and his Greek counterpart, Hephaestus.) His name survives today as one of the very commonest Germanic family names—Smid, Schmidt or Smith.

This prominence, however, lay in the future: the Bronze Age smith was a useful but hardly an important member of the community, as bronze itself was of only minor economic importance, too dear for any purpose where stone or bone would do. In Germania, as in other parts of barbarian Europe, a major use was for items of personal adornment like brooches and belt buckles. But it was also forged into blades for *kniba-* (knives) and *segith-* (sickles—the Germanic word survives as "scythe")— no sharper than stone blades, but far less brittle, and much easier to resharpen, by rubbing them on a *hwatyastainaz* (whetstone). Bronze was also cast into *akusyo-* for tree-felling, and fabricated into horse bits and *swerda-*. These long blades would have been invaluable in hand-to-hand fighting, but were probably beyond the means of the average warrior, being wielded only by such tribal leaders as the *kuningaz* and *erilaz.*

Much more economically significant was the Iron Age, which reached central Europe (by then pretty certainly occupied by the Celts) around 700 B.C. and spread to Germania a few centuries later. Iron was harder to fabricate than bronze, but it held an edge better and above all was much cheaper. It was forged (it could not then be cast) into such things as saws, chisels, knives, swords, helmets and—perhaps most significantly —plowshares: iron-tipped plows could till the soil more deeply than their wooden predecessors, and could also cultivate stony soils that would have blunted or broken wooden plows.

In Celtic central Europe, the cheaper and better tools brought something of a boom, judging from the richer funeral offerings found in burials from the period. Population increased markedly, leading to an almost explosive expansion, reaching Asia Minor on the east, where Gaulish Celts founded the kingdom of Galatia (to whose inhabitants St. Paul would address a famous epistle) and Great Britain on the west. (Many of these western regions were probably already Celtic, thanks to an earlier wave of migration, whose linguistic traces survive in modern Erse and Scots Gaelic, as those of the Iron Age Celts do in Welsh and Breton.)

To Germania, however, the Iron Age at first brought hard times. Some experts ascribe this to the disruption of Bronze Age trade patterns, in which Germania imported *aiz and *tinam and exported amber (*glasam, whence "glass") and fabricated bronzeware. A more important factor, I suspect, was climatic deterioration: around this time temperatures dropped, the growing season shrank, and bogs expanded to cover some croplands. Archaeological remains show a poorer and perhaps sparser population, and also include the seeds of wild plants, evidently gathered to supplement the dwindling grain crops.

The impoverishment of Germania probably explains why the Celts never overran it, as they overran (at least temporarily) most other parts of Europe: there was nothing there that they wanted. Their modest northward expansion, into modern Czechoslovakia, is reflected in the first reasonably certain linguistic evidence of Celtic-Germanic contacts: Common Germanic *isarno- (iron) clearly derives from Celtic *isarnos. The Celtic term may originally have meant "sacred metal," suggesting that the Celts first encountered the stuff as meteoritic iron; parallels exist in other tongues.

Other Germanic borrowings, probably from the same period, include *rik (from Celtic *rix), a ruler or other powerful person. Since powerful people are seldom poor (and vice versa) it later begot "rich," but retains something like its original sense in "bishopric" (the district ruled by a bishop) and the German *Reich*. Celtic *dunum, enclosure or hill-fort (found in historic Gaulish town names like Lugdunum, modern Lyons) became Germanic *tun, whence "town."

These words and a handful of others are the only linguistic evidence of Celtic-Germanic contacts which, at the lowest estimate, must have endured for centuries. Yet from what we have already said about the dynamics of words, such sparse borrowings are not surprising. The Celts knew few things the Germans didn't (*isarnos being a notable exception), and both natural environment and technology differed little between the two peoples. Soon, however, both the Celts and the Germans collided with a people that knew a lot of things they didn't know: the Romans.

What brought Romans and Germans into contact was, first, Roman expansion. This had already been going on for centuries when it achieved what was, for the Germans, its culmination: Julius Caesar's conquest of Gaul (roughly, modern France) around 55 B.C., which brought the Roman frontier to the Rhine and in some places beyond it. Meanwhile, the Germans had begun a less spectacular advance of their own. Thanks in part to an improvement in climate and in part, no doubt, to their adoption of the iron plow, their food supplies and population increased, and they began pressing south from their old homeland, overrunning some Celtic tribes and pushing others into Gaul. By the beginning of the Christian era, the two-way advance had brought the Romans into contact with such unquestionably Germanic tribes as the Batavians, Frisians and Marcomanni, and with the tribal confederation that wiped out the Roman army of Publius Varus, somewhere near the Elbe, in 9 A.D.

Though some German historians have made much of this first recorded German blitzkrieg, it was probably of only minor historic importance, since there was in fact little chance that the Romans either could or would have conquered Germania. The country, as Tacitus noted, "either bristles with forests or reeks with swamps"—terrain that might well have defeated much abler generals than the hapless Varus. Nor would the Roman conquest have been worth the trouble; merely maintaining a permanent garrison would have strained the land's resources, with nothing left over for "tribute"—the taxes that were the real payoff for Roman imperialism.

But if the Romans couldn't, or didn't care to, conquer the Germans, the latter equally could not then conquer the Romans. The standoff deflected German expansion toward the east, where by the third century it had pushed as far as the Dneiper. Stretching now from the North Sea to southern Russia, and from Scandinavia to the Roman frontier, Common Germanic inevitably evolved from a fairly uniform tongue into three distinct, though still closely related, languages. North Germanic (ancestor of the Scandinavian tongues) covered most of Norway and Sweden; East Germanic (which included Gothic and several other extinct dialects) covered eastern Europe and southern Russia. West Germanic, ancestor of all the other modern Germanic tongues, including English, was spoken from the coasts of the North Sea and western Baltic south to the Roman frontier.

For some centuries, Roman-German relations along the frontier remained relatively peaceful, despite a certain amount of raiding back and forth. Roman traders penetrated deep into Germania, while increasing numbers of Germans moved into Roman territory. At first they came individually; thus young Germans not infrequently enlisted for a hitch in the Roman army, returning home (if they survived) with whatever they had managed to pick up in the way of loot and Roman culture. Later, whole tribes were settled in the borderlands, as military allies against their more turbulent kinfolk to the north and east: by the third or fourth century, several million Germans are thought to have resided within the empire.

This prolonged contact with Roman civilization could not help but bring Latin words into the Germanic (especially West Germanic) vocabulary. However, it was not the Latin that some of us learned in school—the elegant literary language used by such writers as Vergil, Cicero and Tacitus—but an informal, often slangy dialect spoken by Roman soldiers, minor officials and merchants throughout the western Empire. The merchants were known as *caupones*, small traders, borrowed into Germanic as **kaupa* (whence eventually "cheap"), and as *mangones*, dealers (with overtones of "connivers"). This begot the Germanic verb **mangoyan*, which we find in such British compounds as "fishmonger" and "ironmonger" (hardware dealer); it has retained—or regained—its original bad vibrations in "scandalmonger," "rumormonger" and "warmonger."

The traders and dealers moved their goods by ship, or on the backs of pack animals—the *asinus*, Germanic **asiluz* (ass), and *mula*, which the Germans borrowed unchanged. Packaging for the goods included the *cista*, Germanic **kisto-* (chest), the *saccus*, Germanic **sakkuz*, and the large jar called an *amphora*, Germanic **amfor-*. The goods themselves were, surprisingly, the very same things that Germanic peoples are still importing from Latin Europe: *uinum* (Germanic **winam*), *olium* (Germanic **oli-*, then meaning specifically olive oil) and *caseus* (Germanic **kasyo-*, cheese). This last would naturally have been quite different from the soft, perishable **yustaz* that the Germans had long known in their own land: hard, rather salty cheeses like today's Parmesan and Romano. Other valued commodities were spicy *piper*, its name borrowed ultimately from India, whence traders shipped it to the Mediterranean, and *cuprum* (Germanic **kupar*, copper).

In exchange for these and other goods, the traders would have taken the Germans' amber, furs (**fella-*, whence the technical furriers' term "fell") and especially slaves: significantly, *mango* often meant not simply "dealer" but "slave dealer." The German economy was still largely based on barter, but Tacitus noted that "the border population . . . value gold and silver . . . and are familiar with some of our coins." We now know that these coins penetrated far beyond the border; thousands have been dug up in Scandinavia alone. Latin *moneta,* coin (whence "money"), begot Germanic *munita,* whence eventually "mint," meaning first "coin" but later the place it was made. Whether bartered or sold for coins, goods such as *caseus* must have been sold by weight—Latin *pondo,* Germanic *pundo,* whence "pound."

The Germans of the early Christian Era, like many Germanic-speaking people today, were also impressed by Latin achievements in the *coquina* (kitchen); they borrowed the word (as *kokina*) along with much of its equipment and many of its raw materials. Roman kitchenware included the *catillus,* Germanic *katiluz* (kettle); *patina,* Germanic *panna; cuppa;* and *discus,* Germanic *diskaz* (dish). This last, however, was probably borrowed from military rather than civilian kitchens: its literal meaning was the round, flat quoit that the Greeks (from whom the Romans had borrowed the word) were always tossing about. Calling a mess tin a quoit sounds like typical soldier's humor, of the sort that later called a small bomb a pomegranate ("grenade") and still later turned another bomb into another fruit ("pineapple").

Roman cuisine included such then-exotic materials as *caula* (whence "kale," which in Scotland still means "cabbage," as well as the "cole-" in "coleslaw"; *caula* itself later supplied the "cauli-" in "cauliflower"). Sometimes the *caula* was stewed up with a *coccus,* Germanic *kukkaz* (cock), later modified to *kiukinam* (chicken). The Germans also coined their own word for the noisy male of this useful new domestic bird: *hanon,* singer (from the same root as "chant"). Modern German *Hahn* retains the original sense, but in English the word somehow became transferred to the singer's clucking mate. The stew may have been flavored with *menta,* Germanic *minta,* perhaps with *petrosilium* (parsley) and certainly with *unio,* Germanic *unyo* (onion). (*Unyo* and several other words mentioned here passed from West Germanic into Old English, but were later replaced by quite similar words borrowed from French or Medieval Latin.) Other dishes were fried in *oleum* or *butyrum* (butter), borrowed unchanged.

If German women were cooking with *kaula,* *minta* and *unyo,* then they or their husbands were surely growing these plants—another word borrowed at this time. Latin *planta* originally meant "sole" (of the foot), but by the time the Germans encountered it, it meant a shoot or seedling firmed into place ("planted") with the foot. In the frontier areas, at least, the Germans were also planting new trees, the *ceresia* (Germanic *keresya,* cherry—whence also German *Kirschwasser,* cherry brandy), the *prunus*

(Germanic **plum-*), the *castanea* (Germanic **kastinya*, chestnut) and even the ornamental *rosa*. Most especially, the Germans planted *winegeards*, combining the Latin "vine" with the Germanic original of "yard" and "garden." These would have been located along the Rhenus and Mosella rivers and in parts of Rhaetia and Noricum (modern Austria)—then as now the only areas along the frontier warm enough for grapes to ripen.

Roman contributions to the evolving Germanic life-style and vocabulary were not limited to trade, food and farming; they included the *matta* that covers a floor, the *theca* (tick) that covers a mattress, and the comfortable *puluinus* (Germanic **pulwi-*, pillow). The Roman *cattus* (Germanic **kattuz*) proved invaluable in controlling the Germanic **ratt*). (Whether this creature—the European black rat—originated in northern Europe is uncertain, but its name is Germanic, from the same ultimate root as Latin "rodent.")

In Roman towns along the frontier, including such prosperous communities as Augusta Trevorum (Treves) and Colonia Agrippina (Koln), the Germans also learned about urban life. In their own lands, says Tacitus, they did not "even tolerate closely contiguous dwellings," while the Romans built a kind of row house called a *uicus*. A secondary meaning, "village," begot Germanic **wik-*, town, surviving now only in place names such as Britain's Warwick, Prestwick and Ipswich. Some dwellings, and certainly permanent Roman fortifications, were constructed of brick or stone, mortared with sand and *calx* (Germanic **kalk*), lime—nowadays "chalk," either a kind of limestone or its chemical cousin used on blackboards). Houses were often roofed with *tegulae*, (Germanic **tiegla*, tile). Urban life also brought such amenities as the *vitula*, Germanic **fithula*, ancestor of the fiddle, and the musical *pipa*, ancestor of the recorder, though the term was eventually transferred to almost any hollow tube. (We find its original sense in the proverb "He who dances must pay the piper.") In exchange, the Germans contributed the **harpon* (probably something like the small "Irish" harp), whose name passed into Latin and thence into the Romance tongues.

Civilization naturally had its price: for Germans living within the empire, taxes, and for those trading with it, the duties levied by the *toloneum* (customs house), Germanic **toln-*, whose modern descendant still levies tolls on our bridges and superhighways. The Romans, of course, had their own superhighways, the superb *stratae viae* (paved roads) along which troops could be quickly marched from one place to another. The Germans borrowed the term—probably from soldier's slang—as **strata*, whence "street," which in English originally meant a paved highway—

often a Roman road or what remained of one. One of these, Watling Street, still appears on some English maps; parts of it, widened and repaved, are still in use along Britain's A5 between London and Chester. Distances along the *strata* were measured in *mille pasuum* (thousands of paces), which the soldiers who trudged them clipped to *milia,* Germanic **milya,* whence "mile."

Other borrowed terms that we owe to the tens of thousands of Germans who over the centuries fought either in or against the Roman armies are *pilum,* javelin, Germanic **pil-* (whence the piles that support a wharf or house); the *uallum,* Germanic **wal-,* originally a rampart of heaped earth topped by stakes, thrown up around a legionary camp (whence "wall"); and the *puteus,* a pit (often with a sharpened stake at the bottom) dug to hamper enemy movements, whence Germanic **puttya,* whose meaning broadened over the centuries to encompass almost any roughly circular excavation.

A less certain but plausible contribution was a word for drink—a subject of great interest to soldiers in all ages. Roman soldiers drank *uinum* when they could get it, but if they couldn't were doubtless willing to settle for whatever was being poured, including German *aluth.* One can imagine a bunch of legionaries elbowing their way into a frontier tavern and demanding *biber* (drink, from the same Latin root as "bibulous"). The German tavernkeeper may well have assumed that this was Latin for the **aluth* that was all he stocked; the misunderstanding (if that's what it was) gave rise to Dutch and German *Bier* and English "beer"—originally, a synonym for "ale"—which eventually made its way back into two of the Romance tongues as French *bière* and Italian *birra.*

Perhaps the most curious Germanic borrowing from the Romans was neither food nor drink nor building material nor soldiers' terms, but the seven days of the week. The Germans had a calendar of sorts, reckoning time by the **yaram* (year) and the **mannoth* (from the same root as "moon"), though we don't know what, if anything, they called those months. They also had words for three of the four seasons (Tacitus says they had no word for autumn): **langtinus,* the time of lengthening days, whence "Lent"; **sumaraz;* and **wintruz.* They may even, conceivably, have divided the lunar **mannoth* into four quarters (corresponding to the moon's phases) of about seven days each. But they don't seem to have had names for those days.

The Romans did, naming them after the sun, the moon and the gods Mars, Mercury, Jove, Venus and Saturn—names that anyone familiar with one of the Romance tongues will recognize in their modern disguises.

The Germans took over the names, but not, as with other Latin words, by direct borrowing, but rather by the process called "loan translation," in which the foreign terms were translated into their Germanic equivalents. Thus *dies solis* and *dies lunae* became **sunnondagaz* and **monandagaz*, and the Roman gods were replaced by their Germanic equivalents, Tiw, Woden (the Wotan of Wagner's *Ring* cycle), Thor or Thunor, and Friga. Their only problem was with Saturn, for whom there was apparently no German equivalent, so that *dies saturnae* is still Satur(n's)day.

Probably the last Germanic borrowings from Rome were a few words relating to Christianity. Germania itself was not converted to the new religion until some centuries after Rome had fallen, but by 400 A.D. most Germans living within the empire had become Christians. Their word **kirika,* from Greek *kyriyakon* via Latin, produced both "church" and the Scottish "kirk." Other possible ecclesiastical borrowings include *crucem* (cross), *monachem* (monk), *episkopos* (bishop) and *nonna* (nun).

The Germans' role in the destruction of the Roman Empire is too well known to need retelling in detail. The simplest way of describing the process is a combination of German overpopulation and Roman financial instability.

The climate of Germania continued to improve during the early centuries of the Christian era; at least one expert believes it may have been warmer than at present as early as 200 A.D. For this and other, less understood reasons, food supplies continued to increase, producing a still larger population that was almost compelled to expand. North there was nothing to attract anyone, west was the sea, and south were the Romans, so that (as we noted earlier) the main movement was initially into the eastern lands of southern Russia. During the fourth century, however, the East Germans were thrown back by the Huns, whose domination of eastern and central Europe may be reflected in a single borrowed West Germanic word, **kokor,* the quiver in which these ferocious mounted warriors carried their arrows.

Driven westward, the Germans had no place to go but Roman territory —sometimes peacefully, as allies settled in the borderlands, but often violently. The result was greatly increased pressure on the Roman armies —and on the rickety financial structure that supported them. Emperors seeking to increase the military budget found themselves confronted by large-scale tax evasion by the rich landholders. Since the rich wouldn't pay taxes and the poor couldn't, the burden was saddled on the middle classes—forcing increasing numbers of *them* below the poverty line. Chronically short of money, and therefore of soldiers and military materiel, the emperors were increasingly pushed back into the richer and more defensible lands of the eastern Mediterranean.

In about 408 A.D., as one minor incident in this eastward withdrawal, the last mobile Roman troops were pulled out of the province of Britannia. Soon afterward, a wave of Germans poured across the lower Rhine to occupy the Low Countries and northern Gaul—meaning that there was now no way of replacing the British legions, even if the emperors had had troops to spare; the provincials were therefore officially notified that they would have to sink or swim on their own. Briefly, they stayed afloat, maintaining a semblance of the civilization that Rome had built in their far-off island. But at last that civilization was swept away by the westernmost waves of the Germanic storm tide—the people called the English, who brought with them the dialect of West Germanic that would become the tongue we speak today.

4. THE SECOND CONQUEST

From West Germanic to Old English

❧

I like the Anglo-Saxon speech
With its direct revealings
It takes a hold and seems to reach
'Way down into your feelings.

—EUGENE FIELD

"An Anglo-Saxon, Hinnisy, is a German that's forgot who was his parents."

—FINLEY PETER DUNNE

THE West Germanic dialect (or group of dialects) that entered Britain during the fifth century is sometimes referred to as Anglo-Saxon, as in the verse that heads this chapter. That term, however, is a later, scholarly invention; there is no evidence that the actual speakers of "Anglo-Saxon" ever called it anything but English. We call it Old English, to distinguish it from its descendants, the Middle English of medieval times, and the modern English whose beginnings date from the sixteenth century.

Yet to refer to these as "descendants" of Old English raises something of a paradox. As we've already noted, more than half the vocabulary of modern English is not "native" (i.e., derived from Old English) but borrowed. In addition, much more than half the vocabulary of Old English (some say as much as 85 percent) has vanished, leaving no descendants. Yet the tongue we speak today is still English, for two good reasons.

First, the syntax of modern English, though differing in many ways from that of Old English, is closer to it than to the syntax of any other language—including those that have contributed the majority of our words. Second, the "native" part of our vocabulary is a good deal more important than might appear from the mere number of words it encompasses; we must also take account of how often these words are used, and with what effect.

Some years ago, a group of scholars at Brown University ran a com-

puter analysis of over a million words of modern English prose, ranging
from scientific papers to sports articles in the daily press. The computer
counted more than fifty thousand different words, over half of them (as
you would expect) not native but borrowed. But the picture changed
radically when the machine was programmed to print out the words in
the order of their frequency of use: of the hundred most common words,
every one was native; of the next hundred, eighty-three were native. One
can, if one works at it hard enough, talk at some length about everyday
things in nothing but homegrown words—as I've been doing right here,
starting with "One can." *But it is* quite impossible *to* conduct *a* conversation *in English on any* subject *whatever without bringing in the* simple, *everyday*
words of our native vocabulary—*witness the* italicized *words in this* sentence.

If our native words are syntactically powerful beyond their numbers,
they are also powerful in another way: taken as a group, they stir the
feelings in a way that the borrowings do not—a fact well known to those
skilled at using our native tongue to persuade or inflame. Listen, for
example, to Mr. Churchill in 1940:

"We shall fight on the beaches, we shall fight on the landing grounds,
we shall fight in the fields and in the streets, we shall fight in the hills; we
shall never surrender." Every word of this is pure English, save only the
final French trumpet peal of "surrender."

Or Abraham Lincoln in 1865: "With firmness in the right, as God gives
us to see the right . . ." with only half a word ("firm-") borrowed. Or
Franklin Roosevelt in 1933: "The only thing we have to fear is fear itself"
—pure English. Turning to poetry, we have Francis Scott Key on that
morning in 1814 when he spied his flag still waving over bombarded Fort
McHenry:

> *Oh say, can you see, by the dawn's early light,*
> *What so proudly we hailed at the twilight's last gleaming?*

with "proud-" the only borrowing, and that nearly a thousand years old.
Or, in a more intimate vein, Elizabeth Browning:

> *How do I love thee? Let me count the ways.*
> *I love thee to the breadth and depth and height . . .*

with "count" the only immigrant. Or the purely English words that ac-
company our gravest moments: "With this ring, I thee wed, to have and

to hold, from this day forward, for better, for worse . . . in sickness and in health . . ."; "The Lord is my shepherd; I shall not want . . ."; "Earth to earth, ashes to ashes, dust to dust . . ." And along with these "formal" usages we have such informal but heartfelt utterances as "Drop dead," "I love you, darling," "Up yours," "Thank God," and a dozen others. The homegrown words of our tongue are those that spring most quickly to our lips when we speak straight from the heart. As, indeed, I have just spoken in the preceding, purely English, sentence.

The tens of thousands of words that the English-speaking peoples have borrowed from friends, neighbors and enemies around the world are a precious heritage, which has enriched our tongue beyond any other. There is not, and never was, any virtue in "getting back to pure Anglo-Saxon"—a nineteenth-century fad whose only surviving monument is Lewis Carroll's jibe, in *Through the Looking Glass*, at "Anglo-Saxon attitudes." Indeed, many of our greatest writers are conspicuous for their ability to mingle homely, blunt English words with the elegant expressions of French and the stately vocabulary of Latin. But when all is said and done (pure English, that), these words are chiefly the ceremonial or celebratory garments and bejeweled ornaments that adorn and embellish our language. It is the old words handed down from the West Germanic of the North Sea coasts that are the *flæsc* (flesh) and *blod* and *ban* (bone) and *guttas* of English—and its *her* (hair) and *hyd* as well.

Remarkably, English retained its basically Germanic character despite the later conquest of England, and its domination for several centuries, by French-speaking Normans. Hardly less remarkable is the fact that this Germanic tongue became established in England at all. The coming of English may seem like the inevitable result of the Germanic conquest of England, yet examined more closely, the result was not quite so inevitable as it looks.

Britain, before it became English, was a province of the Roman Empire (it included modern England and Wales but not Scotland). Its history closely paralleled that of the neighboring province of Gaul (roughly, modern France). Before the Romans, both regions were inhabited by peoples speaking Celtic tongues. About half a century before Christ, Gaul was conquered by the Romans; about half a century after Christ, so was Britain. Both provinces became "Romanized," their economies integrated into the trading network of the empire, with new or expanded towns and cities serving as centers of marketing, manufacture and administration. They were no less Romanized in language: most people, especially in the towns, learned to speak or at least understand Latin, though many of them, especially in the countryside, still used their Celtic tongues at home. In both areas, Latin achieved linguistic dominance because it was the language of government, of the army, of most traders and of anyone who could read or write: none of the Celtic tongues of Gaul or Britain was ever written down.

When the Roman Empire disintegrated, Gaul was overrun by several waves of Germanic invaders and eventually conquered by the coalition of West Germanic tribes called the Franks; somewhat later, Britain was conquered by another coalition of West Germanic tribes, the English. Yet in Gaul, Latin survived to become French; in Britain, it vanished, to be replaced by English. To understand the reasons for these quite different linguistic developments, we must examine the ethnic and linguistic history of Britain both before and after the Roman era.

The first inhabitants of the British Isles who have left any linguistic traces are a non-Indo-European people, sometimes called the Iberians, though their connection with the historical Iberians of southwestern Europe is problematical. About all we know of their language is the name (perhaps their tribal name) that they gave to the island of Iveriu, which was eventually shortened to Eire, which was Anglicized to Ire-land. Britain itself may have been named by the same people; the word is certainly not Indo-European.

Like most of western Europe, Britain was overrun by several waves of Celtic conquerors. The aborigines, if they survived at all, may just possibly be represented by a tribe the Celts called the Atecotti, meaning something like "very old people," who in Roman times lived somewhere north of the Roman border.

The Celts, speaking various dialects of a tongue called British (after the island), occupied most of the island when the armies of "I, Claudius" invaded it in 45 A.D. (Julius Caesar's brief invasions of a century earlier were not serious attempts at conquest, but mere image-building). With the Roman takeover of Britain came bilingualism. Latin was spoken by virtually all the British upper classes in both town and country—that is, by those people with the strongest motives, both practical and snobbish, for acquiring the language and life-style of their new rulers. But in the towns, at least, even workmen (presumably natives) knew the language well enough to scrawl graffiti in informal but grammatical Latin. Those Britons who continued to use their native tongue still borrowed Latin words, as the Germans were also doing, but more extensively: to the Germans, the Romans were primarily neighbors; to the British, they were masters. Several hundred of these borrowings are found in "Modern British"—the Welsh tongue, known to its speakers as Cymric.

Britain's first contacts with the Germanic tribes, sometime during the third century, was with the *Saxones,* the name under which the Romans lumped various piratical raiders from the North Sea coastal lands. These folk almost certainly included the ancestors of the English, but at that time were interested in loot, not conquest. The first English actually to settle in England, soon after the Romans departed, were equally unconcerned with conquest: they came around 425 by invitation, from a British "king" known as Vortigern. His name is Celtic, and translates as "over-king," suggesting that he was a British "emperor" heading a coalition of local "kings"—Romanized British aristocrats—to defend the civilized parts of the island against its enemies. There were plenty of those: "Saxons" on the east, Irish on the west, and Picts—un-Romanized Britons—on the north; the latter were soon reinforced by immigrant Irish warriors known as Scotti.

Later commentators wrote scathingly of Vortigern's supposed stupidity in inviting the "Saxon" enemy within the gates. In fact, hiring one group of barbarians to help fight off another was standard operating procedure all over the later Roman Empire. Vortigern's strategy worked well enough: with the help of his "Saxon" (English) mercenaries, he managed to beat off the attackers and give the civilized parts of Britain twenty years of peace.

Unfortunately, the sequel was equally standard. Once the threat of invasion was past, the British aristocrats fell to bickering and intriguing among themselves, meanwhile relapsing into the traditional aristocratic practice of tax-dodging. Vortigern's invaluable English troops found their pay and rations cut and concluded, not unreasonably, that they had better seize farmlands on which to raise their own food. The British resisted; the English called in reinforcements from their kinsmen across the North Sea. The struggle remained indecisive for some years, until the English at last invited some three hundred British leaders to a peace conference—and massacred them every one. This ended the war for the moment, leaving the English in control of much of eastern England. It also led some fifty thousand Britons to abandon their homeland for northwest Gaul, where they settled between the rivers Sequana (Seine) and Liger (Loire). The emigrants included many of the relatively well-to-do and literate—i.e., Latin-speaking—Britons. This is confirmed by the sixth-century British chronicler Gildas, who denounced them for carrying off books that he could no longer find in Britain.

Despite the departure of many of its natural leaders, British resistance soon revived, led by a certain Ambrosius, one of the surviving aristocrats. Around 475, he was succeeded by an even abler general, Artorius, who after twenty years of fighting smashed the English army at the battle of Badon Hill (probably somewhere near Bath). Despite this victory, however, the British were no longer strong enough to expel the English completely. Instead, the island was in effect partitioned: the English held the southeast coast, and the eastern region still known at East Anglia; the British retained control of the rest of the country, including the Thames Valley, which formed a sort of wedge between the two groups of English. Artorius seems to have established a major garrison near London at what is now Colchester: the old British town of Camulodunum—Camelot.

Artorius—King Arthur—and his "knights"—heavily armed cavalry—brought a generation of peace between Britons and English, and also beat off various attacks from the Irish, Picts and Scots. But they could not undo the effects of a century's invasion, massacre and emigration: the disruption of the British economy and the decline of its towns—centers of Latin speech. At Arthur's death, the British-controlled sections relapsed into what was by now their "normal" state: a collection of petty "kingdoms" run by warlords more interested in ripping off or knocking off their neighbors than in containing the English. The final blow was an epidemic of plague, spread from Gaul and Spain by the merchant ships that still occasionally reached the island.

As the British grew weaker, the English grew stronger. They controlled some of the most fertile land in Britain, enough not only to support them but also to attract additional English immigrants. They escaped the plague, since they had little contact with the British and none at all with Gaul and Spain (their sparse trade was with their cousins across the North Sea). A renewal of the war and an English victory were inevitable, though it took some centuries to establish English control over the whole of England (Wales remained unconquered until the Middle Ages). Linguistically, the mopping-up process is not finished yet: several hundred thousand British subjects still speak Celtic tongues—the Gaelic speakers of northwestern Scotland (whose language is akin to Erse, not British) and, farther south, the descendants of those whom the English called the *Wealsc* (/wailsh/—meaning, ironically, "foreigners"). In their own tongue they called themselves Cymry, from British *combroges*, "fellow countrymen." Another group of *wealsc* survived for some centuries in far-western Cornwall; their dialect of British, Cornish, was still spoken there as late as the eighteenth century.

The British emigrants to Gaul, now reinforced by additional refugees, continued to speak British (or a mixture of British and Latin) for a while. In the French region now called Normandy, they gradually became assimilated into the native, Latin-speaking population, leaving as their main linguistic heritage a dozen villages called Bretteville—"British-town." Farther west, however, the immigrants found the land virtually deserted (as the result of earlier social disturbances) and kept their language, as do some of their descendants, on the rocky peninsula still called Britain—in French, *Bretagne* (Brittany). But the original Britain was now irrevocably England, as Gaul, thanks to its conquest by the Franks, was now France.

Yet we speak English, while the French do not speak Frankish (a Germanic tongue) but a Latin-derived language. The reason is that relatively few Franks actually settled in France; most remained east of the Rhine, where Germanic tongues are, of course, still spoken. Their interest was less in land than in taxes and tribute, which they collected in France through the existing administrative apparatus manned by literate, Latin-speaking Gallo-Romans. The English, by contrast, were very much interested in land, at first (in Vortigern's time) from necessity, later from simple greed—and, perhaps, because the devastated economy of Britain had nothing else to offer. Meanwhile, as they moved in, the Latin-speaking Britons moved out, taking the Roman tongue with them.

The English who would from now on determine the linguistic future of England were a mixed bag: Jutes (originally from Danish Jutland), Saxons (from the coastal region of Germany still called Lower Saxony) and probably scatterings of other groups. Their main component, however, seems to have been the Angles, originating in the section of Denmark still called Angeln, literally an "angle" in the coast. But all, or virtually all, of these peoples spoke dialects of the tongue they called *Englisc* (/eng-glish/).

According to tradition, different sections of England were settled by different tribes: Kent (the original settlement) by the Jutes, and the rest of southern England by the Saxons, various subgroups of which gave their names to the English counties of Essex (i.e., East Saxons), Middlesex and Sussex, and the Old English kingdom of Wessex. Elsewhere, the Angles supposedly dominated. Whether matters were arranged quite so neatly is doubtful, but the tradition seems linguistically valid in that people in the three areas spoke different dialects of *Englisc*. We know this because soon after 600 A.D. the language began to be written down, thanks to the arrival in England of literate Christian missionaries.

The English were not totally ignorant of writing before they arrived in Britain. Like other Germanic peoples, they scratched occasional inscriptions on boards cut from the beech tree (and sometimes on more durable objects). They called such an inscription after their name for the tree, *boc*, and later applied the word to much lengthier written documents. The original *bec* (plural of *boc*) were written in the angular Runic letters that some ingenious Germanic chieftain or priest had developed from one of the Mediterranean alphabets. But the inscriptions themselves, judging from the few that have survived, were little more than graffiti, along the lines of "This is a good sword" or "Here so-and-so was killed." Writing, then, was the most marginal of activities in late Germanic and early English society; its systematic, routine use had to wait on the coming of Christianity, many of whose priests and virtually all of whose higher officials not only spoke Latin but could read and write it.

Which is to say that we have now reached a radically new stage in examining the history of our native tongue. Thanks to the written records of Old English, we know its vocabulary and syntax with far more certainty and in far more detail than we do those of Common Germanic or (even less) Indo-European. But that is by the way: a language is far more than a collection of words and rules for combining them, just as a radio is far more than a collection of transistors and an assembly manual. For our more remote, illiterate linguistic ancestors, we have only the parts, not the whole; the English, by contrast, speak to us through their writings in their own voices: the laws, chronicles, poems and life stories that turn the abstractions of linguistics into the utterances of a people.

The appearance of written English, however, confronted the language with a problem that still plagues us: spelling. Nearly all writing systems are based on some set of symbols that represent, more or less accurately, the sounds of the language they record (Chinese is a notable exception). But as we know, different languages use different sets of sounds. And when a set of symbols designed to represent the sounds of one language is pressed into service to convey the somewhat different sounds of another—which is the rule rather than the exception in linguistic history—things get complicated.

The symbols used to record Old English were basically the Roman alphabet, devised to represent the sounds of Latin, which it did quite well. Old English, however, included various "un-Roman" sounds, notably the two we now write TH (THis, THin). The churchly scribes who first grappled with this problem were ingenious enough to borrow two symbols from the Runic alphabet, þ and ð. Unfortunately they were not ingenious enough to use the two letters with precision, so that either one could stand for either TH sound. This may seem to us rather sloppy, but is typical of the way writing systems evolve: as a rule, they are devised, or modified, for the use of people who *already* know the language being written, and for whom, therefore, it is unnecessary to (literally) spell out every detail.

The scribes also invented another special symbol, Æ, to represent the "flat A" in such words as *baeþ*, pronounced like its modern equivalent, "bath." Two other English sounds, though not present in Classical Latin, were used in Late Latin, and were therefore written in the Late Latin (and modern Italian) fashion: /sh/ was written SC, as in *scip* (ship), and /ch/ as C followed by I or E, as in *cild* (child), or usually at the end of a word, as in *ic*, /itch/ (I). Elsewhere, C had the same value it originally had in Latin, /k/, and still often does in English: as in *carfull* (careful). SC also had its modern English value /sk/ in a few words like *ascian* (ask).

Other Roman letters represented two or three different sounds: thus F stood for either /f/ or /v/, H for either /h/ or the /kh/ sound in Scottish "loCH" and the Yiddish-American "CHutzpah," while G sometimes stood for /g/, sometimes for /y/, and sometimes for a guttural sound impossible to convey except to a phonetician or a Dutchman, in whose language it is still used.

Even the experts disagree on many details of Old English pronunciation. Their (and our) knowledge of Old English phonetics is based in part on what the letters were presumed to stand for in Latin, in part on the subsequent phonetic evolution of the language; we have no Old English tape recordings. The uncertainties are further compounded by the existence of at least three different Old English dialects (whose differences were mainly phonetic), which, moreover, were written down over a period of some five centuries (600–1100 A.D.), during which time their sounds must have changed appreciably. For instance, there is good reason to believe that when the English arrived in Britain they had not yet acquired the sound /ch/, so that *cild* was pronounced /keeld/ and *ic* was pronounced /ik/ (resembling modern German *ich*).

Old English syntax was even more intricate than its spelling. As noted earlier, it was not unlike Latin syntax: nouns were inflected in four "cases" (as against the usual five in Latin), which in theory identified the noun as subject, direct object or indirect object of a verb, or expressed possessive and similar relationships; the inflections also differentiated between singular and plural. Interestingly, the old Indo-European dual number, extinct in Latin, survived in a few Old English pronouns: thus "I" was *ic*, "we" (two) was *wit* and "we" (more than two) was *we* (pronounced /weh/).

In theory, then, each noun had eight different inflections (four singular, four plural); in practice, many of these had begun to "fall together" phonetically, meaning that their inflectional endings were no longer distinctive. (This was also true of Classical Latin, but to a much smaller degree.) For example, of the eight theoretical forms of *sunne* (sun), five were identical *(sunnan)*. Which is to say that Old English syntax could no longer rely on inflection to indicate most syntactic relationships, but was rather forced to depend on word order, as we do. In fact, its word order was not all that different from our own.

Old English did, however, retain the old Indo-European system of grammatical gender, which we so comfortably do without. Nouns were still classified more or less arbitrarily as masculine, feminine or neuter: *mann* was masculine, but so was *wifman* (women), while *wif* (woman, wife) was neuter. Adjectives, pronouns and articles (a, the) had to agree with the noun they referred to in case, number *and* gender, meaning 4(cases) ×2 (numbers)×3 (genders) or 24 theoretically different forms. In practice, as with the nouns, many of these forms no longer differed in reality. In fact, we usually find the adjective in an Old English sentence precisely where we find it today: right before the noun.

Old English verbs were also inflected fairly elaborately. Rather than delve further into Old English syntax, however, we can more usefully take a couple of actual passages in the language, translate them as literally as possible into modern English, and see how the two compare. Most of the words will at least look somewhat familiar—those that have vanished completely from the language are shown in [brackets]—but their sounds are something else. About the only useful thing I can say about them is that most of the consonants have their modern values, while most of the vowels don't; beyond that, you're on your own. As a further aid, however, I have noted changes in the meaning of some "familiar" words in parentheses.

Ond Pharaones dohter cwaeð to hire: [*Underfoh*] *þis cild one fed hit me*
And Pharaoh's daughter quoth to her: take this child and feed it me(-for)

ond ic sylle   *þe þine mede.*   *þaet wif [underfeng] þone*
and I "sell" (will give) thee thy meed (reward). The woman took the

cnapen,   *ond hine fedde ond sealde*   *Pharaones dehter*
"knave" (boy) and him fed and "sold" (gave) Pharaoh's daughter(-to).

Ond [heo] hine lufode ond hafde   *for sunu hyre, ond nemde his namen*
And she him loved and "haved" (had) for son her, and named his name

Moises, ond cwaeð : [Forþamþe] ic hin of waetere [genam].
Moses, and quoth : Because I him "of" (from) water took.

Some points worth noting:

1. For certain words, inflectional forms imply relationships which the translation must show by prepositions; thus the inflectional form *dehter* implies "to [the] daughter" as *me* implies "for me."

2. Some words have changed their meanings radically. Thus the verb *sellan,* represented here by *sylle* and *sealde,* then meant simply "give"; its modern meaning was expressed by *sellan wiþ weorþe,* give with worth—i.e., with a price. Likewise, *knapen* still had its old "Folkish" and Common Germanic meaning of "boy"; its later evolution into "knave" may reflect the widespread feeling that boys are often up to no good.

3. *Sylle,* here translated as "will give," could also mean simply "give"; there was no formal way of denoting future time in Old English. We still sometimes use the present tense of verbs in this way: "If he comes, I (will) go."

4. The word order, as already noted, is pretty close to modern English; the main difference is in the position of pronouns, so that (for example) *sunu hyre* corresponds to "her son." Occasionally, however, the verb at the end of the sentence falls (as in modern German)—e.g., *genam* (took).

Here is another selection, familiar enough to most readers to make a full translation unnecessary; I will therefore translate only the first words and some especially tricky ones later on:

> *Fæder ure, þu þe eart on heofunum*
> (Father our, thou that art in heaven)
> *Si* (be) *þin nama gehalgod.*
> *Tobecume* (let-come) *þin rice* ("Reich"—kingdom)
> *Gewurþ* (let-happen) *þin wille*
> *On eorthan swa swa* (so so) *on heofonum*
> *Ure gedægwamlican* (every-daily) *hlaf* ("loaf") *sylle* ("sell")

us to dæg, ond forgyf us ure gyltas swa swa we forgyfað
ure gyltendum (guilt-doers). *Ond ne gelæd þu on costnunge*
(temptation) *ac* (but) *alys* ("loosen"—free) *us of yfele. Sothlice* (soothlȳ).

(The last word is a literal translation of Latin—originally Hebrew—*Amen*, which of course entered the English vocabulary later in its own right.)

Summing up the words used in these two selections, we find that some have disappeared outright from English (e.g., *underfoh, costnunge*), others have disappeared but, on close examination, are seen to consist of still-familiar words in unfamiliar combinations (*to-be-cume*).

Of those that survive in English, some have changed their sense (e.g., *sylle* and *cnapen*). A more subtle shift is seen in *gyltas,* which then meant "offenses," later, the state of having committed an offense ("his guilt was clear") and, more often nowadays, the anxious awareness of having committed an offense—real or imagined ("I'm full of guilt"). Still other words have retained the same sense, and even the same spelling but (and here you'll have to take my word for it) have changed their sound. *To* and *us* still mean "to" and "us," but rhyme with modern "toe" and "puss" ("us" is still pronounced that way in parts of England). In fact of the fifty-odd different words in these two passages, only one, *for,* is unchanged in both sound and sense.

Quite as striking as the changes in the words that are there are the words that are not there: the borrowed terms from French, Latin and elsewhere that loom so large in our modern vocabulary. The archaic, virtually extinct *mede* would now be expressed by "reward" or "due," both French, while in the Lord's Prayer we miss the equally French "trespasses," "temptation" and "deliver." Which is to say that the vocabulary of Old English was still overwhelmingly Germanic. The only exceptions were the Latin words mentioned in the last chapter, borrowed from the Romans before the migration, a few dozen more borrowed from Latin after the coming of Christianity to England, and a bare handful borrowed from the Britons.

This handful reflects the fact that there was relatively little mixture between the two peoples. The British resisted as long as they could, and in defeat preferred to withdraw—into Cornwall, Wales and France—rather than serve their conquerors. In addition, they knew few things that the English felt any need to know, or borrow words for. Significantly, the sparse English borrowings—perhaps a dozen—include three terms referring to features of the English landscape that the English could *not* have known in their flat, often marshy, homeland: *crag, torr* (a high rock) and *cumb*, a deep hollow or valley (it survives mainly in place names such as my birthplace, High Wycombe). British **hukk* was borrowed as English *hogg* (probably referring to a particular age or sex of pig), and British **assan* was borrowed as *assa*, replacing West Germanic **asiluz* (both of course originally borrowed from Latin). Another probable borrowing was **puca*, an evil spirit, very likely invoked as the standard alibi of British slaves when their English masters complained that something had turned up "missing"; eventually, it begot Puck, England's legendary mischief-maker. But these and a few other words are all our language has to show for the centuries-long British occupation of England.

Place names, however, are another story, since they cling to the land long after those who coined them have vanished or been absorbed by later conquerors. Most English river names are British, not English (some are pre-British—i.e., non-Indo-European). There are half a dozen Avons —"river," in British—while others derive from British words meaning "stream" or simply "water."

Not a few English towns, and even some counties, have names harking back to British or Roman-British times. London was originally *Lon-dunum* (?wild-beast town) and Lincoln was *Lindum Colonia*, a colony of Roman veterans settled in the British district of *Lindum*. *Dubris* became Dover; *Regulbium*, Reculver; and *Cantium*, Kent. This last derives ultimately from a prehistoric Celtic **kanto-*, meaning either "border" or "white." Either would fit: the chalk cliffs of Kent are indeed the white border of Britain.

Several dozen place names were generated by a complicated, three-way interaction among British, Latin and English, involving the Latin word *castra*. In Julius Caesar's time, this meant the fortified camp thrown up by Roman troops on the march; later, it was applied also to permanent Roman forts, in Britain and elsewhere, and was borrowed into British. These permanent *castrae* were usually located in or near existing British towns, but in any case soon generated their own communities of people doing business with the military: provision merchants, craftsmen, wine-sellers and whores.

During the long British-English wars, the British transferred their word for "fort" to any town that was (or could be) fortified and could thereby serve as a military strongpoint. The English picked it up as *ceaster* (/kaste-air/ and later /chaste-air/), a word that has now vanished from English, but survives in the many English town names ending in "-chester," "-caster" and "-cester," all marking the sites of Roman towns. These Latin-British-English endings are usually combined with a shortened version of the British-Roman name, itself often derived from a British tribal name. Thus the chief town of the Durotriges was *Durnovarium,* later something like *Durnoceaster,* and now Dorchester. *Uenta Belgarum* became *Wentaceaster,* modern Winchester; *Mamucium* became Manchester; *Branodunum* (whose Celtic -*dunum,* town, marks it as a pre-Roman settlement), became Brancaster; while the Roman naval base of *Portus Adurnia* became Portchester. (Neighboring Portsmouth is still a naval base.)

The town of Chester itself presumably meant something like "*the* fort," which is precisely what it was in Roman times: the island's largest military base, from which the legionaries could keep watch both on the turbulent, half-barbarian Britons of northern Wales and on Irish pirates conning their ships up the Dee or Mersey.

The majority of English town names, of course, date from later on, and are strictly English (or in some cases, Danish; more on that later), but at least one of them suggests a dim awareness that it was not the first town on the site. When the English settled amid the ruins of Roman *Isurium,* they called *their* town Aldborough—"Old Town"; the site was certainly "old" by English standards.

Though the English vocabulary of around 600 A.D. was almost free of borrowed elements, apart from place names, it was by no means a sparse vocabulary. The English retained the old Indo-European habit of making new words out of old ones: joining two words, or a word and one or more prefixes and suffixes, to yield a new meaning. In the Lord's Prayer (though the text dates from a couple of centuries later) we have *gyltendum,* "guilt-doers," which we express by the cumbersome "those who trespass against us." The single word *heah,* high, was incorporated into more than a dozen expressions, including *heah-borg,* "high-hill"—mountain; *heah-bliss,* "high-bliss"—exultation; *heah-burg,* principal town; *heah sæ,* "the high seas"—deep sea; *heah-heort,* "high-hearted"—proud; *heah þrea,* "high-threat"—panic, and *heah-stræt,* highway (from the Roman *strata via*)—whence eventually the village High Street that is England's equivalent of America's Main Street.

Particularly striking in Old English wordmaking is the wide use of prefix-verb combinations. The simple verb *settan,* set, was compounded into *asettan,* place or put; *besettan,* appoint; *forsettan,* obstruct; *foresettan,* place before; *gesettan,* garrison (a fort) or people (a town); *ofsettan,* afflict; *onsettan,* oppress; *tosettan,* dispose; *unsettan,* put down; and *wiþsettan,* resist. Some of these prefixes have vanished from English, and nearly all of them have ceased to be "productive"—that is, though they survive in old compounds they are no longer used to produce new ones. Thus *wiþ-,* in the sense of "against," "back," is still used in "withdraw," "withstand" and "withhold", but all of these date from the twelfth century or earlier. However, the change is more apparent then real: most of these old prefixes also did duty as prepositions, which have now become adverbs, in which capacity they combine as readily with verbs as they once did as prefixes. Thus the variations on *settan* listed above are paralleled by modern "set down" (in writing), "set to" (music), "set out" or "set off" (on a journey), and so on.

Old English suffixes have stood up better: nearly all have survived, and many of them are still used to generate new words. Thus -y (originally -*ig*) remains the standard way of converting a noun into an adjective (e.g., "dirt-y"), and -ly (from -*lice*) is equally standard to change an adjective to an adverb (e.g., "strange-ly"). Other examples includes -*leas* (e.g., "moneyless"); -*ung*, now -ing, in hundreds of verbal nouns and adjectives; and -*had* (e.g., "sisterhood"). Less common, and also less productive, are -*full* (e.g., "careful"); -*sum* (e.g., "winsome"); -*dom* (e.g., "kingdom"); -*scipe* (e.g., "friendship") and -*wise* (e.g., "sidewise")—though this last became something of a joke suffix few years ago, producing such advertising locutions as "media-wise" and "budget-wise." Cliché-wise, we can well do without it.

These combinatorial techniques of wordmaking gave Old English bards an abundance of synonyms: Old English poetry is conspicuously rich in compound metaphors, or metaphorical phrases, for familiar concepts. The sea was the whale-road, the sea-surge, the water's back, the wave's rolling and more than a dozen others; a ship might be the sea-wood, the wave-runner, broad-bosomed, curved-stemmed, foamy-necked.

Metaphor is, of course, a virtually universal feature of poetry, but for the Old English bard it served a special function, as an aid to memory, through the poetic device of alliteration. Among the English, as among other preliterate or barely literate peoples, poetry was recited or sung, not read. But to recite a poem of any length—the Old English epic *Beowulf* runs some 3,000 lines—puts an impossible burden on the memory unless the structure of the poem itself helps "remind" the bard of what is coming next. Mnemonic devices of this sort include meter—regular patterns of long and short or stressed and unstressed syllables—and rhyme.

Old English poetry did not rhyme, and made only modest use of meter; its bards relied mainly on alliteration's artful aid, with several words in each line starting with the same sound. (If a word began with an unstressed syllable, the alliteration applied to the following syllable.) A few lines from *Beowulf* will give some of the flavor:

> STraet waes STan-fah, STig wisode
> Gumum aetGaeder, Gud-byrne scan
> Heard, Honlocken, Hring-iren scir . . .
> (The road was stone-paved, the way well-shown
> To the band together. The war-shirts shone
> Hard, locked by hand, the ring-iron bright . . .)

Clearly a poet committed so heavily to alliteration had to have at his disposal a wealth of synonyms, from which he could choose one with the right initial sound for a given line.

Given the very considerable native resources of Old English, it had no pressing need to borrow extensively from other tongues, and in fact did not do so until after 900 A.D. Earlier borrowings overwhelmingly concerned new things and concepts to which the English were exposed when they came into more regular contact with civilized Europe; most of these were in one way or another related to the Church, the main agent of that contact.

The conversion of the heathen English to Christianity began in 587, when the Roman missionary Augustine (not to be confused with the North African St. Augustine) landed in Kent. Not long afterward, missionaries from Ireland began the conversion of the northern English, with the process essentially complete before the end of the next century. The dual sources of English Christianity are reflected in two Old English words for its central symbol. Both ultimately derived from Latin *crux,* but the Irish version yielded *cros,* while an earlier, West Germanic borrowing gave *cruc* (/crooch/). The latter has vanished from the language, surviving only in the London street of Crutched Friars—friars with crosses on their robes.

The Church, along with bringing literacy to the English, also brought renewed contact with Latin, the language of literacy all over western Europe, and of course of the Scriptures and the Mass. Old English borrowings from Church Latin extended from 600 to 1100 A.D., and eventually totaled more than four hundred words.

A large group of these, naturally, dealt with the Church itself and the new doctrine it propagated. For some of these concepts, no borrowing was needed: the English already knew about *God* and *hefen, synn* and *hel.*

Moreover, the missionaries were shrewd enough to translate some distinctively Christian concepts into familiar English terms. *Forgyf* in the Lord's Prayer is a literal translation of Latin *per-donare,* whence "pardon" (interestingly, both *per-* and *for-* come from the same Indo-European root); and Latin *evangelium,* literally "good news," became English *godspell,* whence "gospel." Even the elusive and bewildering concept of the *sanctus spiritus* became the *halig gast*—eventually to bewilder still further some generations of Sunday-school children, for whom a ghost, holy or otherwise, had become something you see on Halloween. In the same way, the Church artfully blended some of its own important festivals with existing native ones. The Germanic spring festival in honor of the goddess Eostre became a celebration of the Resurrection, while the old midwinter Yule festivities were consecrated to Christ's birth—though even today they retain some of their pagan character as a time of heavy eating and drinking.

But many Christian terms did not translate easily into English, so that we get the borrowings *preost* and *biscop, nonne* and *munuc, engel* and *diafol, maesse* and *ymen* (hymn), *candel* and *altar,* along with some dozens of others. Indeed most of the English "technical" vocabulary of Christianity and its scriptures originated in these borrowings.

A few ecclesiastical words passed fairly rapidly into the general vocabulary—the *caeppe* that covered the shaven heads of the clergy, and the *purple sioluc* (silk) of their vestments. (The English also had their own, earlier word for "purple," *fisc deag,* literally "fish dye," referring to the Mediterranean shellfish that tinted the garments of Roman emperors and aristocrats—those "born to the purple.") Even more generally useful were the new plants and agricultural technologies brought by the monks—the *persoc* (peach) and *pere* trees, the useful root crops *radisc, bete* (these beets —now called chard—were a primitive variety grown for their leaves; the modern beet—in England, "beet-root"—came much later) and (tur)-*naep,* the *cucumer* and *fic* (fig) and a score of other ornamental or useful plants. Prominent among the new introductions were herbs, then used as much for new introductions healing as for cooking: *fenol, savery* and *gingifer* (ginger), along with the *box*-tree, whose name was later transferred to a container made from its wood, eventually to one made from cardboard and even—in a song popular some years ago—to little houses allegedly made from equally ticky-tacky materials.

Improvements in farming technology were reflected in the *mattuc* (mattock), *sicol* (a new type of reaping hook with a toothed edge) and *culter* (coulter), a blade set in front of the plowshare that could cut into root-matted or heavy clay soils that simpler plows could not penetrate. Easily the most important of these innovations was the *mylen*. The water mill was a real technological breakthrough, for it was the first new source of energy for mankind since the ox was hitched to the plow. Originally the *mylen* only ground grain, replacing the hand-turned *cweorne* (quern), but during the Middle Ages its power began to be used in a host of manufacturing processes as well. As early as the eleventh century, there were more than a thousand mills in England, a small, "underdeveloped" country.

The monks' and nuns' concern with the sick and other unfortunates is reflected in such borrowings as *aelmysse* (alms), *cancer* (canker—an infected sore), *fefor* (with the second F pronounced /v/), *sponge* and *plaster* (at that time, a sticky ointment). Equally, the Church's dominant role in education and literacy show up in the borrowings *scol*, the *maegister* (/my-stair/) who taught there, *paper*, *fers* (verse) and the Latin-English compound *grammatic-craeft* (grammar).

A few borrowings seem to reflect trading rather than religious contacts with western and southern Europe. These include the *market* and the *ancora*, with which a ship, rather than being hauled ashore, could be moored in deep water—a prudent precaution in those turbulent times. The English also borrowed the names of three shellfish still used extensively in Mediterranean cookery: the *ostre*, *musle* and *lopyster*. Since all three were common in English waters, it is hard to see why these words should have been borrowed; conceivably, the ancestral, heathen religion of the English had tabooed the eating of shellfish, as Orthodox Judaism still does.

The very sparseness of these commercial borrowings reflects what history and archaeology tell us: trade did not then loom very large in the English economy. Moreover, such trade as existed was mainly with the Low Countries, whose Germanic dialects were still hardly distinguishable from Old English. And trade with more southerly areas would have involved mainly commodities whose names had already reached English via West Germanic borrowings—*win*, for instance. The main English export, then and for centuries later, was *wull*.

The Latin brought by the Church stimulated expansion of the English vocabulary indirectly as well as directly, by introducing new concepts which English writers employed in loan-translations. Most of these, however, were later replaced by the very Latin expressions that originally inspired them; we now say "preface," not *fore-spraec* ("fore-speech"), "collaborator" rather than *mid-wyrhta* ("with-worker"), and "expel" rather than *utdræfen* ("out-drive"). In some cases, however, the Old English loan-translation has remained side by side with a (later) borrowing; we still use both "withstand" *(wiþstandan)* and "oppose."

These rather sophisticated linguistic developments reflect a surprising fact: by the eighth century, England (along with Ireland) was perhaps the most intellectually and culturally advanced land in western Europe. English and Irish missionaries were active in the conversion of Germany, and when Charlemagne sought teachers to revive learning in his immense Franco-German empire, he looked to England for them.

England was prosperous and cultured because it remained relatively peaceful, despite a fair amount of infighting among the kingdoms into which it was divided. Its remote and island situation saved it from the repeated invasions that disrupted and at times devastated large parts of western and southern Europe: those of the Avars, Byzantines, Lombards and Arabs. At the end of the eighth century, however, both England and Ireland faced attack by a people for whom the sea was not a barrier but a highway: the *Norþmenn.*

These were the inhabitants of Sweden and Norway who, not long after the English migrations, expanded into Denmark as well. As with earlier Germanic expansions, this one seems ultimately to have stemmed from improvements in climate, leading to more food and thus more people. All these peoples spoke very similar dialects of Old Norse, the direct descendant of North Germanic.

The Norse were skilled shipbuilders and seamen, and as such played an important role in reviving trade in northern Europe, carrying furs, walrus ivory and slaves southward to exchange for *vin* and other luxuries. Unfortunately they soon discovered that when trade was slack, or even when it wasn't, their maritime skills were as useful for raiding as for trading. The most accessible target for their raids was western Europe—especially England.

The Norse raids began in 787 A.D. with the sacking by a few ships of a monastery in northern England, but escalated into organized attacks by hundreds of "keels." Inevitably, raiding evolved into conquest. The Norwegians took over parts of Ireland, Scotland and northwestern England, but had relatively little impact on English life or language, since all three areas were still largely or entirely Celtic. The Danes, however, moved into northern and central England and almost managed to seize the rest of the country; they were beaten back only through the persistence and military skill of Alfred, King of Wessex. The result was a virtual partition of England roughly along the line of *Watling Stræt,* the dilapidated but still passable Roman road from London to Chester. North and east of this line was the Danelaw, owing nominal allegiance to Wessex, but in practice virtually independent, as its name implies ("law" itself comes from Old Norse *lagu*).

Nonetheless, the statesmanship of Alfred and his descendants fairly rapidly reconciled the newcomers and the English, thereby helping to bring about a revival of culture and learning. Alfred himself refounded numbers of monasteries sacked in the Danish wars, and established new ones—and monasteries were the chief source of the hand-lettered books of the time. To further encourage education, Alfred (well nicknamed "the Great") conceived the radical notion of using English as the basic medium of instruction in reading and writing, rather than the Latin used elsewhere in western Europe. To this end, he himself began learning Latin when nearly forty and thereafter translated, or had translated, many important Latin works into English. Not the least of these was *The Ecclesiastical History of the English People,* by the eighth-century St. Bede. For secular history, Alfred instituted the so-called Anglo-Saxon Chronicle, which began with a rather fanciful account of English history since Julius Caesar, but was carried forward, year by year, for more than two and a half centuries, giving a clear, and usually quite believable, account of current events. The English were beginning to acquire a sense of their own identity.

Unfortunately, the gradual reunification of England did not do away with the "Norse menace"; various free-enterprising pirate fleets continued to harry England, despite the best efforts of Alfred, his sons, grandsons and great-grandsons—or the worst efforts of his great-great-grandson, Ethelred, surnamed "the Unready." His modernized nickname conceals a bitter Old English pun. *Ræd* meant both "counsel" and "plan" (of action); the English therefore rechristened King *Ethelræd* ("noble counsel") *Unræd* ("no plan").

Contemporary chronicles describe King No-Plan as treacherous and a womanizer, but neither trait distinguishes him from other, more successful political leaders before and since. Ethelred's problem was that he didn't know where to stop: he double-crossed not only his enemies but also his allies and potential allies; eventually, nobody trusted him, and effective English resistance became impossible. The results are eloquently summed up in the Chronicle for the year 1010:

". . . When they [the Norsemen] were in the east, the English army was kept in the west, and when they were in the south, our army was in the north. Then all the councilors were summoned to the king . . . to decide how this country should be defended. But even if anything was decided, it did not last even a month. [No plan!] Finally there was no leader who would collect an army, but each fled as best he could, and in the end no shire [county] would even help the next. . . ."

Unable to resist, the English sought to buy off the invaders with "Danegeld," which we would call protection money. The first payment was the substantial sum of £10,000, equivalent in purchasing power to several million modern dollars, but every year or two the Danes returned—with their hands out. The escalating payments eventually carried the total to something like $100,000,000, an almost incredible sum for a country the size of England with a still-simple economy.

But even these extortions didn't solve the problems, since (as Kipling would much later put it)

> *When once you have paid him the Danegeld*
> *You never get rid of the Dane.*

Shortly after Ethelred's death, in fact, England was conquered by the Danish king Knut, (Canute), not without help from some of the English themselves, who evidently hoped that he would at least bring peace. He did: between 1016 and 1035, England, now part of a northern empire including Denmark, Norway, Scotland and Wales, enjoyed a generation of peace and prosperity. Able though Knut was, however, he could not incorporate England permanently into the Scandinavian sphere of influence—which would, among other things, have radically altered the subsequent development of the English tongue. On his death, the kingdom passed to a son of Ethelred's, Edward, as pious as his father had been vicious, but no less incompetent. It would take another conqueror, like Knut, of Scandinavian blood, but of French speech, to permanently end the Norse menace, unify England—and link it firmly to western, not northern Europe.

Amid all this turmoil, the Danish immigrants in the Danelaw were settling down in their own villages, identified today by hundreds of English town and village names incorporating Norse words. Most prominent are *by*, farmstead (e.g., Derby, and no less than seven Normanbys), *thorp*, hamlet (e.g., Laysingthorpe), *toft*, plot of land (e.g., Lowestoft) and *gata*, road (e.g., Harrogate). These Danish settlements, however, were scattered among the older English communities, meaning that once memories of the initial, inevitably bloody settlement had faded, the two peoples began borrowing one another's tools, marrying one another's sons and daughters—and, naturally, picking up one another's words. This last process occurred the more easily because the two languages were quite similar (they had been separated for less than a thousand years); they may even have been mutually intelligible in part.

The fusion of English and Danes might conceivably have led to a sort of Anglo-Norse hybrid tongue, but in fact English eventually prevailed. One reason was numbers: there were still plenty of English in the Dane-law, and few Danes outside it (the presence of some of them in London is attested by the name of one of its better-known churches, St. Clement Danes). Moreover, the Danes, unlike the English, were virtually illiterate. Some of them knew the old Runic alphabet and even carved a few inscriptions in it, but we have not a single document from the period written in Old Norse. As a result, the Danes lost their native tongue within a century or two (though it survived in parts of Scotland for much longer), but not without substantially changing their adopted language.

The influx of Norse words into English was a gradual process and, like other kinds of linguistic change, affected speech before it showed up in writing. And even the written documents are somewhat deceptive: those dating from the late ninth and tenth centuries, immediately following the Danish settlements, are nearly all in the dialect of Wessex, where Danes were almost nonexistent. From this sort of evidence, we would have to conclude that only about forty Norse words entered Old English; they include "law" (and "outlaw") and *batswegen*, boatman—whence "boat-swain." Yet several hundred other borrowings must have entered the spoken English of the Danelaw, though many of them are not attested in writing until the fourteenth century.

Measuring the impact of the Norse borrowings is complicated by the similarity between Old Norse and Old English, meaning that philologists cannot always be sure which language contributed which word. They are certain of some nine hundred still in general use; hundreds more are probably Norse, while Norse words found only in regional dialects of central and northern England (i.e., the Old Danelaw) and Scotland are numbered in the thousands.

An almost infallible marker of borrowed Norse words is the consonant group /sk/. As we noted much earlier, this group passed unchanged from Indo-European into Common Germanic, but in the West Germanic tongues was later softened to /sh/—though Old English masks the change for us by spelling the new sound SC. Thus Common Germanic **skipam* and **fiskaz* produced old English *scip* and *fisc*, but in Old Norse, most isolated of the Germanic tongues, the corresponding words were *skip* and *fisks.* This phonetic marker identifies such Norse borrowings as *skil, skinn, sky* and *skoltr* (skull), which the English called the *brægnpanne* ("brainpan"). Less certain phonetic pointers are "hard" /g/ and /k/, which in Old English had often evolved into /y/ and /ch/. Thus Norse *egg* eventually replaced Old English *æg* (/ey/), *giva* (give) replaced *gevan* (/yevan/) and *geta* (get) replaced *gietan* (/yehtan/)

These and nearly all the other borrowings are simple, everyday words, confirming that the English and Danish populations mixed rapidly and thoroughly. Indeed the English even borrowed some Norse family terms, though these are normally among the most deeply rooted words in any language: *husbondi* ("house-master") and *syster* (replacing Old English *sweoster*). Pronouns are another class of words not often borrowed, but here borrowing filled a real need. The Norse originals of "they," "their" and "them" replaced Old English *hie, hiera* and *him,* which were confusingly similar to *he, hiere* and *him* (he, her and him). Even so, the replacement was gradual; as late as the fourteenth century, Chaucer was using both the Norse and the English terms.

Often the Norse borrowings did not drive out their English equivalents; instead, both survived. Thus the Scots say "kirk," with the Norse /k/, while the rest of us say "church," with the English /ch/. Norse "skirt" originally meant the same as English "shirt," but soon dropped below the waist; equally distinctive in meaning are Norse *deya* (die) and its English equivalent, *steorfa,* which survived to become a particular way of dying (starve), and English *baeþ* and North *baðask,* which became "bask"; many of us still like to bask in a bath.

In other cases, the Norse terms supplied English with useful pairs of synonyms or near-synonyms: English "whole" and Norse "hale," "rear" and "raise" (you can do either to a child), "shatter" and "scatter" (both of which happen if you drop a plate), "sick" and "ill," "carve" and "cut," "wish" and "want," "craft" and "skill," "hide" and "skin." The Danes did not merely change our vocabulary; they enriched it.

They did something even more fundamental to English: they simplified it, through the elimination of inflections. Though Old Norse and Old English differed only modestly in their basic vocabulary, their inflectional endings were quite different. And as anyone who has ever tried to learn an inflected language (e.g., German, Russian, Latin) can testify, it is precisely the inflections that are hardest to keep straight. Partly this is because we aren't used to inflections, but that can't be the whole reason, because the process operates both ways: foreigners whose native tongues are more heavily inflected than English still have trouble with even our few inflections, constructing sentences like "He go to New York." For similar reasons, young English-speaking children have trouble with "irregular" inflections, saying "I goed" rather than "I went."

If you have trouble keeping track of inflections in a foreign tongue, you are likely either to drop them entirely or to mumble them into a vague "uh" sound—which is precisely what happened to most English inflections in the centuries following the Danish invasions. If the inflections can't easily be dropped without confusing the meaning—e.g., the inflections that distinguish singular from plural in nouns—then the foreigner is likely to "regularize" them by reducing them all to a single, easily remembered pattern, like the child who says "I goed."

Plurals in Old English were formed in many different ways: *stan* (stone)/and *stanas*, but also *nama* (name)/*namen*, *scip/scipu*, *sunu* (son)/ *suna, fot* (foot)/*fet*. We still say "feet," of course, but all the other plurals have been regularized along the lines of *stanas:* "names," "ships" and "sons."

Equally indispensable—and almost equally confusing for the Danes— were the Old English inflections distinguishing past from present in verbs. The majority of verbs (called "weak," for reasons known only to grammarians) formed the past tense by adding *-de* or *-ede*, as in *fyll* (fill), *fyllde*. The minority of "strong" verbs used vowel shift (ablaut)—and the shifts were different for different verbs; thus *drife, draf* (drive, drove) but also *helpe, heolp* (help, helped) and *hleape, hleop* (leap, leaped). Confronted with this confusing system, the Danes did what you'd expect: transformed strong verbs into weak ones with the "normal" *-de* ending. In fact, modern studies have shown that between 1100 and 1200 A.D., nearly a third of the three-hundred-odd strong verbs in English were thus transformed, and the process continued almost unabated until about 1500. These figures, moreover, are based on written documents; the changes must surely have occurred even earlier in speech.

We cannot fairly credit the Danes with *all* this syntactic simplification. As noted earlier, Old English was already considerably simplified as compared with Indo-European, and further simplification was brought about later, through the assimilation of another bunch of foreigners, the Normans. Nor, indeed, do the Danes deserve "credit" for the change: they weren't trying to reform English but merely doing what came naturally —learning the new language as best they could, meaning that they ignored or altered such of its features as they found too confusing. Nonetheless, it is a fact that English syntax underwent as much simplification in the five hundred years following the Danish settlements as it had in the previous five thousand. If English grammar is today somewhat easier to master than French or German grammar (and *much* easier than Russian grammar), a major reason is surely the linguistic difficulties of those Norse hoodlums-turned-good-neighbors.

5. THE THIRD CONQUEST

English and French

✍

... an event ... which had a greater effect on the English language than any other in the course of its history.

—Albert C. Baugh

I followed my duke ere I was a lover
To take from England fief and fee.
But now the game is the other way over;
But now England has taken me.

—Rudyard Kipling

OF the thousands of American and British soldiers who invaded Normandy on June 6, 1944, I doubt that many devoted any thought to another cross-Channel operation, in the opposite direction, some nine centuries earlier. Yet the Norman invasion of England—1066 and all that —had a more profound effect on the future of England than D-day 1944, and a far more profound effect on the English language. The Norman Conquest unified England in a way that no native king, even the great Alfred, had managed to do, brought it permanently within the economic and cultural orbit of western Europe, and grafted a vigorous offshoot of the French language onto the sturdy Germanic roots of English, thereby enlarging the English vocabulary by thousands of words.

Before examining this key event in the history of our native tongue, however, we need some background. Specifically, where did the Norman French of England's new rulers come from? Immediately, of course, it came from Latin (which, incidentally, has heavily influenced the English vocabulary in its own right)—but where did Latin come from?

Some time before 1000 B.C., a group of Indo-Europeans migrated from central Europe into Italy. Like other such migrations, this one produced a regional dialect of Indo-European, known as Italic (comparable to Common Germanic far to the north), which itself rapidly split into several dialects and languages as the newcomers spread over Italy, conquering and absorbing the earlier inhabitants. Some of the ancient Italic tongues, such as Oscan and Faliscan, have survived in a few inscriptions, but only Latin has left extensive written records. The earliest of these date from around 600 B.C., when Latin-speakers acquired a version of the alphabet devised by the Greeks a century or two earlier (this in turn was based on the still earlier Phoenecian alphabet).

Even at this time, Latin and the other Italic tongues had already borrowed words from the native Italians for distinctive features of their environment and culture. Notable among these were the *oliua* tree and the *oleum* pressed from its fruits, the *uinea* and the *uinum* fermented from *its* fruits, and the patient *asinus* on whose back both wine and olive oil could be carried to market. These and some other words of the northern Mediterranean coastal lands may derive from some ancient "Mediterranean" tongue carried westward by the first farmers to reach the region. A few may represent still earlier borrowings from farther east; thus *asinus* may go back to the Sumerians of Mesopotamia, who first domesticated the animal they called *anshu* about the time the Indo-European migrations were beginning along the Danube.

At the beginning, the Latin-speaking Italics, called Romans from their chief city, were but one of many small tribes and tribal confederations scattered over Italy. Some time after 900 B.C., in fact, they were subjugated (from Latin *sub iugum,* under the yoke) by the Etruscans, a non-Indo-European people, perhaps originally from Asia Minor, but then centered in the region of Italy still called Toscana (Tuscany). Under their rule, the Romans would surely have borrowed some Etruscan words, but we can seldom identify these as such: a few Etruscan inscriptions have survived and can even be "read" (they are written in another version of the Greek alphabet), but not understood, since Etruscan is related to no known tongue. Latin *populus,* people (whence also "population," "popular" etc.), is probably Etruscan, as is the root *merx-,* having to do with com*merce*— whence also "merchant," the Roman god Mercury (patron of merchants— and thieves) and the planet and element named for him. Other possible Etruscan borrowings are *carcer,* prison (whence "incarcerate")—the sort of word that subject peoples often borrow from their rulers—and *ferrum,* iron (the Etruscans were notable ironworkers), whence various modern scientific terms and the chemical symbol for that element, Fe.

Other non-Indo-European words in Latin—borrowed or invented we shall never know—include the "nursery" word *amma,* mother, whence "amiable," "amateur" and even "aunt"; *bassus,* low, whence both "base" and the low-voiced bass singer, and *battuere,* beat, whence "com*bat*," "battle," the batter we beat up in our kitchens and even the bat with which English and Americans beat balls. Others that have passed into English by one route or another include *dorsum,* back, whence both the dorsal fin of a fish and the en*dorse*ment we write on the back of a check; and *mappa,* cloth, whence such diverse words as "map," "mop," "napkin" and "apron" (originally "napron").

Gradually, by a combination of brutal military skill and political acumen, the Romans made themselves masters of Italy, conquering and absorbing the Etruscans, the other Italic peoples, the Gaulish Celts of the Po Valley—who as late as 390 B.C. had been formidable enough to sack Rome—and the flourishing, highly civilized Greek cities of southern Italy and Sicily. All these conquests of non-Latin-speaking peoples must have had much the same effect as the later English absorption of the Danes: a radical simplification of Latin syntax. The literary Latin still taught in some schools was, as noted earlier, a highly inflected language, but there is good evidence, in the form of graffiti, that as early as the second century B.C. most Romans were using a much more streamlined version in which (as in the modern Romance tongues) inflectional forms were vanishing, being replaced by prepositions and a more rigid word order. This was Vulgar Latin, literally the tongue of the *vulgus* or common people— though some of the graffiti written in it were pretty vulgar at that.

Thus for some six centuries prior to the fall of the Western Roman Empire, Latin existed in two sharply distinct social dialects. The upper classes used formal, literary Latin for writing, and for speaking among themselves, though most of them almost certainly understood Vulgar Latin and could speak it well enough to communicate with their social inferiors. (Interestingly, the writer Suetonius, a notable purveyor of historical gossip about the early empire, mentions that the Emperor Augustus—who had spent most of his young manhood in military camps, where Vulgar Latin was the lingua franca—continued to use some of its forms, expressing "in Rome" with a preposition rather than the appropriate inflection.) The rest of the *populus* spoke Vulgar Latin—and scribbled it on walls and potsherds.

In our terms, it was rather as if nearly all English and American writing today was in the style of the King James Bible, complete with "thou sayest," "he sayeth" and so on, while almost everyone but the Power Elite *spoke* modern English. Odd as this seems, there are plenty of linguistic precedents in the past and even the present; thus the literary language of modern Greece, called *Katharevousa,* differs considerably from the *Demotiki* or common speech, though the latter is increasingly coming into use for popular writings.

Both forms of Latin, despite their differences, shared an important trait with Old English and most other Indo-European tongues: the formation of new words by joining prefixes to verbs and (less often) nouns. Modern English has taken over thousands of these Latin compounds, some dating back to Roman times but others formed much later out of Latin elements.

Thus from the verb *cadere*, fall, comes *ad-cadere*, "on-fall," whence the accidents that (sometimes literally) fall on or befall us. *De-cadere*, "away-fall," yielded the decadent people or institutions that have fallen away from past greatness or virtue; *co-in-cadere*, "with-in-fall," the coincidence whereby two things unexpectedly "fall in" with one another. *Capere*, take, has given us the *parti-*cipants who take *part* in something, as well as the *de-*ception that takes *away* our money—or our faith in the deceiver. *Cernere*, sift, produced the *dis-*cerning person who can sift *out* sense from nonsense; *fusus*, poured, the *trans-*fusion poured *across* from one person to another. And *plicatus*, folded, begot the *com-*plications of many things folded in *with* one another, the *du-*plicate or *two-*fold document—and the duplicity of the two-faced person.

Positus, put, yields the *ex-*posure of something put *out* to public view (or the ravages of the weather), not to mention the *pre-*position put *before* a noun; *secutus*, followed, yields the *ex-*(s)ecutive who follows *out* the decisions of legis-lators ("law-proposers") or boards of *di-*rectors (those who "guide *away*"—from trouble, presumably). *Solutus*, loosened, gives us the solution that loosens the knotty difficulties of a puzzle or problem, and the *dis-*solute person who has loosed himself *away* from normal restraints —a loose fellow, in fact. Finally, *specere*, look at, has begotten the *de-*spicable person we look *down* on—and who, in *retro-*spect (looking *back*), we should have been *per-*spicacious enough to see *through*.

All these compounds are com-posed (put together) of native Latin elements. Another major component of the Latin vocabulary, however, consisted of several thousand words borrowed from Greek, which brings us to yet another member of the Indo-European family. The Greeks, it is thought, were originally a pastoral people resembling and perhaps akin to the Kurganians discussed in Chapter 2. Around 2000 B.C., they swept into Greece from the Balkans, conquering various native peoples whose non-Indo-European tongues are known only from borrowed words in Greek, such as the Greek equivalents of "wine" and "olive," as well as "hyacinth," "narcissus," "mint," and many place names, including those of such historic cities as Athens and Corinth. Other exotic words came into Greek from trade with the Semitic lands of the eastern Mediterranean; these include *khrysos*, gold, whence the golden-petaled chrys-anthemum.

Ancient Greek, even more elaborately inflected than Latin, became the medium of the most brilliant literary and intellectual achievements the western world had yet seen. Under Alexander the Great and his successors, the entire eastern Mediterranean was brought under Greek rulers, who brought with them both Greek culture and the Greek language, which in the mouths of the local populations rapidly became simplified into the *koine dialektos* or common speech (note the parallel with Vulgar Latin).

Latin borrowings from Greek must have begun with Rome's absorption of Greek colonies in southern Italy, during the third and second centuries B.C., but reached their full stride only after her conquest of the eastern Mediterranean, shortly before the Christian Era opened. The Romans regarded the conquered Greeks somewhat as a Texas millionaire today might regard a Bostonian—with mingled admiration and contempt. On the one hand, the Greeks *had* been conquered, and were therefore obviously somewhat effete; on the other, their art, literature and philosophy were undoubtedly impressive, beyond anything Rome could (or ever would) produce. By the time the empire was in full swing, a knowledge of Greek and its literature had become as essential to the educated Roman as a knowledge of Latin would much later be to the educated Englishman.

Under the circumstances, borrowed Greek words were naturally most numerous in formal, literary Latin (speakers of the vulgar tongue didn't go in much for literature or philosophy), but as Roman traders, sailors and soldiers began circulating through the new provinces, words from the Greek *koine* began infiltrating into their speech as well. In particular, the *koine* was the language of Christianity (which started as an overwhelmingly lower-class religion) and the New Testament, and was thus the ultimate source of many Christian terms later borrowed, through Latin, by the West Germans and English. "Church" comes from Greek *kuriakos doma*, God's house; "priest" from *presbyteros*, elder (**prester* in Vulgar Latin); while "bishop" is from Greek *episkopos*, overseer (**biskopus* in Vulgar Latin). The *skopos* is the same root we find in "telescope" ("far-seër") and "microscope" ("small-seër").

Both literary and Vulgar Latin survived the fall of the Roman Empire, but in different ways. The former begot the Church Latin of the mass and of St. Jerome's monumental translation of the Bible, from Hebrew and the *koine*, which we have already seen as a source of words in Old English. Church Latin also served during the Middle Ages as a lingua franca among churchmen and other educated people throughout western

Europe, both in speech and in theological and scholarly writing. Vulgar Latin evolved into the Romance tongues.

As the language of soldiers, traders and those who dealt with them, Vulgar Latin was inevitably a racy, slangy tongue, borrowing terms from native peoples and playing games with its own vocabulary. Thus *tabula*, plank, became the "plank" you sit at to eat or write, while *caballus*, nag, the Roman cavalryman's slang term for his mount (of obscure origin), completely displaced Latin *equus*, and eventually yielded "cavalry," "cavalier" and even "chivalry"—the same sort of ameliorative change that also elevated Germanic "knight" and "marshal."

In Gaul and parts adjacent, Vulgar Latin borrowed from the Celtic dialects collectively known as Gaulish, but no more than a few hundred words altogether. The Gauls, after all, knew few things that Romans needed or wanted to know, and their tongue had no social prestige whatever (Roman writers describe it as "harsh"—meaning that they didn't want to be bothered learning it). Vulgar Latin *pottus* (whence "pot" and "potter") is from Gaulish, as are *carrum* or *carra*, wagon (the Celts were notable wagon-builders; some of their productions actually had wooden roller bearings in their axles), along with the *carpentarius* who built it, who eventually expanded into a builder of anything in wood. Vulgar Latin *multo*, sheep (whence "mutton"), is another borrowing from the Gauls, who in turn seem to have borrowed it from some earlier, non-Indo-European people, as the Germans borrowed "sheep," "ram" and "lamb." Other Gaulish terms that have passed into English are *pettia*, piece, and *tanno-*, oak, whence the tanning done with the bark of oaks and other trees, containing tannic acid. Possible borrowings from Gaulish—the lack of written records makes it impossible to be certain—include the Latin originals of English "change," "mine" (for metals) and "javelin."

Vulgar Latin, spoken from the Balkans to Spain, inevitably evolved regional dialects, a process that was underway by the second century A.D. It was facilitated by the fact that Vulgar Latin was never written down (apart from a handful of graffiti), since writing is always a conservative influence on linguistic change, and was further accelerated by the breakdown of communications as the Western Empire disintegrated under the shock of the Germanic invasions.

These warriors brought their own words into one or more of the Vulgar Latin dialects. Though relatively sparse in number, the terms give an all too vivid picture of conditions during the empire's death throes.

They include the linguistic originals of the *helmet* and *scabbard* with which the Germanic *warrior* armed himself, the *garrisons* he set as *wardens* to *guard* his conquests and the *heralds* (originally, "army leaders") who led him in *war*—or *murder*. Other Germanic borrowings of the time look innocuous until you discover their original meaning: "mar" meant to distress, "haste" meant violence or fury, while "wait" meant watch as an enemy—"lie in wait." Perhaps the most evocative of these seemingly bland words is "robe," which originally meant "booty" (it is cognate with "rob"); one imagines the invaders, during the sack of a town or villa, stripping the robes from the dead or, perhaps, the living. Other borrowings that may reflect the activities of the brutal and licentious German soldiery are "haunch" and "teat"—matters of overriding interest to nearly all soldiers once the fighting is done.

The return to quieter times as the invasions simmered down are signaled by such Germanic borrowings—found in French and sometimes other Romance tongues—as the originals of "mason," "garden," "sturgeon," "roast," "bacon" and "paw." Another peacetime borrowing, "grape," is rather puzzling—the French certainly knew much more about grapes and their culture than their Germanic conquerors—until you discover that it comes from *krappon,* a bent hook (cognate with the cramp that twists your muscles) used to harvest bunches of grapes. Later it became the bunch itself (which is what *grappe* still means in French) and finally, in English, one fruit on the bunch.

By the eighth century A.D., the Vulgar Latin of northern and central France had evolved into the *langue d'oil,* now more often called Old French. This was distinguished from the *langue d'oc* of southern France, the ancestor of Provençal, which is more like Spanish, Italian and (especially) Catalan than it is like French. (*Oc* and *oil* were respectively the southern and northern words for "yes.") It was the Norman dialect of the *langue d'oil* that William, Duke of Normandy, and his knights brought into England in 1066.

Normandy was the French equivalent of the Danelaw. Scandinavian pirates had made themselves quite as obnoxious in France as in England; the high (or low) point came during the ninth century, when Ragnar Hairy-Breeches sailed his fleet of 120 ships up the Seine and sacked Paris, then sacrificed a hundred prisoners to the Norse god Odin, to discourage French counterattacks. He withdrew only on payment of seven thousand pounds of silver—in modern terms, something like $10,000,000. But the French, like the English, never got rid of the Danes (actually, this lot of pirates was Norwegian), who settled down around the mouth of the Seine and on the Cotentin peninsula to the west. The French, succinctly, called the new settlements "pirate-land."

In 912 A.D., on the principle of setting a thief to catch a thief, the French king Charles the Simple formally recognized the occupation and designated the Norse chieftain Hrolf (Rolf, Rollo) as first Duke of *Normandie.* The experiment worked better than such things usually do: though the Norman dukes long remained turbulent and troublesome subjects of the French crown, they did serve as a shield against their still-piratical kin. Northern France changed from a target of Norse predation to a base for Norman conquests elsewhere—notably, southern Italy and England.

The Normans spoke Old Norse originally, like their kinsmen in the Danelaw, but shifted to French within a couple of generations—surely one of the fastest cases of linguistic assimilation on record. (According to tradition, Hrolf's son and successor had to arrange for his own son to be *taught* Norse.) The Norse were probably a small minority in their new home, and certainly an illiterate one. Nor did they know anything the French population felt the need to know—apart, perhaps, from their unquestioned military skills. One of the few Norse words borrowed into French was **hernest,* Old French *harneis,* originally meaning provisions for an army, later the equipment of a soldier and eventually, that of a horse.

Contacts between England and Normandy, separated by only sixty to a hundred miles of water, remained peaceful, and grew increasingly close, for a century. Ethelred No-Plan married a sister of the Duke of Normandy, and sought refuge with his brother-in-law when he was finally, and deservedly, kicked out of England. His son, Edward the Confessor, spent much of his youth in Normandy, and has been described as "almost more French than English." On his return to England, he brought with him numbers of his Norman chums, whom he furnished with lucrative positions at court—to the considerable irritation of the English, who then as now took a dim view of foreigners. These and other cross-Channel influences brought a few Old French words into Old English; *batt* (club) may have been one of them. (There is reason to think that the English were already playing some sort of game with a *batt* and a **beall,* as they have been doing ever since.) Another borrowing was *prud,* which in Old French meant "brave" or "gallant" (so we still speak of "proud banners"), but which the English, observing the Normans at court, gave the sense of "overbearing."

Edward, unlike his father Ethelred, had little interest in women; he did not marry until he reached forty, and produced no children (there is some reason to doubt that he ever tried). On his death, the English *witena gemot*, or Council of Wisemen—a sort of primitive parliament—was faced with two possible choices as his successor. One was Edward's nephew, Edmund, only thirteen years old; the other was Edward's brother-in-law, Harold, Earl of Wessex, who though not of royal blood was the most powerful man in the kingdom and probably the ablest. Having had their fill of feeble or incompetent kings, the *witena gemot* unanimously picked Harold, who may also have been Edward's own deathbed choice.

There was, however, a third claimant, Edward's second cousin by marriage: William, Duke of Normandy. William claimed—and apparently believed—that Edward had promised him the throne years earlier; he also claimed—and perhaps believed—that Harold had sworn to support his claim. (Some historians doubt that Harold had sworn any such thing; others believe he did, but under compulsion—he was William's "guest" at the time.)

What William failed to grasp was that Edward's alleged promise and Harold's alleged oath were alike beside the point. In England, the *cyning*, like the earlier Germanic **kuningaz*, was still one of the "royal kindred" *elected by the leaders of the community*—that is, the *witena gemot*. Whether that body formally considered William's claim we do not know; the minutes of the last meeting, if any were kept, are missing. But if they did, they must surely have rejected it almost without discussion: William's hereditary claim to the throne was even more tenuous than Harold's—and he was a Norman, a breed of which the English leaders had had quite enough under Edward.

William knew nothing of English legalities—Normandy, unlike England, had no written law code—and cared less; moreover, he had let it be known publicly that he was due to succeed Edward. At stake, therefore, were both his fierce pride and his "image," at a time when a ruler's prestige could make the difference between ruling and being deposed by force. If the English would not give him his "rights" he would take them.

William was Harold's equal as a leader, and his superior in brutal ruthlessness. To conquer England, he needed both qualities, as well as a large helping of luck; amphibious warfare across the Channel was a chancy business even in 1944, and this was 1066. His own knights and nobles, in fact, showed little enthusiasm for the venture.

William therefore began by cooking up a political deal with the Pope. By promising to be the latter's vassal, he induced His Holiness to convene a kangaroo court in Rome which, without bothering even to consult the English, decided that William was the rightful King of England. (It is pleasant to report that the Pope eventually got exactly what he deserved for this bit of ecclesiastical connivery: nothing; William's political IOU turned out to be uncollectable.)

With the Pope's blessing in hand, William was able to gather together a sizable expeditionary force, composed of most of the unemployed knights in northern France—some, perhaps, moved by religion, but most by the loot and English land that William promised them. At that point, luck took a hand.

Harold, well aware of William's preparations, mobilized both the small standing army and the *fyrd,* a sort of militia including most of the able-bodied men in southern England, armed with whatever weapons they could lay hands on. But for week after week, William failed to arrive, held in Norman harbors by northerly winds. With harvest time approaching, the *fyrd* dispersed to its homes—and Harold suddenly found himself facing a second, quite independent invasion. This was led by the King of Norway, Harald Hardrada, whose name translates roughly as Harold the Ruthless. The same north wind that kept William in Normandy brought Harald's ships south from the Norwegian fjords, to sail up the Humber and capture York.

By a stupendous forced march, Harold (of England) brought his army north and virtually wiped out the invaders—only to learn that a shift in the wind had carried William across the Channel. Another forced march placed the English across William's path at Hastings, where, after a see-saw day's battle, they were defeated and Harold killed. With him died any hope of organized English resistance; by a combination of threats, promises (most of them worthless) and terror, William rapidly brought the rest of the country under his sway.

Over the long run, the Norman Conquest may have been good for the English, as it certainly was for their language. Over the short run, it was a disaster, beginning with several hundred thousand deaths in the years following 1066, from war, starvation and disease, and ending with Normans in total control of the country. Norman nobles replaced English—who were, indeed, lucky if they retained their lives; Norman castles (built by English forced labor), filled with Norman soldiers, served as strong-points to "pacify" the English countryside. Norman bishops and abbots took over the English church, Norman clerks the English government, and Norman merchants and craftsmen a good deal of English commerce. The English, with some exceptions, were limited to the lower ranks of society—peasants, serfs or outright slaves.

The social status of the two groups was naturally reflected in what they talked about. As Sir Walter Scott noted in *Ivanhoe,* the English *swin, sceap, cyna* (cows) and *calfru* tended by the peasantry became the Norman-French *porc, moton, boef* and *veel* served up on the lord's table. The Englishman lived in a humble *cot*(tage); the Norman, in a French *maneir* ("manor"—mansion) or *castel.* The English did most of the *werc;* the Normans enjoyed most of the *leisir*—and the *profit.* In short, life for the Normans was relatively *aisé;* for the English it was *hard*—a word whose sound has changed little for more than a thousand years.

The actual situation was not quite as bad as these linguistic contrasts might suggest. Once William had completed his brutally efficient pacification, he made some effort to rule in accordance with English law, which he took the trouble to have codified. Unfortunately, he was ill equipped by upbringing to understand either the English or their law. Like most great lords of Continental Europe, he was virtually an absolute monarch in his own lands, ruling by right of birth—and the sword. The English kings, as we have seen, ruled by right of birth *and election,* and the *witena gemot* that elected them was merely the highest of many "moots" (assemblies) through which a sizable part of the population participated in local and what we would call county government. The English, indeed, were groping toward the idea that even the king was bound by the law—a notion that William would have considered laughable if not outright immoral.

But traditions often outlast kings, as this one did. It became customary for William's successors, whatever their private reservations, to formally accept on oath the "ancient laws" of England; indeed, William's great-great-grandson, John, was *compelled* to put his acceptance of English tradition in writing.

John was unquestionably the nastiest piece of work ever to occupy the English throne—as treacherous as Ethelred, as ruthless as William, and as personally vicious as both of them put together. His main achievement was to bring together a coalition of English barons, townsmen and common folk, none of whom much liked or trusted the others, but all of whom disliked and distrusted the king even more, and who, in 1215, forced him to sign the Great Charter that spelled out limitations on the royal power. Under one of its provisions, the king pledged that "no freeman shall be seized, or imprisoned, or dispossessed, or outlawed, or in any way brought to ruin; we [the king] will not go against any man nor send against him, save by legal judgment of his peers or by the law of the land." Another pledged that "to no man will we sell, or deny, or delay, right or justice."

Some modern historians have attacked the Charter as a "reactionary" document, on the ground that it increased the power of the feudal nobility against that of the crown. But this view, I think, ignores a central fact of history: what actually happened often matters less, in the long run, than what people think happened. The Charter did not in fact permanently curb the power of the king or (even less) the nobility; many more centuries, and much bloodshed, would be needed for that. What it did do was give the average Englishman a sense that he had some sort of formal, "unalienable" right to be ruled by law, not a ruler's whim; that even the most powerful should have limits set on their power. The Charter planted a seed in men's minds that, long afterward, flowered in England's unwritten constitution and our own written Bill of Rights.

All that, however, was still far in the future. From the point of view of language, the most notable effect of the Norman Conquest was to convert England, almost overnight, into a bilingual country. The upper classes spoke French; before long they were joined by those of the English middle and lower classes who had regular dealings with them: tradesmen, manor "foremen" and the like. French was also essential to anyone with ambitions of rising in the social scale. The rest of the population continued speaking English at home and among themselves, though many of them doubtless learned to understand French if not speak it; likewise, many of the upper classes doubtless learned to understand, if not speak, English.

It is worth emphasizing, however, that medieval bilingualism in England (or anywhere else) was not associated with the linguistic nationalism that has raised such hell in modern times—bitter disputes in bilingual Belgium and Canada, actual bloodshed in multilingual India. The notion that subject peoples "ought" to speak the language of their rulers simply didn't exist. Rome, the prototypical empire, included peoples speaking scores of different tongues, while the subjects of Charlemagne's short-lived "Roman" empire (late eighth century) spoke at least two major dialects of Old French and several dialects of German. Thus when the Normans looked down on the English, as they often did, it was as social inferiors, not as speakers of another tongue. And if the English resented the Normans, as they often did, it was because they were oppressive and grasping, not because they spoke French. For nearly two centuries after the Conquest, both communities did what came naturally, speaking their birth tongues by preference but learning the other if they needed to— or, in some cases, no doubt, simply because some of their childhood playfellows spoke it.

Given the disparity in numbers—despite the direct and indirect casualties of the Conquest there were still far more English than Normans—one might have expected French to fall out of use within a few generations, as Norse had done in Normandy. However, any tendency toward rapid linguistic assimilation was checked by the fact that the Norman nobles, from the king down, owned lands in France as well as England, and spent much of their time living or fighting across the Channel. Indeed, by the mid-twelfth century, the King of England controlled (at least in theory) more of France than did the King of France; his French subjects may have outnumbered his English ones. Thus the French influence remained strong.

Had this situation continued, England might well have taken over the speech of its conquerors, as Gaul had earlier adopted Latin. It didn't, for two reasons. The first was intermarriage: almost immediately after the Conquest, some of the men-at-arms, knights and even barons that William had brought with him began taking English wives. (Those who "commuted" across the Channel may well have had families—legitimate or otherwise—in both countries.) Thus as early as 1177, a chronicler could write that "the two nations have become so mixed that it is scarcely possible today, speaking of free men, to tell who is English, who is of Norman race." The second reason was another achievement of the unpopular King John, who shortly after 1200 managed to lose virtually all his possessions in France to the French crown. Individual nobles still owned lands in both countries, but pressure from both French and English kings rather quickly ended this practice, in effect requiring the lords to make up their minds to be either French or English. Both English and French nationalism were further boosted by the outbreak of the Hundred Years War between the two countries in 1337.

English kings after John still often took French wives and often appointed their French in-laws to high offices in court and church. But this merely fanned antagonism toward the French among the native-born English, whether of Norman, English or mixed stock. Thus in 1252, Bishop Grosseteste (of Norman blood, as his French name—"big head" —attests) could denounce Henry II's imported French favorites as "not merely foreigners; they are the worst enemies of England. They strive to tear the fleece and do not even know the faces of the sheep; *they do not understand the English tongue . . .*" (emphasis added). A few generations later, Edward I, attempting to whip up national feeling against the King of France, declared that it was "his detestable purpose, which God forbid, to wipe out the English tongue."

By 1300, in fact, nearly everyone in England spoke English, and only a minority also spoke French. A poet of the period, writing, significantly, in English, reported that

> *Lewede men cune Ffrensch non*
> *Among an hondryd, unneþis on.*
> (Of French the common men know none;
> Among a hundred, scarcely one.)

As for the "uncommon" part of the population, the decline of French is attested by, among much other evidence, the production around 1285 of a small treatise for *teaching* children French "which every gentleman ought to know." Clearly every gentleman did *not* know it by birth; equally clearly, whether or not he knew French, he certainly knew English. Around 1325, the writer William of Nassyngton summed up the linguistic situation in a passage which, to spare the reader's patience, I have translated rather freely:

> *Latin can no one speak, I trow*
> *But those who it from school do know;*
> *And some know French, but no Latin*
> *Who're used to Court and dwell therein,*
> *And some use Latin, though in part,*
> *Who of French have not the art,*
> *And some can understand English*
> *That neither Latin know, nor French.*
> *But simple or learnèd, old or young,*
> *All understand the English tongue.*

Indeed even the minority who continued to speak French along with English spoke a provincial dialect, Norman French, that had been further provincialized by two and a half centuries of semi-isolation. Chaucer whimsically notes that his Prioress spoke French fluently, but

> *After the scole of Stratford-atte-Bowe,*
> *For French of Paris was to hir unknowe.*

Fortunately, there was no Académie Française in those days; one trembles to think of its sulfurous comments on the *franglais* of fourteenth-century England.

In 1356, the mayor (French *maire*) and aldermen (Old English *aldor-menn*) of London ordered that court proceedings there be held in English, not French; six years later, Parliament extended the principle nationwide, because "French is much unknown." In 1385, Parliament was opened in English, and in the same year the scholar John Trevisa could write that "in all the grammar schools of England, children leave French to construe and learn in English"; even fifty years earlier, instruction had been entirely in French. The change, said Trevisa, had "advantage on one side and disadvantage on another side. Its advantage is that they learn their grammar in less time than children were wont to do; the disadvantage is that now children of grammar school know no more French than does their left heel." (I have, of course, modernized Trevisa's English and spelling.) Advantage or disadvantage, English had triumphed.

But it was far from the Old English spoken at the court of Edward the Confessor some three centuries earlier. The most notable difference shows up vividly in a resolution of the London guild of brewers, from around 1420, in which English is formally adopted as the language of their meetings:

> Whereas our mother tongue . . . hath in *modern* days begun to be *honorably enlarged* and *adorned;* for that our most *excellent* lord King Henry the Fifth hath, in his *letters missive* and *divers affairs touching* his own *person*, more willingly chosen to *declare* the *secrets* of his will [in it], and for the better understanding of his *people* hath, with a *diligent* mind, *procured* the *common idiom* . . . and there are many of our craft of brewers who have the knowledge of writing and reading in the said English *idiom*, but others [i.e., Latin and French] . . . they do not in any wise understand; for which *causes* . . . it being considered how the greater *part* of the Lords and trusty *Commons* [i.e., Parliament] have begun to make their *matters* to be *noted* down in our mother tongue, so we also in our craft, following in some *manner* their steps, have *decreed* in *future* to *commit* to *memory* the needful things which *concern* us. [spelling modernized]

As the reader has undoubtedly guessed, all the italicized words in this rather pompous document are borrowed from French, assimilated, where necessary, into English syntax. Thus "honorably" combines a French root with the English adverb suffix -ly; "touching" incorporates the English participle suffix -ing; while "enlarged," "adorned" and half a dozen other verbs include the English past suffix -ed. (The seeming English plural -s of "letters" and "secrets" is not really a case of assimilation, since such plurals were even commoner in French than in English.)

The earliest recorded English borrowings from Old French following the Conquest are mostly the sort of words that underlings pick up from their bosses. English *esclaves* (slaves) and *servants paid homage* to the *barun* or other *noble* who *governed* them, and learned to say *sire* and *ma dame* (my lady) when they waited on *table* at a *feste*—which might be enlivened by *stories, rimes* and *lais* told or sung by a *menestral*. The Church, which no less than civil life was dominated by the Normans, was another source of early borrowings; it was there the English *prayed,* were *baptized,* given *penance* and *absolution,* and listened to *sermuns* by the *persone* of the *paroche* or a traveling *frere* (friar). Two centuries after the Conquest, some nine hundred French words, mainly of these general types, were already being used in English writing, and probably many more in English speech.

But as increasing numbers of the upper classes began learning English, they brought into it French words not by hundreds but by thousands. Many of these naturally reflected their high social status and the preoccupations that flowed from it. As the language of *cort, cuncil* and *parlement* (literally, "talking place"), French contributed such words as *royal, corone* (crown) and *autorité, tresoror* and *mareschal, subget* and *alligeance, oppression* and *liberté, rebelle* and *traitour.* To be sure, old England's *cyning* was still the *king,* as the *cwen* was the *cwene;* an *eorl* was still an *eorl* (though his wife was now a *contesse*), and a *cniht* a *knyght,* with little more than a change in spelling. But the far more elaborate structure of Continental feudalism had added *prince(sse), duk, duchesse, marchis* and *barun* to the English nobility. It was the Norman rulers who decided on *werre* or *pais,* while Norman *captains* (originally, "head officers," from Latin *caput,* head) commanded the *armée* and *navie* and led their *sergeants, archers* and other *soldiers* in *bataille, siege, defense* and *retrait.*

The French of the law courts contributed almost the entire cast of characters in any English-speaking court today: *plaintif, defendant,* the *atorneys* on both sides, and naturally the *juge* and *jurée;* only the witnesses were English—though their *testimonie* was French. No less French are most of our *legal offenses,* from *misdemeanors* through such *felonies* as *larcenie, assault* and *perjurie;* even Old English *morþor* was replaced by French *murdre* (from the same Germanic root).

From the French-speaking *clergé* came more ecclesiastical words: *confession, chapelain* and *co(n)vent,* and the *encens* burned before *images* of the *Creatour, Saviour* and *seints. Sermuns* and theological writings contributed *virgine, temptation, damnation* and a host of other words whose -ion endings (ultimately from Latin *-ionis* or *-ionum*) stamp them as French.

People who *dressed* in the *faciun* naturally borrowed from French (as indeed they still do), from *embroidered kerchiefs* to *robes* of *satin* or *velewet* trimmed with *furre* or *lase* to *botes* and even *galoches* for the feet—the latter then meaning the wooden *patins* (pattens) that kept a lady's feet out of the mud. The most affluent *adorned* themselves with *costly juels* of *diament*, *perle*, *rubi* or *turqueise* (the "Turkish stone").

The upper classes *dined* as well, and as French, as they *dressed*, not only on the meats mentioned earlier, but on *venison*, *bacon*, *saussiche*, *tripe* and *pouletrie*, not to mention *makerel*, *sole*, *perche*, *sturgeon* and *salmon*. These, along with *soupes*, were *saisoned* with *erbes* such as the *percely*, *sauge*, *rosmarine* and *thym* of the old song, or perhaps with *mostarde*. The meal might include a *salade* of *letus* or (later) *endive* dressed with *oile* and *vinegre*, and close with such *confections* as *tartes* or *gelys*, fruits such as *cheris*, *peches* or *grapes* in season and dried *rasins*, *dates* and *figues* at any time. But only the wealthiest could afford such costly imports as *orenges*, *lymons* and *sugre*, or such *espices* as *sinamome* or *nutemuge*, which in those days were almost literally worth their weight in gold.

The lower classes, perhaps 90 percent of the population, enjoyed no such mouth-watering *repasts*, but made do with English *brede*, *ale* and *chese*, eked out with *bean* or *pease* porridge, *stockfish* (dried cod or haddock) and perhaps some *flesch mete* on *halidays* (holy days).

When they were not ruling, fighting, dressing or eating, the upper classes could *solace* their *leisour* in *dancing* to the *melodious musique* of *lut* and *tabour*, laugh at the antics of *jugelers* and professional *fols*, play at *chess* (or *checkers*, though the word then referred not to the game, but to the pattern of its board), and, inevitably, engage in *dalliance*. This last amusement, however, was happily not limited to the upper classes, as Chaucer makes clear in several of his tales.

The amenities of upper-class life contributed yet other words. Words from the kitchen, such as we find in Chaucer's description of the Cook:

> *He coulde* roste *and sethe and* broille *and* frye,
> *Maken* mortreux *and wel bake a* pye.

(Mortreux was a thick soup.) Words from the *panetrie: plate*, *saussier* and *gobelet*. Words from just about every other room in the house, from *celer* to *garite: table* and *chaier* (the lower classes sat on English *stoles*); *lampe* and *chaundeler; blaunket*, *cuilte* and *materas*. Words from the *stables: harneis*, *rene* and *staloun*. Words from the *kenils: spaynel* and *mastif*. Words from the *parc* or *forest* where the lord set his *faucon* at *fesaunt* or *plover*.

Words from *art* and *musique*, like *peynting*, *colour* and *tone;* from architecture, like *porche* and *piler;* and especially from the world of *lettres: prose* and *poetrie, tragedie* and *comedie,* and the *penne, enque* and *parchemin* with which *scolers* compiled *tretises* on *geometrie, gramere* and *logique.* Words from *medicine,* like *fisicien, surgien, palsie, jaundice,* and the *terrible pestilence* that in 1348 wiped out at least a quarter of the English people.

And, finally, hundreds and thousands of plain—and sometimes fancy —words: nouns from *action* to *waste,* as abstract as *substance* or *manere,* as homely as *grein* and *buket,* along with *courage* and *cuardice, plesir* and *peine;* verbs like *count* and *cover, coveite* and *crye;* adjectives like *faint, feble, fiers* and *ferme.* (The adjectives in particular filled a real need: Old English had relatively few of them.)

Altogether, between 1100 and 1500 A.D., more than ten thousand French words passed into the English vocabulary, of which 75 percent are still in use. Thousands more came from Church and scholarly Latin, and another thousand or two from Dutch and Low German (more about these other borrowings later). At the same time, hundreds of Old English words disappeared from the language: *bleo* was replaced by French *colour, lyft* by French *aire,* and so with *here* and *armée,* and *anda* and *envie.*

For all these borrowings, however, a lot of the ancestral English vocabulary remained in use. The philologist Albert C. Baugh has put the matter neatly, pointing out that the English, of whatever social class, still "*ate, drank* and *slept,* so to speak, in English, *worked* and *played, spoke* and *sang, walked, ran, rode, leaped* and *swam* in the same language." They still lived in *houses* with *halls, rooms, windows, doors, floors, steps* and *gates,* and (along with the homely English foods mentioned earlier) consumed *salt, fish, butter, wine* and *pepper*—though the last three, as we know, had been borrowed much earlier from Latin. Equally, the Englishman's *spirit* might be French but his *mind* was still English, as were his *body* and nearly all its parts: *arms, legs, hands, feet, eyes, ears, nose* and *mouth,* plus *brain, liver, lungs, arse* and *ballocks.*

English words and suffixes also formed compounds with the French borrowings; indeed, the two languages produced their mixed progeny as easily and quickly as did the thousands of Anglo-Norman marriages. French *gentil* (wellborn, whence "genteel") appears in (written) English in 1225, and within a century has been joined by such Anglo-French compounds as *gentlewoman, gentleman, gentleness* and *gently;* similarly *faith* begot *faithful* and *faithless, faithfully* and *faithfulness.* French *common* was grafted onto English *-weal* by 1330, and in another fifty years French *battle* had hooked up with English *-axe.*

To these Old English survivors, we can add all modern English pronouns, articles and prepositions, and nearly all the conjunctions. The latter now included a few hybrids like *bicause* (English *bi-* plus French *cause*), but also such new and purely English formations as *nevertheless, however* and *notwithstanding,* though the last of these may be a loan translation from French *nonobstant.*

Syntax also remained English. For example, adjectives continued to precede the noun, as in Alfred's day, rather than follow it as in French (a few exceptions survive today; thus law-French has given us *attorney general* and *court-martial*). But it had become a much simpler syntax, through its almost total loss of inflectional endings.

This major shift in English syntax has begotten a number of curious explanations: notably, the suggestion that since English was for some two centuries after the Conquest a language of illiterates, ignorant folk unaccustomed to making fine linguistic distinctions, its inflections vanished because its speakers didn't know any better. Since, as a matter of history, the illiterate English peasant of 900 A.D.—not to mention the illiterate Russian peasant of 1900 A.D.—used elaborate inflections routinely, this explanation owes more to snobbery than to science.

A less snobbish but not much more illuminating explanation points out that writing is almost invariably a conservative force in language, because it tends to freeze word forms. Thus, since English was little written between 1066 and about 1300, change could progress more rapidly than it otherwise would have done. Which, though undoubtedly true, doesn't explain why the change took place at all.

The loss of English inflections actually began in prehistoric times, when the eight "cases" of nouns in Indo-European were reduced to the four of Old English—not all of them, as we've seen, any longer distinctive; the same goes for the reduction of Indo-European singular, dual and plural to Old English singular and plural. But nobody knows how or when these losses occurred, or why. The simplification of English syntax moved into high gear only with the assimilation of the Scandinavian immigrants of the ninth and tenth centuries, as we saw in the last chapter.

The assimilation of French-speaking immigrants inevitably intensified this loss of inflectional forms, the more so in that French, being derived from Vulgar Latin, had already lost most of its own noun inflections, though it was still well endowed with verb inflections. It is perhaps not coincidental, then, that by the end of the fourteenth century, English noun inflections had become hardly more noticeable than they are today, while verb inflections like "I go, thou goest, he goeth" hung on for another couple of centuries.

French also helped simplify English syntax in another way, by reducing the few "live" inflections of English, like the plurals of nouns and the past tenses of verbs, to largely uniform patterns, as against the diversity of these inflections in Old English. Quite apart from the normal tendency of foreigners to simplify life for themselves in this way—it's far easier to remember one inflectional pattern than half a dozen—the enormous influx of French nouns and verbs had to be syntactically assimilated by being given English inflections. For nouns, whose plural in French was normally formed by adding -s or -z, assimilation was no problem, since most English nouns did the same, meaning that in the combined vocabulary the great majority of nouns now used this form. Probably as a result of this, even some of the native English nouns with irregular plurals became "regularized"; thus Chaucer used both the old, irregular *yeer* (years) and the new *yeres*.

In verbs, the "weak" past inflection -ed became almost equally dominant. Of the several thousand French verbs borrowed into English, all but one were assimilated as weak verbs, and the single apparent exception (strive, strove, striven) is itself problematical. (Though usually derived from Old French *estriver,* it could equally descend from an unattested Old English **striv(i)an,* which has close relatives in both Dutch and German; the French word itself is almost certainly of Germanic origin). And, as with the nouns, native irregular (i.e., "strong") verbs continued to shift into the regular form; thus "cloven" had been joined by "cleaved" as early as the fourteenth century, and likewise with *mew*/ mowed, *wrought*/ worked and so on.

A no less important result of French influence, though indirect, was the loss of grammatical gender. Old French had retained the Latin masculine and feminine genders (the neuter had vanished), while Old English had all three. Confusion grew out of the fact that too often corresponding words in the two languages had different genders. Thus English *blaed* was masculine, while its French replacement, *flour* (flower) was feminine, and the same was true of English *here* and its French replacement, *armée.* On the other hand, the feminine English noun *firen* was edged out by its French equivalent, the masculine *crime.*

This was confusing enough for people of either tongue seeking to master the other, or to borrow words from it. Even worse confusion arose from the fact that both French and English adjectives were inflected for gender—and with quite different inflectional endings. Imagine, then, the problem of mentally replacing an English noun with a French one (as people must often have done) and then adding an adjective, which was supposed to agree with the noun in gender. Did that mean the gender of the English noun, or of its French replacement—assuming anyone remembered by this time? And having decided this, how was the adjective to be inflected—in the English or the French fashion?

This confusion is by no means imaginary: it shows up in medieval documents written in French, but by English-speakers, or by French-speakers who, like Chaucer's Prioress, knew not the French of Paris. Genders get badly muddled, so that phrases like *le avant dit Aliz* (the aforesaid Alice) uses the masculine *le,* though Alice herself was surely feminine.

How much the abandonment of grammatical gender in English was due to conscious efforts to resolve this confusion and how much to the general loss of inflectional endings (which by itself would have abolished gender distinctions for most adjectives) we do not know. But certainly by the fourteenth century English had done away with these artificial distinctions entirely, and has been all the better for it ever since. We have, indeed, retained gender in a few pronouns, but it is now *natural* gender: "he" and "she" refer to male and female people (or sometimes animals) respectively, while "it" refers to everything else.

A more ambiguous result of the fusion of French and English was a marked slackening of word formation in the Old English style. The verb prefixes so common in Old English either vanished altogether, as did *to-* and *a-* (as in *to-berstan,* burst asunder, and *a-colian,* grow cold), or survived only in existing words while ceasing to form new ones. A few of the latter, like over- and under-, have more recently undergone a modest revival. (e.g., "overact" a dramatic part, "undersell" a competitor). To some extent the loss was made good by prefixes of Latin origin, such as counter-, dis-, trans- and re-, though these are now used as much with nouns and adjectives as with verbs. Ultimately, it was more than made good through the characteristic modern English construction of verb + adverb, as with "go in," "go out," "go away," "go through" (with something) and hundreds of other examples. Most Old English suffixes also ceased to form new words, though a few, like -ness and -ly, are alive and productive to this day.

Exactly why the English changed their habits of word formation so radically is something we can never know for sure. One reason may be that it ran counter to French linguistic habits; though French inherited scores of prefix + verb combinations from Latin, it produced few new ones. But the most obvious reason is also the most probable: with all these brand-new words at one's disposal, why go to the trouble of thinking up new combinations of old ones? If a word comes readily to your tongue or pen, as thousands of French words now did to those of most English people, why hunt about for a native synonym?

6. THE FIRST FLOWERING

Chaucer, Caxton and "Good English"

⟨❧⟩

> No lover of poetry can spare Chaucer, or should grudge the short study required to command the archaisms of his English, and the skill to read the melody of his verse.
>
> —RALPH WALDO EMERSON

> What's in a name?
>
> —WILLIAM SHAKESPEARE

ENGLISH borrowings from French did not end with the assimilation of the French-speaking upper classes during the thirteenth and fourteenth centuries; they have continued down to the present day, as witness such twentieth-century borrowings as "ambience," "fuselage," "quiche" and "auteur." Borrowing words is a little like borrowing money: the more you do of it, the easier it gets—especially since borrowed words, unlike borrowed francs, pounds or dollars, need not be repaid. Some philologists have expressed this thought in less homely terms by saying that the initial surge of French words into English broke a "barrier" to further borrowing. But this, I think, makes an abstraction of a human reality.

The only "barrier" to word-borrowing is in the minds of the borrowers. Foreign words are often hard to pronounce, and even harder to remember, if (as is common) they have no roots in the native vocabulary. Thus, as we've seen, most borrowings before the Conquest, by the English and their ancestors, concerned new things and ideas, for which their own tongues had no words.

But if a language, out of some peculiar historical circumstance, has already incorporated large numbers of words from some foreign source, the barrier crumbles, in that new words from the same source, or related sources, will likely resemble words already assimilated, and can therefore pass into the vocabulary much more easily. Having, so to speak, established a line of credit at a particular linguistic bank, people will be apt to return to it, or one of its branches, for additional loans.

It is this commonplace human tendency to prefer the familiar to the unfamiliar that, I think, goes far to explain our continued borrowing from French, from the other Romance tongues, and especially from the parent of all of them, Latin.

Granted, the English had ample opportunities for borrowing Latin words from the very beginning of the Middle Ages. Until the sixteenth century, it was the language of the English Church and its scriptures, read from the pulpit on Sundays and holy days, spoken by churchmen and -women among themselves in convent and cloister. For even more centuries it was the language of scholars; as late as 1687, Isaac Newton published his great treatise on physics under the title *Principia Mathematica,* not *Mathematical Principles.* But the same opportunities for borrowing existed in Germany and Scandinavia, yet were taken far less often.

A single example can help explain the difference. In the sixteenth century, some German scholar felt the need for a word meaning "beyond human capacities." Knowing the Latin term *superhumanus,* but presumably doubting its acceptability to those he wrote for, he translated its outlandish elements into familiar German ones, as *übermenschlich,* whence ultimately Nietzsche's and Hitler's *Übermensch,* which George Bernard Shaw translated into English as "superman." Most Latin terms have entered German by this technique of "loan translation," even as, much earlier, some had entered Old English.

A century or so after *superhumanus* was translated into German, it was borrowed directly into English, as "superhuman." In truth, however, the "borrowing" amounted to little more than a reshuffling of long-familiar elements of English: "human" had been in our vocabulary for three centuries, and "super-" (as in "superabundant") for more than two. Much the same could be said of most Latin terms taken into English, both earlier and later.

Unlike English and French, however, Latin was never actually spoken by more than a tiny minority of Englishmen; as a result, its influence on our language has come mainly through theological and scholarly writings. As these works began to be translated into English, during the thirteenth and fourteenth centuries, they revealed serious gaps in the English vocabulary—especially, words expressing philosophical, abstract or learnèd concepts. Translators in King Alfred's day had confronted the same gap, and had filled it partly by borrowing but mostly by loan translations from Latin, such as *fore-spraec* (preface) and *midwyrþa* (collaborator). But terms of this sort had dropped out of the English vocabulary during the centuries when it was used only by the uneducated, with scholarly discourse conducted in either Latin or French. Thus translators in the thirteenth century found, as one of them put it, that "there ys many wordes in Latyn that we have no propre English accordynge thereto." The simplest solution, given the large store of Franco-Latin linguistic elements now in the language, was simply to take over the "Latyn" word, with whatever phonetic and other assimilation seemed necessary to make it into a "propre English" one.

Thus the fourteenth-century translation of the Latin astrological treatise *De Proprietatibus Rerum* ("On the Properties of Things"), made by John Trevisa—cited earlier as a commentator on the decline of French in England—contains several hundred Latin words hitherto unknown in English. Theological translations (notably, of the Bible) made about the same time, by such religious reformers as John Wycliffe, added over a thousand. Other contributions came not from translations but from original works, by scholars who wrote in English but knew Latin, and who therefore naturally and easily used a Latin word if they were stuck for an English one. Still more came, indirectly, through French, which was itself borrowing Latin words quite heavily at this time, for much the same reasons we have been discussing.

In this way, hundreds of Latin words passed into English between (roughly) 1200 and 1400; a brief sampling will suggest their scholarly sources: "adjacent," "custody," "frustrate," "history," "inferior," "lunatic," "moderate," "necessary," "prosecute," "rational," "solitary," "summary," "testimony," "ulcer" and "zenith."

The last of these leads to yet another source of English words: Arabic. During almost the entire Middle Ages, the Moslem world, stretching from Spain through North Africa to the Near East and even parts of India, was the world's most advanced civilization west of China. Arab armies, beginning in the seventh century, had grabbed some of the world's richest croplands—those of Mesopotamia and the Nile Valley—and had also seized control of nearly all the trade routes between East and West, through which the silks and porcelains of China, the spices of India and the Indies, and the gold, ivory and incense of Arabia and East Africa reached Europe. The Arab world, moreover, was little troubled by invasion; indeed, Arab incursions into Europe had helped keep that continent in turmoil during the Dark Ages.

The Arabs' initial conquests included some major centers of Greco-Roman culture (e.g., Alexandria), while later merchants and travelers brought new ideas and technologies from India (notably, the "Arabic"—actually Indian—numerals we now use) and even China (e.g., the magnetic compass). Regrettably, the Arabs' brilliant civilization declined almost as fast as it rose, into the kind of absolutism and religious fanaticism so common in the Moslem world today. But while it lasted it was a rich source of new things and ideas—and therefore new words—for Christian Europe.

Since England, unlike the Mediterranean lands of Christendom, had little direct contact with the Arab world, it borrowed few Arab words "from the source." Its borrowings were at second hand, via French or Latin, meaning that by the time they had passed into English they had been phonetically (and sometimes syntactically) assimilated not once but twice. As a result, the English word often has a tenuous resemblance to its Arabic original. "Zenith" derives from Arabic *samt arras* (path overhead), "zero" from *cifr* (whence also "cipher" and "cypher"), "caliber" from *qalib* (casting mold) and "algebra" from *al jebr* (the reunification—referring to the solving of equations). An important Arab technical contribution was *al inbiq* (the still, whence the alchemist's alembic) with which both Moslem and Christian scientists distilled *al koh'l* (the essence). The most notable of their products was the alcoholic essence of wine (i.e., brandy), whose striking effects won it quick adoption as a medicine, indeed a "water of immortality." Like most medicines of the time, it didn't make patients better, but it certainly made them *feel* better.

Trade contacts with the Moslem world supplied the *zasforan* (saffron) that still seasons and colors the cuisine of Mediterranean Europe (it was also used as a dye), the *naranj* that yields our breakfast juice, and the leafy green *isfinaj* that has triggered so many dinner-table wrangles between parent and child. A less "controversial" vegetable was *al kharshof* (the artichoke). Crusaders as well as traders brought back to Europe Arab notions of comfort—notably the *matrah* (pillow), on a heap of which one could recline at ease, as we still recline on mattresses. Sometimes the pillows were heaped in *al qobbah* (the alcove). Also from the Crusades, perhaps, came *amir a'la* (higher commander, whence "admiral").

Other borrowings from Arabic take us to more remote lands and tongues. The sweet and costly *sukkar* that Arab traders originally imported from India comes from Sanskrit *sharkara,* itself a non-Indo-European word very likely borrowed from the mysterious Indus Valley people overrun by the Sanskrit-speaking Aryans around 1500 B.C.; their tongue was probably akin to the Dravidian languages spoken in southern India today. A more certain Dravidian borrowing via Arabic is the *qandi* made from *sukkar.* Oddly enough, however, the cane from which sugar and sugar candy were derived is not from Arabic; it reached English through a far different route, and from a far more remote time. The

Sumerians, who built the world's first civilization in Mesopotamia around 3500 B.C., called the tall reeds that filled the swampy parts of their homeland *gin* (as in "begin"). The Babylonians who succeeded them as lords of Mesopotamia borrowed the word as *kanu,* which passed into Greek as *kanna* and thence to Latin, whence we get, via Old French, the canes used for walking (and, in England, to chastise some recalcitrant schoolboys), and, via one or another of the Romance tongues, a host of words referring to long, narrow and more or less hollow things, including "cannon," "canyon," "canal" and "channel." In "canon law" we have the old reed in a new guise: a measuring rod used to enforce a standard.

Also from the Middle East, but via Arabic, comes the Persian *shah mat* (the king is dead), whence "checkmate" and "check" in all its senses, from the checks on a checkerboard or a checked fabric to the checks we use to pay our bills and which, at least in theory, check our expenditures so that they don't exceed our incomes. The ream by which we measure quantities of paper comes from Arabic *risma* (bundle of clothes)—bewildering unless we happen to know that the new technique of making paper out of rags, rather than papyrus, reached Europe from China through the Moslem world. Finally, the alchemy of alembics, alcohol and *al qaliy* (the ashes—a traditional source of alkali) may take us back to the ancient Egyptians, the mythical originators of alchemy; they called their country *Khemet* (the black land—i.e., the fertile Nile Valley contrasted with the barren "red land" of the desert). Other borrowings from Arab scientists include nearly all our names for the stars, from Aldebaran to Zubenelgenubi—though most have been garbled into words that no Arab would recognize.

As these examples show, English (and other European) borrowings from Arabic were nearly all of the "normal" type—i.e., they concerned things that the Arabs knew and the English didn't. In sharp contrast are the borrowings from French and Latin we have already surveyed: though some of them unquestionably filled gaps in the English vocabulary, many not only enlarged but also enriched that vocabulary, by supplying synonyms for existing English words. Thus by the middle of the fourteenth century, English was well on the way to acquiring a double and even a triple vocabulary, in which a homely native English word was paralleled by a French equivalent (sometimes, but not always, more literary) and a scholarly Latin one. English "rise" is matched by French "mount" and Latin "ascend," and similarly with such triplets as kingly/royal/regal, ask/question/interrogate, fast/firm/secure, goodness/virtue/probity, holy/sacred/consecrated, work/labor/exertion, and scores of others.

The Middle English of the fourteenth century was still not modern English; its syntax, though much simplified from that of Old English, still differed from ours in some respects, and its phonetics in more, while a good deal of its vocabulary has either vanished or changed in meaning. But in one vital respect it had probably already attained the most notable characteristic of English: a vocabulary richer than that of any other tongue. The stage was set for the first great flowering of English poetry, culminating in Geoffrey Chaucer.

Writing about Middle English poetry raises a painful dilemma: how does one convey its sounds, which were markedly different from those of modern English? If you translate it into modern English, you get the words but not the music; if you don't, you must try to give the reader a quick, and not very palatable, cram course in Middle English phonetics. Reluctantly, I have decided that the latter alternative is simply not practicable in a book of this length. Emerson may have been right in saying that only a "short study" is needed to master Middle English, but it is still a good deal too long for this chapter. I shall therefore give only a few samples of actual Middle English, with a few tips on how to pronounce them; other selections will be translated as literally as possible while preserving rhyme and meter. (Readers interested in pursuing the matter further, in order to get the full flavor of Chaucer and other Middle English poets, are referred to John Gardner's excellent book cited in the Notes on Sources at the end of this book.)

The fourteenth century was an unlikely time for a literary renaissance, and the small realm of England, still on the outskirts of civilization, an even more unlikely place. The distinguished historical writer Barbara Tuchman has accurately described the fourteenth century as "calamitous." The climate of northern Europe, balmy for several centuries, had turned colder and wetter; crops were sparser, the common people (that is, most people) had less to eat, and in years of really bad harvests, sometimes starved. This was the more true in that the population of Europe had increased to the point where, even in good years, it could consume every bit of food that could be raised with the existing technology, as in many parts of the "Third World" today.

Periodic local famines were bad enough, since given the enormous cost of land transport they could seldom be relieved by shipping in surplus crops from other areas. Far worse was the Black Death—a pandemic of bubonic plague which between 1347 and 1353 wiped out at least a quarter of Europe's population, with smaller outbreaks later in the century accounting for as many again. It was far and away the worst disaster in history—it destroyed a larger part of the population than World Wars I and II combined—and is unlikely to be equaled except by a nuclear war.

Along with Death, Famine and Pestilence, the Fourth Horseman, War, was also abroad. The Hundred Years War between England and France broke out in 1337, and smaller but no less brutal local conflicts harried Spain, Italy and the Rhineland, in the last of which Jews were massacred by the thousands. Even when wars were broken by truces—as the Hundred Years War several times was—peace was not much of an improvement: soldiers of fortune on both sides went into business on their own, ravaging and pillaging as free-enterprising ruffians.

Ironically, however, these calamities to some degree canceled one another: plague and war together solved the population problem. Though thousands of farms passed back into wilderness, those that remained tended to be concentrated on the most fertile lands. Food production dropped, but in many places less radically than the population, so that those who survived often ate better.

The century was also a great deal more calamitous in some places than in others. The devastation of the Hundred Years War, and of its hardly less destructive truces, fell almost entirely on France; England escaped with only a few coastal raids. Moreover, English armies were victorious almost until the end of the century, so that the country was enriched by tens of millions of dollars (modern values) in loot and in ransoms paid over by noble POWs.

These English victories must have done much to crystallize England's national identity and lift its morale. Compared to France, it was poor in population and resources, but it was the French who were getting beat, time after time. Perhaps for the first time, though certainly not the last, the English began to suspect that God was an Englishman, and that any Englishman could lick three foreigners. At Crécy, the first great battle of the war, the English army had indeed beaten a French one three times its size, while at Poitiers the odds were more like five to one.

These English victories against all the odds reflected a fundamental shift in military tactics, which in turn were linked to important changes in English society. The French still relied on their knightly armored cavalry, but the English had discovered that the six-foot yew bow and yard-long arrows of the foot soldier—the first armor-piercing missiles— could stop a cavalry charge in its tracks. English peasants were less brutally oppressed, on the whole, than their French counterparts, and therefore less feared by the upper classes, meaning that they could be allowed a much more prominent role in war. The English knight or noble in no way considered the yeoman his social equal, but still granted him considerable respect—especially in view of his proven performance on the battlefield.

Even closer relationships grew up between England's nobility and gentry and the middle-class merchants and artisans who supplied its victorious armies. These classes, in turn, found the nobles wholly admirable—as long as victories kept the profits rolling in; later, when the English armies stopped winning, the middle classes discovered that taxes were unbearable.

This burgeoning national consciousness and national unity could not and did not survive the war-born prosperity that engendered it. But while it lasted, it helped make the fourteenth century in English letters the very opposite of calamitous. The connection between national morale, national prosperity and national artistic achievement is, indeed, hard to spell out precisely, but there are enough historical examples to make such a relationship probable if not inevitable. One thinks, for example, of the spectacular outburst of Athenian art and literature following the Greek victory over Persia early in the fifth century B.C., and, much later, the no less spectacular literary achievements of Elizabethan England, in which growing prosperity at home was equally combined with military victories abroad.

One might say that the fourteenth century was the time when English society temporarily "got it all together." The same was true, and more permanently, of the English tongue. Its French, English and Latin elements were rapidly fusing into a unified, diversified and rich vocabulary, and the poets who used it, after a long period of vacillation, finally achieved something of a consensus on the basic form of poetry: metrical, rhymed verse.

Almost immediately after the Conquest, the new-fangled Continental device of rhyme found favor among some of the few poets who still wrote in English. Others, however, either didn't know how to handle rhyme or didn't care to; one Ormm, writing around 1200, used blank verse. Others mingled rhyme with alliteration, as English poets would continue to do for centuries afterward. Around 1350, alliterative verse in the true Old English tradition underwent a brief revival, as in the epic poem *Sir Gawain and the Green Knight*—though even here the author tosses in an occasional rhymed stanza for variety. William Langland's socio-religious homily *The*

Vision of Piers Ploughman, from a generation later, does not make even this much concession to rhyme: the sound of its somber alliterated lines would have been recognized by the pre-Conquest bard of *Beowulf.* (For an example, see page 128.)

Given the new surge in national awareness of the fourteenth century, one could easily conclude that these alliterative poets were consciously trying to revive Old English literary traditions, but there is no evidence of this whatever. Rather, there is good reason to believe that those traditions had never vanished. Significantly, the language of William Langland and the anonymous author of *Gawain* mark them as natives of northern England, precisely the areas where Continental influence was weakest and the English-Scandinavian alliterative tradition strongest. There, old sagas such as *Beowulf* must have continued to be sung among the common folk (doubtless with the language updated from time to time), with occasional newer poems composed in the same style.

But the center of English civilization and letters, then as for centuries to come, was in the south, where rhyme, though often accompanied by alliteration, was dominant. A delightful example is this anonymous ode to spring, dating from around 1300. To get its flavor, you must give the vowels their "Continental" values: A=/ah/, E=/eh/, I and Y=/ee/, O =/oh/, and U and OU =/oo/. Also, some E's now silent in English were pronounced as /uh/; I have indicated these as ë. Now try it:

> *Lenten* [Spring] *is come with lovë to toune*
> *With blosmen and with briddës roune* [bird's song]
>   *That all this blissë bringeth*
> *Dayës-eyës* [daisies] *in this dalës*
> *Notës suete of nyghtegalës*
>   *Ech foul* [fowl] *songë singeth.*

The lilting words must surely have been set to some lost tune; they almost sing themselves. (Note, by the way, the lovely metaphor concealed in modern "daisy": its bright blossoms are the "day's eye.")

The dominant fourteenth-century literary tradition of southern England culminated in the towering figure of Geoffrey Chaucer. He was undoubtedly familiar with Langland's works (which rivaled his own in popularity), but was himself a Londoner and a poet of the court, still semi-French in culture. Chaucer himself knew French well enough to translate a long epic on courtly love, *Le Roman de la Rose,* and his original poems masterfully mingle the French and English elements of the language, adapting Continental verse forms to the rhythms of colloquial, educated English.

Chaucer, arguably one of the half-dozen greatest poets of the western world, was what we'd now call a Renaissance Man: soldier, diplomat, civil servant and the first major European literary figure outside of Italy (France's great rogue-poet, François Villon, comes from the next century). He knew astronomy and mathematics well enough to compose a treatise on the astrolabe (a predecessor of the mariner's sextant), and enough alchemy to write knowledgeably about it in *The Canterbury Tales*, and had also studied law and probably what would now be called business administration.

The son of a well-to-do but otherwise undistinguished London merchant, Chaucer in his teens became part of the "household"—a sort of mini-court—of Lionel, third son of Edward III; a few years later, he shifted to that of John of Gaunt, Duke of Lancaster, Lionel's younger brother. How this came about is unclear; by some accounts, Chaucer's association with Gaunt began rather disreputably. Chaucer's wife-to-be, Philippa, had supposedly been Gaunt's mistress, and was allegedly pregnant by him when he had to go off to the war in France. To preserve the proprieties, she was married off to the talented young commoner whose poems were already beginning to attract attention. On this assumption, the first child of the marriage was not actually Chaucer's but Gaunt's— and therefore the king's granddaughter.

Be that as it may, Philippa's younger sister, Katherine, unquestionably became Gaunt's mistress a few years later (eventually, after twenty-five years of unwedded bliss, his wife), so that Chaucer was in effect Gaunt's brother-in-law. The duke, one of the most powerful men in England, was the poet's sponsor and protector, as well as friend, as long as they both lived (they were born and died within a year or two of one another; Chaucer's dates are ?1340–1400). Gaunt's influence, along with Chaucer's own diplomatic and administrative abilities, ensured that the poet would never know want. (However, his humorous "Compleynt" addressed to his empty purse—"Be heavy again, or surely I must die"— shows that, like most of us, he was sometimes short of ready cash.)

Unlike Langland, Chaucer was no radical reformer, but what would nowadays be called a middle-class liberal, of the best sort: a loyal servant of the crown, but also a cool observer of the human comedy, with a sharp eye for hypocrisy and pretentiousness. He wrote no sermons—which, necessary though they sometimes are, seldom make good art—but was always ready to plant an unobtrusive pin in the important and self-important, while recognizing and applauding the humble and virtuous.

Chaucer certainly knew the dark side of fourteenth-century life: the Black Death had killed several members of his family during his childhood, and, like his young protagonist, the Squire, he had been to the wars "In Flanders, in Artois and Picardy," where he had fought and been taken prisoner. Then, and on later, diplomatic trips to France, he would have seen firsthand the destruction wrought by the Hundred Years War. In Spain he would have seen Pedro the Cruel and his rivals torturing and butchering one another with that peculiarly Spanish viciousness that would one day be systematically deployed in the Inquisition. Finally, his journeys to Italy would have shown him the mercantile aristocrats of that fragmented land eliminating their rivals and relatives in the style later called Machiavellian (a term rather unjust to that grimly ironic political realist).

We see the calamities of the fourteenth century briefly in the "dark imagining of villainy" in "The Knight's Tale":

> *The smiler with the knife inside his cloak;*
> *The burning stable, sending up black smoke;*
> *The treacherous, secret murder in the bed;*
> *The open war, with wounds all gaping red . . .*
> *The throat-slit carcass, hid behind a fence;*
> *A thousand slain—and not by pestilence;*
> *The tyrant who his prey by force has reft;*
> *The town demolished—there was nothing left.*

Yet when we think of the first great master of our native tongue, we do not ponder such horrors: it is springtime, and we are on the road to Canterbury. In England (as elsewhere in northern Europe), spring marked the end of frost and sleet, of a season spent huddling over smoky fires, eking out the fall harvest which, even with the fasting season of Lent to help, often barely lasted through the winter. No wonder, then, that English poets have ever celebrated the season. "Summer is a-coming in, loudly sing cuckoo" they sang in 1200 A.D., in a round whose joyous melody has fortunately been preserved. A century or so later, it was "Just between March and April, when blossoms begin to blow," and "Lenten is come with love to town." And so, in Chaucer's masterwork, the gentle showers of April have struck to the roots of March's drought, bathing in their moisture the day's-eyes, marigolds and primroses that will soon burst into bloom, and the woods ring with the melodies of birds that can scarce sleep for excitement. What better time indeed to shed the chill and damp of housebound winter, to follow the growing sun out of Aries into Taurus, to "go on pilgrimages" to the great shrine of Thomas à Becket in Canterbury, through the burgeoning farmlands and blossoming orchards of Kent: to see the earth being reborn? And what better company than that nine-and-twenty gathered at the sign of the Tabard, across the Thames from London town, "Of sundry folk, gathered as might befall/ In fellowship, and pilgrims were they all"?

Chaucer was not the only writer of his day to show us a collection of his contemporaries. "Long Will" Langland's long visionary poem begins with

> *. . . a fair field full of folk*
> *Of all manner of men, the poor and the rich*
> *Working and wandering, as the world asketh.*

But these folk are but generalized types; Chaucer gives us a living portrait gallery of individual men and women.

And what a gallery it is! First the "perfect, honorable knight" who "loved all chivalry/ Truth and honor, freedom and courtesy," and had fought bravely in Russia, Prussia, Lithuania, Turkey, Algiers and half a dozen other places. Yet even as we read the poet's encomium, we catch the glint in his eye—and wonder whether even the most "perfect" warrior could have managed to be in quite so many places in one lifetime. His son, the "Squyer," is "a lover and a lusty bachelor"—there were plenty of his sort at court—so hot for love that, like the springtime birds, he scarcely sleeps.

The "Marchaunt" is drawn from life; as a customs official in the port of London, Chaucer dealt with him daily. Riding proudly beneath his "Flemish beaver hat"—most English trade was with Flanders and the other Low Countries—he speaks always of his profits, never of losses, keeping his front of prosperity "so well set/No man could tell when he was deep in debt." No less familiar to the poet, and indeed to us, is the "Man of Lawe," rich in fees, elegantly dressed, busy about his clients' affairs, *and yet,* says the poet with a wink, *he semëd bisier than he was.*

Another familiar figure is the "Doctour of Phisyk," who, like his professional brethren in all ages, "knew the cause of every malady"—a claim that, given the still-unchecked ravages of the plague, must have made the poet's audiences grin sourly. The more sophisticated among them would have chuckled at Chaucer's enumeration of the doctor's medical studies, for along with such recognized authorities as Galen and Avicenna they included Asclepius—a legendary Greek who left no books that even the most learnèd physician could have consulted. Like some other doctors, Chaucer's medical pilgrim enjoyed a mutually profitable association with the apothecaries (pharmacists), and "Since gold's a potent medicine, we're told,/ Therefore he had a special love for gold."

The Shipman—skipper of a merchant ship—hailed from the West Country, sailing out of Plymouth or Falmouth, but his counterparts would have been visible enough to anyone with business around the London waterfront: tanned of face, with seaman's knife hung on a lanyard around his neck, able to "calculate the tides, currents and dangers"—and no less expert at filching wine from the casks he brings from Bordeaux. He is equally skilled in coping with the raiders and outright pirates that thronged the narrow seas around England: "Whenever he fought and held the upper hand," says the poet grimly, "By water he sent them home to every land."

The "gentil Mauniciple"—steward and purchasing agent for a group of London lawyers—is, like the Shipman, not overburdened with conscience. He buys victuals for his learned masters for cash or credit, but always manages to come out ahead of them. Though they are

> *Able to administer the rent and land*
> *Of any lord that dwells in our England . . .*
> *In any circumstance that might befall—*
> *Yet this same manciple could fool them all!*

Is it not a fine example of God's grace, says the poet, deadpan, "That such a common fellow's wits outpace/ The wisdom of a heap of learnèd men?" His courtly hearers, most of whom doubtless had personal experience of both cheating stewards and conniving lawyers, must have roared.

Even the bit players among the townsmen do not escape the poet's sardonic eye. His five prosperous tradesmen, clothed in the liveries of their guilds, their knives ornamented with silver, were each of them "fit to have been an alderman," at least in their own estimation. Chaucer, son of a merchant, knew—none better—how such men scrabbled for social position, often prodded by their wives, who found it "full fair to be called madame" and walk in church processions with a train borne regally behind them. The bourgeois would-be gentleman was not invented by Molière in the seventeenth century (or, indeed, by Chaucer in the fourteenth; Roman satirists like Petronius knew him well).

The tradesmen have brought with them their own Cook, whose culinary skills the poet recounts at length, while noting that he has a "mormal" (ulcer) on his shin. When I first read Chaucer years ago, this last seemed to me an odd and superfluous bit of naturalistic detail—but I underestimated the poet's powers of observation. It happened that while writing this book I spent some time in the hospital, where I shared a room with a youngish man under treatment for an ulcerated varicose vein on his shin. By profession he was—a cook. In the twentieth century as in the fourteenth, cooks must spend much of their working day standing, with varicose veins and "mormals" a regular occupational risk.

The rural pilgrims are no less lifelike, and lively, than the Londoners; Chaucer knew them all from several years spent as a justice of the peace in Kent. The skinny, choleric Reeve, foreman of a manor in fertile Norfolk, knows all the tricks with which farmhands and tenants try to cheat the lord of his just (or anyway, legal) due, and enough tricks of his own to have made himself rich: "There was no auditor could see through *him.*" The Miller, brawny, burly and boozy, is no less a rogue: "Well could he pilfer grain, for thrice his fee." Millers lived mainly by grinding other people's corn, for a supposedly fixed percentage, but—as "The Reeve's Tale" later makes clear—unless you looked very sharp, your grain poured into the hopper above the millstones was likely to be much diminished when it emerged as flour below.

Surpassing them all is Chaucer's most memorable character, the "Wyf" of Bath—broad-hipped, ruddy, her hat as broad as a soldier's round shield, garrulous, free-spoken and sexy. In Chaucer's day, *wyf* meant both "wife" and "woman," and this one is both—in spades. Five times married (not to mention "other company in youth"), as skilled in managing husbands as in weaving fine cloth, she is ready to take up "the old dance" of matrimony again, if opportunity knocks a sixth time. Meanwhile, as a wealthy widow, she occupies herself with pilgrimages and—we can hardly doubt—with the far-from-religious activities for which these outings (comparable to a modern shipboard cruise) were notorious. "She had," says the poet meaningfully, "passed over many a foreign stream" and "did much wandering on the way." Five centuries before feminism, she has liberated herself to the point, indeed, where she is in some ways a holy terror. When she is in church of a Sunday, with ten pounds of kerchiefs adorning her head, woe betide any woman who pushes ahead of her to the communion rail. And in matrimony, she has learned well the lesson that woman's most deadly weapon is moral ascendancy: keep a man busy apologizing for his own faults (real or invented) and he'll have neither time nor breath to talk of yours. A ripe dame, in every sense!

The clerical members of the pilgrimage fare even worse than the laity under the shafts of the poet's wit. Chaucer was unquestionably a deeply religious man, as were most of his contemporaries. (An exception was the "Doctour of Phisyk," of whom we are told "His study was but little on the Bible"; doctors of the time were often suspected of being closet atheists.) Yet poet and audience alike were always ready to enjoy a pot shot at religion's ministers on earth. The contradiction requires a brief explanation.

During the fourteenth century, the Catholic Church (which was, of course, the only church in western Europe) had reached the lowest point in its long history. As landlords controlling perhaps a third of the land in western Europe, its higher clergy were no more moved by Christian charity than were secular nobles. Few of these officials honored their vows of chastity or poverty; most enjoyed absentee "benefices"—revenues of up to twenty parishes whose daily pastoral duties were shoved off onto ill-paid ordinary priests. Of the greed and high living of its monks and friars, we shall hear plenty from Chaucer himself.

At its higher levels, in fact, the fourteenth-century Church amounted to little more than a business for selling salvation—and almost everything else—at a price. Abbacies, bishoprics and benefices could all be had for a consideration; one well-connected young man was consecrated as a bishop without troubling to be ordained a priest! For what might be called the mass market, the Church peddled indulgences and pardons which, for cash on the line, provided absolution for any sin, actual or prospective.

For the English, clerical corruption was doubly infuriating because most of these ill-gotten gains went to foreigners in Rome or, even worse, in French Avignon, where disorders in Italy had forced the papacy to flee in 1305, thereby converting the Pope into a French puppet. The culminating scandal was the installation, later in the century, of two competing popes, in Avignon and Rome, who busily hurled anathemas at one another. Adding insult to injury was "benefit of clergy," a legal principle under which no clergyman, however corrupt or even criminal, could be tried in any but a Church court—meaning he could expect little or no punishment. This went down especially hard in England: the old principle that everyone was bound by the same law, though often bent in practice, was still accepted in theory by nearly all lay Englishmen.

During Chaucer's lifetime, clerical abuses led to a powerful movement for Church reform, led by the scholar John Wycliffe but backed by a large proportion of the rank-and-file parish priests and protected, if not actually supported, by John of Gaunt himself. These "Lollards," as they were called, were ultimately suppressed as subversive heretics—many of them were connected with radical movements among the peasantry—but the religious abuses that inspired them continued to evoke contempt and hatred among all classes.

Chaucer was no Lollard, but he was also no fool—he was thoroughly aware of clerical corruption, and sophisticated enough to distinguish between the corrupt higher clergy and the ordinary "working" priests, themselves often victims of their superiors' rapacity. We see such a priest in *The Canterbury Tales*, the "poor parson" of a village—diligent in the care of souls, patient in adversity, who, far from screwing the last farthing of tithes from his parishoners, shares what little he has with the poorest of them. Unlike some other churchmen, "He was a shepherd, not a mercenary." He does not turn over the revenues of his parish to some grasping bishop and run off to London in search of a better job. Rather, he feels bound to set an example to his flock—"If gold can rust," he notes, "then what will iron do?"—while it is shameful to have "A shitty shepherd tending his clean sheep." This admirable man, and his brother, the no less humble plowman, are the only pilgrims to escape without at least a glancing dig; the poet sums him up in one of his most telling couplets:

> But Cristës lore, and his apostles twelvë
> He taughte—and first he folwed it himselvë

Almost as admirable is the young Clerk of Oxenford University (roughly equivalent to a modern graduate student), in threadbare coat, bestriding a horse "as lean as is a rake" and he himself "not very fat." No more than the Parson is he concerned with personal advancement, but rather loves learning. However, like many young scholars, he takes himself rather seriously, for which reason, perhaps, he does not completely escape the poet's sardonic eye:

> He knew philosophy, both new and old,
> But all his learning got him little gold.

—a jibe that to Chaucer's affluent audience must have had rather the flavor of "If he's so smart, why ain't he rich?"

The "Prioresse"—deputy head of a convent—at first glance seems to get off almost as lightly as the Clerk. She is a familiar enough figure: a maiden lady of a certain age, perhaps disappointed in love (as her gold brooch with the motto *Amor Vincit Omnia*—"Love Conquers All"—suggests), rather ostentatiously pious, rather overrefined, speaking French —though not "the French of Paris"—and lavishing affection on her "small dogs that she fed/ With roasted meat, or milk and fine white bread." One has to read her description a couple of times to realize that Chaucer is up to his old tricks: satire through the most delicate, deadpan overstatement. The Prioress is *so* dainty, *so* "charitable and piteous"—"she was all conscience, with a tender heart"—yet her charity is limited to animals: a mouse caught in a trap, or her yapping lapdogs, better fed than most Englishmen, who probably inspired more than one surreptitious kick from her less "piteous" fellow pilgrims.

With the Monk and the "Frere" (Friar), the poet really hits his anticlerical stride. The former, like most of his kind, cares nothing for the old monastic rule of poverty, study and hard work:

> *Why should he study, driving himself mad,*
> *Upon some book in cloister daily poring,*
> *Or labor with his hands, however boring?*

Rather, he is devoted to "venery"—the hunting of game but also, perhaps, what we know it meant in later times: the hunting of women (Chaucer notes immediately that he is "a manly man"). We find an even likelier pun in "Of pricking and of hunting for the hare/ Was all his lust . . . " To Chaucer's audience, "pricking" meant hard riding—in both senses; the "hare" he pursued may not have been so innocent either. But whatever game was hunted by this plump prelate, fairly sweating with good living, piety clearly took a distant second place:

> *And when he rode, men might his bridle hear*
> *Jingling in a whistling wind as clear,*
> *And just as loud, as does the chapel bell . . .*

The Friar, Chaucer tells us flatly, loved "wantonness" and "dalliance," and "knew the taverns well in every town." His main interest, however, is cash. He is a "limitour"—licensed, for a fee, to collect money from the pious within certain geographical limits—and makes a good profit from his franchise. Unlike friars of an earlier day, he spends no time with the sick and needy, but rather consorts with merchants and country gentlemen who love good eating and drinking. To them he is humble and well-spoken, and also understanding in setting penance. He knows that

> *. . . many a man may be so hard of heart*
> *He cannot weep, though sore his sins may smart.*
> *Therefore, instead of weeping, or of prayers,*
> *They can give silver to the needy freres.*

Last, but by no means least fragrant, of the ecclesiastical pilgrims are those two beauties the "Somnour" and the Pardoner, surely the original Odd Couple of literature: the first with his fire-red, pimply face, ugly enough to scare children, smelling of "garlic, onions, also leeks" and the strong red wine he relishes; the latter pop-eyed, beardless by nature ("I think he was a gelding or a mare"), his goat's voice bleating out a love song with the summoner's boozy bass trumpeting in counterpoint.

A summoner was part process server, for a Church court, and part cop. Like any modern crooked cop, he would for a consideration "forget" to deliver a summons; equally, he could threaten to give one for some invented crime, unless his palm was crossed. This Summoner has picked up a few Latin legal tags that he uses to overawe the unlettered, and also bellows out "when he had drunk his fill of wine" (pretty much his normal state, one gathers). He is a bit of an amiable pimp, permitting "for a quart of wine/ Some chum of his to have his concubine," and more than a bit of a con man.

The Pardoner is as big a crook as his good buddy the Summoner and, as becomes apparent later on, a hypocrite to boot. The wallet at his belt is stuffed with pardons "come from Rome all hot"—we'd say "hot off the press"—plus other choice bits of religious merchandise such as the Virgin's veil—actually a pillow case—and some pig's bones he calls the relics of a saint. With his well-oiled, pious sales talk, he can get more money from a "poor parson" and his congregation in one day than the parson gets in two months.

> *And thus with phony flattery and japes*
> *He made the parson and the people his apes*

—made monkeys of them, in fact. Yet this "noble ecclesiastic" is an eloquent preacher:

> *Well could he read a lesson or a story*
> *But best of all he sang the Offertory . . .*
> *Collecting silver, as so well he could;*
> *For that he sang both cheerfully and loud.*

(It is perhaps worth noting that it was the activities of just such a pardoner —a peddler of papal "indulgences"—that inspired Martin Luther's final break with the Church a century and a half later.)

For those unfamiliar with *The Canterbury Tales*, it is, as the title indicates, a collection of stories. The night before the pilgrims set out, the Host, landlord of the inn where they have foregathered, announces that he is joining them, and proposes that to pass the time along the way each pilgrim should tell two tales going and another two returning. (If Chaucer actually intended this grand design, he never came close to it; the collection includes only twenty-three.) This literary device was common during the late Middle Ages; a well-known example is Boccaccio's *Decameron*. What puts Chaucer's tales in a class by themselves is the variety of the tales and their tellers, and especially the prologues and epilogues that intersperse them, in which the other pilgrims comment on the tale just told, and often on its teller or one of their other fellow travelers.

Given the lively, indeed gamy, cast of characters that Chaucer introduces in his own lengthy "Prologue," some of the tales themselves are frankly disappointing. Several are high—or at times very low—comedy, but others are less than enthralling literary satires, takeoffs of various verse forms or philosophical ideas of the day, no doubt funny enough to those who knew the originals but often meaningless to us who don't. "The Parson's Tale," not surprisingly, is a straight sermon in prose; "The Monk's Tale" is little more than a catalogue of various historical figures who fell from high places, so tedious that the Knight at last cuts him short. And even some of the best tales, though full of individually vivid incidents, are broken by reflections on morality or the human condition. These were standard medieval literary devices, and some of them are high poetry, like the "smiler with the knife" passage quoted earlier. To a modern taste, however, they often break the flow of the narrative.

But though in the tales themselves Chaucer is still half a man of the Middle Ages, in the prologues and epilogues spoken by his pilgrims he foreshadows the vivid realism of Elizabethan drama. In their energetic,

comic and at times near-violent byplay, they further illuminate the na-
tures of the people we have already met in the main "Prologue." A high
point, naturally, is the Wife of Bath's prologue, in which she sets forth
at length her philosophy of sex and marriage, with copious firsthand
illustrations. Another is the Pardoner's prologue and epilogue. Having
fortified himself with a quart of ale, he brazenly recounts all the "false
japes" with which he cons the public. He no less brazenly dilates on the
perennial theme of his sermons, "covetousness is the root of all evil,"
holding himself specially qualified to preach on that text: there's not
much *he* doesn't know about covetousness.

> *For I myself, though full of vice and sin*
> *A highly moral tale for you can spin . . .*

After telling his tale—and a good one it is—he then passes, without
shifting gears, into a sales pitch for his holy relics, and urges the Host,
as the most sinful man present, to come forward and (for a price) kiss
them. The Host, whatever his other transgressions, is unquestionably
both short-tempered and free-spoken, and his suggestions as to who
should kiss what, and what parts of the Pardoner's anatomy might well
be converted into another "holy relic," cannot, as they say, be reprinted
in a family publication.

Indeed, the same goes for many incidents in the tales, dealing as they
often do with the perennially comic subjects of adultery and cuckoldry,
in language that leaves nothing to the imagination. The Miller, describing
a young clerk's advances to the young wife of his elderly landlord, tells
how "stealthily he grabbed her by the cunt"; later on, the young woman,
seeking to discourage another suitor, arranges that in the dark he will
"kiss her naked ass." It is ironic to reflect that had Chaucer written this
sort of thing in 1950, he could not have been published in any English-
speaking country.

Matters were evidently quite different in the fourteenth century: none
of this raw and rowdy comedy draws any reproof from the rest of the
pilgrims, not even the delicate-minded Prioress. Chaucer himself does
offer us a semi-apology, noting that the Miller was a vulgar fellow speaking in his own vulgar manner—which is certainly true. Therefore, the
poet tells his hearers,

> *. . . think not that I speak*
> *From evil intent, but rather must rehearse*

All of these tales, for better or for worse,
Or falsify the things I speak of here . . .

One's first reaction, since both the Miller and his tale are after all the
poet's own invention, is "Who does he think he's kidding?" One's second
is that Chaucer is up to his old rhetorical sleight-of-hand: rather than an
apology he is giving us a come-on, saying, in effect, "Listen closely,
friends—this is a juicy one!"

If one can draw a moral from such immoral goings-on, it is that English,
like every other language on the face of the earth, deals with the earthy
as well as the sublime, with the whole range of human activity and experience, "low" or "high." Some nice-minded folk find this distressing, or
profess to do so; a generation ago, a California politician won himself
some nice publicity by denouncing a new dictionary as "an encyclopedia
of sex perversion," because it gave the names of things that millions of
people had been doing for years. It is therefore worth reminding ourselves that our first great writer was great partly because he strove to show
people as they are, rather than the bloodless, sexless phantoms some
would like them to be.

The fourteenth century, apart from producing Chaucer, was remarkable in a very different way: it was the time when the English, or most of
them, acquired family names. Whether these can properly be considered
part of the English language is arguable; certainly the only ones that
appear in our dictionaries are the handful that have been converted, in
one form or another, into ordinary nouns or verbs: Lynch, Boycott,
Shrapnel, Wistar(ia) and the like (their exact etymologies can be found
in any large dictionary). On the other hand, we use these words every day
and all have at least one of our own; moreover, closely examined, they
can tell us some interesting things about how our ancestors, genetic or
linguistic, lived in past centuries. For all these reasons, they seem to me
worth a look.

In England of a thousand years ago, as in Homeric Greece of a couple
of thousand years earlier, family names were unknown. Communities
were small enough, and given names diversified enough, so that if one
spoke of Egbert or Ethelreda everyone in the village knew who was
meant. If any ambiguity remained—or for aristocrats proud of their lin-
eage—the given name might be supplemented by a surname, "So-and-
so's son" (or daughter). We find names of this sort in *Beowulf* (Herogar
Healfdenesone), in the Norse sagas (Leif Ericson, who founded the first
European settlement in America) and in the protagonist of Sigrid Und-

set's trilogy set in medieval Sweden, *Kristin Lavransdatter,* just as we do among the much earlier Homeric gentry (Achilles Peleiades—"son of Peleus"). Common folk were more likely to be identified by nicknames; some of the Norse sagas are inhabited by characters whose names translate as Dirty Eyolf, Cockeye Ulf, Loudmouth Thord and the like. (Any resemblance between these nicknames and those of some prominent Prohibition Era Americans is perhaps not wholly coincidental; in manners and morals there was little difference between tenth-century Vikings and twentieth-century gangsters.) Perhaps the most evocative of these Viking nicknames is that of Leif Ericson's maternal grandmother, Ship-bosom Thorbjorg. Picture the prow of a Viking ship . . .

English surnames of this type (at least those that have come down to us) are less colorful; they mainly refer to hair and complexion (Black, Brown, White), stature or build (Little, Biggs, Crane) or mental characteristics (Sharpe, Jolly, Fox). The "son of " names, by contrast, are exactly paralleled by scores of modern family names like Johnson, Thompson (Tom's son) and the like. Note, however, that until the fourteenth century these surnames (literally, "extra names") were still not *family* names, because they did not pass from one generation to the next. The son of Edmund Egbertson, Alfred, would be Alfred Edmundson, while *his* son would be surnamed Alfredson, and so on. Likewise, the son of John Black might be surnamed Black if he took after his father, but (say) Read if he favored his red-headed mother, or something else entirely, based on some peculiarity of his own.

As the Middle Ages drew on, this system grew increasingly confusing. A major reason was that people for some reason began limiting themselves to a bare handful of given names: those of saints, like John, Peter and Thomas, or prestigious ones borrowed from the Norman aristocracy, like William, Richard, Henry and Robert. As a result, almost any village might include (say) a dozen Johns and Thomases and smaller but still substantial groups of Richards, Williams and Henrys. As some villages grew into towns, the Johns might increase to scores, of which a sizable number might beget Johns in their turn—with judges and tax collectors hard put to it to tell one of these John Johnsons from another.

One way out of the difficulty was to use nicknames, as already discussed. Another was to use different forms of the father's name, often dropping the "son" as well, so that along with Johnson one got Johns, Jones, Jenks, Jenkins (from the pet name John-kin) and Jackson. Particularly prone to such mutations, for some reason, were Richard and Robert.

The first has given us not only Richardson and Richards but Dix, Dixon, Hicks, Hickson, Higgs, Higgins and Higginson; the second, along with Robertson and Roberts, begat Robbins, Robinson, Robb, Robson, Hobbs, Hobson, Dobbs, Dobbins and Dobson. As will be seen, these names normally derived from the father's name; the English, like the Indo-Europeans long before them, reckoned descent in the male line. One of the few exceptions is Maggs or Meigs ("son of Meg"), and even this may have been first applied to a child who, as the Victorians would delicately put it, had no father.

Yet another way of diversifying surnames was to use the person's place of residence; thus we have Brooks and Rivers, Hill and Dale (or perhaps Coombes, from the old British word for "valley"), Forrest, Wood, Grove and Shaw (a copse or thicket), Mills and Church. When the continued growth of towns, plus the social disruption of the Black Death, drew people from their native villages, they would face the perennial question addressed to the stranger in town, equivalent to "Where ya from?" A native of one of the dozens of Burtons in England might then be known as John of Burton, or simply John Burton. Some historic American names of this type include Washington (from a village in County Durham), Lincoln (from the town or county) and Cleveland (from a town in Yorkshire). Names of the old "son" type gave us Presidents Jefferson (Geoffrey's son), Jackson, two Johnsons and Nixon (Nick's son). A less historic geographical name is Claiborne, from the onetime manor of Clayburn in Northumberland, whence my ancestors presumably migrated to Norfolk, where they first appear in public records.

By far the most interesting surnames, however, are those identifying people by what they did for a living. To be sure, the commonest occupation—peasant or villein—contributed no surnames, precisely because it *was* so common, and likewise with plowman. No less common was mather (mower); the few families of that name must be descended from local mowing champions. (The same root has given us "aftermath"—originally the second mowing of hay.) We do find a modest number of Yeomans—countrymen of more than average position—and Franklins, representing the few rich farmers; the type was unforgettably limned by Chaucer: "It snowèd in his house of food and drink/ And every dainty that a man could think." But the surname Farmer comes from tax farmer—tax collector.

Most rural occupational surnames were drawn from the specialized workers found mainly on the larger manors: Shepherd, Calvert (calf-herd) and Coward—no poltroon, but a cowherd. The kitchen garden contributed Gardner, and the lord's woodland, Forrester and Parker, while inside the manor house were the Cook, the Lardner, in charge of the larder, and the Butler ("bottler"), in charge of potables.

During the early Middle Ages, rural communities were largely self-sufficient, but by 1300 they were increasingly becoming caught up in the web of trade. Commodities flowed from country to town, where they were processed by a wide spectrum of specialized craftsmen, with finished goods flowing back to the country, or sometimes overseas.

Thus livestock brought into town by John Driver were turned over to John Slaughter or John Butcher, or perhaps to John Bacon, specialist in pork products; these same tradesmen also dealt in game, supplied by John Hunter or John Fowler. The odoriferous stock in trade of John Fisher, however, would have been relegated to a separate shop or market stall. The hides of the slaughtered livestock, removed by John Skinner, would be processed by John Tanner with the oak and willow bark supplied by John Barker; the resulting leather supplied the shops of John Shoemaker, John Glover, John Sadler the harnessmaker and John Girdler the beltmaker.

Grain, the major staple, was processed by John Miller (or Milner) and after him by John Baker or Baxter (the suffix -ster was originally feminine, as in "spinster"; eventually it was applied to either sex, reflecting the decline of gender distinctions in English). Alternatively, grain might be taken over by John Brewer or Jane Brewster, fermented in the vats made by John Tubman, stored in the barrels of John Cooper, and eventually served up by John Taverner or John Inman, in drinking vessels made of leather, earthenware made by John Potter, or wood turned on a crude lathe by John Turner.

Wool had been the principal English export commodity since before the Conquest, but there are few Woolmans (most Wool- and Wol- surnames have to do with wolves, not wool); the trade was managed by John Marchant and John Chapman—the latter the linguistic and occupational descendant of the Roman *caupones* who had traded with the ancestral Germans across the Rhine. During the fifteenth and sixteenth centuries, however, exports were increasingly of cloth, not wool. The textile business added to our cast of "townies" John Weaver (or Webber, or Webster) and John Dyer (or Dexter). More specialized skills, too intricate to recount here, were practiced by John Shearer (or Sherman), John Fuller, John Tucker and John Walker. The work of all these craftspeople was organized (and often financed) by the capitalists John Draper and John Mercer, who then arranged for it to be hauled to the coast by John Carter and John Porter, for onward conveyance by John Shipman or John Marner (mariner), in craft made by John Shipwright and rigged by John Roper.

Timber, another major English resource, was seldom if ever shipped overseas: it was too valuable as construction material and fuel, and far too heavy to haul any distance in a land where paved Roman roads were now but a dim memory. Felled by John Woodman or John Hacker and cut into beams and planks by John Sawyer, it was then worked by John Carpenter or John Wright (though this word, cognate with "wrought" and "worked," sometimes meant any skilled craftsman). More specialized woodworkers were John Cartwright and the wagon (wain) makers John Wainwright and John Wayne, assisted by John Wheeler.

Frame buildings would be erected by the local "wright," those in more costly stone and brick by John Mason. Roofs, depending on local taste and materials, would be installed by John Thatcher, John Slater or John Tyler. The occasional lead roof (e.g., of a church) was the work of John Plummer (from Old French *plommier*, lead worker); "plumbing" in our sense would not arrive for some centuries.

The metal trades were, of course, led by John Smith. He worked mainly in iron and steel, from ore dug by John Miner and John Pitman and smelted by John Bloomer (ingots are still called "blooms") and John Steele, with charcoal supplied by John Collier. (In a few large towns such as London, the last of these might deal in actual coal, used for heating but not yet for smelting.) More specialized craftsmen were John Farrer (farrier), who shod horses using nails made by John Naylor (most wooden objects were pegged together with "treenails"), and the knifemaker, John Cutler. Metal goods for the luxury trade were made by John Brasher, the brass founder, John Goldsmith and John Silver.

Roaming the narrow streets of Chaucer's London, or one of the larger towns like York or Bristol, one could buy a besom (broom) from John Bessemer, shoes from John Shoemaker or John Chaucer (from Old French *chaussier*), crockery from John Crocker, or a horn spoon or horn-windowed lantern from Jack Horner, while John Chandler's shop would supply both greasy tallow candles and the better grade made from the products of John Waxman. Seasonings came from John Spicer, John Pepper and especially John Salter, whose wares supplied not merely flavor but the means of preserving meat and sausage (literally, "salted") through the winter. For cleanliness one would seek out John Soper, for a haircut, John Barber, who also pulled teeth and performed simple surgery—the only kind then possible.

A common sight would be a detachment of soldiers bound for the French wars—John Bowman, John Archer, John Speare and John Ballester with his arbalest (crossbow). Their helmets and breastplates would have been made by John Armour and his assistant, John Frobisher, who polished (furbished) the finished goods; other members of the embryonic military-industrial complex were John Bowyer and John Arrowsmith, or his competitor, John Fletcher, which meant the same thing.

The clergy would appear in the persons of John Priest, John Abbot, John Monk and John Parsons. Normally, these names were applied either to the men themselves or to their servants, but some of them were doubtless borne by people who were the living proof that clerical celibacy was less than absolute.

Market day or a festival might bring dancing in the streets to the music of John Piper, John Harper, John Fidler and drum-beating John Taber. Recreation for the thirsty was provided by John Taverner or the establishments of John Swann and John Bull—named from their painted inn signs. Too many drinks might bring one into the hands of John Constable and John Gaylor (gaoler), while less combative celebrants might end the evening at the whorehouse run by John Hollier or, more often, Madam Jane Hollister. And if anyone was unfortunate enough to succumb to all this excitement, he would be buried by John Sexton and have his knell rung by John Toller.

Though these and many other medieval surnames have survived to the present, as late as 1300 most of them were still not family names. Indeed, a single person might bear half a dozen names in his lifetime: young John, born in Sheffield, might begin life as John Harrison (after his father), be nicknamed John Bigg when he got his growth, join the army as John (of) Sheffield, return from the wars as John Bowman, and, having invested his loot in a horse and wagon, finish life as John Carter. To take a real case, Chaucer's grandfather, son of Andrew le Taverner (presumably an innkeeper), was himself known at various times as Robert le Saddler, Robert Chaucer (not from his occupation, but from his residence in London's Cordwainer—leatherworker—Street) and Robert of Dennington, from a Suffolk village where he was born, or lived, or held property.

Such fluid surnames, however, were beginning to make life altogether too complicated for lawyers and judges, especially in disputes concerning the ownership and inheritance of property—a problem that must have been aggravated unbearably by the Black Death, in which whole families were wiped out, leaving no obvious heirs, while other families migrated from village to village or village to town. Significantly, Robert Chaucer's (or Robert of Dennington's) son John, and his grandson, Geoffrey, used the name Chaucer all their lives, though neither had any connection with either the leather trade or with Cordwainer Street.

Many American and English family names are not English at all, of course. In England, the majority come from other parts of the British Isles, though names like Fleming, French and Holland point to immigrants from the Continent. The Welsh have contributed Evans (their version of Johns) and Owens, and also their distinctive prefix for "son of," *ap*. The prefix, however, has almost invariably merged with the name, and is sometimes further disguised by phonetic alteration. Thus we have Welsh Rhys (usually pronounced, and often spelled, Reece) and Price (apRhys), Howell and Powell, Richards and Pritchard, Evans and Bevan, Owen and Bowen. The Welsh LL (pronounced approximately /hl/) underwent phonetic assimilation, giving us both Lloyd and Floyd, while Shakespeare's Captain Fluellen was as close as an English tongue could get to the old Welsh name Llwellyn.

Some of the commonest Welsh names, however, were originally English, either borrowed from or bestowed by English overlords. In addition, the Welsh for some reason heavily favored a very few family names, so that in some North Wales villages today every other person seems to be named Jones, Evans, Thomas or Williams. The result is often the appearance of an extra, personal surname of the old type, whereby letter-carrying Evan Evans the Post can be distinguished from undertaking Evan Evans the Box, Evan Evans Gladys (after his mother) and Evan Evans Llangollan (from his birthplace).

The Scots and Irish too have their own version of "son of"—Mac or Mc; indeed the Irish also have O, meaning "grandson of" or "descendant of." But most of these prefixes are attached to names of the same paternal and occupational types we have already seen in England: Macauley means "son of the smith," and McPherson "son of the parson." A few, however, take us back to the old, resounding tribal names of the Indo-Europeans (both Ireland and the Scottish Highlands remained essentially tribal until a few centuries ago). Thus McCormack means "son of Chariot-Lad," McGoldrick "son of High-Temper," and McRory "son of Red-King."

Since this is a book about the English language, we cannot reasonably devote much space to the innumerable family names in England and (especially) North America that are neither English nor Celtic. Worth noting, however, is that most of them follow the same patterns we have been describing, drawn from paternal names, nicknames, places of birth or residence, and occupations. English Blacks and Browns are matched by German Schwartzes and Brauns, French Lenoirs and Lebruns ("the black" and "the brown"), Italian Neros and Brunos and Hispanic Negróns and Morenos. "Son of" turns up in Slavic *-ski* or *-vich* or *-ich,* Armenian *-ian,* and the almost omnipresent Hispanic *-ez.* The ancestors of the infamous French fascist Pierre Laval must have hailed from the town of that name, as the Berliners originated in Berlin and the Genoveses in Genova (Genoa). The Bouchers are descended from some French butcher, the Pfeiffers from a German piper, the Profumos from an Italian perfumer, the Molnars from a Hungarian miller—and the Jewish Schechters and Schactmans from a *schochet,* the ritual slaughterer or kosher butcher.

The throngs of Johnsons, Jacksons and Joneses on American immigration rolls are matched by McShanes, Gianninis, Gianopouloses, Ivanovs, Johanssons, Hennings, Jandas, and Janowskis. And John Smith, that ancient, archetypical craftsman, passed through Ellis Island thousands of times as Sean Gough, Jean Lefevre, Giovanni Ferrari, Juan Herrero, Ivan Kuznetsov, Hans Schmidt, Jan Kowalski and Janos Kovacs.

Our names, part of our own personal past, are, like other words, also part of the past of some tribe or community or nation. And in names, as in many other human basics, peoples don't seem all that different.

The fourteenth-century English renaissance, alas, turned out to be a false dawn. Even before its close, the darkness had begun creeping back: the war in France was going badly, and England's brief national unity was fragmenting into quarrelsome factions of crown, nobles, Church, and commons (the townsmen and lesser gentry), whose only point of agreement was the importance of keeping the *real* commoners—the peasant majority—in their place. In this confused and increasingly nasty conflict, one can seldom distinguish good guys from bad guys; most of the participants were both, or neither: either they were doing the right thing for the wrong reasons or vice versa.

Yet there is this to be said about the unprincipled and often brutal conflicts of fifteenth-century England: they were generally carried out within the forms of law—findings of the courts, or acts of parliament. True, courts were often intimidated, and parliaments often packed by bribing or intimidating electors (not difficult, given the small number of people able to vote), yet even the worst leaders of the time never thought of simply abolishing these institutions. Hypocrites they were, perhaps, yet there is something to be said even for hypocrisy. It has been described, correctly, as the tribute vice pays to virtue—and the mere fact that vice feels compelled to pay that tribute says something about the state of civic virtue among a people. As long as that people believes that a government restrained by law is important, it stands a reasonable chance of getting, or regaining, such a government. Cleaning up elections, abolishing repressive laws and reforming corrupt courts is never easy—but it is still a lot easier than trying to reform or abolish a ruling elite that has never known any law but its own greed.

For all that, the fifteenth century was a bad time for limited government in England, and not much better for the English language. The borrowing of Latin words expanded far beyond need or reason, with poets vying to introduce the most eccentric terms taken from what one critic sourly called "half-chewed Latin." A good, or at least vivid, example of this "aureate" (gilded) diction, whose glittering vocabulary half conceals its leaden substance, comes from the Scottish poet Dunbar:

> *Hale sterne superne! Hale, in eterne*
> *In Godis sicht to schyne!*
> *Lucerne in derne, for to discerne*
> *Be glory and grace devyne;*
> *Hodiern, modern, sempitern . . .*

but we need not further belabor the point. (Readers with a morbid interest in literary monstrosities will find most of the unfamiliar words in *The Oxford English Dictionary.*)

This sort of thing naturally begot a reaction that at times reached equal heights of silliness. Around 1450, a somewhat batty bishop, one Reginald Pecock, proposed to "purify" English of its Latin and Latinate elements, even as his modern counterparts in other lands seek to purify their own tongues of English infiltrations. Instead of "impenetrable," he proposed the Old English–style compound "ungothroughsome"; another suggestion was the monstrous "not-to-be-thought-upon-able." But the English, though they had by this time lost the French war, had not lost their sense of humor: Pecock's eccentric proposals were swept away on a tide of laughter. French and Latin words were so embedded in the English vocabulary that extracting them was not merely "not-to-be-thought-upon-able" but downright impossible—a borrowed word used since 1300.

The fifteenth century also saw several historical developments important for the subsequent development of both English society and the English tongue. The first was the expulsion of the English from France, under the inspiration of Jeanne d'Arc. This was obviously a blessing for France but also, in the long run, for England, since it forced the English to concentrate on improving their own country instead of trying to run someone else's. The immediate result, however, was less benign: a series of struggles over the succession to the English crown (the Wars of the Roses), largely fought by the bellicose nobles and professional soldiers whose greed and machismo had hitherto expressed themselves mainly across the Channel. Yet even this turned out to be something of a disguised blessing: it killed off a lot of the turbulent feudal lords whose perennial wrangling had checked the growth of a strong, efficient central government.

Far more important for England and for English than the noisy clash of feudal armies was an unobtrusive event of 1476: the return of the merchant William Caxton from the Low Countries, where he had learned the new craft of printing. Caxton's introduction of printed books to England was obviously the first step in spreading literacy and knowledge to wider sections of the population. Less obviously, it raised a question that has bedeviled us ever since: what is "good" English?

Neither Caxton nor anyone else put the matter in those words, of course, yet the problem was real enough. English was not then (and probably never had been) a single, uniform language, but a collection of regional dialects, some of them barely intelligible to one another. As early as 1300, the anonymous author (or perhaps editor) of the poem *Cursor Mundi* notes that he, a native of northern England, has translated it from a southern original:

> *In southern English was it done,*
> *But I have turned it to our own*
> *English, of our northern breed*
> *Who other English cannot read.* [my translation]

Chaucer, too, was aware of the problem: he introduces his "lytele boke," *Troilus and Crisedye,* with the famous lines

> *And since there is such great diversity*
> *In English, and the writing of our tongue,*
> *I pray to God that none shall miswrite* thee . . .

There were four major dialects in medieval England (and probably twice as many minor ones). Northern covered England north of the river Humber, and parts of Lowland Scotland as well. Between the Humber and the Thames and Severn lay two related dialects, East and West Midland, while southern England was divided into Southern and (in the southeast corner) Kentish. The differences among them, involving mainly phonetics and vocabulary, are too intricate to be worth discussing here, apart from noting that Norse loan words were inevitably much more numerous in Northern and East Midland—the old Danelaw.

By Chaucer's day, a more or less standard written language had begun to emerge from this welter of regional and local tongues—basically, the East Midland dialect. The reasons are not far to seek. First, the Midland dialects had resemblances to both Northern and Southern. As John Trevisa noted in 1385, "men of middle England, as it were partners of the ends, understand better the side languages, Northern and Southern, than Northern and Southern understand each other." The *East* Midland region, moreover, was the richest and most populous part of England, containing her largest city, busiest port and seat of government (London) as well as one of her two great universities (Cambridge); the other (Oxford) lay on the border between Midland and Southern. The London version of East Midland gained added prestige as the language of the court —the king's English, in fact. It was not "pure" East Midland, however; the city's steady growth attracted migrants from all parts of England, notably the north, some of whose words and grammatical forms passed into the local lingo.

The growth of printing, inevitably centered in London, could only strengthen the influence of this dialect. But it also forced printers into sometimes difficult decisions. As long as books were hand-copied, any given copy was likely to be read by only a modest number of people, mostly of similar speech. But printed editions of hundreds and eventually thousands of copies had to be sold to people of quite different speech habits. It was therefore up to the printer—who in those days doubled as publisher, editor and translator—to decide which forms to favor.

Caxton's account of how he grappled with this problem is so trenchant and witty as to be worth quoting at length. (Interestingly, though only a century separates him from Chaucer, I have had to do little more than modernize the spelling: his syntax and vocabulary are close enough to ours to make a full translation unnecessary.) His account comes from his preface to *Eneydos,* translated from a French version of Vergil's Latin epic, *The Aeneid.*

After divers works made, translated and achieved [i.e., completed], having no work in hand, I [was] sitting in my study where lay many and diverse pamphlets and books, [and it] happened that to my hand came a little book in French, which late[ly] was translated out of Latin by some noble clerk [i.e., scholar] of France. And . . . I deliberated, and concluded to translate it into English, and forthwith took a pen and ink and wrote a leaf or two, which I [then] oversaw again to correct it.

And when I saw the fair and strange terms therein, I doubted that it would please some gentlemen who late[ly] blamed me, saying that in translations I have [used] overcurious terms which could not be understood by common people, and desired me to use old and homely terms in my translations. And fain would I satisfy every man, and to do so took an old book and read therein, and certainly the English was so rude and broad that I could not well understand it. . . .

Certainly our language now used varies far from that which was used and spoken when I was born. . . . [Moreover] the common English that is spoken in one shire varies from another. So much [so] that in my [own] days [it] happened that certain merchants were in a ship in [the] Thames . . . and for lack of wind they tarried at [the] Foreland and went on shore to refresh them[selves]. And one of them, named Sheffield, a mercer, came into a house and asked for meat [i.e., food], and specially he asked after eggs. And the goodwife answered that she could speak no French. And the merchant was angry, for he also could speak no French, but would have had eggs, and she understood him not. And then at last another said he would have "eyren," [and] then the goodwife said she understood him well. Lo, what should a man in these days now write: "eggs" or "eyren"? [The two words are respectively the Northern—ultimately Norse—and Southern forms.]

Certainly it is hard to please every man, by reason of diversity and change of language. For in these days every man that is [of] any reputation . . . will utter his communication and matters in such manners and terms that few men shall understand them. And some honest and great clerks have been with me, and desired me to write the most curious terms that I could find. And thus, between plain, rude and curious, I stand abashed. But in my judgment the common terms that are daily used are lighter [i.e., easier] to be understood than the old and ancient English. . . . Therefore . . . I have reduced and translated this said book into our English, not overrude, nor curious, but in such terms as shall be understood, by God's grace, according to my copy.

To all of which any modern writer or editor can only cry "Amen!" We prepare our copy for the press, and hope that with or without God's grace it will be "in such terms as shall be understood." We grapple with the literary efforts of men of "reputation"—scientists, academics and bureaucrats, public and private, who in the 1980s as in the 1480s still utter their "matters in such manners and terms that few men shall understand them." Faced, like Caxton, with "diversity and change of language," we wonder, in effect, whether to write "eggs" or "eyren." Like him we would fain satisfy every man—and find the job no easier than he did.

But even as we wryly recognize our kinship to this English pioneer in "mass communication," we see that he is grappling with a basic problem engendered by those same communications: who are we trying to communicate with, and how can we best do it? What, in fact, *is* good English, and by what standards, and who sets the standards? As we shall see, there are no easy answers to these questions, and no answers of any kind that will serve for all times and places. But to say that the answers are elusive does not mean that, as some modern authorities claim, the questions are unimportant; to dismiss as trivial the question of good English is to blind oneself to what Caxton saw so clearly, five hundred years ago.

7. "THE VERIE HEIGHT"

Shakespeare and the King James Bible

⟡

I doe not think that anie language, be it whatsoever, is better able to utter all arguments, either with more pith, or greater planesse, than our English tung is.

—RICHARD MULCASTER, 1582

Oh brave new world, that has such people in't.

—WILLIAM SHAKESPEARE, 1612

THE years between the crowning of Henry VII in 1485 and the death of his great-great-grandson, James I, in 1625 brought unparalleled achievements to both England and its language. When Henry was crowned, England possessed a mere three and a half million people; its largest urban center, London, had perhaps sixty thousand souls, with most of its other towns little more than overgrown villages. Militarily it was feeble compared with the "great powers," Spain and France; indeed, it was at times threatened by its much smaller neighbor, Scotland.

By 1625, England's population was close to five million, while London's had quadrupled, making it Europe's largest city north of Naples. Scotland was no longer a threat, but united with England under one king. And if Englishmen argued about the conduct of the king, and Scots about the virtues of the union, the government was at any rate stable and solvent. On the international scene, England had taken on the Spanish Empire, Europe's richest and most formidable power, and fought it to a draw—in terms of English war aims, a victory.

During this same period the English tongue became the instrument of a constellation of writers never surpassed in England or anywhere else. Compared with French, Spanish or even German, English was still a minor language, little spoken outside the British Isles, and not universally even there (Celtic tongues still dominated Ireland, Wales, the Scottish Highlands and parts of Cornwall, while the Shetlands and Orkneys spoke a Scandinavian dialect). But it had already crossed the Atlantic, to the continent where its speakers would one day far outnumber those in the mother country.

The rise of England (and with it, English) toward greatness was compounded of many things, not all of them unique to that country. Over most of western Europe, new towns were springing up and old ones were expanding, as improvements in technology spurred production in both town and country. Moreover, a series of Atlantic explorers had opened up the sea route around Africa to India and the Spice Islands, transatlantic passages to the teeming fisheries off Newfoundland and, after 1492, the uncountable riches of two new continents. These discoveries shifted the center of Europen commerce from the Mediterranean to the Atlantic, to the immense profit of the lands fronting on that ocean—initially, Spain and Portugal. Over the long run, however, England and its English-speaking colonies would be the chief beneficiaries.

How England first overtook and then far outstripped both Spain and another Atlantic power, France, is a complicated story. One important reason was a sort of provincialism: a growing disinclination to involve itself in European wars unless England itself seemed under threat; this led the English to focus most of their energies on internal development and overseas commerce and expansion. No less important, I think, was something in the English tradition and character—call it good sense, good temper or a genius for compromise—which spared it the extremes of religious and political fanaticism that sapped the energies of other Atlantic lands.

It would be ridiculous to suggest that the English-speaking peoples had or have some sort of rooted objection to bloodshed: the Native Americans, among others, know better. But I think it fair to say that when it comes to *internal* conflicts, whether of politics or religion, they have managed matters with a good deal less bloodshed than have most other peoples. Dissidents in religion and politics have been suppressed, and sometimes killed, though even then usually according to the letter if not the spirit of the law. They have not been exterminated. However oppressive the government—and that has sometimes been pretty damned oppressive—it has almost always conceded the mass of its opponents the right to life, if not always to liberty and the pursuit of happiness.

In Spain, by contrast, conformity was enforced by the sword and stake. In the same year that Columbus discovered America, the Spanish crown gave its Moslem and Jewish subjects the option of conversion to Catholicism, exile—or burning. Most chose exile, thereby stripping Spain of some thousands of skilled artisans. Even as a flood of gold and silver was about to begin pouring in from America, Spanish fanaticism was ensuring that little of the new wealth would be put to productive use. Instead, the combination of stagnant productivity and a rapidly expanding money supply gave Spain just what you'd expect: the highest inflation rate in Europe.

The same sort of fanaticism inflicted generations of cold and hot religious war on France, which reached its low point in the massacre of some thirty thousand Protestants during one bloody week in 1572. (Subsequently the French replayed this murderous scenario several times, notably during the Terror of 1791 and the suppression of the Paris Commune in 1871.) A few generations later, religious conflict in Germany helped fuel the Thirty Years War, which between battle, disease and famine may have destroyed as much as half the population. Meanwhile, the English followed the advice that a great Frenchman would one day offer his countrymen: they cultivated their own garden, often with the help of fugitives from fanaticism elsewhere. Among these were Flemings, Germans and French Huguenots (Protestants), the latter of whom brought the word *refugie* into English.

Yet with every allowance for geography and national temper, part of England's rise toward greatness was due to sheer luck: a run of able, or at least competent, rulers. The usurper Henry VII was as devious a man as ever sat on the English throne, but as skilled at kingship as at intrigue. His son, Henry VIII, gets only passing grades as a king—his machismo once again embroiled England unprofitably in France—but was served by a series of brilliant ministers. *His* two immediate successors, the sickly adolescent Edward VI and the religious fanatic Mary I, both had the grace to die within a few years of their accession, while Mary's successor, Elizabeth I, was a genius by any definition, a pacifist by inclination, and anything but a fanatic; she had, she declared, no desire "to open windows into men's consciences." Happily, her reign was one of the longest in English history.

Good luck, good management and good sense helped England to enjoy a century of rising prosperity. The wool trade, for centuries the backbone of its foreign commerce, expanded, and, moreover, the wool was increasingly exported not as raw material for foreign looms but as cloth— meaning more jobs and profits for the English. England's economy, in fact, was rapidly evolving into what would later be called capitalism, with all that implies. The process, as summed up by a writer of 1590, "has made of yeoman and artificers, gentlemen, and of gentlemen, knights, and so forth upward, *and of the poorest sort, stark beggars"* (emphasis added). Then as later, prosperity had its price—in this case, the impoverishment of thousands of small farmers and farm laborers whose lands had been "enclosed" by wealthy landholders, and often converted from farmland into sheep pasture, requiring almost no labor. A bitter jest of the time noted that where once men had eaten up sheep, now sheep ate up men.

The "beggars," whom now we would call the unemployed, periodically rioted against the "tyrants" who "grind our flesh against the whetstone of poverty." Ben Jonson's Volpone, that expert financial manipulator, employed the same image when he remarked that he had "no mills for iron, oil, corn or men, to grind them into powder." Other writers shrugged their shoulders, declaring, in terms not unfamiliar today, that "a citizen, however he may be noted for covetousness, and a corruption of trading, yet under color of private enriching himself he laboreth for the common good." Measured by the expanding gross national product, there was a good deal of truth to this view, but the "common good" generated by covetousness was a lot more common to some than to others.

Nonetheless, the "average Englishman," in town if not in country, was certainly better off. One bit of evidence is the growth of the new industry of printing. Within a century after Caxton had first set up his press, the old, expensive handwritten book had almost vanished, while its printed successor was becoming almost a necessity for the middle as well as the upper classes. Books, pamphlets and half-penny, single-sheet "broadsides" poured from the presses, first by dozens of titles, then by scores, then by hundreds. And education expanded along with publishing: the more there was to read, the more "point" there was to learning how— and the more readers, naturally, the more point in publishing more books. Though we have no reliable statistics, it is likely that by 1600 nearly half the English population had achieved at least minimal literacy, while higher education, though still limited to a small minority, had grown in proportion.

These developments inevitably influenced both the English language and its literary products, as we shall see in a moment. Curiously, however, one of the most striking changes in English during the period had nothing to do with social history, prosperity, printing or anything else; it just happened. The Great Vowel Shift of the sixteenth century, though it occurred on the very threshold of modern times, is every bit as mysterious as the prehistoric Great Consonant Shift several thousand years earlier. Without going into elaborate details, it involved a change in nearly all the English vowel sounds. In Chaucer's day, these had been mostly close to their "Continental" values, /ah/, /eh/, /ee/, /oh/, /oo/. By Shakespeare's time, they had shifted almost to their modern values, and even closer to those of the English spoken in Ireland today, so that "clean," for example, was nearer /klane/ than /kleen/.

These changes were most noticeable in the accented vowels. Unaccented ones tended to fall together into a single, indeterminate /uh/, as they still do—witness, for example, the indicated vowels in "elEgant," "Upon" and "dramA." Others simply disappeared—notably, the unstressed final E's of Middle English, in which *clene* (clean) was pronounced /kleh-nuh/, and, somewhat later, many of the E's in the past suffix -ed, so that "walked," "talked," and "showed" became monosyllables.

Syntax changed less radically: the really radical change—loss of inflection—was already largely complete. Anyone who has read Shakespeare (or any of the other great Elizabethans) has doubtless noticed that his syntax is not always ours; thus when Polonius asks "What do you read?" we'd say "What are you reading?" and when Macbeth mutters "Our fears in Banquo stick deep" we'd say "*of* Banquo," or "*concerning* Banquo." But such minor differences are seldom important enough to obscure the meaning, even if they don't "sound right" to our ears; the obscurities in Elizabethan literature are overwhelmingly semantic: words now obsolete, or used in a different sense. Thus when the horrified Macbeth cries to the ghost of Banquo, "Thou hast no speculation in those eyes" he is evidently not talking about playing the stock market—the commonest modern use of "speculation"—but rather of vision, from the Latin verb *specere*, look at (we find the same basic meaning in "inspect"—"look into"). But note, too, that Shakespeare probably chose this word (rather than the flat "sight" or "vision") because of its additional sense, "contemplation," thereby reminding us that murder destroys not merely sight but the mind that contemplates what is seen.

The main development in English (apart from its phonetic changes) was merely a continuation of what had been happening for some centuries: a further expansion of its already oversize vocabulary, both by borrowing and by making new words out of old ones. Many of the borrowings came from Latin, some from Greek, and not a few from other European tongues.

The Latin borrowings, of course, continued a process already operating vigorously in Chaucer's day and earlier, but the source was somewhat different. Whereas Middle English had borrowed mainly from Church

Latin, the new wave of words came rather from the classical Roman writers, whose works had become popular all over western Europe as part of what we now call the Renaissance.

This gradual but profound social and cultural revolution involved, among many other things, the breakup of the old, relatively fixed categories of medieval society ("It has made of yeomen and artificers, gentlemen, and of gentlemen, knights . . .") and, consequently, of medieval thought as well. New social classes—notably, the "gentlemen" of the commercial and manufacturing sectors—were making their weight felt in political and cultural life, new technologies and arts were being developed, a new world was appearing—figuratively in the expanding urban centers, and literally across the Atlantic. To try to make sense of all these novelties, scholars and laymen alike sought out new ideas and theories. One source was the study of the natural world, by such figures as Galileo and the great Italian anatomist Vesalius; in England, by scientists like William Harvey, who discovered the circulation of the blood, and William Gilbert, pioneer in the study of magnetism. Another source was the literature of the classical world, whose rich, sophisticated societies often seemed more "relevant" to the new Europe than its own recent past.

Literate Europeans with a "classical education" read Roman and Greek authors in the original. Others—the great majority—had, like Shakespeare, "small Latin and less Greek," and read the translations that poured in increasing numbers from the multiplying presses. It was, as one would expect, mainly via these translations that the new words entered English, as earlier borrowings had originated in translations from Church Latin. Thus most of them started out as scholarly terms, but many sooner or later passed into the "general" vocabularies of educated (and often uneducated) English-speakers.

"Tonic," for example, was borrowed in the seventeenth century with the meaning "pertaining to tension," which is about the way that doctors still use it. In another century, it had acquired the additional meaning of "restoring the *tone* of the body," which soon begot a noun: the medical "tonic" taken for this purpose. Late in the nineteenth century, one of these tonics, containing quinine, became (with alcoholic additions) a favorite tipple of British pukka sahibs in India and points east—which is essentially the same tonic we buy in six-packs at the supermarket.

The classical borrowings of the sixteenth and seventeenth centuries numbered in the thousands. "Pure" Latin words included "capsule," "dexterity," "agile," "expensive," "habitual," "insane," "excavate" and "meditate." Others reflected earlier Latin borrowings from Greek; they included "atmosphere," "autograph," "climax," "critic," "parasite," "pneumonia" and "skeleton." And a few were taken directly from Greek, such as "anonymous," "catastrophe," "ostracize" and—"tonic."

Interestingly, some of the borrowings were actually reborrowings. A notable example was Greek-Latin *discus,* whose borrowing into Germanic yielded English "dish." A medieval reborrowing, which we find in Chaucer, yielded "desk," while seventeenth-century re-reborrowings gave us both "disk" (i.e., of the sun or moon) and "discus," which at last restored the original Greek sense.

Though Latin was the main source of Renaissance (and post-Renaissance) English borrowing, other important contributions came from its descendants, the Romance tongues, chiefly French. This had, of course, long since disappeared as a spoken language in England, but not a few educated English had picked up at least a smattering of it through travel or reading. Shakespeare had no inhibitions about writing an entire scene of Henry V in French—including some uninhibited French-English puns to tickle sophisticates in the audience. Many of the French borrowings, in turn, had previously been borrowed from Italian or Spanish.

The authentic French words that entered English at this time are a mixed bag; they include *bigot* (originally, a religious hypocrite; later, a religious fanatic, of which there were plenty in France), *detail,* and *choc* (shock—originally, a military encounter). Franco-Italian borrowings, however, often recall the repeated sixteenth-century French invasions of Italy: they include *bataglione,* (French *bataillon*), *bastione/bastion, brigata/ brigade, infanteria/infanterie* and the verb *rebuffare/rebuffer.* Indeed, not a few French infantry brigades and batallions were rebuffed from Italian bastions—often by the Spanish troops which then occupied much of Italy. From these tough opponents the French acquired the *granada/grenade,* which could blast a hole in a *palisada/palisade.*

But English also borrowed directly from Italian and Spanish (and in a few cases from Portuguese). Italy's contributions remind us that the Renaissance began there, bringing it preeminence in the arts and in architecture reflected by such words as *balcone, cupola, portico, cameo, fresco, stucco* and *violino,* along with the *violinista* who played it. These and most other Italian borrowings came either from literary Italian or (what amounts to almost the same thing) the dialects spoken by educated Florentines and Romans. A few, however, came from the version of Italian spoken in the great city at the head of the Adriatic which for most of the Middle Ages was the largest and richest in Europe west of Constantinople. Venice gave us (naturally) the *laguna* in which it and its satellite islands are situated, the *gondola* that plied its waters (from a word meaning "to rock") and a dialect term for a gondola race that is now the yachtsman's regatta. From Venice also is the *ghetto* in which its Jewish population was required to live, and the *casino* ("little house") in which more fortunate Venetians won—or lost—fortunes. The Venetian gold coin called *zecchino* has declined into the glittering sequin that ornaments ladies' garments, while a smaller coin, *gazeta,* gave its name to the gazette purchased with it. "Arsenal," finally, reminds us that Venice's commercial wealth was based on sea power: the Venetian Arzenale was for some centuries the largest naval dockyard in the world.

In contrast with most Italian borrowings, taken from the arts of peace, those from Spanish are more likely to reflect the arts of war, stemming from the long English-Spanish conflict that culminated in the near-destruction of the Spanish *Armada* (fleet). The war was fought by trade *embargos,* as well as by *desperados* who stormed the *barricados* with *bravado.* ("Desperado" originally meant "desperate adventurer," an apt description of such semipiratical English admirals as Drake, Hawkins and Raleigh.)

A large number of borrowings from Spanish and Portuguese, however, reflect the discoveries by these peoples of a host of new birds, beasts, plants and foodstuffs. Some came from Portuguese exploration of West Africa, where they found the native cultivating the *banana* and the *inhame* (/eenyame/—yam), and hunting the improbable-looking *zebra.* (The first two, and possibly the third, are thought to derive from native African words, but these have not been identified with certainty.) The bulk of such exotic borrowings, however, came from the New World, via Spanish.

Some of the new names for new things were simply Spanish coinages. Thus the burrowing creature seemingly clad in plate mail was christened *armadillo,* literally "little armored man," while an American relative of the crocodiles somehow acquired the innocuous title *el lagarto,* the lizard. Usually, however, the Spaniards followed the normal linguistic habit of people in strange lands, borrowing native words and assimilating them to the phonetics of their own tongue.

The first Spanish contact with Native Americans (whom Columbus mistook for Indians) was with the Taino Arawaks of Hispaniola, Cuba, Puerto Rico, Jamaica and the Bahamas. They grew *mahiz,* and also *patatas* (sweet potatoes; the Spanish later applied the same word to the quite different tubers grown in Peru). The Taino also fished from *canoas* and reclined in *hamacas,* smoking rolls of aromatic leaves they called *tabaco* (some dictionaries derive this word, against all probability, from Arabic).

The amiable Arawaks were no match for European arms and diseases; within a few generations they had vanished, though their blood still flows in many natives of the Greater Antilles. The *Caribales* (Caribs) of the Lesser Antilles were a rather tougher proposition, thanks in part, perhaps, to their alleged habit of eating the bodies of slain enemies, which brought a variant of their name, *Canibal,* into Spanish and English. They also, of course, gave their name to the sea that washes the Antilles, and their word *huracan* to the spectacular tempests that still lash its waters every summer.

Cortez' conquest of Mexico, richest of the Native American societies, brought other new words. Notable among them were three food crops, the *cacahuatl* (cacao) tree, whose fruits yielded the brownish paste *chocolatl,* still a prime ingredient in Mexican cookery; the scarlet-fruited *tomatl,* and the oily, pear-shaped *ahuacatl* (literally, "testicle"). The Spaniards, in a fanciful bit of folk etymology, transformed this to *avocado* (literally, "advocate"), from which the English, in an even wilder flight of fancy, contrived "alligator pear"—presumably because the fruit, like the reptile, is tough-skinned and lives in the tropics.

From a much different source, but no less evocative, are the words that reached English from the lowlands (nether lands) across the North Sea, whence the English themselves had come centuries earlier. There was nothing exotic about these words: most of them derived from the everyday needs of trade, mainly in wool and cloth, which even before the Conquest had accounted for most of England's foreign commerce. From the Middle Ages on, moreover, Flemings (natives of modern Belgium and Holland) had migrated into England, often encouraged by the English crown, which valued their clothmaking skills. Other Flemings served as mercenaries in English armies, while Flemish merchants settled in London and other North Sea ports. (A descendant of one such immigrant, Sir Alexander Fleming, would win world reknown as the discoverer of penicillin.) A later wave of immigrants arrived during the sixteenth century, when Spain tried to impose religious conformity on its Flemish dominions by the kind of terrorism shown so vividly in Brueghel's *Slaughter of the Innocents.*

Other contacts came through sailors (until the mid-seventeenth century, most ships plying between England and the Low Countries were Flemish- or German-owned) and soldiers: England and the Netherlands were first allied against Spain and later, when the Spanish threat had receded, fought a war over the control of North Sea shipping.

The North Sea tongues from which English borrowed were Flemish-Dutch (two names for the same language), spoken in modern Holland and Belgium, and the closely related Low German, spoken in the coastal lowlands to the east. For convenience, the entire group of borrowings is sometimes lumped together as "Low Dutch," a term doubly appropriate in that they were far from the elevated, scholarly terms borrowed from Latin; some, as we shall see, were very low indeed.

Among the earliest Low Dutch borrowings were the *pak* or *bale* in which wool was shipped. A little later came the *spole* on which the spun-wool thread was wound, the *wagen* in which the *vrecht* (freight) was transferred from *docke* to *mart* or warehouse, and the *dalers* in which merchants often settled their accounts. (This last was a Dutch abbreviation of *Joachimstaler*, a coin minted at the German silver-mining center of Joachimsthal.) More specialized terms from the textile industry were the *noppe* (nap) and *selfegge* (selvage) of the woven cloth, and the *vollersaarde* (fuller's earth) used to dry-clean it.

Of course, trade flowed both ways. An early import from the Lowlands was air-dried *stockvisch* (stockfish); later came cambric, the fine linen woven at Kamerijk (now French Cambrai), and the coarser linen called *doek* (duck). Still later came *brandewijn* ("burned"—distilled—wine), which English drinkers shortened to "brandy," and another liquor, distilled from grain, that the Dutch called *genever*, from the juniper berries used to flavor it, but which impatient English sots clipped to "gin."

Sailors' lingo contributed such items of ship's *takel* as the *boline*, *boeg* (bow) and *boechspriet* (bowsprit), the *schoop* used for bailing small craft (Dutch SCH is pronounced /sk/) the *boom* to which sails were attached, the verb *splissen* (splice), and various types of craft such as the *sloep, jacht* and *jol* (Dutch J is pronounced /y/). Some enterprising *schippers*, seeking to dodge English customs duties, would *smuggelen* their cargoes by night into English creeks. But a smuggler whose *luk* had run out might *splitten* his *sloep* on a *rif* or sandbank. ("Split," originally a purely maritime term, has since branched out in all directions: a board or a political group can split; profits, stocks or bottles of wine can *be* split; while an extra-small bottle is *a* split.)

Dutch-Flemish soldiers contributed *holster, aenslag* (onslaught), *belegeren* (beleaguer) and *vrijbuiter*, whose freebooting activities had nothing to do with boots but a lot to do with booty. (The same word, after a bewildering series of phonetic and semantic shifts, has ended up in American English as our legislative filibuster—though freebooters in the original sense are also not unknown in those bodies.) When soldiers on *verlof* (furlough) joined Dutch and English sailors to *busen* (booze) over flagons of *brandewijn* and *genever*, they must have raised quite an *oproer*.

The speech of sailors (or soldiers) is, well, salty: many tavern discussions must have touched on *fokkinge* and *kunte*. Equally "low" Dutch contributions were *krappe* and *bugger*, the latter of which the Dutch had earlier borrowed from French. (The full pedigree of this word, starting with Latin *Bulgarus*, Bulgarian, is given in the notes.) Somewhat later, a more respectable segment of society contributed a few terms reflecting Dutch artistic achievements of the seventeenth and eighteenth centuries: the printmaker's *etsinge*, and the artist's *ezel* (literally, "ass"), which like its namesake patiently bore its burden—the canvas on which the painter was rendering a *schets* (sketch) or *lantskap*.

Even discounting the Low Dutch contributions, borrowings into the English vocabulary between 1500 and 1700 numbered more than ten thousand. Not content with this bounty, writers and ordinary folk alike mined their own tongue for even more new words. In part, this process was no more than an unstudied (and usually unconscious) development of simplified English syntax to its logical conclusion. Since nouns, verbs and adjectives had by now lost nearly all their distinctive inflectional endings, a word could easily be shifted from one syntactic category to another with no change (except, for some adjectives, the addition of -y, and for most adverbs, -ly). And this is exactly what happened: nouns became verbs, verbs became nouns, old nouns like "gaud," "gloom," and "shade" begot the new adjectives "gaudy," "gloomy" and "shady," and adjectives at times even became verbs, as with the Franco-Italian borrowing "incarnadine," which Shakespeare made a verb to describe what Macbeth's bloody hands would do to the sea. Some writers went even further, consciously reviving archaic or obsolete words like "astound" and "doom," or simply inventing new ones. Thus "braggadocio," though it sounds like an Italian borrowing, is actually the name that Edmund Spenser gave a braggart in his poem *The Faerie Queen*.

The flood of new words inevitably produced a reaction, in which some critics and writers stigmatized them as "inkhorn terms" (from Latin and Greek), "oversea language" (from the Romance tongues) and archaic "Chaucerisms." As early as 1549, Thomas Chaloner, a writer and translator, belabored writers who "serche out . . . four or fyve disused woords of antiquitee . . . to the end that who so understandeth them maie repute him selfe for more cunnyng and litterate: and who so dooth not shall

. . . esteeme it some high matter, because it passeth his learnyng." The writer who drops in "woords of antiquitee" to flatter or overawe his readers is by no means extinct; William F. Buckley is one name that comes to mind.

Writing a few years later, another literary man, Thomas Wilson, de-nounced the "farre journeyed gentlemen" who, "like as they love to goe in forraine apparrell, so they will pouder their talke with oversea lan-guage." He also paid his respects to those that "wil so Latin their tongues, that the simple . . . thinke surely they speake by some revela-tion." As an example of the latter, he quotes a letter from a gentleman applying for an ecclesiastical benefice; a fragment will suffice: "Pondering and expending and revoluting with my selfe, your ingent affabilities and ingenuous capacity for mundaine affaires, I cannot but celebrate and extol your magnifical dexteritie . . ." Wilson may have invented this particular horrible example, but there can be little doubt that some real gentlemen were expressing themselves in similar "magnifical," Latinate effusions. So, to this day, do many of our lawyers, sociologists and gov-ernmental and corporate bureaucrats.

Insofar as the critics were attacking self-consciously fancy talk, over-loaded with elaborate new terms, one can sympathize with them com-pletely. Wilson, among others, made the additional point that the obses-sive use of new and unfamiliar words made for obscurity, not clarity, and urged that "wee . . . speake as is commonly received: neither seeking to be over fine, nor yet living over-carlesse, using our speeche as most men doe," a sentiment that rings as true today as it did then. Some, however, objected to new words simply because they *were* new, as did the classical scholar Sir John Cheke. "I am of the opinione," he wrote to a literary friend, "that our own tung sholde be written cleane and pure, unmixt and unmangled with borowing of other tungs." The good knight's "opin-ione" would have been more persuasive had not this word, along with "mixt," "mangled" and "pure," come from earlier "borowing."

Eventually, of course, criticism began striking a balance. Thus the writer and translator George Pettie summed up the matter wittily when he noted that if borrowings "should all be counted inkpot termes, I know not how we should speake any thing without blacking our mouths with inke: for what word can be more plaine than this word *plaine,* and yet what can come more neere to the Latine? . . . What more commun than *rare,* or less rare than *commun,* and yet both comminge of the Latine?" He then put his finger on what we now know to be the principle governing all linguistic innovation: "But you wyll say, long use hath made these woords curraunt . . . *why may not use doo as much for these* [newer] *woords . . . ?"* (emphasis added).

Though Pettie did not say so explicitly, he must have known that many of the new words had not been brought into English frivolously, but (in the words of his contemporary, the educator Richard Mulcaster) out of "pure necessitie in new matters"—as, indeed, had been occurring with English and its ancestors ever since the Germanic migration to the Baltic. A case in point is some of the Italian and Spanish military terms already mentioned: the author of a late sixteenth-century treatise, *Discourse of Warres,* noted that for many aspects of the subject "I have no other names than are given by strangers, because there are fewe or none at all in our own language."

Mulcaster, however, went further: English, he declared without apology, acquires new words not only out of "necessitie" but also out of mere "braverie to garnish itself withal." He was echoed by Pettie, who noted that borrowing was "the ready way to inrich our tongue and make it copious, and it is the way which all tongues have taken to inrich themselves." As other critics noted, Latin in particular had enormously "inriched" itself by borrowing from Greek.

English has been enriching and "garnishing" itself through borrowing ever since, and, I think, only a remarkably impoverished or pedantic spirit can object to a new word simply because we don't really need it. To adopt a purely functional view of language, eschewing any ornamentation, is to make the same mistake as Le Corbusier when he defined a house as "a machine to live in"—which may perhaps define a house but certainly not a home. Languages, no more than houses, are mere machines: they are for enjoyment as well as use, and a judicious amount of "garnish" is part of that enjoyment.

Sometimes, of course, the garnish is applied overlavishly, with ornaments ill chosen. But time has a way of taking care of these problems. Sooner or later, either usage makes a new word "curraunt" or disuse makes it obsolete. And the rate of attrition is high: of the more than ten thousand new words brought into English during the sixteenth and seventeenth centuries, only about half are still in use. But it is a valuable half—and not only to scholars. Of the four dozen Latinate terms that Wilson mocked in his anonymous (or fictitious) letter in "magnifical" English, the survivors include such far from scholarly terms as "celebrate," "fertile," "confidence," "native" and "antique."

Why some words survive and others, equally useful (or equally pretentious), perish is, as the philologist Albert C. Baugh reminds us, one of "the things about language that we cannot explain." Occasionally the reason is obvious: Spenser's invention "bellibone" (fair maid, apparently from French *belle et bonne*) vanished within a generation, surely because it sounds like something neither fair nor a maid. But why did "impede" survive and its opposite, "expede," disappear—especially since we have since had to contrive a substitute, "expedite"? If "disagree" and "disabuse" are still acceptable, why not "disaccustom"? Nobody will ever know the answer.

If we can draw a moral from all this, it is perhaps that people who find some new word or usage objectionable might profitably conserve their energies by ignoring it. On past performance, the odds are at least even that before very long the novelty they find so obnoxious will have slipped out of the language as mysteriously as it slipped in. Writers who overload their works with modish, "in" words will always be fair game for the critic —and should be—but the words themselves are likely to confound the most prescient purist: thus the verb "contact" is still going strong after half a century of denunciation.

Just as the growth of printing nourished and was nourished by the growth of literacy, so the expansion of the English vocabulary stimulated and was stimulated by another major sixteenth-century development: the use of English, not simply in poetry and relatively informal prose, but as a medium of learnèd, scholarly discourse. Even in Chaucer's day, almost the whole of what we'd call the academic community was made up of Latin-speaking "clerks" (clerics), whose power in intellectual life was not unconnected with the Church's immense power in economics and politics. It was, of course, Henry VIII who broke that power during the 1530s, by confiscating church lands. At the same time, by cutting the ties of the English Church to Rome, he unwittingly struck a blow at the Roman tongue. Church services were now conducted in English; even more important, the Bible was translated from Latin into English.

In itself, translation meant little: as we know, Wycliffe and his friends had made an English translation almost two centuries earlier, and parts of the Scriptures had been translated into Old English long before that. The new translations, however, were "official," endorsed by both Church and state (except during the brief reign of Mary I, when English Bibles were burned), and were printed in tens of thousands of copies. Any literate Englishman could, and nearly all did, read the Bible in his own tongue. And if English could express those ideas which, in any Christian nation, were still deemed the most important in the world (and express them, moreover, with profound eloquence), who would dare say that any other ideas were beyond its scope?

Those few scholars who did say this were helped by the growing popularity of Latin authors and the expanding formal study of Latin (which, in fact, remained a staple of English secondary and university education almost until today). Latinists who valued their specialized learning, and the academic prestige it supported, often downgraded English as "vulgar," a word whose original meaning, "popular" (as in "Vulgar Latin"), was already shifting to "commonplace" or "unrefined."

Mulcaster among others argued forcefully against such snobbery, noting dryly that even the best Latinists were really more at home in English: "He that understands Latin very well can understand English farre better, if he will confesse the truth, though he can Latin it exceeding well." (Note, by the way, the typically free-and-easy syntax, in which "Latin" serves as both noun and verb.) While not condemning the study of Latin as such, he insisted that to learn it merely as a medium of scholarly discourse was waste motion: "Is it not in dede a mervellous bondage to become servants to one tung for learning sake . . . whereas we maie have the verie same treasur in our own tung, with the gain of most time?" In summary he declared, "I love Rome, but London better, I favor Italie, but England more, I honor the Latin, but I worship the English." There is no language, he declared flatly, that "is better able to utter all arguments, either with more pith, or greater planesse, than our English tung is." Not only was English becoming a great language: increasing numbers of those who used it were beginning to appreciate just how great it was.

The final, and perhaps decisive, blow to Latin was economic. For every Englishman who could read Latin, a dozen could read English, and booksellers (as publishers were then called) naturally were aware of this. As early as 1567, one of them wrote to the author of a Latin manuscript that "though, sir, your book be wise and full of learning, yet peradventure it will not be so salable." This great-great-grandfather of publishers' rejection letters will evoke the sympathy of any author who has faced the complaint that his book is "not so salable." Yet the bookseller had a point: like any modern publisher, he was not in business for his health, let alone the author's. Nor, indeed, were authors unconcerned with this point: they wanted their books to sell, or at least to be widely read. Thus Roger Ascham, as distinguished a classicist as he was an educator, yet wrote of "Englishe matter in the Englishe tongue, for Englishe men," out of concern for "the pleasure or profit of many."

By the end of the century, some writers had become very directly concerned with the "pleasure or profit" not of their readers but of themselves. These were something new on the literary scene: men (not, so far as we know, any women) who made their living—such as it was—from writing. They were the authors of the first "pop" literature: tales of roguery and lovers' misfortunes, broadsides hawked at streetcorners, and even pamphlets on theology, whose sales were swelled by the growing religious controversies among the various shades of "Puritans" (more or less radical protestants) and between them and the conservative Established Church, which though now English in language was, as some saw it, still half-Roman in doctrine.

The quality of the popular tales and doggerel was pretty low for the most part. One critic satirized the hack writer who "sitting in a bawdy house . . . writes of God's judgments," or whose "ballads go out in single sheets, and are chanted from market to market to a vile tune and a worse throat, whilst the poor country wench melts like her butter to hear them," or offers the "stories of some men of Tyburn" (criminals were hanged there, and their supposed life stories were often hawked during their executions) or "monsters out of Germany."

Pop literature has clearly not changed all that much in four hundred years. We still have innumerable stories of rogues and criminals, though they are seldom hanged and sometimes not even caught, and certainly no shortage of monsters, though more often from outer space than from Germany. And the flick of a switch will bring us the airborne ballads of many a singing group, chanted to a vile tune and a worse throat, that still melt some wenches like butter.

Some Elizabethan pop writers, like some of their modern counterparts, wrote junk because they could do no better, but all of them wrote it because it was the only way to keep bread and cheese on the family table. The educated audience for more sophisticated books was still small, and writing for it remained essentially what it had been for Chaucer: an avocation for those with some other source of income. Even Shakespeare, that literary Everest, made most of his modest fortune as a theatrical producer, not from the printed editions of his plays. His younger contemporary, Ben Jonson, called poetry "a mean mistress," while another poet, Michael Drayton, denounced the publishers as "a company of base knaves, whom I both scorn and kick at"—a thought that has at least crossed the minds of many writers since.

Though the professional writers turned out little but junk, it would be a mistake to leave the matter there. Manure is junk of a sort, but it can make flowers grow. Similarly, it is at least arguable that the Elizabethan outpouring of pop literature helped form the soil out of which the truly great writers of the age could blossom in all their glory. Some, indeed, borrowed from the "pops" directly: Marlowe lifted the plot of his *Doctor Faustus* from one of the German horror stories mentioned earlier. More broadly, pop literature, by intensifying people's acquaintance with and awareness of words and their use, helped some of them toward an appreciation of those who could use words supremely well.

Be that as it may, there can be no doubt that a sizable part of the nation became, for a while, positively drunk on words. As the modern writer John Moore has said, "philosophers were splitting hairs with them, actors were gloriously ranting them, poets were doing conjuring tricks with them and prose writers . . . were so bemused by the sound of them that they let the sense go hang. Mountebanks at streetcorners invented new words for old ills." According to a contemporary commentator, the very beggars "select and choose out words of vehemence, where by they . . . adjure the goer-by to pity their cases." In this sort of atmosphere, it is not too hard to comprehend the long line of Elizabethan and post-Elizabethan literary marvels—Spenser, Sydney, Dekker, Marlowe, Jonson and, overtopping them all, the butcher's son from Stratford, whom Jonson, himself no mean playwright, would memorialize as "The applause, delight, the wonder of our stage."

Shakespeare is unique in the original sense of that rather hackneyed word: one of a kind. Neither England nor any other land has produced his equal, and if the English tongue has a claim to being the greatest communicative instrument ever devised, the fact that it served his genius is surely a major reason. Admittedly, England has produced only one Shakespeare, but, as has been said, no other country can claim even that many.

There is little one can say about the man that has not been said already —often several times: he has supported a major academic industry for some generations. Perhaps his most obvious quality is the extent of his vocabulary: more than twenty thousand words all told, ranging from the most intricate Latinate and Romance polysyllables to the simplest homespun terms—"taffeta phrases, silken terms precise" contrasting with "russet yeas and nays and honest kersey noes" (russet and kersey were the plain cloth that clothed the commoners, as silk and taffeta did their betters). Consider Macbeth, horrified at his murder of Duncan:

> *Will all great Neptune's ocean wash this blood*
> *Clean from my hand? No, this my hand will rather*
> *The multitudinous seas incarnadine . . .*

The magnificence of "great Neptune's ocean" gives way to the simple "wash this blood clean from my hand," and surges to a new peak in "the multitudinous seas incarnadine." The multitudinous seas—wave after wave after wave to the horizon that beckoned Drake and the other great adventurers, and the ornate adjective, "incarnadine," transmuted into a verb by a stroke of the pen. Or the tortured mutterings of the sleepwalk-ing Lady Macbeth, whose lyrical, near-hysterical "All the perfumes of Arabia will not sweeten this little hand" gives way to the monosyllabic, childlike—and therefore doubly chilling—wonderment of "Yet who would have thought the old man to have had so much blood in him?"

Reading and rereading Shakespeare, one is perpetually struck by how casually he tosses off some of his best phrases. In *Measure for Measure,* Beatrice, one of the cleverest and therefore most delightful heroines that ever trod stage, says lightly, "There was a star danced, and under that was I born" (how can one *not* fall in love with a woman who could say that?). Hamlet, swapping jokes with the courtiers who, he senses, seek to manip-ulate him as passively as the fretted lute, puns "For though you can fret me, yet you cannot play me!" In just eight words of dialogue Shakespeare can chill our blood with looming horror:

> *Macbeth:* Duncan comes here tonight.
> *Lady Macbeth:* And when goes hence?

Paralleling Shakespeare's felicities of sense are those of sound—his exploitation of the rhythmic possibilities of English, which in turn depend largely on the varying lengths of English syllables. As we have seen earlier, the phonetic structure of English is considerably more complex than that of most languages, with its syllables ranging from the simple vowel or vowel-plus-consonant type to a "double" vowel (diphthong) sandwiched between four or more consonants. In languages such as Spanish and Japanese, where most syllables are of the simple types, poetry has a flowing, "musical" quality, pleasing enough to some ears, yet lacking in rhythmic shifts and variety.

The same was true to a considerable degree of Middle English. In Modern English, by contrast, the loss of inflectional endings, along with other phonetic changes, has, as it were, repeatedly compressed two sylla-bles into one. An example is Chaucer's *sma-le fou-les,* whose four syllables have shrunk to two in its modern equivalent, "small fowls," which, how-ever, still occupy the same rhythmic "space" as before. The length of modern English syllables ranges from the quick, unaccented "a" through "put," "burr," "rude," "rolls" and "strolls"—and there are probably longer monosyllables I haven't thought of.

See, then, how Shakespeare uses English rhythms to underscore the sense of what he is saying. Here is Macbeth, tasting the bitterness of the tyrant's life:

> *Tomorrow and tomorrow and tomorrow*
> *Creeps in this petty pace from day to day . . .*

where the equal syllables of the repeated "tomorrow," echoing the endless, tedious flow of time, contrast with the crawling, drawn-out "creeps." And here is Anthony, addressing the corpse of Caesar:

> *Oh mighty Caesar, dost thou lie so low,*
> *Are all thy conquests, glories, triumphs, spoils*
> *Shrunk to this little measure?*

Note how the accelerating beat of "conquests, glories, triumphs" pauses on the longer "spoils" and is cut short by "shrunk," as Caesar himself has been cut short. Or Richard II, defeated and stripped of his crown:

> *You may my glories and my state depose*
> *But not my griefs; still am I king of those*

where the majestic rhythm of the first line is halted by the long-drawn-out "griefs," followed by the prolonged, echoing L's of "still," telling us that for Richard "still" means "forever."

Or, turning to the sonnets,

> *This time of year thou may'st in me behold*
> *When yellow leaves, or none or few do hang*
> *Upon those boughs that shake against the cold,*
> *Bare, ruined choirs, where once the sweet birds sang.*

The smoothness of the first line gives way to the syncopation of "yellow leaves" and "or none or few," climaxing in the jagged rhythm of "shake against the cold," like leafless branches trembling in the wind, followed by the drawn-out "bare" and "choirs," as bleak as the ruined monastery churches that Henry VIII had left scattered across England, and giving added poignancy to the simplicity of "where once the sweet birds sang."

No less extraordinary than the richness of Shakespeare's words in both sound and sense, for which the language itself is surely entitled to some credit, is the richness of the ideas he clothes in them—for which, perhaps, the intellectual climate of his England also deserves some credit. Among other things, he was an intensely political writer—not, of course, in the sense of peddling some political thesis, but rather in his perennial concern with the basic questions of politics: what is the proper way to run a country, how is power to be transferred (a very live issue in a land whose virgin queen had no direct heirs), and how does an honorable man deal with an unjust or incompetent government? We see all these questions raised explicitly in the great series of historical plays, *Richard II, Henry IV,* parts 1 and 2, and *Henry V.*

It is in the third of these that we find a dialogue which tells us much about English political attitudes, then and now. Henry V has been crowned, and the Chief Justice of England, who had had him arrested and jailed during his dropout days as Prince Hal, is understandably nervous now that the dropout holds royal power. Yet he speaks out boldly, saying to the king's face that he was simply upholding the king's law, and would do so again. The king replies, magnanimously,

> *Happy am I, that have a man so bold*
> *That dares do justice on my proper son;*
> *And not less happy, having such a son*
> *That would deliver up his greatness so*
> *Into the hands of justice.*

Now it is doubtful whether the historical Henry V ever said anything of the sort—or would have, in such circumstances. The point is rather that both Shakespeare and his audience believed that this was what a proper king should and would say: that even the heir to the throne should be subject to the law, like anyone else. It was not an idea that would have been widely accepted in most other parts of Europe.

The concern with political fundamentals runs through most of the poet's other serious plays: the problem of an able but overambitious ruler (*Julius Caesar*), the problem of a murderous usurper (*Macbeth*) and the same problem seen from a quite different perspective in Shakespeare's most complex and intellectually sophisticated play, *Hamlet.*

The Freudians have done an ill turn to both the Prince of Denmark and his author by emphasizing Hamlet's alleged desire to sleep with his mother, rather than the very real and complicated moral and political dilemmas he faced. Claudius, though certainly something of a sensualist, is portrayed as a competent and respected ruler, *and accepted as king by the Danes.* His marriage to the widowed queen was arguably "incestuous" by Church law—as Henry VIII had claimed of his own first marriage—but not, apparently, by the law of Denmark, whose nobles, the king notes, "have freely gone with us along" in this.

Comes now Hamlet, an intellectual, a humanist and a prince. He resents the man who has supplanted his own beloved father, and resents even more his mother's hasty remarriage, as would almost anyone—with no need for Freudian complexes. Suddenly he is told, privately, by something claiming to be his father's ghost, that the king he so dislikes is in fact a murderer and a usurper. Being an intelligent, sensitive man, however, he knows well enough that the "message" may not be from the dead but from his own living resentment. Being a politically astute man, he also knows that with no evidence but the secret "testimony" of a ghost, he cannot move openly against an anointed king. There were no impeachment laws in the sixteenth century: a ruler could be removed only by coup d'état or assassination. A coup would need the support of powerful nobles, but they, in the person of Polonius, support the king. As for assassination, Hamlet knows what any Englishman with any knowledge of English history knew: once you start killing people, it's hard to stop. Moreover, either a coup or assassination risks bringing down the whole structure of government, leaving the land open to foreign enemies. Which, in the event, is what happens: with king, queen and crown prince all dead, Denmark is taken over by Fortinbras of Norway.

In such circumstances, only a fool would charge ahead thoughtlessly, and Hamlet is anything but a fool. Torn not simply by his own psychological conflicts but also by real dilemmas, he hesitates—and at last is forced to act, too late.

It would be a ludicrous oversimplification to call *Hamlet* merely a political drama; it is that, and a personal tragedy, and a comedy of manners, and several other things. But it is even more ludicrous to describe the prince, as did the prologue to Olivier's magnificent film portrayal, as "a man who could not make up his mind." This proverbial indecisiveness has even given us the adjective "Hamlet-like"; a juster appraisal would recognize that Hamlet was Hamlet-like mainly because he faced impossibly difficult moral and political choices.

Even beyond Shakespeare's sensitivity to language, and to political-moral problems, is his humanity, which more than anything else makes him "not of an age, but for all time." In his early plays, to be sure, the characters are often stock white hats and black hats, but as he mastered his trade they acquired all the complexitites and inconsistencies of real life. However admirable, they can sometimes be foolish or vacillating; however despicable, they retain the virtue of courage, like Macbeth.

Shylock, for example, is from one angle a half-comic, half-sinister figure—which is about the best a Jew could hope for in the Christian world of that day. (The protagonist of Marlowe's *Jew of Malta* is totally sinister.) But Shylock is something more: a man who has been deeply wounded by the arrogant, self-righteous Antonio, and whose villainy is explicitly portrayed as the consequence of his injuries. Macbeth, ready to murder for ambition's sake, hesitates at the crucial moment, and even his chilling wife cannot at last sustain in sleep her steely waking composure. Falstaff, that cowardly, gluttonous braggart, is given one of the play-wright's most moving speeches, in which he reflects on the brutality of war and the "honor" that goads men to it:

> Honor pricks me on. Yea, but how if honor prick me off when I come on— how then? Can honor set to a leg? no: or an arm? no: or take away the grief of a wound? no. Honor hath no skill in surgery, then? no. What is honor? a word. What is in that word honor? . . . air. A trim reckoning! Who hath it? he that died o'Wednesday. Doth he feel it? no. Doth he hear it? no. It is insensible, then? yea, to the dead.

Soon after, surveying the contorted features of the slain Sir Walter Blunt, this gross, shrewd old man observes, "I like not such grinning honor as Sir Walter hath. Give me life." The whole passage should be required daily reading for those modern statesmen who peddle brinksmanship or worse in alleged defense of "that word honor."

Viewing men and women from all sides, Shakespeare naturally sees their sexual side, and not a few of his lines, properly understood, are among the bawdiest (or, if you like, the dirtiest) in English, and as such have deeply perturbed some eminent critics. The prissy John Dryden, for example, though recognizing the poet's greatness, deplored his wit as "not of gentlemen; there was ever something that was ill-bred and clown-ish in it." This, mind you, was in the late 1600s, when such "gentlemen" as the Earl of Rochester were turning out poems and plays that even today would win a triple-X rating.

Other critics have "excused" Shakespeare's bawdry as mere pandering to the "groundlings" (lower-class members of the audience), as if the quality never thought or talked about sex. Finally, in 1818, an English editor, Thomas Bowdler, decided to act instead of criticizing: he prepared a sanitized edition of the plays omitting "those words and expressions . . . which cannot with propriety be read aloud in a family"—and in so doing, gave English a new verb.

The truth is that Shakespeare's sexual humor crops up at every social level: not merely in the mouths of his clowns, but from Hamlet, who jokes with Ophelia about "country matters" (with the obvious pun very much intended), and even from the highborn, virginal Beatrice. It is specially rife among the young nobles of Verona, in that lyrical tragedy of young love *Romeo and Juliet,* ranging from Mercutio's brilliantly outrageous reply to a request for the time ("the bawdy hand of the dial is now upon the prick of noon") to rather labored sexual puns which remind us that Romeo and his good buddies were, after all, teenagers.

If Shakespeare, the universal man, is one towering peak of English literature, the other—no less universal in a very different way—is the King James Bible, published in 1608. Here are no quips, sexual or scholarly, nor any taffeta phrases, but the unadorned Word of God, couched in the plainest, homeliest English: where Shakespeare used over twenty thousand words, the King James makes do with less than half that number. But what words they are, and how splendidly compounded!

The English Bible is, of course, not an "original" work but a translation, from Hebrew (Old Testament) and from the Greek *koine* (New Testament), and it would take a pretty sophisticated knowledge of both tongues to say how much of its eloquence stems from the original and how much from its translators. At the very least it must surely equal the originals; it is impossible to imagine anyone saying better, in any tongue, what the King James says so well. For example, Ruth's reply to the widowed Naomi, who has urged her to return to her own people:

> *Entreat me not to leave thee,*
> *Or to return from following after thee,*
> *For whither thou goest, I will go,*
> *And where thou lodgest, I will lodge;*
> *Thy people shall be my people,*
> *And thy God, my god;*
> *Where thou diest, will I die*
> *And there will I be buried.*

The "parallel" construction, in paired lines, is a common feature of ancient Hebrew poetry, but not, I think, the subtle variations within and among the parallels, like variations in music: *"Whither* thou goest" shifting to *"Where* thou lodgest," "Thy people shall be my people" contracting to "Thy God, my God," "Where thou diest" recapitulating the earlier theme of "Where thou lodgest," but with *"I will* lodge" inverted to *"will I* die," while the final "and there will I be buried," breaking at last from the strict parallelism and shifting from active to passive voice, serves as a sort of coda.

Or feel the anthem-like beat of Isaiah's magnificent vision, as relevant today as when James' canons and bishops translated it "out of the original tongues":

> *They shall beat their swords into ploughshares,*
> *And their spears into pruning hooks,*
> *Nation shall not lift up sword against nation,*
> *Neither shall they learn war any more.*

Like Shakespeare, the Bible can say a lot in a few words; it manages to sum up the whole moral duty of mankind in eleven:

> *. . . to do justly,*
> *and to love mercy,*
> *and to walk humbly . . .*

One could write volumes on the subject and get no nearer the heart of the matter: justice, impossible to define precisely, yet something nearly all of us intuitively know lies at the root of social relations; mercy, because simple justice is not always enough ("Use every man according to his deserts," says Hamlet to the devious Polonius, "and who should scape flogging?" Who indeed?). Justice is the fair bargain between buyer and seller, utterly essential in human relationships, but mercy is the gift whose cost we do not count. And, finally, humility, which I take to be a reminder that we are, after all, not gods or God, but men and women, and therefore fallible; that our estimates of what is truly just or truly merciful are liable to error, and that we owe our fellows that extra bit of consideration which leaves margin for that error. (As Oliver Cromwell a generation or so later would thunder to his fellow parliamentarians, "I beseech ye, consider that ye may be mistaken!")

The companion to the Authorized Version of the Bible, and its equal in literary power, is the Book of Common Prayer, largely the work of the religious martyr Thomas Cranmer (as the King James, though produced by a committee, depended heavily on the pioneering translation of another martyr, William Tyndale). For some, indeed, its marvelous words strike even closer to the heart because they are linked with life's most intense moments, from the baptismal "renounce the devil and all his works" to "With this ring, I thee wed" to the final "Earth to earth, ashes to ashes, dust to dust."

Incredibly, even the Bible has not escaped the bowdlerizers. In 1833, Noah Webster produced an edited version in which "give suck" was replaced by "nourish" (one wonders how the ladies of his denomination nourished their babies) and "stones" (testicles) by "peculiar members." A Quaker Bible published a few years earlier did not go quite that far, but did segregate from the rest of the text those passages "unsuitable for a mixed audience." Since these earnest Christians surely believed the Bible to be the Word of God, one is forced to conclude that they considered God to be in the dirty-book business.

Sadly, none of the subsequent Biblical translations have come anywhere near the power of the King James. Twice during the past century have church committees tried to update the language of the older work and make its sense reflect modern knowledge of the ancient tongues. Both times thay have produced versions that are scholarly, modern and flat. Ruth now says "Entreat me not to leave you, or to return from following you; for where you go I will go and where you lodge I will lodge . . ." The words are there, but not the music.

Why these modern translations have fallen so far short of what they could be is beyond the scope of this book. Why the King James did *not* fall short, but remains, like Shakespeare, not of an age but for all time, is surely due, among other things, to its appearance at a particular stage in the development of English, summed up four hundred years ago by Richard Mulcaster. "I take this present period of our English tung," he wrote, "to be the verie height thereof. . . . Whatsoever shall becom of the English state, the English tung cannot prove fairer, then it is at this daie." To which all of us, Christians and unbelievers alike, can surely cry "Amen!"

8. A SEARCH FOR ORDER

Trying to Make English Behave

Some method should be thought on for ascertaining and fixing our language forever. . . . I see no absolute necessity why any language should be perpetually changing.

—JONATHAN SWIFT (1712)

. . . sounds are too volatile and subtile for legal restraints; to enchain syllables and to lash the wind are equally the undertakings of pride, unwilling to measure its desires by its strength.

—SAMUEL JOHNSON (1755)

THE seventeenth century brought abrupt, often wrenching and sometimes bloody changes to England, changes that finally confirmed the basic character of English government: limited, not absolute in its powers. The same changes (though no one suspected it) would in the next century also confirm the English tongue in *its* basic character: plastic, irrepressible and more than a little anarchic. Just as the Stuart kings tried and failed to make the English obey their arbitrary orders, so, half a century later, some eminent writers and critics would try and fail to make the English language obey their arbitrary rules.

James I, first of the Stuarts to rule England (he was James VI of Scotland), managed in less than a quarter century to infuriate his subjects more than all his Tudor predecessors (save only the fanatical Mary) put together. In part, this was simply bad luck: Elizabeth I was an exceedingly tough act to follow. Mainly, however, it was the man himself: intelligent, well educated but (as a much later poet would put it) "learnèd in all things, wise in none"—the classic case, in fact, of a man with brains but very little sense. At a time when even modified absolutism was going out of fashion in England, James actually sought to outdo his hardnosed Tudor predecessors in this respect, but without the hard common sense that had let them get away with it. Henry VII, though he had seized the crown by force, preferred to hold it by maneuver, connivery and a few judicious judicial murders. His son, one of the most imperious kings in

English history, was not so imperious as to forget that his subjects could be pushed just so far. Finally, Henry VIII's younger daughter, Elizabeth, got her way through a combination of brains, blarney and bullying. If argument failed, she fell back on feminine charm or, as a last resort, her superb command of English in the abusively imperative mood: Gloriana in a rage could reduce strong men to tears.

James, with no firsthand knowledge of the English (he had spent his first thirty-five years in Scotland), sought to rule them by the French theory that kings were not merely anointed by God but were responsible to Him and nobody else. It was not a script that had ever played well in England; in the seventeenth century, with the middle classes yearly growing in wealth, self-confidence and political savvy, it soon had the audience muttering and eventually booing. James himself managed to rule without Parliament for most of his reign, and died in his bed. His son, Charles I, was not so lucky: his father had sown the wind, and he reaped the whirlwind—a civil war that cost him his head.

In Henry IV, Shakespeare could declare, to general approbation, that even the heir to the throne was not free to do anything he pleased; at Charles' trial for high treason in 1649, Parliament applied the same rule to the throne itself. Charles, indeed, correctly protested that there was no law under which he could be tried; the revolutionary tribunal that convicted him ensured that from then on there would be.

For nearly twenty years, revolutionary England managed without a king, ruled first by parliament, then by a minority parliament purged of its right-wing members, an event that gave "purge" its modern, political sense. (Unlike many modern purges, however, this one was bloodless; the ousted members lost their seats but kept their heads.) At last, when factions in and out of parliament grew too contentious, Oliver Cromwell took over as a somewhat reluctant military dictator, ruling as Lord Protector from 1653 to 1658. His son and successor, Richard, was not the man his father was (he was known, in fact, as "Queen Dick"); after two years of mounting confusion, the exiled son of Charles I was recalled to the throne as Charles II.

On the face of it, nothing had changed; in fact, almost everything had. Charles II, fortunately for himself, was also not the man his father was, but shrewd, flexible and gifted with a sense of humor. Urged by his brother to rule in the old, highhanded Stuart fashion, the former exile remarked with a grim smile, "Do you go on your travels, brother; I have already been on mine." When brother succeeded to the throne as James II, he tried the experiment, and was indeed sent on his travels—permanently—by the "Glorious Revolution" of 1688, which put an end to the Stuart dynasty and set William and Mary on the throne. The revolution was not only glorious but also bloodless—thereby testifying that the real power in England indeed lay with parliament, not with any king.

It has remained there ever since: for three centuries, English political conflicts (and there have been plenty of them) have centered on who should control parliament, and in whose interest. And they have been fought out, almost always with words, not weapons, on the common ground shared by virtually all Englishmen and -women: whoever holds the power is subject to the limits imposed by law and custom.

In one dizzying half century, England had swung from near-absolutism to parliamentary moderation to parliamentary dictatorship to military dictatorship to cautious monarchy to incautious monarchy to limited, constitutional monarchy. Those who valued money or social prestige found political agility essential. As early as 1678, the sardonic Samuel Butler could write:

> *What makes all doctrines plain and clear?*
> *About two hundred pounds a year.*
> *And that which was proved true before*
> *Proved false again? Two hundred more.*

A generation or two later, taverns rang with the tale of the surefooted clergyman whose only religious principle was "That whatsoever king may reign/ I'll still be Vicar of Bray, sir!" In such an atmosphere, not a few people began to feel that the important thing about government was that it should be orderly and stable, whatever its precise political complexion. And certain literary men, perceiving what they deemed to be an unsettling amount of change in the English language, became concerned about making it equally orderly and stable. Or trying to; stable government, it turned out, was more easily come by.

The question of imposing some sort of order on the rambunctious English tongue had been raised as far back as 1550, in the area of spelling. Nowadays, if we want to know how to spell a word, we look it up in the dictionary; in the sixteenth century, there was no such resource, and many people tended to spell pretty much as the spirit moved them at the moment: the writer Robert Greene, in one of his popular pamphlets on "coney catching" (we'd say "trimming a mark" or, more formally, "fleecing a victim") managed to spell "coney" nine different ways.

Most of the time, things weren't as bad as that. The influence of printing had already established a considerable area of common custom in orthography (the study or science of spelling)—for example, the use of the "silent E" to indicate differences in the length and quality of vowels (e.g., rat/rate, bit/bite). Unfortunately, however, printing had come in before the Great Vowel Shift was complete, so that printed books tended to reflect the pronunciation of 1500 rather than 1550. As Benjamin Franklin remarked much later, "the orthography of our language began to be fixed too soon."

The partial divorce between sound and spelling led a number of scholars to devise schemes whereby English could be spelled as it was spoken. None of them succeeded because, in the words of one reformer, of "their differing so farre from the old." And there was no way out of it: English speech in 1550 already differed pretty "farre" from that of 1500, and changing orthography to reflect those differences would have meant forcing writers and printers to unlearn the habits built up over half a century. And neither then nor later did anyone in England have either the authority or the power to do this; it would have taken a military dictator like the much later Kemal Ataturk, who in the 1920s forced Turkey to shift from the Arabic to the Roman alphabet.

Eventually Richard Mulcaster, with his usual common sense, declared publicly that giving English a truly phonetic spelling was a lost cause: every attempt to impose radical new schemes against established custom "hath alwaie mist, with loss of labor." Which has not, unfortunately, deterred various scholars, critics and cranks from periodically tackling spelling reform. Their schemes have been rationalized on various grounds: that English spelling is altogether irrational; that it is the least phonetic in the world; that devising a truly phonetic spelling is practicable, and that doing so would be a Good Thing, since it would save who knows how many child-hours a year in our schools. In fact, every one of these statements is false—indeed, Mulcaster saw through two of them four hundred years ago.

English spelling is obviously irrational in spots; a few minutes' thought will supply any number of examples of the same sound being spelled differently ("meet" and "meat") or different sounds being spelled the same ("meat" and "great"). One can even conjure up imaginary monsters like GHOTI, which spells "fish"—GH as in "touGH," O as in "wOmen," TI as in "moTIon." But amid the apparent madness of our spelling there is actually a great deal of method. "Feet," "beet" and "discreet" are not only spelled like "meet" but rhyme with it, and the same goes for "meat," "heat" "seat" and "beat," and a score of other phonetically consistent spellings. No doubt it is ridiculous that GH should ever spell /f/, but it almost always *does* spell it (when used at the end of a word), if it is pronounced at all. (The only exception I can think of offhand is "hiccough"—which is now often spelled "hiccup.") And TION always spells /shun/.

Whether English spelling is *more* irrational than that of any other language is arguable, but it is certainly not alone in its irrationality. The French, for instance, manage to spell the simple sound /o/ in eight different ways, though five are used only at the ends of words (the spellings in question are O, AU, EAU, -OT, -OS, -AUT, -AUX and -EAUX). And the few Irish who can write their ancestral tongue, *Gaedhlige* (Gaelic), use an orthography even madder than our own. "O'Flaherty" is *O Flaithbherataigh*, "O'Shea" is *O Seaghdha* and James Joyce would have spelled his name *Seamus Seoigheach* had he written in *Gaedhlige* rather than English.

The mere mechanics of contriving a truly phonetic spelling for English are forbiddingly difficult because, as Mulcaster noted, "letters can express sounds . . . no fuller than the pencil can the form and lineaments of the face." This is especially true of English, because its sounds considerably outnumber the available letters, meaning that "phonetic English" would have to employ perhaps a dozen additional—and unfamiliar—ones. Alternatively, we could employ the International Phonetic Alphabet, which has the advantage of being familiar to philologists around the world, and the disadvantage of being unfamiliar to almost everyone else. To write in the IPA aʊə ˈspeliŋ iz moʊst knˈfjuziŋ ("our spelling is most confusing") would be even *more* confusing to everyone but the experts; in fact, every one of us would have to relearn reading, at a cost of who knows how many hundreds of millions of man- and woman-hours.

Moreover, before embarking on any such project for spelling the way we pronounce, we must consider another question: Who's "we"? The vehicle that most of us drive about in is a car to most Americans and Canadians, but a *cah* in New York, a *caa* (with a long flat A) in Boston, something like a *cau* in London, a *carrh* in Edinburgh, a *cyah* in Mississippi, and God only knows what in Sydney or Cape Town. The Texas dressmaker who uses *pens* to *pen* up the *him* is matched by the New Englander who'll tell you that Cape *Caud* is surrounded by *wotta,* and my wife's Aunt Janie from Liverpool, who used to make *loovly spoonge-*cake. There are some twenty distinctive English dialects knocking about the world; are we to devise a different spelling for every one of them?

But let us ignore that. Let us suppose that somehow all we English-speakers have reached agreement on one dialect that will serve as the basis for a truly phonetic English spelling. Let us suppose that we have further agreed on the details of a phonetic spelling for that dialect, and that as of, say, January 1, 2000, all children in the English-speaking world will be taught that system and no other, and all books will use the new spelling. The inevitable result would be that well before January 1, 2100, every English book published before the year 2000 would be obsolete, readable only by specialists: Shakespeare, the King James Bible, Jane Austen, Dickens, Mark Twain, Hemingway and Virginia Woolf would be as inaccessible to our great-grandchildren as Chaucer is to us today. Unless, of course, all their books were reprinted in the new spelling, at a cost of who knows how many *billions* of man-hours.

Finally, having hypothetically done all this, we should, in another couple of centuries, have to do it all over again; indeed, Mulcaster recognized four centuries ago that one century's phonetic spelling is another's arbitrary spelling. For proof one need only glance at Chaucer, whose spelling (if you understand its conventions) conveys quite accurately the sounds of Middle English, yet renders a quite different set of sounds if read according to our own conventions.

For a rational perspective on our admittedly less than rational spelling, we need to ask what spelling, and writing generally, is supposed to accomplish. The answer, as true when writing was invented some five thousand years ago as it is today, is that writing bridges time and space: it enables people to "speak" beyond the range of their own voices and the span of their own lifetimes. Written English still serves these purposes, enabling London to write letters to Sidney and San Francisco and Dallas to cut deals with Aberdeen and New Delhi, and all of them to enjoy the riches our writers have heaped up over the past four centuries and will continue to pile up in the future. And it does this formidable job not in spite of its spelling but because of it, in the sense that no radical revision of English orthography, however scientifically contrived, could do it half so well, if at all.

Though phonetic English spelling is (as Mulcaster long ago recognized) an impossible dream, uniform spelling is not. Writing communicates across time and space because it employs a code, however imperfect, for translating sounds into symbols and vice versa. And clearly communication will be easier, quicker and more accurate if everyone is using the same code. In the seventeenth century, nobody put the matter quite like that, but the advantages of uniform spelling were so obvious that by the middle of the century it had been virtually accomplished—not by any man's decree, but through the gradual, unspoken agreement of writers, editors, printers, critics and schoolmasters. Not for the first time, and certainly not for the last, the English had muddled through to an imperfect but serviceable solution.

If a uniform system for translating sounds into symbols is invaluable, then so, surely, is a uniform system for combining words into statements —that is, a uniform syntax. Like uniform spelling, this was (and is) a complicated question, since even in the seventeenth century English dialects varied somewhat in syntax (though less, I think, than in phonetics). Indeed, there seems to have been some variation, or at least ambiguity, even within some dialects, to the point where the poet Dryden could complain in 1679, "I am often put to a stand, in considering whether what I write be the idiom of the country, or false grammar."

What gave the question of true or false grammar a special urgency was the continued expansion of literacy and printing. By 1700, at least half the adult population of England could read, and the number of books printed each year was probably at least four times what it had been in 1600 (the number of *copies* printed had of course increased even more). The next half century saw the appearance of printed magazines and newspapers. And writers for all these "media" (to apply a twentieth-century word to an eighteenth-century phenomenon) wanted what every writer still wants: to be read and understood.

If, in 1700, you were chatting with another resident of your native town or village, understanding was no problem: both of you would almost certainly use the same syntax, acquired in childhood, and any unclarity of meaning could be quickly resolved by asking, "What do you mean?" The writer preparing his copy for the printer was in quite a different situation: he was addressing himself to people he had never seen and in all likelihood never would see. If they found his syntax obscure, they could not cross-question him, but would likely damn him for an ignoramus and resolve never to read him again.

Seen in this light, the problem of distinguishing true from false grammar (or, as we now say, good English from bad) was obviously a real and important one. Unfortunately, efforts to solve it became entangled in all sorts of irrelevant matters: social snobbery and the British class system, the pulling and hauling of political factions, and the desire of some eminent Englishmen to stop the clock of history and return to the Good Old Days.

The decades after the Restoration in fact saw a series of proposals to standardize not only English syntax but English vocabulary as well. The instrument was to be a royal academy, modeled on the newly formed Académie Française, whose declared aim was to work "with all possible care and diligence to give definite rules to our language." An English academy could surely do as well, and once the rules had been drawn up, that would be that. In the words of Jonathan Swift, the most distinguished proponent of the scheme, "some method should be thought on for ascertaining and fixing our language forever."

Swift complained that during the Revolution English had been corrupted by "an infusion of Enthusiastick jargon" (the language of radical religious enthusiasts whom we'd call counterculturalists); he was no happier with the aristocratic supporters of the Restoration, whose "licentiousness . . . from infecting our religious and morals, fell to corrupting our language." Hence the need for an academy that would "fix" the language in perpetuity, if possible returning it to the Good Old Days of a century earlier, before all these unsettling social and linguistic changes had occurred. (Ironically, some critics of those earlier days had seen *Chaucer's* English as the standard from which the language had been "corrupted"; equally, a century after Swift other critics sought to return to the English of *his* day.) "I see no reason," he wrote, "why any language should be perpetually changing."

Now Swift, one of the best-read men of his time, knew perfectly well that his English was not the English of Shakespeare, which in turn was not the English of Chaucer. How on earth could he have supposed that a language which had been "perpetually changing" in the past could be stopped from doing so in the future?

When a brilliant man embraces an evidently ridiculous literary scheme, one may reasonably suspect that he has something on his mind beside literature. What Swift had in mind was the state of the English nation—politics, manners and morals—all of which had changed repeatedly in his lifetime and, in his view, seldom for the better. A Tory by conviction and a pessimist by temperament, he increasingly saw change itself as the enemy. When he declared that "it is better a language should not be wholly perfect than that it should be perpetually changing" he could with equal conviction have said the same thing about government.

In savage satires like *Gulliver's Travels* (which in its unexpurgated form is far from the kiddies' book it is usually considered today) he sought to rally public opinion against social change; in his proposal for an academy he sought to enlist the Tory government in the task of stopping linguistic change. And, like some modern intellectuals, he was prepared to help the government do its duty, for a suitable consideration.

Dryden, an earlier partisan of an English academy, had already noted rather disingenuously that the Académie Française had been "indowe'd with large privileges" by the French king, Louis ("*I* am the State") XIV. In 1712, Swift, in a long and obsequious letter to the Earl of Oxford, Lord High Treasurer of England, staked his own claim to similar privileges. Praising the earl for his "publick thrift" (we'd say "balancing the budget"), he still urged him to set aside some of the money saved for pensions (we'd say "grants") to literary men of distinction who could "discover a Vein of true and noble thinking." Louis XIV, he noted significantly, "bestows about half a dozen pensions to learned Men in several parts of Europe, and perhaps a dozen in his own kingdom." One wonders what Swift the social satirist would have said to Swift the pension-hunting sycophant had they met under other circumstances; perhaps what Swift himself had written a few years earlier: "Satire is a sort of glass, wherein beholders do generally discover everybody's face but their own."

Swift and other Tory intellectuals had issued the challenge; one John Oldmixon, "in the name of all the Whigs," accepted it. He did not attack the notion of an academy directly, though he denounced Swift as unfit to play any part in it. Rather, he shrewdly directed his fire against his opponent's weakest point: the idea that English could be permanently frozen. "I should rejoice," he declared, ". . . if a way could be found to *fix our language forever,* that like the *Spanish* cloak, it might always be in fashion." But "this would be doing what was never done before, what neither Roman nor Greek, which lasted the longest of any in its purity, could pretend to."

In the face of this and other denunciations, the idea of an academy still lingered on for nearly half a century, despite the growing feeling, as expressed by the grammarian Thomas Sheridan, that it was "unsuited to the genius of a free nation." The coup de grace was finally delivered by Samuel Johnson, Swift's successor as an unofficial, one-man Supreme Court of English letters. Johnson was no less a Tory than his predecessor, but he had the advantage of fifty years' hindsight, which had demonstrated, first, that the Académie Française had not in fact stabilized the French tongue, and, second, that neither England nor its language was bound for hell in a handbasket, as the misanthropic Swift had thought. Johnson had the further advantage of a detailed and intimate acquaintance with the English vocabulary, past and present, acquired in the compilation of his great dictionary. In his preface to that work, he permanently disposed of the notion that English could ever be stopped from changing.

Some of his friends, said Johnson, had expected that his dictionary "should fix our language, and put a stop to those alterations which time and chance have hitherto been suffered to make in it." He himself had started out with the belief that this could be done, "but now begin to fear that I have indulged expectations which neither reason nor experience can justify. . . . We laugh at the elixir that promises to prolong life for a thousand years; and with equal justice may the lexicographer be derided, who being able to produce no example of a nation that has preserved their words and phrases from mutability, shall imagine that his dictionary can embalm his language, and secure it from corruption and decay. . . .

"With this hope . . . academies have been instituted . . . but their vigilance and activity have hitherto been vain; sounds are too volatile and subtle for legal restraints; to enchain syllables, and to lash the wind, are equally the undertakings of pride, unwilling to measure its desires by its strength."

Having thus effectively buried the idea of an English academy, it remained only to supply its epitaph, which Johnson did in a later letter. The tombstone, had one been erected, would have read

Here Lies

THE ENGLISH ACADEMY

*"the decrees of which every man would have
been willing, and many would have
been proud to disobey"* —s.j.

R.I.P.

Though Johnson had buried the academy, every generation still seems to raise up a new crop of Swifts eager to save English from the alleged corruption worked by time and chance, protesting the introduction of new words, or the acquisition of new meanings or new pronunciations by old ones. Yet their invariably futile efforts do not dispose of the problem of standardizing *current* English usage, including both vocabulary and syntax. The advantages of this were perfectly clear to eighteenth-century grammarians and critics; the question as they saw it was not whether to establish standards but how.

As far as vocabulary was concerned, the sole possible standard was usage: the only way to tell what a word means is to determine what people use it to mean. And since it was obviously impracticable to poll some ten million Britishers individually on how they used words, lexicographers were compelled to depend on the words of men (and a few women) that had appeared in print. The resulting consensus left the "lower classes" almost unrepresented, and professional writers much overrepresented. No doubt there was a certain amount of social snobbery wrapped up in this, but wrapped up in the snobbery was an assumption that was no less persuasive for being unconscious: that those who had demonstrated their ability to use words with precision and eloquence were the best examples to follow in deciding how words *should* be used.

The instrument for standardizing vocabulary was the dictionary. The word itself had been in English since the thirteenth century, but in different senses: lists of "hard" or unusual words, in English or other tongues, or "translation" dictionaries (English-French, Latin-English, etc.). It was only in the eighteenth century that it occurred to anyone to produce a comprehensive inventory of English words with their meanings and derivations.

Among these first lexicographers, Johnson was unquestionably the chief. His dictionary was not the first modern English dictionary, but it was by far the largest (forty-one thousand words) and best that had yet appeared. It was also, remarkably, almost a one-man job, and as such was inevitably inaccurate in spots (its etymologies in particular were sometimes absurd). At times, too, it reflected its author's strong personal prejudices: thus he defines "pension" as "An allowance made to anyone without an equivalent. In England, it is generally understood to mean pay given to a state hireling for treason to his country." Johnson had reason to regret this bit of lexicographical exuberance when he later accepted a pension from George III, though in all fairness he deserved every penny of it for his services to the English tongue.

Standardizing syntax was more complicated. As with vocabulary (and for the same reasons), the guiding principle was necessarily usage, but there was apparently more variation in syntactic usage, even among the educated, than in vocabulary. Some grammarians sought to resolve the inconsistencies by "the rule of reason"—which didn't get them very far, since neither English nor any other language has ever followed such a rule. The other "final authority" was Latin syntax. To begin with, a knowledge of Latin was the mark of a gentleman; moreover, since nobody had spoken the language for centuries, its rules were not going to change, as those of living tongues had a perverse habit of doing. Dryden had foreshadowed this approach in the seventeenth century when he remarked that sometimes he had to translate an idea into Latin to decide on the correct way of expressing it in English.

This idea, too, was bound to fail: the fact that a particular syntactic structure made sense to the Romans evidently says nothing about whether it can, or should, make sense to us. Indeed, it probably *won't* make sense to us: the famous opening sentence of Caesar's *Gallic Wars, Gallia est omnis divisa in partis tres,* is good Latin, but its literal translation, "Gaul is all divided into parts three" is certainly not good English.

For all that, the Latinists did manage to saddle English with a few quite arbitrary rules, some of them still taught in schools, though observed rigorously only by pedants. For example, the "grammatical" reply to the question "Who's there?" is, by Latin syntax, "It is I," but nearly all of us naturally say "It's me."

Even weirder was another Latinate rule, that it is wrong to ever split an infinitive. The reasoning here (if you want to call it that) was based on the fact that Latin infinitives were single words (*amare,* to love; *dare,* to give), and therefore *couldn't* be split—hence in English, where they were *not* single words, they shouldn't be split. To some literary snobs even today, splitting an infinitive is deemed the mark of the beast; the definitive comment on this was made by, I believe, James Thurber, on the margin of a proof "corrected" by an officious editor: "When I split an infinitive, it's going to damn well stay split!" Yet another Latin "contribution" to English grammar is the rule that a preposition is a bad word to end a sentence with. The definitive comment on *that* was made by Winston Churchill: "This is the sort of nonsense up with which I will not put!"

More serious than these minor examples of literary prissiness was the Latinists' attempt to jam English grammar into the Procrustean bed of Latin rules, through an elaborate structure of pretense that managed to confuse some generations of schoolchildren. For example, as we've noted earlier, Latin nouns possessed a number of different inflectional forms, called cases, which expressed syntactic relationships that we indicate by prepositions or position; Old English, too, had similar "case" inflections. Well before the eighteenth century, English had lost virtually all its noun inflections, yet the Latinists insisted that nouns were still "inflected," the difference now being only that all the inflections looked the same. The theory recalls the lunatic who claimed that Shakespeare's plays were not written by Shakespeare, but by another writer of the same name.

This and similar grammatical fictions were wittily—though not, alas, permanently—disposed of by the critic William Hazlitt. "It is roundly asserted," he wrote in 1829, "that there are *six cases* in the English language. . . . Now in the Latin language there are no doubt a number of cases, inasmuch as there are a number of inflections, and for the same reason (if words have meaning) in the English language there are none," because "there is no inflection or variety whatever in the terminations." Yet pedagogues still insisted, Hazlitt continued, that the noun "case," for example, actually has six cases: "A case, Of a case, To a case, A case, O case . . . though the deuce of any case [that is, inflection of the noun] is there in the case." For all that, however, it took some time before the grammarians cudgeled their brains enough to solve the Case of the Missing Cases—by recognizing that they were gone for good and (more recently) that it was good they were gone.

The quotations from Hazlitt, however, demonstrate a much more important point: English syntax *had* become standardized, not by the theorizings of pedagogues but by the same process of muddle-cum-consensus that had earlier standardized spelling. His remarks make perfect sense according to modern usage, as, indeed, do those of Johnson quoted earlier, though the style of the latter is rather more elaborate and formal than most people would use today.

The long, often acrimonious arguments over how English *should* be written did not, of course, inhibit increasing numbers of the English from writing it. Poetic drama, indeed, had been going downhill since Shakespeare's day, a process that was merely accelerated by the twenty-year closing of the theaters (as a threat to morals) during the Revolution. In exchange, however, came the post-Restoration flowering of prose comedy, some of it almost as "licentious" as Swift had complained (though still fairly tame by modern X-rated standards), but increasingly, in the hands of such skilled practitioners as Congreve, Sheridan and Goldsmith, a lively and witty satire on current manners and morals that many of us still enjoy seeing in revival.

The decline of poetry on the grand scale was, in my admittedly minority opinion, given further impetus by Milton's attempt to produce an English equivalent of Dante's *Divine Comedy*. The received view, of course, is that he is the greatest English poet after Shakespeare; to me, his *Paradise Lost* and *Paradise Regained* merely demonstrate anew, and at wearisome length, the truth that good sermons seldom make good art. Admittedly, Milton was operating under difficulties: not simply his growing blindness, but a more basic, "ideological" problem. As a devout revolutionary, he was naturally on the side of Satan, "in dubious battle" against the heavenly Establishment; as a no less devout Christian, he was, no less naturally, on the side of the angels. But ideological confusion neither explains nor, in my view, excuses the stuffing of his text with indigestible Scriptural and classical allusions, or his total lack of either wit or humor. When Milton was not laboring to be "poetic" he could be eloquent, as some of his prose works demonstrate, but if he ever cracked a joke, or even a smile, the record fails to show it.

The torch of poetry was for a while kept burning by the shorter works of such writers as Herrick, Suckling, Marvell and Donne, much of it lightweight stuff compared with *Hamlet* but no less delightful for that. George Herbert even demonstrated that it was possible to write moving poetry about religion—perhaps because he did not harangue his readers but stuck to his personal feelings. Yet the day of poetry as the major form of English writing was clearly done. By Alexander Pope's time in the early eighteenth century, what we see is only poetry in the technical sense: in fact it is a series of rhymed epigrams, though often quite good epigrams. Already, and despite brief revivals in the early nineteenth and early twentieth centuries, poetry was well on the way to becoming what it is today: a distinctly minor branch of English letters.

But the shrinkage of English poetry was more than matched by the expansion of English prose. Leaving aside the low-grade prose fiction of the Elizabethan pop writers, it began with what may loosely be called essays, if the word can be stretched to cover the melancholy meditations of Robert Burton, the crisp worldly wisdom of Francis Bacon and the philosophical sonorities of Sir Thomas Browne. These were followed in due course by the acid criticism and fantasy of Swift and the elegant, deadpan historical humor of Gibbon's *Decline and Fall.*

Meanwhile, Aphra Behn, the first professional woman writer in English, had more or less invented the modern novel, though it took her successor, Daniel Defoe, to put it on the literary map. Behn had been anticipated by Cervantes, but where *Don Quixote* is an isolated monolith in Spanish literary history, Behn's *Oroonoko* and other works, though far inferior to Cervantes' masterpiece, were the first of a long line. Richardson combined narrative with moral reflections, Fielding speeded up the narrative and downplayed the morality, Sterne thumbed his nose at both narrative and morality (as in *Tristram Shandy*), and Jane Austen's acute and witty observations of country society established her as the first important woman writer in English. If we then survey the multiplying English and American novelists of the later nineteenth and twentieth centuries, we can only exclaim with Macbeth, "What, will the line stretch out to the crack of doom?"

All these literary activities, exciting though they were, involved only a small minority of the English, most of whom were pursuing the traditional British occupation of business as usual: improving their farms with new breeds of plants and animals, sending out ships and manning counting houses in the ever wider pursuit of trade, and increasingly, as the eighteenth century wore on, spurring the productivity of the manufactories that before very long would be explosively enlarged by the force of expanding steam.

England's vocabulary expanded along with its economy, spurred by new trade and cultural contacts, new commodities, new knowledge and new processes. Perhaps the strangest of these influences, however, was the one that didn't happen. The Celtic tongues of Ireland, Wales and the Scottish Highlands, like Sherlock Holmes' dog in the nighttime, did nothing (to the English tongue)—and that, as the great detective might have said, was the curious incident. Geographically these countries were the closest to England, and politically too: Ireland and Wales had been under English rule—after a fashion—since the Middle Ages, and the Scots had been neighbors for as long.

As one would expect, a fair number of Celtic words were taken into the vocabularies of English-speaking Irishmen, Scots and Welsh, but only a bare handful of these trickled into the general vocabulary of English. *Bog* was borrowed from Scots Gaelic in the thirteenth century (and later reborrowed, even more appropriately, from boggy Ireland); *bard* and *clan* are Welsh and Scots respectively, from the fourteenth century, while *glen* filtered down from the Highlands in the fifteenth. These terms were used mainly in poetry, and indeed still have a literary flavor, but three later borrowings have become naturalized in anything but poetic contexts. The Scots *sluaghghairm,* war cry, became the modern politician's and advertiser's "slogan," while Scots *uisgebeatha,* water of life, still flows down English and American gullets as "whiskey." Most recently, Irish *fainne,* ring, became attached to "fawney-rigging," a confidence trick involving a fake—phony—gold ring. But this is just about all English has to show for its centuries-long contact with the Celtic fringe of Europe.

From 1650 to the present, the main source of borrowed English words, except in the scientific field, has been the same as it was from the Conquest on: French. One reason for this was the economic and military decline of Spain during the seventeenth century, which left France the major Continental power, and one increasingly disposed to throw its weight about; her Bourbon kings found that activity much more glamorous than the grubby business of promoting agriculture, manufacture and trade. The English, though they preferred these latter activities, had by this time muddled their way into a long-term policy of maintaining the "balance of power" (the phrase in this sense dates from 1701). That is, they cared very little what happened across the Channel as long as no one country was running things. And since the only country with a chance of doing so was France, English and French armies periodically found themselves confronting one another with *pique* (pike) and *mosquet;* both words came into English in the sixteenth century, but the weapons themselves remained in use for much longer, the musket until well into the nineteenth. Later, the contest expanded with English and French empire-building, from Canada to India. This protracted conflict, which was settled only by Waterloo, brought numbers of French military terms into English to join those borrowed earlier: *fusillade, corps, manoeuvre, havresac, cantine* and *espionage.*

But France was much more than a perennial military and colonial rival: she was the cultural center of the Continent, her tongue spoken by diplomats and courtiers across Europe, her foods, fashions and dances adopted by sophisticates and social climbers everywhere; Louis XIV's spectacular palace at Versailles became the inspiration of every megalomaniacal king, prince or grand duke who could squeeze enough out of his tax receipts to imitate it. Part of every upper-class Englishman's education was a trip to Paris, where he could quaff *champagne,* attend the *ballet,* and ogle the *blonde* and *brunette soubrettes* with the eye of a *connoisseur* —preferably without a *chaperon.* England's eighteenth-century French connections also contributed a miscellany of useful terms like *dentiste, routine, publicité, boulevarde* and *piquenique.* The Victorian era brought another influx of Englishmen into France, seeking the pleasures that, if not precisely forbidden in England, were at least frowned on by the formidable matriarch who presided over the expanding empire. The result has been wittily summarized by John Moore, in his lively book *You English Words* (the italics, however, are mine):

> Fashion brought over such words as *crêpe, beret, suède, cretonne, rosette;* French chefs taught us *sauté, mousse, fondant, gratin;* soldiers laid down *barrages* and issued *communiqués.* . . . Society mingled only with the *élite,* was *chic,* went to the *matinée,* attended *premières,* dined in *restaurants,* made its daughters *debutantes* and found them suitable *fiancés,* maintained its *prestige,* deplored *enfants terribles* and kept its *amour propre.* The century ended . . . in a rather *macabre* and *fin-de-siècle* mood.

English travel and trade in Europe were not, of course, limited to France, but terms borrowed from other European tongues mainly described things peculiar to the lands in question. An important exception is Italy, which has given us, among other words, virtually our entire technical vocabulary in the field of music, from *pianissimo* to *fortissimo* and from *largo* to *prestissimo.* But from Norway we took only its *fjords,* from Iceland its *geysirs,* and from Russia its word for "plains," *step',* as well as *tundra*—the latter in turn borrowed from the Lapps who inhabit those bleak, treeless barrens in Europe's far north. One Russian word, however, has expanded far beyond its original specialized meaning. Its ultimate source was some enormous bones dug up in southern Russia, which the local Tatar inhabitants called *mamont* (earth) in their tongue (it is related to Turkish), apparently believing that the creature lived underground as a sort of super-mole. Russian savants recognized that it was rather a super-elephant, but borrowed the word, the source of our modern "mammoth" political rallies and movie productions.

A scattering of "general" English words comes from a few other European tongues. The Hungarian town of Kocs, pronounced /coach/, gave us the name of a carriage, and *vampir* comes from (where else?) Hungarian Transylvania, though the real-life original of fiction's most famous vampire was a Romanian. When the French crown hired Croatian (*Hrvat*) mercenaries, their name was applied to their linen neck scarves, becoming French *cravate* and English "cravat." During the seventeenth century, trade and military contacts with the Turks introduced the curious brownish beans that could be ground and brewed into *kahveh*—a drink that in England and other parts of Europe rapidly acquired the popularity of pot today, and was viewed just as sourly by some of the older generation.

Chinese *t'e* was less popular in England than coffee until an unsuccessful attempt to ship it into Boston led to a glut on the English market, sending the price down to within middle-class means. The English still prefer tea to coffee—and for the most part brew it much better. Much more costly than tea was the fine porcelain that the wealthy served it in, at first imported from the Orient as China ware, but later manufactured in English potteries as simply china. English merchants in the China trade sometimes had the bad luck to run into Malay pirates en route; those that survived brought back the Malay term for fighting furiously, *amoq.* Eventually, some merchants established permanent trading stations in Malay-speaking lands—offices and warehouses often stockaded in *bambu* and called by the native term for "enclosure," *kampong,* whence such modern enclosures as the famous "Kennedy compound" on Cape Cod. (The chemist's "compound" is a much earlier borrowing from quite a different source—ultimately, Latin *componere,* put together.)

From his explorations in the South Pacific, Captain Cook brought back the Melanesian term for "forbidden," *tabu* (which has given us a noun and a verb as well as an adjective), and the first reports of the extraordinary, bounding *kangooroo,* whose name has been applied to a court, official or otherwise, that, shall we say, leaps to conclusions. The convicts who later settled Australia discovered the surprising *bumarin,* a club that, if carelessly thrown, could return to strike the thrower, whence our invaluable verb "to boomerang."

Traders, explorers and colonists also, of course, picked up hosts of native terms for the fauna, flora and other distinctive features of these exotic locales, but these are used mainly by naturalists or by English-speaking inhabitants of these far-off lands; few people outside Australia, for example, have much occasion to discuss wallabies or wombats. Thus Australia's unofficial national anthem, "Waltzing Matilda," tells of a *billabong* (pond, waterhole) beneath a *coolibah* tree, where a tramp fills his *billy* (water can), but then comes to grief through stealing a *jumbuck* (sheep)—all borrowed from various aboriginal tongues. (American English has borrowed just as heavily from Native American languages; these will be considered in the next chapter.) Finally, English colonists in South Africa took from the hardnosed Dutch Calvinists who had preceded them there the words *spoor, trek* and *veldt* (literally, "field").

British colonization in North America, Australia and Africa were, of course, part of the process now called imperialism (the word itself dates only from Victorian times). It is currently rather fashionable for English-speakers to deplore their imperial past and even to indulge in a bit of breast-beating over it. In defense of the English, it is worth noting that they were doing only what the Greeks, Chinese, Romans, Aztecs, Arabs and Turks had done before them, what the Portuguese, French, Dutch and Russians were doing at the time, and what several "Third World" nations have been doing over the past thirty years.

Whatever may be said about the morality of imperialism, there can be no doubt that the English practiced it more successfully than anyone before or since, and—on the whole—less brutally. (Australia and North America are notable exceptions to this rule. However, the worst atrocities against these native peoples were perpetrated not by British governments but by the local colonists and, in North America, by the U.S. government.) Far and away the greatest success was the conquest of India during the eighteenth and nineteenth centuries. Even at the height of the empire, the population of that subcontinent probably exceeded that of all other British colonies put together, and its contribution to our vocabulary is equally preponderant.

The earliest channel for that contribution was, naturally, trade, which in earlier centuries, and through various channels, had given us such words as "pepper," "sugar" and "crimson," the last ultimately from Sanskrit *krmi*, worm, referring to the insects from which a crimson dye was made. Later mercantile borrowings included *tekka* (teak), *jhuto* (jute), and the *goni*-sack often made of jute fiber, as well as calico from the port of Calicut (not to be confused with the modern city of Calcutta), and the gaily printed textiles called *chint* or, collectively, "chints."

Many more words, however, were borrowed by the several hundred thousand Englishmen who over the generations visited or lived in India as traders, soldiers and colonial officials, often with their wives. These Anglo-Indians incorporated many native words into their vocabularies, as can be seen in the Indian stories of Kipling, and carried some of them back home. These included terms for exotic things, like the highly seasoned stews called *kari*, the spicy relish *chatni*, and the Indian word for dense forest, *jangal*. (Its etymology is startling: originally it meant "desert," whence "uncultivated land," and then "forested land.")

A fair number of Indian words, however, gradually made their way into ordinary, everyday English. They include the American cowboy's bandanna, from Hindi *bandhnu* (tie-dying), and the dungarees worn these days by practically everyone under or over thirty, from a coarse cloth woven in Dungri, the *pae jamah* that many of us sleep in (the word and the garment were both originally borrowed from the Persians), the *khat* we sometimes sleep on, the *shal* draped over ladies' shoulders in chilly weather, the yachtsman's *dingi*, and the one-story *bangalo*, often with a *varanda* attached (the last had been previously borrowed into Hindi from Portuguese).

A sinister Hindu religious sect, which combined piety and profit by ceremonially murdering and robbing prosperous travelers, gave their name, Thugs, to modern, less pious specialists in violence. Hindi *lut* became English "loot," which Kipling, to the horror of his Victorian readers, described as a principal aim of British soldiers in India ("That's the thing that makes the boys get up and shoot!"). Strangest of all was the Indian word for a pond or open cistern used in irrigation, *tankh*. Its origins are controversial: some authorities consider it an indigenous word, others a borrowing from Portuguese *tanque* and ultimately from Latin *stagnum*, pond (whence, of course, "stagnant"). But its subsequent evolution is even more remarkable. Transferred to England, which had no use for irrigation, it became a large, usually metal container for any kind of liquid—whence the oil and gasoline tanks we fill today at increasingly exorbitant prices.

Enter now Winston Churchill, who during World War I was promoting, against the violent opposition of the British high command, a new invention: a self-propelled gun enclosed in a steel box, which, it was hoped, would break the murderous stalemate that was destroying a generation of young men in the trenches of the Western Front. As a "cover name" to conceal the project from the enemy—and probably from the British generals as well—Churchill or one of his associates suggested "tank," a name that has stuck to its modern, much-modified descendants. Odd changes in meaning are almost routine in philology, but this shift, in a mere hundred years, from peaceful irrigation to armored warfare is a bit dizzying.

A minor but historically important incident in the long British occupation of India was the discovery, by Sir William Smith, that the languages of central and northern India were related to those of Europe. This laid the foundations of Indo-European philology, which has enabled us to trace the roots of English back eight thousand years (see Chapter 2).

All these foreign borrowings through trade, empire-building and contact with French culture, while fascinating and often colorful, are far outweighed in sheer numbers by those from medicine, science and technology, which from the sixteenth century on brought first a trickle, then a stream and at last a flood of new words to match the new knowledge. Some were borrowed from Latin, like the biologist's *genus* and *species*, others from Greek, like the physician's "tonic," and a few (mostly dealing with minerals) from German, like *Quartz* and *Feldspath* (feldspar) and the metals *Nickel* and *Kobalt*—the last two from the malignant elves *Nickels* and *Kobolds*, who supposedly supplied these then-worthless ores to medieval miners.

The great majority of the new words, however, were new coinages, almost invariably from Latin or Greek roots. Thus, to take just one example, Greek *hydor*, water (it is cognate with the English word, despite the phonetic differences), contributed "hydrophobia" and "hydrography" in the sixteenth century, "hydrostatics" and "hydrocephalus" in the seventeenth, "hydrogen" in the eighteenth, and subsequently "hydroxide," "hydrocarbon," "hydrolysis," "hydroplane," "hydrocortisone" and "hydroponics," to name only a few of its compounds.

Collectively, these scientific terms coined from the classical tongues have added well over a hundred thousand words to English, but most of them are little used by people outside the various "-ologies" (ultimately from Greek *logos*, discourse, hence "science of "). The ordinary mechanic, whose skill and labor, no less than the scientist's curiosity and the capitalist's "covetousness," made the Industrial Revolution possible, employed (and employs) a quite different vocabulary, consisting mostly of homely, familiar words that acquired specialized meanings. He dealt with the nuts and bolts of technology—from Old English *hnutu*, the kind of nut you eat, and *bolt*, a heavy arrow—with the shafts (Old English *scæft*, spear shaft) and pulleys (Old French *polie*) and screws (Old French *escroue*) of the new industrialism. The steam engine, whose invention and early adoption made England for a while the industrial and commercial master of the world, combined Old English *steam* with Old French *engin* (originally, any mechanical or similar device produced by human *ingen*-uity), while the railway, which put the steam engine on wheels and revolutionized land transport, combined Old French *reille*, iron bar, with Old English *weg*, path—the latter stemming ultimately from Indo-European **wegh-*, transport in a vehicle.

Yet other words entered English from slang, as Thackery borrowed "snob," or through writers' coinages, like Lewis Carroll's "chortle." The results can be seen when we compare Johnson's dictionary of 1755 with the monumental *Oxford English Dictionary* (informally, the OED), published in twelve volumes between 1884 and 1928, with a supplement to bring it up to date published in 1933. (Three volumes of a much more elaborate supplement were published in 1972, 1976 and 1982; a fourth, completing the alphabet, is promised for 1985.) Johnson's dictionary included some forty-one thousand words, the OED *ten times* that number, with another thirty-three thousand in the original supplement. The supplement currently being published will add over a hundred thousand.

Since the OED includes all words used in English since 1150, a sizable proportion of its entries—at a very rough guess, perhaps 25 percent—have dropped out of use. On the other hand, it omits most slang terms, a good deal of the specialized jargon of particular trades or professions, and thousands of terms limited to America, Australia and other non-English but English-speaking lands, or to local dialects in England and elsewhere. What we are talking about, evidently, is a total current vocabulary, in all the English-speaking lands, of over half a million words!

Obviously neither you nor I nor anyone, not even professional lexicographers, "knows" anything like all these words, nor will any one of us have occasion to use more than a small fraction of them. Nonetheless, one is reminded of the advertising slogan of a famous American newspaper with a notably massive Sunday edition: "You don't have to read it all, but it's nice to know it's all there."

The OED is an extraordinary work quite apart from its mere size, which even photographically reduced fills two fat volumes. It includes not only the definitions and etymologies of other large dictionaries, but quotations from English writing, dating from before the Conquest to the early twentieth century, illustrating every nuance of meaning and usage. Simply by reading and collating these fragments—a million and a half of them!—one could, given time, reconstruct the entire history of English over the last thousand years, and much of the history of the society that has begotten it; a browse through them, in fact, is worth some hours of anyone's time. "Liberty," for instance, takes us back to Caxton ("Fredome and lyberte is better than ony gold or syluer") to a pamphleteer of the English Revolution ("The Prize which We now play for is The Liberty of the Subject") to John Locke, theoretician of the Glorious Revolution ("The Liberty of Man, in Society, is to be under no other Legislative Power, than that established by Consent in the Commonwealth") to Benjamin Franklin, laying the intellectual groundwork for the American Revolution ("Those who would give up essential liberty, to purchase a little temporary safety, deserve neither liberty nor safety.") "Liberty of conscience" goes back to 1580, "civil liberty" to Milton in 1644, and "liberty of the press" to 1769, when the great legal commentator Blackstone called it "essential to the nature of a free state."

We get an earthier view of English from the obsolete word "swive," now replaced by the very commonest of our "four-letter words"—what the writer Dashiell Hammett euphemized as "a short, guttural verb." It takes us back to the amorous young woman of Chaucer's "Miller's Tale" (*Thus swivëd was the carpenteris wyf*) and, even earlier, to a legendary king of Germany, a sort of raunchy Old King Cole, memorialized in an old ballad:

> *Richard of Alemaigne, whil that he wes kyng*
> *He spend al is tresour opon swyving . . .*

Reading further, we come on a rather startling seventeenth-century report that in a Scottish translation of the Bible, the Book of Genesis was rendered as "The Buke of Swiving"—which, considering the number of times that one or another patriarch in that book "knew his wife, and begat," is not wholly inappropriate.

In sharp contrast to the permissive Middle Ages, in which ladies and gentlemen could chuckle over tales of swiving, is the atmosphere of Victorian America, which we find reported under "roach" (i.e., cockroach; the word also has three other, quite independent, meanings). A writer from 1840 assures us that " 'Cockroaches' in the United States . . . are always called 'roaches' by the fair sex, for the sake of euphony" —that is, so that the dreadful syllable c--k should not soil their lips. The same perverse propriety crops up again under "unmentionables," which meant "trousers" to the Victorians, because of the unmentionable areas they covered.

From time to time the OED even regales us with little vignettes of some section and period of English society, as under "sham." This was originally a slang term that appeared rather suddenly in English during the 1670s. Nobody knows its origin (Swift, who detested it, believed it had been invented by "some pretty fellows"—fops), except that it seems to have some connection with "shame"—"sham" in some English dialects. A writer of 1734, however, gives us etymological chapter and verse, in an account which if it isn't true is certainly, as the Italians say, a fine invention. The original meaning of "sham," he tells us, was "a Town Lady of Diversion, in Country Maid's Cloaths"—which attested to her innocence, and therefore to her health. She, "to further her Disguise, pretends to be so *sham'd.*" Young men involved in commerce with her would eventually discover that she was neither innocent nor healthy, whence "it became proverbial, when a maim'd lover was laid up, or looked meagre, to say he had met with a *sham.* " Whence the innumerable shams of all sort that have plagued us from the seventeenth century until today, including "sham zeal" (1724), "sham battle" (1839)—and the sham morality of those who proclaimed their virtue publicly by substituting "roach" for "c--kroach."

Like hundreds of other words of more or less dubious origins, the noun "sham" survived its critics, and begat an adjective and a verb to boot, because people found it both useful and colorful. Of all the kinds of liberty of which we English-speakers are perennially and, on the whole, justly proud, not the least is liberty of speech: the freedom not only to say what we choose, but to choose the words we use to say it.

9. ONLY IN AMERICA

English Leaps the Atlantic

❧

When we Americans are through with the English language, it will look as if it had been run over by a musical comedy.

—FINLEY PETER DUNNE

England and America are two countries separated by the same language.

—GEORGE BERNARD SHAW

IN 1582, Richard Mulcaster, while defending the value of the English tongue, was forced to concede that it was still little known outside England. In 1599, the poetaster Samuel Daniel, with true Elizabethan grandiloquence, speculated on the glorious future of this little-known language:

> And who in time knows whither we may vent
>   The treasure of our tongue? To what strange shores
> This gain of our best glory shall be sent,
>   T'enrich unknowing nations with our stores?
> What words in th' yet unformèd Occident
>   May come refin'd with th' accents that are ours?

Eight years after Daniel penned these limping lines, Captain John Smith, an explorer, soldier of fortune and spinner of prodigious tales, founded the first permanent English settlement on the "strange shores" of the "unformèd Occident" and began a process that would ultimately shift the center of gravity of English some thousands of miles westward. But the American branch of English, whose speakers now outnumber those of all other varieties of the language put together, would become by no means English in its "accents"—and, in the long-held view of most English critics, anything but "refin'd" in its vocabulary; indeed, some have denied that it is English at all.

Of course the American language, including the version of it spoken in Canada, *is* English. It differs noticeably from the mother tongue in phonetics, but only in its vowels; the consonants remain virtually identical. The vocabularies of the two tongues, counting words used in one but not the other, or used in both but in different senses, have diverged in several thousand instances, but are identical in tens of thousands. And in syntax the two are indistinguishable apart from a few minor points of usage (e.g., English "different to" versus American "different from"). Even in speech, educated Americans and Britons communicate fairly easily, while in writing, where almost identical spelling conceals the phonetic differences, ease of communication is attested by a vigorous, two-way transatlantic commerce in books of all sorts.

The first English settlers, in the colony named for the late, great Virgin Queen (their settlement was named for her successor, James I), were a motley crew. Southern folklore has it that most or anyway many of them were "Cavaliers," meaning landed gentry if not outright nobility. However, since the English gentry and nobility were mostly doing very nicely at home, they would have been mad to seek out the privations, diseases and hostile natives of the New World, which collectively made an immigrant's chance of surviving his or her first year no better than fifty-fifty.

Even the "better element" among the colonists was seldom of much social status; typical of them is one William Claiborne, who arrived in Virginia in 1621 and subsequently founded the first European settlement in what is now Maryland. (He was subsequently dispossessed by Lord Baltimore, who had better political connections, as essential then as now.) Though various relatives of mine have sought to engraft William into the gentry of Northumberland (ultimately, into the family trees of the dukes of Normandy and the kings of Scotland), all we know for sure is that he was the younger son of a not very successful London tradesman, trained as a surveyor, who, like millions of immigrants after him, came to America to seek his fortune. (Unlike most of them, he found it, though it is now long gone.) Most of his fellow colonists were even less genteel —out-of-work laborers and artisans, shady characters a jump or two ahead of the law, and some out-and-out jailbirds.

The point is worth emphasizing because the character of these early immigrants—respectable middle-class at best, neither respectable nor middle-class at worst—would be largely duplicated in the later colonies up and down the coast from Virginia, and would inevitably be reflected in both the nature of the language they brought with them and its subsequent development. Though the majority were at least minimally literate, few were even moderately learnèd (Claiborne, who had studied at Cambridge, was one of the few). Their language, therefore, was not, as has sometimes been said, the tongue of Shakespeare, but the plain, homely English of the King James Bible, at its best capable of eloquence but seldom marked by elegance.

The settlers, moreover, had few books—and little respect for bookish scholars. From their first landing, they encountered plants, animals, crops and climates that were not *in* the books, and could be coped with only through hard-bought experience, a situation that would recur periodically over the next two centuries as their descendants made their way across an enormously diversified continent. The result was that pragmatic, cut-and-try philosophy that has characterized American attitudes to both life and language ever since.

Finally, the colonists were on the whole a tough, aggressive and obstreperous lot; milder-mannered folk were unlikely to emigrate, and unlikely to survive if they did. Which is to say that the settlers were even less prone than their stay-at-home contemporaries to accept the dictates of Authority, in language or anything else.

Not that Authority would have had much of a chance in any case. The colonists, as Thomas Jefferson would later point out, were confronted with "new circumstances . . . which . . . call for new words, new phrases, and the transfer of old words to new objects." The most obvious of these circumstances was the natural world: the dozens of new birds, beasts and plants that the colonists had never seen and needed names for. Sometimes they coined them from their own tongue, but as often as not did what migrants to new lands generally do: asked the natives, "What do you call that?"

The Native Americans whom the English found in possession of the land—and dispossessed from it as quickly as possible—did not, as some people still believe, all speak "Indian," but several hundred different languages and dialects, some as different as English, Chinese and Swahili. However, the coastal tribes from Canada to the Carolinas all spoke related tongues belonging to the great Algonquian linguistic family. It was therefore from one or another of the Algonquian languages that the settlers drew names for the ring-tailed *aroughcoun*, the striped *chitmunk*, the odoriferous *squnk* and the tail-hanging *aposoun*, whose habit of discouraging predators by playing dead begot the later American metaphor "to play possum." The burrowing *ochek* was assimilated as "woodchuck," and the aquatic *musquash* as "muskrat." Colonists to the north encountered the wide-antlered *moos*, for which English in fact already had a name: the Scandinavian elk was virtually identical. But few Englishmen had ever seen an elk, and its name was eventually tacked onto a quite different American species of deer, also known by its native name, *wapiti.*

Birds and fish were another story: some, like the cod and mallard, were identical on both sides of the Atlantic, while others were enough like English species—at least to the eyes of homesick colonists—to pass under the old name or some variant, whence such names as "robin," "red-headed woodpecker," "oyster" and "striped bass." A marine exception was the oily menhaden, apparently named from a native word meaning "fertilizer," for which it was used by the Algonquians and is still harvested by the ton today. Unfamiliar birds, on the other hand, were more likely to be named from their calls—birds are more often heard than seen—whence our chickadee, flicker, bobwhite and whippoorwill. Most of the trees, though not English species, were, like fish and birds, enough like European species so that English names, with some modification, would serve. Thus, for example, the white pine and white oak were named for their light-colored wood, the black walnut for its darkish wood and bark, while the southern live oak remained "alive" (i.e., green) all year.

Some trees, however, were beyond the bounds of English experience. One yielded nuts that, pounded in water, made an oily drink that the natives called *pawcohiccora;* the English assimilated this as "hickory" and transferred it to the nuts and the tree, whose tough wood proved invaluable for making such things as ax handles and wagon wheels. Another toothsome nut came from the *paccan,* and yet another from the chestnut-like *chechinkamin* (chinquapin). From the *pasimenan* tree came a fruit which, said Captain Smith, could when unripe "drawe a man's mouth awrie with much torment," though when ripe "it is as delicious as an Apricock"—an opinion still held by the few Americans lucky enough to have tasted wild persimmons. The Creeks, a non-Algonquian tribe farther south, contributed names for the *kutuhlpa* (catalpa) and *ito-opilwa* (tupelo—literally, "swamp tree"). The fragrant-leaved *sasafras,* however, was already known to the English from the Spaniards, who had presumably borrowed its name from some tribe of northern Florida. Sassafras root was valued for its supposed medicinal properties, and English merchants had mounted expeditions to collect it, in New England and elsewhere, some years before Jamestown was founded.

Like sassafras, a name for the natives' main crop plant had also passed into English via Spanish; learnèd men knew it as "maize." The unlearnèd colonists christened it "Indian corn" or "Indian wheat," and found that in the southern colonies it yielded much more copiously than imported

202 / Our Marvelous Native Tongue

kinds of "corn" (i.e., wheat and barley), so that it soon became simply "corn" (in England it is still "maize"). The new corn could be ground into meal and baked into the flat cakes the natives called *apan* (pone); alternatively, it could be soaked in a solution of wood ash, which removed the hulls and softened the grain into *appuminneash*. The English found this tasty but unpronounceable, and therefore simplified it to "hominy," nowadays more commonly ground into the less tasty "grits" that are still a Southern American staple.

The natives' other main crop, kidney beans and similar varieties, had already reached England from Middle America, and was enough like the old English (broad) bean to retain the old name. It was from the natives, however, that the English learned to combine unripe corn, beans and any game that was handy into the savory stew, *msickquatash* (succotash). Another useful native crop was the pumpkin-like *askootasquash*, whose outlandish name quickly shrank to "squash."

Our chief linguistic legacy from the Native Americans, however, is neither beasts nor plants, nor such distinctive items of native gear as the *wikawam, tamahak* and *mohkussin*, but names on the land—the category where the tongues of conquered peoples have always survived the longest. Above all, the names of the rivers, which had flowed before either red men or white men had fished or paddled their waters. Glancing over the map of the North American east coast, one must almost hunt for English or even European river names. The St. Lawrence, St. John and St. Croix were named by pious Frenchmen, the Hudson for the English explorer who hoped it might prove a passage to India, the Delaware for Lord de la Warre, the Charles for Charles I and the James for his cranky, devious father. But far outnumbering these are New Brunswick's Restigouche and Miramichi, beloved of salmon fishermen; New England's Penobscot, Kennebec, Merrimac and Connecticut; New Jersey's Passaic and Raritan; and farther south the Susquehanna, Potomac, Rapahannock, Roanoke, Peedee, Santee and Savannah—to name only the larger streams.

It is to the Native Americans, finally, that we probably owe the nickname by which Americans have become known almost worldwide: "Yankee" apparently derives from the native assimilation of "English" to *Yengees*. Some, indeed, trace the name to Dutch *Jan Kees* ("John Cheese"), a nickname unquestionably applied to Dutch settlers and sailors, but this is more likely coincidence. The Dutch term looks plausible on paper, but its actual sound, /yon *case*/, is less like "Yankee" than the native /yeng-gee/. Moreover, it is hard to see why a nickname for the Dutch, presumably coined by English-speaking sailors and buccaneers, should have been transferred to English-speaking New Englanders, to whom it was first applied.

Whether or not the Dutch colonists of Nieuw Amsterdaam and parts adjacent gave us "Yankee," they certainly contributed a number of other American words, and therein lies a puzzle. The Dutch settlers were never numerous—according to some estimates, no more than ten thousand all told—and were, moreover, concentrated in one small part of the coast. Yet they contributed almost as many words to the American vocabulary as the later-arriving Germans, Italians and Poles put together, who would collectively outnumber them by several thousand to one.

The explanation, I think, lies in *where* the Dutch were concentrated: New York (as the colony was renamed when the English seized it in 1663) was destined to become North America's trading and transportation center. At a time when most goods could be carried economically only by water, it possessed one of the world's finest harbors, linked by a unique network of waterways to a vast hinterland. West and southwest lay the valleys of the Passaic and Raritan; on the east the semiprotected waters of Long Island Sound led to the Connecticut Valley and a dozen shore settlements; while to the north Hudson's broad river (still called by some New Yorkers the North River) led through its own fertile valley past the mouth of the Mohawk. And this river, in turn, led into the only break in the long Allegheny chain of mountains, stretching from Maine to Georgia, that blocked off the coastal lands from the interior. The Mohawk Gap was low enough for easy wagon travel and for the later construction of the Erie Canal, whose opening in 1829 extended waterborne commerce from New York to the Great Lakes, and thus to the entire upper Midwest.

The growth of New York into a mercantile and financial center—eventually also a cultural one—was thus virtually inevitable. Which is to say that any additions to the English language there were likely to spread far beyond the city limits. And so it proved; the New York Dutch have given us the flat-bottomed *schouw* that plied New York harbor and the Hudson, the *slee* used for winter horse-drawn travel, and the *stoep* that still fronts so many old New York houses. The propensity of the Dutch Calvinists, like other godly folk, to pry into their neighbors' affairs gave us the verb *snoep*, while Dutch ghost stories, like the famous Headless Horseman of Sleepy Hollow, contributed *spooke*. New York business gave us *baas*, whence the political boss and the *boedel* (boodle) he amassed, while New York urchins learned to call one another *dom* (stupid), as they still do, though the word has been assimilated to English "dumb." They also picked up the rude exclamation *Pappekak!* (soft shit), later borrowed, in all innocence, as "Poppycock!" by the most eminent English Victorians. And yes, Virginia, there is indeed a *Sinterklaas.*

The Dutch, too, left names on the land. Nieuw Amsterdaam might become New York, but Breukelyn is still Brooklyn, Haarlem is still Harlem, and Jonas Bronck's farm is still the Bronx. And every summer hundreds of thousands of New Yorkers vacation in the Catskill mountains up the Hudson, named for a stream *(kil)* where some Dutch settler once spied a wildcat; other Dutchmen named the Beaverkill and Fishkill.

Another early source of borrowed words was African slaves. These involuntary "colonists" began arriving in 1619—before the Dutch or even the Pilgrims—but their contribution to the American vocabulary was long ignored. One reason was that the slaves spoke a dozen or more different tongues, for many of which dictionaries did not exist until quite recently, so that tracking a possible African word to its source was at best difficult and often impossible. The other reason is that nobody was looking very hard. Some (white) scholars found the notion of African influences on American English actively distasteful, but most of them, I suspect, never thought about it one way or the other. Here, as in most areas of our national life, the Afro-American was, in Ralph Ellison's poignant phrase, "the invisible man."

Some Africanisms, of course, were too obvious to be ignored. The okra plant originated in Africa and so, naturally did its name, though the closest anyone has yet come to its original is West African *nkrumah.* (I use the term "West African"—there is, of course, no such language—partly for simplicity and partly because we often can't be sure which of several West African tongues was the source of a given word.) Other tribes called the plant *ngombo,* whence the "gumbo" soups and stews containing its edible pods. Another agricultural import from Africa was the *nguba,* a strange nut that was not picked from a tree but dug from the ground, attached to the roots of a pealike plant. The English call it "ground nut" and most Americans, "peanut," but to many Southern Americans of both races it is still the "goober" (the word has even been appropriated as a brand name by a maker of chocolate-covered peanuts). "Yam" (from West African *nyam-nyam,* eat) may be another Africanism, though in North America it has been transferred from the African yam (which will not grow outside the tropics) to a variety of sweet potato. Unquestionably African in name are the various small turtles of our South and Midwest called "cooter" (West African *kuta,* turtle), and the pestiferous biting mites of the same region called "chiggers" or "jiggers" (West African *jiga,* flea). The banjo, North America's only "native" musical instrument, actually originated in Africa, and its name may represent a blend of Portuguese *bandore* and West African *mbanza*—likely enough, if one recalls that the Portuguese were the first Europeans to explore that area.

Easily the prize Africanism in American English, whence it has passed into a dozen tongues around the world, is our omnipresent "O.K." For years, lexicographers grappled with this strange term, evolving etymologies that were more ingenious than scholarly. It was termed an abbreviation of the semiliterate expression "oll korrect," slanderously ascribed to President Andrew Jackson, or of "Old Kinderhook," the supposed nickname of another American president, Martin Van Buren (from his birthplace, a Dutch settlement on the Hudson). Eventually, more thoughtful scholars established that "O.K." and various similar terms had been used as far back as the American Revolution—long before anyone had heard of either Jackson or Van Buren. And its source was unquestionably one of various West African expressions such as *o-ke* or *waw-ke*, meaning O.K. It is surely a major linguistic irony that this expression, virtually the trademark of Americans abroad, should derive neither from English nor from any other European tongue, but from the lips of a minority with which most other Americans still prefer to associate as little as possible. (Some more recent African contributions to American English will be discussed in the next chapter.)

Of course, the English colonists by no means neglected their own language in coining new names for new things. Many of these were topographical—features of a landscape both grander and more varied than that known to most Englishmen, though Scots and Welsh would have found it familiar. As the settlers moved inland toward the mountains, they passed through "foothills," and climbed through "notches" or "gaps" across the "divides" that separated one "watershed" from another. Arrived at a likely spot, perhaps on a "bluff" overlooking a "creek" or "branch," the pioneer would cut down trees and "underbrush" to make a "clearing" for his "log cabin," with a "corn crib" in back. All these were English words, or compounds of them, but the meanings were distinctively American.

Life in the "backwoods" also begot some lively metaphors. The hot-tempered fellow who "flies off the handle" could be as dangerous as an ax head that did the same thing. So could the frontier bully who literally put "a chip on his shoulder" and dared onlookers to knock it off. And a misinformed individual, like a 'coon or 'possum hound on a false scent, was obviously "barking up the wrong tree."

The settlers from the beginning set their own English names on the land—seldom, as we have seen, on the rivers, but on virtually all the villages and towns. In the south they tended to favor royalty, with Jamestown, Charleston, Williamsburg, Annapolis ("Anne's city") and Georgetown cataloguing the succession of English monarchs. In New England, the anti-Establishment Puritans, who had come seeking religious freedom (for themselves, that is), more often borrowed the names of their English homes, or of the ports whence they had sailed. Thus the *Mayflower*, outward bound from Plymouth, England, discharged its passengers at what became Plymouth, New England (where, according to a later account, they piously "fell first upon their knees, and then upon the aborigines"). All along the New England coast we find such English port names: Falmouth, Sandwich, Harwich, Chatham and Truro on Cape Cod; Weymouth, Boston and Lynn (from King's Lynn) to the north; and to the west, in the onetime lands of the Narragansett and Connecticut tribes, Newport, New Haven and Milford, plus such monuments to hometown pride as New Bedford and New London, the latter naturally located on the Thames River (pronounced as spelled, however, not /temz/ like its English original).

Along with their language, the settlers brought their old traditions of limited, and partially representative, government. The first colonies were purely private enterprises, financed and controlled by companies of English investors. Initially, they were organized in what some historians have called a "communistic" system, but was in fact simon-pure capitalism: the colonists were to do all the work while the investors got all the profits. Not surprisingly, little work got done. With more realistic arrangements, the colonies prospered and grew. Nominally, they were ruled by governors appointed by the stockholders (later, by the crown), but in practice the governors found it prudent to share their power with the various representative bodies that sprang up almost automatically.

Like similar bodies in England, these "represented" only male property owners, and, like many later American legislatures, were usually dominated by the biggest property owners. However, they remained for the most part limited governments in theory, and even more so in practice, due in no small measure to the fact that most settlers had guns— essential for hunting game, and especially for defense against the dispossessed natives. If, as occasionally happened, a colonial governor waxed too oppressive, the settlers were willing enough to point their weapons in his direction.

The English political struggles of the seventeenth century evoked only muted echoes across the Atlantic. Most settlers were busy clearing new lands, fighting off the lands' former owners and, if they were lucky, making money; their most pressing political concern was to be let alone. Mostly they were, thanks to England's preoccupation, first with its own internal problems and later with the Dutch and French wars, though the latter produced some skirmishing between New Englanders and the inhabitants, both French and native, of New France to the north. English law compelled the colonists to ship to English ports and buy from English merchants, but this was initially no hardship, since the English were equally obliged to buy their tobacco, indigo and rice from the colonies. As colonial population, production and shipbuilding expanded, however, the colonists found these trade restrictions increasingly burdensome, and smuggling grew into a major American industry. Neither Americans nor English were altogether happy with the situation, but neither were they unhappy enough to pick a fight over it, so long as the "French menace" remained a reality to the north.

In 1759, however, this was finally ended by Wolfe's capture of Quebec. The war in which his campaign was a minor incident was an expensive one for England, and at its close parliament voted to levy certain taxes on the colonies to pay for their own defense. At the same time, in order to prevent future costly conflicts with the natives, it forbade the settlement of lands beyond the Appalachians. Many modern British historians have called these measures reasonable, and so in a sense they were. They were also guaranteed to infuriate the colonists. These, though they liked taxes no better than Americans do today, had been levying taxes through their own colonial assemblies for some generations. The new taxes, however, were voted by a parliament three thousand miles away, in which the colonists were unrepresented: *they were being taxed without their consent.* Englishmen of the seventeenth century had not let the Stuarts get away with this, and their eighteenth-century American descendants were not about to let King George do so. As for the ban on trans-Appalachian settlement, immigration and procreation together were doubling the colonists' numbers every quarter century, and to suppose that this swelling tide of humanity could be contained by government decree was to emulate old King Knut (Canute).

The result, of course, was a war, which the Americans, by all logic, should have lost: the English had more guns and powder, far more trained troops, and overwhelmingly more warships. The Americans did know the country, whose unmapped wilderness and violent weather were altogether foreign to British experience. They had also learned from the natives the tactics of what would later be called guerrilla warfare, but this was of little value except for harassing British supply lines and foraging parties. What really turned the tide was a vigorous antiwar movement in England and the intervention of a foreign power—France, which, like some modern great powers, was happy enough to aid a war of liberation in other people's colonies, though not in her own.

The war produced one of the most eloquent pieces of English prose ever written (the Declaration of Independence), a new sense of American national identity, in language as well as politics, and, after a good deal of what would today be called political wheeling and dealing, a governmental structure that remains, after nearly two centuries, perhaps the most strictly limited on earth in theory, and, most of the time, one of the most limited even in practice.

It is currently fashionable among some historians to describe the U.S. Constitution as an aristocratic document whose framers, nearly all of them well-to-do, were mainly concerned with keeping power out of the hands of the "common people." This is true, but it is much less than the whole truth. Aristocratic or democratic, the Founding Fathers almost to a man had the Englishman's ingrained distrust of unlimited government, which had been nowise lessened by their recent experiences with the British crown. Their concern with limiting the commoners' power over government was therefore tempered by a concern for limiting government's power over anyone—whence the elaborate system whereby the separate powers of the executive, legislative and judicial branches check and balance one another. The Fathers were also not unmindful of the fact that many of the commoners still had guns, plus considerable experience in using them—and if pressed too far were willing to use them again, as they did in Shay's Rebellion, which broke out in the very year the Constitution was adopted.

The result of this and other, less violent protest movements was what amounted to a compromise: in exchange for their support of the new constitutional government, the commoners were given the first ten amendments, which for the first time in history wrote into the fundamental law of a nation a detailed list of things that government was forbidden to do.

Another, more ominous compromise concerned slavery. Not a few of the Founding Fathers would have liked to abolish it, but thanks to the political power of the slaveholders, found themselves faced with the unpalatable choice between a national government tolerating slavery and no effective government at all. They chose the former, albeit with misgivings. Jefferson, himself a slaveholder, saw the slavery question as "a firebell in the night," causing him to "tremble for my country when I reflect that God is just."

The limitations on governmental power written into the U.S. Constitution have, over the generations, been strained almost to the breaking point on a number of occasions: Americans have had to relearn repeatedly the old lesson that eternal vigilance is the price of liberty. But thanks to that vigilance—and the shrewdness of the document's original framers—the limitations have survived and, in some respects, even expanded. Over the years, various groups have periodically complained that the federal government had or has too much power over its citizens, but most of these grumblings have emanated from those who disliked government "interference" with *their* power over other people.

This was the case in 1861, the only time in our history when constitutional government was seriously endangered. The causes of the conflict that broke out in that year were complex, but what we would now call the bottom line was the conviction of some white Southerners that the new national administration of Abraham Lincoln threatened their power over their slaves. Akin to this was the hardly less important question of whether a minority that disliked the government could simply cut loose from it—whether, as was said two years later in another great piece of English prose, a nation "conceived in liberty and dedicated to the proposition that all men are created equal . . . can long endure." Four years of terrible bloodshed established that it would endure, and without slavery, though also, alas, without achieving full equality among all its citizens. I believe it will continue to endure. Government in America has not abolished injustice; no government has. It has often worked badly; all governments do. More notable, I think, is the fact that it continues to work at all—something that can be said for very few governments in existence two centuries ago.

Even before the Revolution had created a new sense of American nationhood, some Americans had come to recognize that their language was becoming different from that of England. Early in 1774, an article in the *Royal American Magazine* suggested that the "highest perfection" of the English tongue "is perhaps reserved for this land of light and freedom." The author thereupon proposed the formation of a society that would regularly "correct, enrich and refine" American English, until "perfection at last stops their progress and ends their labor." The anonymous author of this obviously utopian proposal may have been John Adams; at any rate, he made a similar one a few years later, urging the

Continental Congress to establish "the first public institution for refining, correcting, improving and ascertaining the English language"—that is, essentially the same sort of national academy that Swift had proposed for England nearly a century earlier.

Swift's countrymen, as we know, debated but ultimately rejected his proposal; Adams' fellow citizens, far less respectful of academies and authority generally, hardly even bothered to discuss the matter. A couple of nongovernmental "academies" aimed at purifying the language were set up later on, but their influence on American speech remained invisible to the naked eye.

Nonetheless, over the next half century American English did become partly standardized, in a typically pragmatic American way and largely through the labors of a most pragmatic American, Noah Webster. Born near Hartford, Connecticut, Webster started out as a lawyer, but lack of business forced him into schoolteaching. Textbooks, published in England, were in short supply thanks to the war, and in Webster's view, not very good in any case. Seeing a need, he set out with true Yankee ingenuity to fill it. Between 1783 and 1785, while still in his twenties, he published *A Grammatical Institute of the English Language,* consisting of a spelling book, a grammar and a reader.

All three were almost instantly successful, the speller spectacularly so: over the next century its sales are estimated at over eighty million copies, making it the all-time best-seller in English next to the Bible. Since each copy went through several hands, it follows that the vast majority of American schoolchildren during that period must have learned their spelling—and often their pronunciation as well—from this one book. Its royalties, at only a cent a copy, supported Webster comfortably for the rest of his life, enabling him to work full-time at his chosen career of standardizing and giving respectability to American English. His work was crowned by the publication in 1828 of his *American Dictionary of the English Language*—a third again as large as Johnson's, and of course reflecting American as well as English usage in its vocabulary and many of its definitions.

Webster's writings were in one sense a practical man's answer to a practical problem: Britain, he wrote in 1789, "is at too great a distance to be our model, and to instruct us in the principles of our own tongue." But he was also consciously motivated by patriotism, seeing a national language as a means of strengthening the bonds among the widely dispersed—and often contentious—inhabitants of the new nation. As with other Americans of the time (and later), his patriotism sometimes degenerated into silliness, as when he wrote of Britain that "the taste of her writers is already corrupted, and her language already on the decline." This sort of nonsense was perhaps excusable in a country that had just emerged from a bitter war with England, but it has persisted, in politics and sometimes in linguistics, among a certain class of Americans: those who seek to demonstrate their love of country by downgrading other lands, rather as if I should "praise" my wife by abusing other women. For Webster, at least, time—and a year's residence in England—brought a mellowing: in the preface to his dictionary he noted that "the body of the language is the same [in America] as in England, and *it is desirable to perpetuate that sameness*" (emphasis added).

Webster's major contributions to standardizing American pronunciation and spelling were joined by some minor achievements in simplifying the latter. At times, indeed, he flirted with the notion of wholesale spelling reform, but was practical enough to recognize, as had earlier reformers, that it just wouldn't work. However, he made a few improvements. Where two spellings were current in England, he generally picked the simpler, writing "music" and "risk" where some English still wrote "musick" and "risque." In other cases he broke with English practice, dropping the U in such words as "honour" and "favour," so that where the U.S. today has a labor movement, Britain has a Labour Party. Similarly, the British "defence" budget is equivalent to the even more onerous American "defense" budget, and the two peoples go to the theatre and theater respectively. Webster also tried to suppress some superfluous silent E's, as in "medicine" and "determine," but here habit proved too strong.

Webster was something of a crank on his chosen specialty, but there was a lot of pragmatic method in his crankiness. He sensed that in America above all, no single person, no matter how respected, could *impose* standards on the language. Accordingly, says his biographer, he "inculcated his views on orthography and pronunciation upon all occasions. He wrote, he lectured, he pressed home his doctrines upon persons and assemblies. . . . " In 1881, an elderly printer recalled how when he was an apprentice of thirteen, "a little pale-faced man came into the office and handed him a printed slip, saying, 'My lad, when you use these words, please oblige me by spelling them as here: *theater, center,* etc.' It was Noah Webster traveling about among the printing offices, and persuading people to spell as he did. . . . " Webster knew his countrymen: his incessant persuasion got results as the dictates of an academy could never have done.

But not even a Webster, or a hundred Websters, could have standard-ized or contained the American vocabulary, which was expanding as vigorously, if not quite as rapidly, as the country itself. The Americans, in fact, were handling their language in much the same way as the Elizabe-thans had handled theirs, and for similar reasons: an outburst of national pride, national consciousness and national self-assertiveness. Like Shakespeare and his contemporaries, they were giving old words new meanings (as we saw a few pages back), turning nouns into verbs ("advo-cate," "progress," "notice") and vice versa, making verbs out of adjec-tives ("belittle"—apparently coined by Jefferson) and adjectives out of nouns ("lengthy"), inventing brand-new words out of sheer high spirits and delight in "tall talk" ("rambunctious," "hornswoggle") and borrow-ing words from any source that happened to be handy.

Nowhere were these processes so active as along the westward-moving frontier, whose trappers, explorers and pioneering settlers were remote from scholars and schoolbooks, and in contact with new peoples whose vocabularies could be raided for new words. Most westward travel was along the waterways—which, as always, mostly kept their native names. From Buffalo (named for an animal like the European wisant, but with the name itself borrowed from Portuguese, where it referred to quite a differ-ent creature), the westward route led through Lakes Erie, Huron and Michigan to the Chicago River and thence to the Illinois, or via the Fox River (named not for the animal but for a native tribe) to the Wisconsin. Farther south, the "raftsman" or "keelboatman" might start at Pittsburgh (named for an English prime minister), where the Allegheny and Monon-gahela join to form the Ohio, whose current, swelled by the waters of the Muskingum, Scioto, Kentucky, Miami, Wabash and Tennessee, would carry him at last to the great Mississippi, the "big river" (not, as folklore has it, "father of waters"), itself carrying the flow of the Missouri, Illinois, Iowa, Wisconsin and Minnesota. And what was true for the lakes and rivers was true for the new territories and states as these were organized over the decades: half were given native names, as were several Canadian provinces.

But on both the lakes and the Mississippi, the pioneers found that white men as well as red men had been there before them—French *voyageurs* and *coureurs du bois* (woods runners) whom the fur trade had drawn west-ward along the St. Lawrence and Ottawa and later northward from the mouth of the "big river." Until 1803, when Jefferson swung history's biggest real-estate deal, the entire west bank of the Mississippi was still

French territory, and much of eastern Canada was (and is) French in language, though not in sovereignty.

The French contributed some of their own borrowings from the natives —the *caribou* of the far north and the *tobakan* used for hauling goods and supplies over deep snow—but even more from their own tongue. The fur trade between Canada and the west was conducted largely by birchbark canoe, a craft light enough to be carried over *portages* between streams, such as the one between the Fox and Wisconsin rivers where Portage, Wisconsin, now stands. In parts of the Midwest, with hotter summers and less rainfall than eastern North America, the French discovered natural clearings in the forest, which they called *prairies* (meadows), a term that Americans later applied to the enormous, horizon-to-horizon grasslands "across the wide Missouri." Beyond even these great "meadows" the French found strange, flat-topped hills like oversize versions of the earthern mounds *(buttes)* thrown up behind shooting targets, and narrow valleys cut by flows *(coulées)* from spring or summer thunderstorms. Along the lower Mississippi, finally, the French had explored the swampy backwaters that the native Choctaws called *bayuk* (French *bayou*), and had learned to fear the annual floods of the great river, which forced them to build raised *(levée)* embankments to protect their settlements. The small French coin called a *picaillon* begot the contemptuous American adjective "picayune."

Like everyone else, the French left names on the land: Louisiana (originally referring to the entire territory) for Louis XIV, New Orleans for his brother, the Duke of Orleans, and St. Louis for France's national saint. Detroit still lies on the strait *(étroit)* between Lakes Erie and St. Clair (now called the Detroit River), Sault Sainte Marie on the rapids *(sault*—literally "leap") between Lakes Huron and Superior, and Fond-du-Lac, Wisconsin, at the lower end *(fond)* of Lake Winnebago. The Des Moines River enshrines the memory of French missionary monks *(moines),* while far to the west the peak of Grand Teton records the far-from-monkish joke of some woman-starved voyageur: it means "big tit."

An even greater influx of words came when the pioneers pressed beyond the French lands into those seized much earlier by Spain, by this time part of independent Mexico. The English-speaking Americans began as peaceful if sometimes obstreperous immigrants, but their perennial land hunger led to conflicts with the Mexican authorities and eventually to a war denounced by many other Americans, including an obscure Illinois congressman named Lincoln. This new land grab carried the U.S. boundary to the Pacific, and with it the American language and its ever-growing vocabulary.

First, naturally, came Spanish names for the natural world, some of which the Spaniards had earlier borrowed from the Mexican natives: the *coyotl* (Spanish *coyote*), *mizquitl* (Spanish *mezquite*) and the fierce wild pigs called *pekari* (peccary). English, plus a very limited knowledge of zoology, contributed names for the pronghorn antelope (which is not an antelope), the mountain goat (which is not a goat) and the bighorn sheep (which *is* a sheep). But the wild *mestengos* (literally, "strays") were as Hispanic in name as they were in origin: the descendants of horses escaped from Spanish *ranchos*. Equally Hispanic was the topography: a flat-topped mountain was not a butte here, but a *mesa* (literally, "table"), a coulee was a *cañon* ("conduit") and the jagged mountains that loomed, range after range, beyond the High Plains were *sierras* (originally, "saws").

The Mexicans contributed a new breed of cattle that the Americans called "longhorns," for obvious reasons, and along with it most of their cattleman's vocabulary. The Mexican *vaquero* (cowman) became the American buckaroo, complete with broad-brimmed *sombrero* (literally, "shade-maker"), *la reata* (the lasso), *poncho* and the leather leggings called *chapareras* (chaps), useful in riding through *chaparral* (ultimately, from a Basque word meaning "thicket"). Mounted on his *bronco* or piebald *pinto* (literally, "painted"—the Old Paint of song and story) from the old *corral* (probably from Portuguese—ultimately from Hottentot), he guarded the cattle against hungry wolves and natives and tried not to get caught in an *estampida*. Come payday, he might overindulge in *mescal* or *tequila* and end up in the *calabozo* or *juzgado* (hoosegow).

A few more Spanish terms came in with the discovery of gold in California, where the forty-niner panning a *placer* (literally, "reef"—i.e., a river sandbar) might with luck strike a *bonanza* ("prosperity"). But when it came to California's most spectacular natural objects, towering up to 350 feet into the air, both the Spanish and the American imagination failed: the Californians could come up with nothing more eloquent than "redwood" or "big tree," though one species later somehow acquired the name of the great Cherokee chief Sequoyah, who had never been within a thousand miles of one.

The Spaniards, too, have left their names on the American map. Some were purely literal: the snow-covered (*nevada*) sierra of California, the great river red (*colorado*) with the mud of its tributary canyons, and El Paso, from the pass where the Rio Grande, another "big river," cuts through the mountains named for St. Andrew (San Andrés). But most of the names were, like this last, religious, the Spaniards of those days being the most devout (some would say bigoted) Catholics in the world: San Antonio and San Angelo in Texas, San Carlos in Arizona (the "arid zone") and, in California—settled by missionaries who introduced the natives to both Christianity and peonage—a whole calendar of saints, from St. Rose (Santa Rosa) and St. Francis (San Francisco) in the north to St. James (San Diego) near the Mexican border, and, greatest of all, the Virgin Mary, queen of the angels *(reina de los angeles)*. By the river of the Blessed Sacrament (Sacramento), by the town of the Holy Faith (Santa Fé) and by the mountains whose peaks at dawn and dusk flame scarlet like the veritable Blood of Christ (Sangre de Cristo), we English-speaking Americans may know and remember that we were not the first nor yet the second to pass that way.

Spreading across the immense expanses of the new lands, and filling up empty spots in the old ones, the settlers found mountain peaks by the score, rivers by the hundreds, creeks and brooks by the thousands, and founded town and villages on the same scale. All needed names. Some, as always, came from the natives; others were borrowed from great cities in other lands (Rome, London, Paris, Berlin, Canton, Moscow, Valparaiso) or from antiquity (Syracuse, Troy, Utica, Athens, Palmyra) or from the towns the settlers had left behind them: there are Hartfords scattered from Connecticut to Oregon, and Newarks from New Jersey to California. Some were named for national heroes—more than a score of Washingtons and over a dozen Lincolns, plus Jacksons, Grants, Shermans and Lees; others commemorate obscure notables whose memories survive only in the towns they founded or where they were admired. Pious folk named the Lebanons, Canaans and Bethlehems; impious ones, Tombstone, Hangtown (its name, alas, now civilized to Placerville) and the Dirty Devil River. Men seeking riches in the earth named Goldfield and Oroville, Silver Peak and Silver City, not to mention Leadville, Tungsten and Antimony; those mining the great forests for "lumber" (not English "timber") christened Oak Ridge, Pinehurst and Redwood City; those seeking merely to survive in the thirsty Great Basin named Bitter Creek and Badwater, Funeral Peak and Death Valley. Sheer exuberant imagination named Rabbit Ears Pass, Truth or Consequences and Steamboat Springs, on a mountain stream where no steamer ever plied; when imagination failed we got the North Fork of the South Fork. Elk, moose and antelope, wolf and grizzly, left names that survive even where the animals themselves are long gone, as did the tribes now extinct or nearly so: the Nauset, Mohican and Tuscarora, the Kickapoo, Omaha, Mandan, Cheyenne and Arapaho.

Like Stephen Vincent Benét, it is easy to fall in love with American names:

> The sharp names that never get fat;
> The snakeskin titles of mining claims,
> The tall war-bonnet of Medicine Hat,
> Tucson and Deadwood and Lost Mule Flat . . .

They are fraught with magic: tragedy and comedy, the call of the wild and the lure of the city, heroes remembered and forgotten, fortunes made and fortunes lost, the courage, imagination, hardihood and brutality of those who settled the land—and the memory of those who were there before them.

As with the names, so with the language. Politics inevitably gave new meanings to the English words "president," "senate," "congress" and "assembly," which in turn begot the new adjectives "presidential," "congressional" and "senatorial." Likewise from politics are the "spoils system" and "pork barrel"—well known in England, but under other names —and the fabulous "gerrymander," unknown in England, since electoral districts there had not been redrawn since the seventeenth century (both the word and the practice subsequently crossed the Atlantic). This marvelous term derives from the political boss Elbridge Gerry, who around 1800 presided over a notably biased redistricting of Massachusetts. Examining a map of one of the new districts and tracing its bizarrely twisting boundaries, an opponent muttered, "It looks like a salamander!" "No," said another, "a Gerrymander!" Candidates were "dark horses" or "favorite sons," or mere "wardheelers" picked by a "caucus" of the "machine." The fortunate candidate won by a "landslide"; the unlucky one became a "lame duck."

Homesteaders traveled west by "flatboat" or "prairie schooner"— later, the "iron horse"—to plow (not "plough," as in England) the virgin soil of the "corn belt" or "wheat belt." Prospectors would "stake a claim" (originally, by literally driving stakes at the corners) and hope to "strike it rich," but if the claim "petered out" they would "pull up stakes" and seek new diggings that might "pan out" better.

The almost explosive expansion of industry contributed both "payrolls" and "sweatshops," along with such inventions as the "cotton gin," "telegraph," "telephone," "sewing machine," "elevator"—and "electric chair." Speculators in "real estate" made fortunes selling city and suburban "lots" (so called from colonial times, when building sites in new townships were sometimes parceled out by lot). High and low finance contributed "bulls" and "bears," profiting respectively from "booms" and "busts," along with stocks both "gilt-edged" and "watered"—the latter sold, inevitably, in a "bucket shop." The manufacturer's sweatshops, "lockouts" and "yellow-dog contracts" begot "strikes," complete with "scabs" and the "finks" who served as "strikebreakers."

Perhaps the most evocative feature of the new economy and technology was the railroad. Simply in its physical presence, the steam locomotive, its stack belching black smoke by day, its firebox door glaring orange at night, its pounding drivers reeling off more miles in a day than a man could travel on horseback in a week, was the most impressive man-made object that most people had ever seen. As symbol, it was more impressive still, its steel bands binding isolated towns into one expanding nation, its lonesome whistles, echoing between the hills and across the prairies, telling of the far-off places the settlers had once come from, or might one day move to, or might never see.

Though originally an English invention, the American railroad evolved a vocabulary almost totally different from that of the British "railway." Its rails were laid on "ties," not "sleepers"; trains transferred from one track to another on "switches," not "points." The "freight train" (not "goods train") was made up of "cars" (not "waggons")—"boxcars," "flatcars," "gondolas"—while passengers rode not in "carriages" but in plushy "parlor cars" and "Pullmans," or, more often, in plain "passenger cars" or "coaches" with wooden seats.

The railroads begot the "hobo" (nobody knows where his name came from) who "rode the rods" to find temporary work in mine or "lumber camp," or on a "combine" at harvest time; the railroad magnate who charged "all the traffic will bear," as, indeed, magnates and merchants have been doing since Babylon; and the tiny "jerkwater town," one where the hurtling "limiteds" never stopped, but could replenish their boilers at full speed by lowering a scoop into a water-filled trough between the rails—not to mention "main line" and "side track."

As always, a large proportion of the new terms sooner or later fell by the wayside; who now remembers the political verb "to swartwout" (i.e., to emulate a notably corrupt customs official of that name) or the slanderous election-eve rumor, the "roorback" (from an imaginary author cited as the source of one such tale)? Reading through H. L. Mencken's classic *The American Language,* whose most recent revision dates from less than fifty years ago, one is struck by the number of then-current Americanisms that are now obsolete or archaic.

All the new words we have discussed thus far were either English in origin or borrowed from the natives or other peoples whom the Americans found in residence as they overran the continent. But what of the immigrants who, by the tens of millions, helped populate the new lands?

Though most people don't realize it, the largest single immigrant group has been British—English, Scotch and some Welsh—who, since they virtually all spoke English, left no linguistic traces that anyone can identify. American English has, indeed, borrowed from British English since the Revolution, but the bulk of the borrowings are relatively recent, and most of them from books, though it is often impossible to be sure whether a given word crossed the Atlantic in print or by word of mouth. For similar reasons, there are almost no linguistic traces of the millions of Irish driven westward by the devastating potato famine of 1847–48; some of them doubtless spoke Gaelic, but virtually all of them spoke English. The comic "stage Irishman" of the late nineteenth and early twentieth centuries introduced such terms as "begorrah" and "shillelagh," while earlier borrowings may be represented by "blarney" (from Blarney Castle in Ireland) and the *smiderins* ("tiny fragments") we sometimes smash things into, though the first of these, at least, may well have reached America via England, where it was borrowed not long after 1800.

Surprisingly, the contribution of the other, non-English-speaking immigrants to American English is hardly more visible than that of the British or Irish, apart from one limited area of life that we shall get to in a moment. The Pennsylvania Dutch (who were not Dutch but German—*Deutsch*) arrived before the Revolution, yet have given us only the "hex" someone puts on us. To be sure, they have always kept pretty much to themselves, yet we have only a few more words from the great wave of Germans—some five million all told—who spread across the U.S. beginning in 1848, when the liberals of their homeland failed to establish a democratic government. (It was one of these immigrants, Carl Schurz, who brilliantly supplemented the superpatriot's "My country, right or wrong!" with "When right, to be kept right; when wrong to be put right.") The Germans temporarily influenced local varieties of English in such places as Milwaukee, Cincinnati (one section of which was known as "Across the Rhine") and New York's Yorkville: a few generations ago, many English-speaking Americans were at least glancingly familiar with *Biergartens, Turnvereins* (gymnastic clubs), *Sängerfests* (song fests) and other amiable manifestations of German *kultur*. But as German-speaking immigrants gave way to their English-speaking descendants, their language evaporated, leaving as its only residue a few words like *kindergarten* ("children's garden"), "loafer" and its derived verb (apparently from *Landläufer*, "land-runner"—tramp) and "bum" (noun, verb—"bum a cigarette"—and adjective—"a bum deal"). This was originally "bummer," from *Bummeler*, loafer. "Bummer" seems to have passed into English during the Civil War, when it was applied, in no complimentary sense, to the troops of General Sherman (some of them Germans) on the devastating march from Atlanta to the sea, which even today makes Sherman's name anathema to some Georgians. (In defense of Sherman, we should note that he achieved his objective—wrecking the South's economy— while killing very few people; there are worse ways of fighting a war.)

All the millions from other nationalities—Scandinavians, Chinese, Italians, Poles, Hungarians, Slavs and smaller contingents from other lands—have left even fewer linguistic traces, with the single exception of the Jews. These, for a complex of reasons—notably, the high rate of literacy and ingrained respect for learning they brought with them—were among the most "upwardly mobile" of all immigrant groups, in every business or profession they were allowed to enter. (During my own boyhood, virtually all American colleges had quotas limiting the number of Jews they admitted.) The Jews were notably successful in "show business," whose performers and writers have brought a number of Yiddish terms into American English.

Yiddish, though written in the Hebrew alphabet, is actually a dialect of medieval German, with heavy borrowings from Russian, Polish and, of course, Hebrew, still the religious language of Orthodox Jews. Among the Yiddish terms now known to many if not most Americans are *schlemiel* (fool, bungler), *schlimazl* (luckless person, "loser"), *schmuck* (originally, "prick," both literally and figuratively, but now merely an unpleasant schlemiel) and that invaluable noun *chutzpah* (effrontery, squared). The classic example of chutzpah is the man who murdered his parents and then asked the court for mercy on the ground that he was an orphan. (His chutzpah was matched, however, by an ambassador from an Arab state who, during the 1973 oil embargo, complained that his chauffeur had to wait in line for gas.) Americans who don't know the difference between *milkich* and *fleishich* still know that there is something fishy about anything that's not *kosher*, and whether or not they play cards, can tell a *kibitzer* when they see one.

The immigrant contribution to American English becomes noticeable, however, when it comes to eating and drinking; one might say that the only genuine American "melting pot" is a cooking pot. From the Native Americans, as noted earlier, we got hominy, succotash and squash. The Dutch of New York contributed *koolsla* ("cabbage salad"), which, folk-etymologized into "cold-slaw" (because it's served that way), begot "hot slaw," a dish of *cooked* shredded cabbage served in parts of the Midwest. Equally Dutch are the *kraanbere* sauce served with Thanksgiving turkey, as well as the *krulles* and *koekjies* ("little cakes") that we consume at coffee breaks and other times. ("Cookie," by the way, is involved in one of the more bewildering encounters between American and British English. An American cookie is an English biscuit, while an American biscuit is an English scone, except that American pilot biscuit is English ship's biscuit. Clear?)

When we *dunk* a cruller or doughnut, however, we are indebted to the Pennsylvania Dutch, who also gave us *Sauerkraut* ("sour cabbage") and the *Nudel* and *Pretzel.* From the French of Canada we got *chaudière,* literally "caldron," but early applied to the fish or clam chowders stewed up in it. (Its literal sense crops up in Canada's Chaudière River, whose rapids and whirlpools make it a seething caldron indeed.) From Louisiana French comes *jambalaya,* that savory concoction of seafood, ham and other goodies that is New Orleans's answer to bouillabaisse.

The nineteenth-century German immigrants—like all their country-men, valiant trenchermen—brought over what might almost be called the German national dish: *Wurst* (sausage)—*Leberwurst* (now semi-translated into "liverwurst"), dark-red *Blutwurst, Knackwurst* (so tightly packed it cracks—*knackt*—when cut), and of course the *Wienerwurst* or wiener, the almost identical *Frankfurter,* and (in a different category) the omnipresent *Hamburger.* Whether these last three, in their modern U.S. versions, would be recognized by natives of Vienna *(Wien),* Frankfurt or Hamburg is, however, an open question. German too, of course, is the *Delikatessen* where many of these "delicacies" are sold.

The Italians have contributed another American "national" dish, *spaghetti* ("little strings"), along with *ravioli* ("little turnips," presumably from the shape of some varieties) and, for the connoisseur, a dozen other varieties of *pasta* (the flour paste from which they are made). From the garden the Italians brought *broccoli* ("little sprouts"—not to be confused with the Brussels variety) and *zucchini* ("little gourds," though they are of course a squash). And how can we forget *pizza* (apparently from *pizzare,* to pinch, which is what the pizza maker does to his dough)?

Mexican cuisine was slow to spread outside the region that some residents still sardonically call "occupied Mexico." Over the last twenty years, however, nearly all Americans have at least sampled the fiery stew originally called *chile con carne* (hot pepper with meat) but now simply "chili." Also from Mexico are the "peppered" *enchilada* (whose *-chil-*, like that of "chili," comes from Native American *chilli*) and *tacos* ("rolls")— both made from *tortillas* ("little round cakes") plus various fillings—as well as the cornmeal-and-meat *tamale* (from Native American *tamalli*).

From the Hungarians we get "goulash" (from *gulyas hus*, "herdsman's meat"); from the Poles, their garlic-laden sausage, *kolbaczi;* from the Russians or (more likely) the Jews, *borschch*—whence the "Borscht Belt" of Jewish Catskill resorts that was the training ground for several generations of night-club, theatrical and movie performers. Unquestionably Jewish are *pastrami* (though the Yiddish word was borrowed from Romanian), *lox,* and the *beygel* (ring) on which it is often served with cream cheese. ("Lox" has a strangely checkered history in English: its Old English version, *laex,* was replaced by Norse *lax* in the thirteenth century, which was in turn displaced by its French equivalent, "salmon." "Lox" itself, meaning "smoked salmon," was reborrowed during the present century.)

Americans tired of home cooking have long patronized their friendly local Chinese restaurant, for *chow mein* ("fried noodles," with the same Chinese root as "chow," food) or *chop suey* ("mixed pieces"), though the latter is seldom seen these days, having been replaced by more authentic (and tastier) Chinese dishes, such as *moo-goo-gai-pan* ("mushroom-chicken-slice"). And in our larger cities, at least, the gourmet can usually turn up a tolerable Scandinavian *smörgäsbord* ("open-faced-sandwich-table").

When we pour out the drinks, our linguistic choice is less varied. The basic American "hard liquor" is still whiskey, ranging from the finest Scotch malts to the skull-blasting "white lightning" ("looks like water and kicks like a mule") of the southern mountains, distilled, of course, by moonshine to evade the "revenooers." More temperate drinkers stick to wine or beer, whose names are English, though the beer is not. It is, in fact, the Germans' *Lagerbier* ("stored"—aged—beer), which in the nineteenth century became so popular, thanks to the German takeover of American brewing, that it displaced the heavier, darker brew of the old English type, and is now called just "beer." More recently, whiskey has lost some ground to Russian *vodka* ("little water"), Mexican *tequila* (from the town where it may have originated) and rum, a word whose source nobody knows, though it has been in English, on both sides of the Atlantic, since the seventeenth century.

In language, if not in literature, the period between the Revolution and

World War I was unquestionably the American equivalent of the Elizabethan age. What did the English descendants of the Elizabethans think of our linguistic carryings-on? The answer, in two words, is: not much.

Twenty years before the Revolution, Samuel Johnson was already denouncing a book by an American as "a tract of corruption, to which every language widely diffused must always be exposed." Johnson's own experience and common sense certainly told him that linguistic change was inevitable, but his intense conservatism also told him that any change was likely to be for the worse—especially if it was the work of ignorant provincials, remote from the civilizing influence of London. Johnson considered even the Scots semibarbarous; it would have been surprising had he viewed the Americans any less sourly.

Johnson's view of American English remained typical of English literary opinion for well over a century. Thus in 1808, an English magazine denounced the "torrent of barbarous phraseology" that threatened to "destroy the purity of the English language." Another critic found American writing loaded with "a great multitude of words which are . . . as utterly foreign as if they had been adopted from Chinese or Hebrew." The first criticism was obviously fatuous: how can one talk of the "purity" of a language that had been borrowing from foreign tongues, with both hands, for centuries? The second was simply ignorant: the much-deplored "Americanisms" of the early nineteenth century were, in their great majority, English, not borrowed. Some were English words that had passed out of cultivated use in the old country; thus Americans said "fall" where educated Englishmen said "autumn." Indeed, of the two, "fall" was the more authentically "English"—if the term means anything— being directly derived from Old English, while "autumn" was a French import. Likewise, the phrase "I guess" meaning "I suppose," used by English writers until well into this century as a virtual trademark of eccentric American speech, goes back to Chaucer (*Of twenty yeer of age he was, I gesse*). Others, as we've seen, were old English words with new meanings, while still others were new compounds—but compounded out of English elements, according to the rules of English syntax. "Belittle," target of several critics, was modeled on such respectable English verbs as "befoul," used since the fourteenth century, while "lengthy," another supposed barbarism, was equally analogous to "weighty," used since around 1500.

American commentators, then and later, repeatedly made these points —with an occasional assist from colleagues across the Atlantic—but it made no difference to most English travelers and critics, who continued to berate American English, along with American manners and morals, in terms that were at best unreasonable and at worst viciously dishonest. Frances Trollope, mother of the novelist, reported in 1832 that during her entire stay in America she had seldom "heard a sentence elegantly turned and correctly pronounced." A few years later, Captain Frederick Marryat, author of several well-known naval novels, found it remarkable "how very debased the language has become in a short period." A few years later still, Dickens, after his fabulously successful American tour, wrote that outside New York and Boston, grammar was "more than doubtful" and that "the oddest vulgarisms" were acceptable. Perhaps the lowest blow came in 1863, from Henry Alford, Dean of Canterbury. Though he had never visited America, he bewailed "the process of deterioration which our Queen's English has undergone at the hands of the Americans," and finished by denouncing them for conducting "the most cruel and unprincipled war in the history of the world." Since earlier writers had denounced America for tolerating the slavery which that unprincipled war would abolish, it was clear that for a certain type of Englishman, *anything* America did, in language or politics, was wrong.

In fairness to the less abusive critics, one must concede that at the time they wrote Americans *were* going "hog wild" in reshaping their native tongue, and inevitably so. Not only were they by temperament contemptuous of all authority, but in vocabulary there *was* no authority. That is, there was no substantial cadre of people—professional writers and editors—whose particular business was the skillful, clear and precise use of words. Jefferson himself had noted in 1813 that "We have no distinct class of literati. . . . Every man is engaged in some industrious pursuit, and [learning] is but a secondary occupation. . . . Few, therefore, of those who are qualified have leisure to write." The main reason for this, I think, was that it was then almost impossible for an American writer to make a living (Webster being a notable exception). Americans bought books in quantity, but they were nearly all English books: the American market alone was still too small to yield more than a pittance to the American writer or his publisher. (Needless to say, the *English* bought very few *American* books.)

But having been fair to the English, we must also be fair to the Americans: much of the "American speech" reported by Dickens and many others was certainly never spoken by any American in or out of New York and Boston. As Ralph Waldo Emerson said of Dickens, "He has picked up and noted with eagerness each odd local phrase that he met with and . . . has joined them together into the broadest caricature." We have, in fact, actual records of frontier speech—notably, the utterances, both real and apocryphal, of Colonel Davy Crockett, who served three terms in Congress. Crockett, and his imitators, were sometimes eccentric in their syntax and often extravagant in their vocabularies, but were still nothing like as bizarre as Dickens' alleged Americans.

Examined more deeply, the controversy between British and Americans involved social attitudes as well as language. To begin with, some English still considered the language their private property, part of their queen's expanding empire, which the Americans had somehow misappropriated; the Americans, not unreasonably, felt it was as much their language as anyone else's. Another fundamental difference was exemplified in a dialogue between the British traveler Captain Basil Hall and the aging Noah Webster. To Hall's complaints over the multiplying novelties in the American vocabulary, Webster replied that Americans "had not only a right to adopt new words, but were obliged to modify the language to suit the novelty of [their] circumstances." The progress of language, he acutely noted, "is like the course of the Mississippi, the motion of which, at times, is scarcely perceptible, yet even then it possesses a momentum quite irresistible. Words and expressions will be forced into use, in spite of all the exertions of all the writers in the world."

"But surely," said the rather shocked Hall, "such innovations are to be deprecated?"

"I don't know that," replied Webster. "If a word becomes universally current in America, where English is spoken, why should not it take its station in the language?"

"Because," said Hall, "there are words enough already." His argument was unanswerable, since there was and is no way of defining how many words are "enough." Happily, English speakers at most periods have seldom troubled their heads about the matter; had they done so, the language would hardly be as rich as it is.

An even more fundamental source of conflict was hinted at as early as 1808, by the same writer who had compared Americanisms to Chinese and Hebrew. The Americans, he declared, make it "a point of conscience to have no aristocratical distinctions—even in their vocabulary." That is, they considered "one word as good as another, provided its meaning be as clear." Nowadays, many writers on both sides of the Atlantic would consider this last complaint a concise definition of good English usage, though the author clearly found it shocking. What was really bothering him, as it would bother Mrs. Trollope and dozens of later critics, was Americans' lack of "aristocratical distinctions." Americans didn't talk or (in most cases) write like upper-class Englishmen (no more than did the great majority of the English themselves) and, far worse, *clearly didn't give a good goddam*. Unlike the British lower classes of the time, the Americans didn't "know their place." The attitude persisted until well into this century; in 1908 an American critic summarized it concisely when he declared of the English: "It offends them that we are not thoroughly ashamed of ourselves for not being like them."

By that time, however, English attitudes were already beginning to change. American writers such as Fenimore Cooper (whose frontier novels had an immense vogue in England), Emerson, Hawthorne, Melville, Poe, Whitman and, above all, Mark Twain had demonstrated that while the language they used might or might not be "English" it could certainly produce a lively, vigorous and readable literature. Moreover, and thanks in part to the influence of these and other professional "literati," many of the more eccentric Americanisms had passed out of use. Not a few of the others had passed into British English, despite periodic howls from purists. By the 1920s, some distinguished British literary figures, including Robert Bridges (poet laureate, no less), Wyndham Lewis and Virginia Woolf, began speaking up for American English, finding the "invasion" of British English by Americanisms no disaster, and perhaps even something of a Good Thing. Thus Mrs. Woolf pointed out that Americans were only "doing what the Elizabethans did—they are coining new words." By contrast, she noted, "one may search English fiction in vain for a single new word. . . . All the expressive, ugly, vigorous slang which creeps in among us . . . comes from across the Atlantic." (Actually, Mrs. Woolf underestimated her own countrymen, some of whom had long been coining words at almost the American rate. The difference was that nearly all English writers of the time, if they were aware of these coinages at all, considered them "low" and therefore unfit to be seen in respectable literary company.)

The advent of the talkies—most of them "Made In U.S.A."—brought another upsurge of British viewings-with-alarm, comparable to the later French uproar over *franglais*. The King's English, it was held, was about to be submerged by a tide of transatlantic slang. Nor is the argument done with even now: some English writers continue to deplore American usage, in most cases every bit as ignorantly as that early nineteenth-century critic who compared Americanisms to Hebrew and Chinese.

A recent target is American syntax, which has supposedly been corrupted by our tens of millions of non-English-speaking immigrants; in the words of the British writer Kenneth Hudson, by "the immigrant's literal, but illiterate, translation from his own language, which strikes roots in the country of his adoption." Hudson's particular target in this case was "premodification," whereby "George Shearing, the pianist" is condensed to "pianist George Shearing." Anthony Burgess, also writing during the 1970s, took a similar view of "slow" used as an adverb ("Go slow!"), which he called "U.S. English . . . (undoubtedly via Yiddish)." Here and in other, similar criticisms we find a distinct odor of the anti-Semitism long endemic among educated Britishers.

Since American immigrants, especially the Jews, have long been blamed for all sorts of things they had nothing whatever to do with, I think that "criticisms" of this sort should be seen for what they are: pure wrongheaded ignorance. As we've seen, the immigrants' influence on the American vocabulary has been minimal outside the kitchen; their influence on general American syntax has been almost invisible. The only exception I can think of offhand is the expression "by me," as in "O.K. by me," which is is undoubtedly borrowed from (not "via," as Burgess puts it) Yiddish *bei mir.* "Go slow," on the other hand, is not Yiddish syntax, but rather perfectly good English syntax—good enough, anyway, for Shakespeare ("How slow this old moon wanes"), Milton and Thackeray, among others. As for "premodification," it was, as a matter of history, contrived and popularized not by immigrants but by publishing tycoon Henry Luce and his band of bright, WASPy young men, as a feature of what was called "Timestyle," whose purpose was to give that egregious newsmagazine a trendy, sophisticated flavor.

Though nobody has conducted a poll on the subject, my own feeling is that most British writers today take a less jaundiced view of American English. They may or may not use Americanisms themselves, but see no reason why Americans should not use them. Many, perhaps the majority, would agree with the view put forward by the American critic Brander Matthews nearly a century ago: "A Briticism is none the worse because it is known only to the inhabitants of the British Isles, and an Americanism is not to be despised because it is current only in America. The question is not where it was born, but whether it is worthy to live."

A few years later, the British critic William Archer echoed Matthews, in terms that would also evoke wide agreement in both countries today. "The English language," he wrote, "is no mere historic monument, like Westminster Abbey, to be religiously preserved as a relic of the past; it is a living organism. . . . It has before it, we may fairly hope, a future still greater than its glorious past." And the greatness of that future, he concluded, would depend on "the harmonious interplay of spiritual forces" between the two great peoples who speak and write it.

That interplay has continued across the years, though not always harmoniously; history has made Britons and Americans different peoples, and it could not have been otherwise. Equally, it has made their languages different. But it has not, praise be, made them *that* different, to the point where, as Shaw put it, the two nations are indeed "separated by the same language": British and Americans alike can still share the treasure—past, present and future—of our common tongue.

10. OUR INFINITE VARIETY

Modern Variations on an Old Theme

❦

Age cannot wither . . . nor custom stale her infinite variety.

—Shakespeare

It is impossible for an Englishman to open his mouth without making some other Englishman hate or despise him.

—G. B. Shaw

Every language spoken over a sizable area is subject to regional variations called dialects; English, spoken over a wider expanse of territory than any other language, naturally includes more such variations. American English has anywhere from half a dozen to over a dozen, depending on how fine you choose to draw your distinctions; British English, by some accounts, no less than thirteen. To these we must add Australian English, New Zealand English, West Indian English, South African English and the English dialects spoken by several million upper-class and professional people in India, some other parts of Asia and Black Africa.

Dialects aren't just regional, though most people think of them that way; they can also be social. My small group of London friends—journalistic and literary types—speak differently from a London docker; equally, I, who speak a different dialect from either, also speak differently from those of my New York City neighbors who work as "longshoremen" (not "dockers"). Almost any regional dialect includes two or three such "class" dialects, some of whose features stretch across regional lines; this is especially true of one of the most interesting social dialects in America, Black English.

To oversimplify matters considerably, regional dialects divide the English-speaking world geographically, while class dialects divide it socially. Thus (to take our earlier example), the speech of a New York longshoreman will resemble mine in certain respects (expecially in phonetics and vocabulary) but will resemble those of a Boston or Norfolk longshoreman —or even a London docker—in certain others, especially syntax. All four dock workers, for example, will probably say "he don't" instead of "he doesn't," as I do, but the sound will range from the Londoner's "'e daownt" to the Virginian's "he don'."

What are dialects, and where do they come from? Unfortunately, there is much less hard information on the subject than one would like, and much of the information we have is out of date. The English Dialect Society, for example, got its start during the Victorian age, when many British intellectuals were suffering from what I call the Merrie England syndrome: an idealization of folk songs, folk dances and "folk speech"— that is, the culture of the old English village, supposedly a repository of ancient virtues not found in cities and towns. American dialectologists have mostly followed their example; thus Hans Kurath, until his death a few years ago the high priest of American dialectology, has described the three social levels of U.S. speech as "(1) Cultivated speech, which is most widespread in urban areas; (2) common speech, the language of the large middle class; (3) folk speech, *which is found in rural areas"* (emphasis added). Not a word about "blue-collar" speech, found almost entirely in urban or suburban areas.

Since more than three quarters of the U.S. and British population today live in cities and suburbs, it's obvious that even the most assiduous studies of "folk speech" can tell us little about how most of us actually talk. For instance, one of the terms dialectologists consider a regional "marker" in the northeastern U.S. is "whiffletree" (the bar to which a draft horse is hitched), something that few Americans have ever laid eyes on, even in rural areas (most farmers now use tractors). Again, an aging minority of mostly rural folk may talk of "clabber" (or "loppered milk" or "cruddled milk"); the rest of us buy its nearest commercial equivalent, yogurt. In short, the dialectologists who inhabit this Norman Rockwell world are emulating the legendary foo-foo bird, which flies backward because it doesn't give a damn where it's going but likes to know where it's been.

If a lot of the available dialect data is obsolete or almost so, a lot more of it is far too sparse to support any sort of reliable conclusion. For example, a 1970 study of speech in three Kentucky counties, aimed at (among other things) defining possible speech differences between blacks and whites, was based on interviews with exactly twelve people, only two of them under sixty—and only one a black! Nor is this a uniquely horrible example: the *Linguistic Atlas of New England* (published 1941), supposedly the definitive work on the subject, is based on interviews with 416 "informants," most of whom were also over sixty; the entire city of Boston, with a population of close to a million, is represented by five. Even worse, every one of the five, so far as I can make out, was a WASP—that is, the Irish, Italians, Portuguese and blacks (composing most of Boston's blue-collar and a large part of its white-collar population) were simply ignored.

In short, dialect studies, like other studies of human societies, reflect the investigators' own social preconceptions—in this case, which dialects are worth studying. This fact, in turn, may well reflect an even more basic fact about dialects: they are involved more than any other aspect of speech in questions of power, prestige and snobbery.

A great many dialect studies are misleading in another way: they focus on vocabulary, especially such archaic terms as "whiffletree," "clabber" and the like. People are interviewed with dozens of "What do you call that?" questions, and their answers are charted on maps with lines, called "isoglosses," showing where in a given region one term drops out of use and another replaces it. Sometimes a group of isoglosses will line up fairly neatly, with one set of terms on one side and another on the other. More often, there is little geographical correspondence between one isogloss and another; often *both* terms are current over fairly wide areas. Thus by judiciously selecting one's terms, one can place the boundaries between one "dialect area" and another almost where one chooses.

The main reason for these inconsistencies, I think, is that vocabulary is conspicuously the most fluid aspect of language, as compared with syntax and phonetics. The last, in particular, is something we pick up quite unconsciously in early childhood and is likely to stay with us for a long time, perhaps as long as life itself: few adults can learn to speak a foreign language without an accent, be they ever so fluent in syntax and vocabulary. By contrast, our vocabularies can expand and change for decades; any child, and most adults, can pick up a new word in seconds.

What exactly is a dialect? It has been said that a perversion is any kind of sex the speaker doesn't like, and for many people a dialect is any kind of English they don't speak. Earnest young graduate students inquiring about dialects out in the field are likely to draw responses like "Dialeck? We-uns don't speak no dialeck hyarabouts, but effn you go up the road about tin miles . . . " The truth is, of course, that all of us speak dialects: the elegant Victorian English used by the good ladies and gentlemen of the original English Dialect Society was just as much a dialect as the speech of the picturesque rustics they studied.

My own definition of a dialect—which some experts would disagree with—is a variant of a language with distinctive phonetic characteristics, which may or may not be accompanied by significant differences in vocabulary and syntax. I doubt that there are anywhere on earth two varieties of English differing *only* in syntax, while "dialects" differing only in vocabulary are better classified as argots or lingoes.

The most obvious source of dialects is the same one that helped convert the Vulgar Latin spoken all over Western Europe two thousand years ago into the Romance languages of today: geographical separation. This particular process, however, is much less important today than in Roman or medieval times: for Chaucer's pilgrims, the horseback journey to Canterbury was a lot longer than a modern jet flight from London to Los Angeles—or Sydney, for that matter—while electronic communications carry speech from one part of the English-speaking world to another with the speed of light.

Sometimes dialectical differences do not *develop* in different regions but are rather brought there, by the process known as differential migration —the settlement of different regions by groups with different speech habits. The results are most conspicuous, of course, when groups of settlers speak different languages, as with French-speaking Quebec (settled by the French) versus the rest of Canada (settled mainly by English-speakers). More subtle differences are found when settlers in different regions speak different dialects of the same language. As noted in Chapter 4, the settlement of England by different groups of English (Angles, Saxons, Jutes) is thought to account for dialectical differences in Old English; a more recent example (discussed later in this chapter) is the high proportion of Scots among early English-speaking migrants into Canada, which almost certainly explains some phonetic features of Canadian English compared with other American dialects.

Differential migration can also bring groups with the same dialect into contact with different speakers of other tongues, whether natives or immigrants. These contacts operate most conspicuously in vocabulary, as (for example) in U.S. and Australian English, whose vocabularies differ very markedly in words borrowed from the native peoples of the two continents. English speakers in the southwestern U.S., as we've seen, borrowed heavily from the Spaniards they found in residence, though many of the borrowed words eventually spread throughout the U.S. (thanks largely to the influence of Western novels and films). Such "exotic" contacts may also influence phonetics and syntax; thus some of the distinctive traits of southern U.S. English are thought by many to stem from the large proportion of blacks in that region (more on this later). Having said all this, however, I must add that some of the reasons behind dialectical divergence are as mysterious as those underlying linguistic change in general.

Like the languages of a family such as Indo-European, dialects fall into related groups: the regional and class dialects of Great Britain, those of America, the class dialects of Australia (there are apparently no important regional variants there), and so on. But the relationship is more complicated than that, because the groups diverge from one another "from the top down": that is, the varieties of "upper-class," educated English around the world are much closer to one another in syntax, in phonetics and even in vocabulary than are the less educated dialects. A classic reflection of this fact was the comment of an uneducated "Bajun" (Barbadian) on the radio speech in which Edward VIII announced his abdication: "Mon, he tok just like a culchud Bajun!" In fact, a cultured Barbadian could have communicated quite easily with the king, just as I can communicate easily with friends in Toronto, Houston or San Francisco, and almost as easily with friends in London. On the other hand, put an "uncultured" Barbadian together with the Norfolk longshoreman and the London docker mentioned earlier, and each might well believe that while he was speaking English, the other two were talking some foreign lingo.

As just noted, dialects in Great Britain go back to the English invasions of the fifth century, and are thought to reflect differential migration by tribes or groups of tribes speaking different dialects of *Englisc.* By Shakespeare's day, the original three or four English dialects had split into seven; from south to north they were Southern, Kentish, East Midland, London (basically, East Midland, but with some Northern and Southern influences due to migration into the capital), West Midland, Northern and Scottish.

These sixteenth-century dialect regions have persisted to the present, though the differences among them have been blurred by migrations into urban areas over the past two centuries. Indeed, the differences were probably never as sharp as modern "dialect maps" suggest: each dialect area actually comprised a number of local dialects, so that in traveling from (say) London to York one would hear a gradual change of speech from London to East Midland to Northern. Shaw's Professor Higgins of *Pygmalion* could spot a speaker's birthplace within a few miles, and some nonfictional dialectologists claim to be able to do as well, at least in rural regions, where dialect differences have been most persistent.

Educated London English—which, as "BBC English," is something of a standard for all of Great Britain—is familiar to anyone who has watched a British movie or TV program with upper-class characters. Hardly less familiar, even to Americans, is uneducated or blue-collar London English, or Cockney, at least in its less extreme versions. Few people in the English-speaking world have not seen Shaw's *Pygmalion* or its musical version, *My Fair Lady*, both of which revolve around the differences between the Cockney spoken by Eliza Doolittle and her disgraceful parent and the refined London speech of Professor Higgins and Colonel Pickering.

The most conspicuous phonetic feature of Cockney is its prolongation of long vowel sounds, with single vowels being transformed into diphthongs and diphthongs, into triphthongs. "Again" becomes "agyne," and "now," "naow," the latter blending the vowels of "at," "so," and "boot." Another Cockney feature is the "intrusive R"—the injection of an /r/ after some long vowels, so that "gone" becomes "gorn" and "lost," "lorst," as in the line from the old comic song, "And agyne she lorst 'er nyme." (Some Americans take the English slang term "barmy" —nutty, kooky—to be a case of the intrusive R, and spell it "balmy"; in fact it derives from "barm"—yeast. A barmy person figuratively has yeasty, fermented brains.) Some but not all Cockneys transform the sounds /th/ and /dh/ (as in "THin" and "THis") into /f/ and /v/, as in the catch-phrase "firty-free fevvers on a frush's froat." On the other hand, the "dropped H" (as in "Look 'ere, you!") that some Americans consider "typical" Cockney is found in many other blue-collar English dialects.

A striking feature of Cockney as compared with other English regional dialects is its rapid change over the past 150 years. In Dickens' day, its most conspicuous feature seems to have been the interchanging of /v/ and /w/: the immortal Sam Weller of *Pickwick Papers* introduced himself in court as "Veller" ("Spell it with a wee, Sammy," cried his father); his fictional contemporary the fox-hunting London grocer John Jorrocks, of R. S. Surtees, hunted "wixens" as well as foxes. If there was anything distinctive about Cockney vowels of that time, neither author took note of it. By the time Shaw created Alfred Doolittle, however, soon after 1900, Cockney V's and W's had regained their normal places and vowel changes held the stage; the "firty-free fevvers" consonant shift was apparently still to come.

Cockney has long been used by English writers for comic purposes, with Weller, Jorrocks and Doolittle as notable examples. Indeed, Shakespeare's lower-class characters are almost routinely played in Cockney nowadays, though the text of the plays suggests nothing of the sort. (In a recent production of *A Midsummer Night's Dream*, Puck, the very spirit of rural England, was played as a Cockney!) Kipling, however, used a modified Cockney as a medium for serious verse, and while critics have claimed that the dialect diminishes their poetic impact, a Cockney Kipling fan might well feel otherwise.

As one moves out from London, the dialects tend to grow more phonetically conservative—that is, their sounds often tend to resemble those of Shakespeare's or even Chaucer's English. London, for more than five hundred years, has been where the action was, full of wanderers from other parts of Great Britain and from abroad; social change was rapid, and linguistic change no less so, Cockney being a good case in point. In contrast, there is the West Country dialect of Devon and parts adjacent, which in some respects has apparently not changed for nearly eight centuries. Its most noticeable feature is the shift of initial /f/ and /s/ to /v/ and /z/, producing such utterances as "Did 'e zee the vox?" ("Did ye see the fox?"). This phonetic shift was once found in all the southern English dialects—it has been traced back as far as 1200—but has survived only in the isolated rural West Country. A few southern forms, however, passed into the London dialect and thence into today's Standard English: thus we say "vixen" (not "fixen"), "vane" (as in "weathervane") and "vat." In at least one case, both forms have survived, though neither "vial" (Southern) nor "phial" (East Midland) is much used nowadays. West Country dialect is used extensively in the late R. F. Delderfield's trilogy *A Horseman Riding By;* other Southern dialects with less archaic phonetics are found in Thomas Hardy's novels and some Kipling short stories, notably "The Wish House" and "Friendly Brook," both employing the rural dialect of East Sussex.

There is no very sharp line between middle-class East Midland and middle-class London speech, and none at all between upper-class speech in the two areas; rural speech includes some syntactic peculiarities such as the use of "that" instead of "it" as in "He saw that coming along the road." West Midland, spoken in much of Britain's industrial belt, is rather more conservative; thus almost everyone, regardless of class, retains an earlier vowel sound in such words as "love" and "up," both of which have the vowel of "foot," and are often spelled "luv" and "oop." West Midland of the "extreme," blue-collar variety is spoken by most working-class characters in British films and TV who don't speak Cockney (as in the film *Saturday Night and Sunday Morning*).

Still farther west is the English of Wales. Perhaps a fifth of the Welsh speak their ancestral tongue, a direct descendant of ancient British, but nearly all this group are bilingual. Yet even the Welsh who speak English from birth have taken over from the Welsh tongue a peculiar and unmistakable intonation, either "musical" or "singsong," depending on who is describing it. Also from Welsh are certain characteristic turns of phrase, notably the interjection "look you," which has been almost the trademark of the stage Welshman since Shakespeare's Captain Fluellen of *Henry V*.

In the Northern dialects, phonetic and even syntactic conservatism become more noticeable. The old-fashioned Yorkshireman who says "Tha'll get nowt from me" is almost Shakespearean both in wording ("Thou'lt get nought from me") and in his pronunciation of "nought." Northern dialect shows up in Kipling (notably, in "On Greenhow Hill") and in some of the writings of D. H. Lawrence, himself the son of a Nottinghamshire miner.

Even more archaic are the phonetics of Scots English; "about" and "night," for example, are pronounced much as they were in Chaucer's London (/aboot/, /nikht/). This conservatism reflects the distance of Scotland from southern England, centuries of Scottish-English hostility —by no means extinct today, though the two nations were united under one crown nearly four hundred years ago—and the fact that while many Scots emigrated to England (and other lands), few English cared to settle in Scotland. The Scots vocabulary is also distinctive, and was even more so a century ago, when it included more than five thousand special words; most of these have since dropped out of use except in rural areas. Thanks to these dialectical terms, and the peculiarities of Scots phonetics, some of Burns' poems are almost as difficult for the rest of us as Chaucer.

Many of these Scottish words are cognates of English words that underwent a distinctive semantic (and often phonetic) evolution over the centuries; most of the rest derive from words that have been lost elsewhere in England. A few were borrowed from the "native" language of Scotland, Gaelic (actually, the Gaelic-speaking Scots did not migrate into Scotland from Ireland until after the English had moved into England), of which a few have passed into the general English vocabulary. Another handful were taken from Old Norse: parts of mainland Scotland were under Scandinavian rule until the later thirteenth century, and the Orkneys and Shetlands for a good deal longer than that.

The reason these borrowings are so few is that the Scottish Lowlands have been English-speaking for well over a thousand years and, as the most fertile, populous, and literate part of the country had no compelling reason to borrow words from the Gaelic- and Norse-speaking tribesmen of the north and west. The most numerous survivals of these tongues occur where one would expect: on the land. Loch Lomond and other, less widely sung Scottish lochs use the Gaelic equivalent of (French)-English "lake," while the "Ben" in Ben Nevis and a score of other Scottish peaks is Gaelic for "mountain." Maritime geographical terms, however, are dominated by Old Norse, as the waters around Scotland were long dominated by the Vikings and their descendants. The firths that cleave the Scottish coastline come from Old Norse *fyorth,* the -ay in Sanday, Ronaldsay, Whaley and others of the Orkneys and Shetlands is Norse for "island," while the stormy sounds between the islands are from Norse *sund;* this last has passed into the general vocabularies of both American and British English.

Scots English produced its own literature, but a very modest one. Its only major figure is the magnificent Burns, that hard-drinking "proven fornicator" who somehow became the national poet of a rather sober and God-fearing nation. The poverty of Scots literature in part reflects the centuries-long poverty of Scotland itself, which led many of its ablest sons to seek their fortunes in England and elsewhere, but in part, perhaps, a certain lack of interest or aptitude. Given the Scots' major contributions to British culture in medicine, technology, science and government, it's hard to believe that they could not have distinguished themselves equally in letters had they cared to. Even more important, perhaps, was the fact that from the eighteenth century on, any Scottish writer who cared to make a decent living had to stick pretty much to Standard English, as did such figures as Scott, Stevenson (both of whom, however, used Scottish in dialogue) and Barrie: there simply weren't enough book buyers in Scotland alone.

Ireland, even poorer than Scotland, produced a notable Anglo-Irish literature during the last hundred years, with Yeats, Synge and O'Casey among the major figures. (Shaw and Wilde, though Irish by birth, both wrote in Standard English, of course.) Joyce is a special, indeed a unique case: on the one hand, he is surely the most Irish of writers; on the other, his language, always excepting dialogue passages, is basically Standard English—in *Finnegans Wake,* hardly even English.

The English of Ireland ranges from the educated English of Dublin (which some Dubliners will tell you is the purest English spoken in the British Isles) to the very distinctive brogue of the blue-collar worker and peasant. This last is, like Scots English, phonetically conservative, but the pronunciations it has conserved are quasi-Shakespearean rather than quasi-Chaucerian. The reason is that few Irish learned to speak English until the seventeenth century, and therefore they naturally learned the English current at that time. For some two centuries thereafter, moreover, even most English-speaking Irish preferred their ancestral tongue,

Gaelic; the long survival of this language (still not entirely extinct) explains some peculiarities of Irish syntax. Such constructions as "Is he come with yourself?", "Six yards of stuff for to make a yellow gown" (Yeats), "Is it mocking me you are?" and "I was after cleaning the house" are actually translations from the Gaelic. Gaelic, moreover, lacks expressions equivalent to "yes" and "no," so that the Irishman's answer to the question "Is he come with yourself?" will be "He is" or "He is not."

There has been, so far as I know, little systematic study of class dialects in England—mainly because for the upper-class English, *any* other variety of the language, regional or otherwise, was "low" or at least "lowish," however distinguished the speaker. Even Sir James Murray, editor of the great *Oxford English Dictionary*, remained self-conscious about his Scots accent until the end of his life (ironically, when he returned to Scotland on his retirement, his neighbors thought he talked like an Englishman). Shaw, as we know, had a great deal to say about this linguistic snobbery of the English establishment, but it was far from new in his day: the English were class-conscious, in language and other ways, long before Marx and Lenin invented the phrase. As early as the fourteenth century, the upper-class London dialect of the court seems to have been considered superior to provincial speech; later and more direct evidence comes from the critic George Puttenham in 1589. He advises poets to "take the usuall speach of the Court, and that of London and the shires lying about London within lx. myles, and not much above." Outside this area, he declares, even "the gentlemen and also their learned clerks" mostly "condescend" (lower) their speech to that of "the common people."

The same bias is reflected in Shakespeare's use of dialect: invariably for comic purposes. A good example is the byplay between his three non-English captains in *Henry V*: Fluellen (Welsh), Macmorris (Irish) and Jamie (Scotch). On the one hand, this multi-ethnic group was introduced as a plug for British national unity in wartime, and is thus the lineal ancestor of the multi-ethnic American infantry squad beloved of Hollywood ("Goldberg, take left flank; Di Nobile, right flank; Martinez on point, and Kowalski, you give covering fire."). But brave captains though they were, and for all their contributions to Henry's victory at Agincourt, they were also figures of fun, because they talked funny.

Things haven't changed all that much in four hundred years: to most of the English upper classes, what they speak is "English," while all else is "dialect." Yet the essence of upper-class speech remains curiously hard to define. It is by no means (as one might expect) an archaic, stick-in-the-mud dialect matching the social attitudes of many of its speakers, but

almost as fluid as Cockney itself. Thus Trollope's mid-Victorian aristocrats unself-consciously used locutions like "I ain't" and "He don't" that
would be deemed irretrievably low by their modern counterparts. A later
generation of quasi-aristocrats, as Nancy Mitford entertainingly pointed
out some twenty years ago, felt impelled to develop their distinctive "U"
(Upper-class) vocabulary to distinguish themselves from the upwardly
mobile, "non-U" middle classes: e.g., they said "lunch," not "luncheon,"
"looking glass," not "mirror," and "scent," not "perfume."

The dominance of educated Londonese stems partly from the dominance of London itself over the governmental, financial and cultural life
of Britain. But a major boost came from the great public schools (in U.S.
terms, private prep schools) whose "old boys" (alumni) notoriously dominate all three areas of English life. (It has been said that the main difference between a Tory and a Labour government is that the former is
composed of old boys from Eton, the latter of old boys from Winchester.)

The power of the public schools, in both speech and society, dates from
the nineteenth century, when the old ruling class of landed aristocrats
and gentry, which had ruled England since the Glorious Revolution, was
at last compelled to share power with the up-and-coming middle classes
of commerce and industry. They didn't like the idea—ruling classes never
do—but were shrewd enough, and English enough, to bend to the winds
of change and evolve a compromise. Its terms, which were all the more
binding for being unstated, were that the middle classes (eventually, even
selected members of the working classes) would be allowed a share in
running the nation, provided they—or at least their sons—became public-school "gentlemen" with the speech, manners and fundamental values of their "betters." Out of this compromise there evolved a complex
interaction of language, literature, education and social attitudes which,
I think it fair to say, played a significant role in the industrial decline of
Britain so visible today.

So far as speech was concerned, the compromise was harmless, except
to the sensibilities of middle-class public-school boys, who were given a
hard time by their better-born peers until they lost their "low" regional
accents. Public-school social attitudes were something else, for they centered on the gentry's traditional dislike and contempt for the middle
classes that had broken their monopoly of power, and on their no less
rooted distrust of new ideas. Anyone "in trade" was socially beyond the
pale, while the public schools themselves proudly proclaimed that their
aim was the development of "character" (i.e., gentlemanly social attitudes) rather than "intellect" (knowledge and the capacity for innova-

tion). The schools, and the universities they fed, stressed Latin and Greek, sometimes modern languages such as French and German, literature and some history. "Pure" science was tolerated (in some cases, just barely), but applied science (technology), economics and business administration were ignored: they were the business of grimy types whom no gentleman would invite into his home and whose speech betrayed their dubious origins in Glasgow, Birmingham or Cardiff, and the even grimier proletarians whose labors made the whole social structure possible, but whom a gentleman simply ignored.

As in life, so in literature. Most Victorian English novels are in one way or another about money (will the young hero come into his rightful inheritance? Will the poor but honest heroine manage to make a "good" —prosperous—marriage?) but very few of them show any curiosity about, let alone understanding of, where the money came from. Indeed, some writers went further, deliberately turning their backs on the modern world and regarding nostalgically the "age of chivalry" with its allegedly stable social arrangements and "knightly" ideals of conduct. In language, this nostalgia was reflected in the "Merrie England" syndrome already mentioned, and in literature, by the work of half a dozen writers, most notably Scott and Tennyson.

Now as a personal moral code, chivalry had its points—protection of the weak, women and children first, and so on—but as intellectual equipment for dealing with the problems of English society in the late nineteenth and early twentieth centuries it was about as useful as a suit of armor against a machine gun. The knight, like the Victorian gentlemen and their middle-class imitators who idealized him, did not concern himself with "trade"; his business was to fight—as thousands of British "officers and gentlemen" did, on battlefields even more far-ranging than those where Chaucer's Knight had wielded sword and lance—and to rule —as other thousands of gentlemen did over an equally wide expanse of territory. But the price of admission to military or political leadership in the British Empire became a willingness to downgrade the commercial and technological preeminence that had made that empire possible.

Eventually, of course, the empire crumbled, as empires have a habit of doing, and Britain was left with a well-spoken, gentlemanly, nostalgic ruling class, trained to a knightly role that no longer existed—and, with few exceptions, without the faintest notion of what to do next. In life as in language, it does not pay to confuse style with substance, or the right accent with right thinking.

*   *   *

Considering the size of the United States, it has far fewer dialects than England, and for fairly obvious reasons: English has been spoken in North America for less than four centuries, as against fifteen in the mother country, and in parts of the continent for less than a century and a half. Moreover, the English-speaking inhabitants of North America are notoriously prone to frequent migration, carrying their dialects with them, to the confusion of scholars trying to establish regional boundaries.

How many American dialects exist depends largely on whom you're reading, and whether they focus on phonetics, vocabulary or both. The minimum number is seven, while other scholars distinguish more than a dozen on the Atlantic Seaboard alone. Considering the volume of collected facts the experts are trying to interpret, the confusion is understandable. New England and New York State speak one dialect when they're talking about a small stream (both say "brook," as against "run" or "creek" in other areas), but two when they're talking about a sugar maple ("rock maple," "hard maple") and three when they're talking about cottage cheese ("sour-milk cheese," "Dutch cheese," "pot cheese"). Likewise, Virginians and North Carolinians are likely to speak the same dialect when they say "long" (/lahng/ rather than the /laung/ found to north and south) but a different one when they say "vegetables" (/veggetubbles/ in Virginia and in South Carolina, /veggetibbles/ in North Carolina). Read enough of this stuff and you are likely to end up wondering whether American dialects exist at all.

Of course, anyone who has traveled at all widely in the U.S. knows that they do, and also that dialectical differences between neighboring areas are usually quite subtle. The following account of American dialects is inevitably oversimplified, and is also based almost entirely on phonetics. Vocabulary is, indeed, the fun part of dialectology: it's entertaining to discover, for instance, that a dragonfly in one area is a "snake doctor" in another, a "mosquito hawk" in a third, and a "(devil's) darning needle" in a fourth. Or, to take a more up-to-date example, that a sandwich made with a split loaf of Italian bread is called a "hero" in New York City (you have to be one to eat one), a "grinder" around Boston (you need a good set of them), a "po' boy" in New Orleans (it's all he has for dinner), a "Garibaldi" in Wisconsin (after the famous Italian liberator), a "bomber," "sub(marine)," "rocket" or "torpedo" in various other places (from the shape, obviously), and a "hoagie" in various others (your guess is as good as mine). But the very multiplicity and geographical dispersion of these picturesque terms ensure that they will throw little light on regional differences in American speech.

Starting in the upper right corner of the map, we find the New England dialect, stretching from the valley of the Connecticut on east. (This dividing line, like the boundaries of most other dialect areas, is somewhat arbitrary, and could probably be shifted fifty miles or so either way without doing serious violence to the facts.) To the majority of Americans, its most distinctive trait is the loss of /r/ except before vowels—that is, "cart" is /caht/ and "far" is /fa/, but "carry" is /carry/. However, this trait is not unique to New England. More characteristic is a vowel shift of /au/ to /ah/, so that "caught" and "Boston" sound like /caht/ and /bahston/. In many parts of New England, notably Cape Cod, the reverse shift also takes place ("Cape Caud is surrounded by wotta"). This curious phenomenon, which I call "vowel reversal," is found in at least two other American dialects (though involving different vowels), and as far as I know in no other English-speaking country. Yet another Cape Cod idiosyncrasy is to pronounce "there" not simply without its R, as /theah/, but with an extra syllable, as /they-uh/. One day on a Cape Cod beach, I overheard a lady who had been diving under the incoming waves remark breathlessly to a friend, "I had to staup—I was runnin' out of ey-uh."

Of more restricted currency in New England is the "Boston A," which resembles the A in "calf." On the Boston subway you almost always change at Paak Street unless you're driving a caa, which you paak in a garaage. Quite different, and also of limited currency, is the "Brahmin A" of many upper-class New Englanders, borrowed from upper-class England, in which "grass" becomes "grahss." An archaic feature of New England phonetics, now found mainly "Down East" in Maine, is the pronunciation of "stone" and "home" as /stun/ and /hum/.

West and south of the New England dialect region lies a large area covering western New England, New York State and New Jersey (except for the area around New York City), Pennsylvania, northern Delaware and Maryland, and West Virginia. Most authorities divide this region, which I have chosen to call Midland, into several subdialects, and even sub-subdialects, but in fact the phonetic differences among them are neither very great nor very consistent. All of them pronounce all their R's, all tend to pronounce "hoarse" like "horse," "mourning" like "morning," "Mary" (and sometimes also "marry") like "merry," and "lots" like "lots," rather than New England's /lauts/. Moreover, the boundaries between the various subregions, none too sharp even along the Eastern Seaboard, become increasingly blurred as one moves inland; by the time one reaches the Mississippi, the various Midland subdialects have pretty well blended into what is called "General American," which extends to the Pacific.

The Metropolitan New York dialect is located exactly where its name implies: New York City and adjacent parts of New York, New Jersey and Connecticut. It resembles New England speech in dropping R except before vowels, but otherwise shares none of the New England vowel changes, or those of Midland. Its best-known vowel change is the "New York diphthong" found in the catch-phrase "Toity-toid Street and Toid Avenue." Like many dialectical diphthongs, this one is easier heard than written: it blends the vowels of "but" and "hit." Fifty years ago, the New York diphthong was quite common on the lips of educated New Yorkers, but is now considered a hallmark of blue-collar Metropolitan speech. Also blue-collar is the consonant transformation of the two TH sounds (as in "third" and "the") to /t/ and /d/ ("toid" and "duh"). Older residents of Brooklyn dwell nostalgically on the great days of the Brooklyn (now Los Angeles) Dodgers, fondly known as "dem bums." Blue-collar Brooklyn also incorporates the New York diphthong into its own version of vowel reversal: people often heat their houses with erl boiners, and if the heat goes off, things get in a toimerl.

These and other traits of blue-collar New York speech are tolerably familiar to the English-speaking world through movies and television: they are almost automatically placed in the mouths of gangsters, taxi drivers and other uncouth types, regardless of where the drama is supposedly set.

Southern American is spoken in a great arc stretching from the Midland region down through the lowlands of the South Atlantic and Gulf states into Texas, and up the Mississippi and Ohio valleys almost to St. Louis and Cincinnati: practically, it coincides with the "Old South" of the plantations. Like New York and New England, it drops its R's except before vowels, but handles the vowels themselves like no other region. The well-known "Southern drawl" stretches long vowels into diphthongs or triphthongs, as in Cockney, though the actual sounds are quite different: "yes" (/yess/ in other American dialects) becomes /yeahss/ or even /yeyus/, "class" becomes /clayus/. Words ending in T or TH preceded by another consonant are likely to lose the final consonant, so that "last" and "depth" come out /lass/ and /depp/, though this is commonest among blue-collar and some white-collar Southerners.

Of more restricted Southern currency are the shift of /ah/ to /uh/, making "bomb" and "mamma" into /bum/ and /mumma/. In other parts of the South, /eh/ changes to /ih/ in some words ("Git me a pin and I'll sign it"). Finally, in Texas and some other places, these two sounds take part in a full-fledged vowel reversal: ("I need to pen up the him on that dress.").

The speech of the Southern Mountain region, finally, is described by some experts as Southern influenced by Midland and by others as the reverse—a chicken-and-egg argument that we needn't bother to unscramble. The most isolated parts of the region, inhabited by what used to be called "hillbillies," are somewhat archaic in both phonetics and syntax; thus some people still say "I didn't see aira [e'er a] critter all day" where the rest of us would say "any." But the notion, propagated by some romantics, that the mountaineers speak "Elizabethan English" is, like their favorite drink, moonshine: when their ancestors moved in, Elizabeth had been in her grave for nearly two centuries.

The English spoken by most Canadians differs little from General American, apart from one fairly widespread trait: the diphthong in words like "out" and "about" shifts toward /oo/, yielding something like Scots "oot" and "aboot." Since the Scots played a major role in settling Canada (as one could guess from the names of the Mackenzie, Fraser and half a dozen other Canadian rivers) it would be surprising if their dialect had not left a few traces. Otherwise, however, Canada is too close to the United States (most of its inhabitants live within a couple of hundred miles of the border) to be more than an extension of its large neighbor, linguistically speaking—always, of course, excepting Quebec, most of whose inhabitants continue to speak their own rather archaic dialect of French.

All these regional North American dialects are subdivided into local ones, which unfortunately we have not time to examine. A couple of them, however, are worth a quick look because of their especially tangy flavor. The first is spoken in Bawlamer, Merlin, a large city some forty miles northeast of our nation's capital, Warshnin. Bawlamer kids go to the zoo to see the mighty elfin and the long-necked draff, teenagers go to hoskull, and grownups go to a druckstewer lunch counter for a cole race beef sanrich. Bawlamer ladies warsh their clothes, wrench them, then arn them on an arnin board; their husbands cut the lawn (if they have one) with a paramour. (The terms are taken from a guide published by the city for visiting torsts.)

Another guide has been compiled—with tongue in cheek—by Russell Baker of *The New York Times,* for the use of Yurpeans visiting the U.S. He calls the language American, but it sounds to me like basic New Yorkese —the tongue most Yurpeans encounter on first arrival. A typical guidebook question and answer:

Q. Ahdaya gettuh Rootwun?
A. Dake a leffada nexlite, gwate bloxun daycoride tillya kumdooa big facdree, unyul see toorodes. Dake a rodetudda lef unya cantmissit.

(England, too, has its local dialectical eccentricities. Perhaps the most curious of these is found in one of Britain's larger ports, whose inhabitants long ago formed the habit of tacking an /l/ onto words ending in a vowel, thereby converting their town's original name, Bristowe, into Bristol. As of 1963, at least, they were still at it: a friend of mine swears that during the Cuban missile crisis he spied, chalked on a Bristol wall, the slogan HANDS OFF CUBAL!)

As to the origin of American dialects, the traditional view is that they originated in much the same way as Old English dialects: through settlement by people speaking different dialects of British English. Specifically, New England and the South were supposedly settled from southern and eastern England, the middle states from northern England, Scotland and Ireland—whence, it is held, the "lost R's" of the first two regions as against the pronounced R's of the third.

Examined against the facts, this theory doesn't look very good. The early (before 1700) settlers do, indeed, seem to have come mainly from southern and eastern England, but this proves nothing, since the area included four dialects—East Midland and London, in which R's had been lost, and Kentish and Southern, in which they had not. Moreover, a settler's birthplace doesn't necessarily pinpoint his dialect. William Claiborne (to take an example I happen to know something about) was born and brought up in Kent (meaning that most of his playmates would have spoken Kentish), while his parents were from London and Norfolk respectively (speaking two varieties of East Midland). I'd hate to bet much money on precisely what kind of English *he* spoke.

A second major objection is that if Virginia and New England were settled by people speaking the same dialect (whatever that may have been), their inhabitants ought to sound alike today. In fact, Virginia speech sounds much more like that of the rest of the South, resembling New England speech *only* in its dropped R's. Finally, there is now considerable firsthand testimony that American dialects are actually a fairly recent (since 1800) development.

William Eddis, a traveler reporting in 1770 on his visit to America, described the language of the colonies as "perfectly uniform and unadulterated; nor has it borrowed any provincial, or national, accent from its British or foreign parentage." Seven years later, the Rev. Jonathan

Boucher found in America "the purest pronunciation of the English tongue that is anywhere to be met with," and "a perfect uniformity"; similar reports recur right up to the end of the century: the only really distinctive dialect reported was "among the poor slaves."

A plausible explanation for this uniformity was put forward by a London editor in 1783; it still sounds good two centuries later. English-speaking people, he pointed out, had "assembled in America from various quarters" (i.e., different parts of Great Britain) and "in consequence of their intercourse and intermarriages, soon dropped the peculiarities of their several provincial idioms, retaining only what was fundamental and common to them all; a process which the frequency or rather the universality of school-learning in North America, must naturally have assisted."

Here, then, we have the most likely explanation of Midland and General American. The influence of school learning would have been especially marked in the Midwest and Far West, which were settled by people from many parts of the East, speaking different regional dialects, and many others whose native tongues were not English. Since there was no "Standard" English spoken among the schoolkids themselves, it was natural enough for them to follow the lead of their teachers. This is the more likely in that the normal nineteenth-century method of teaching spelling was by "sounding out" a word, syllable by syllable: "A-D, ad, M-I, mi, admi-, R-A, ra, admira-, T-I-O-N, shun, admiration." General American still "follows the letters" more than other American dialects, or than British Standard English, in which /sec-re-ta-ry/ is clipped to /sec-re-trih/, and /i-o-dine/ to /i-o-din/.

For dialects that don't follow the Midland–General American pattern, it makes more sense to look at individual cases, rather than seek a general explanation.

New England is the one area where a plausible case can be made for the migration theory. First, it is the only area where a majority of the early settlers did, perhaps, speak the same or closely related dialects: those whose origins can be traced came mostly from London and the East Midlands, areas where Puritanism was especially strong. Second, it is the only area where some eighteenth-century visitors claimed to have heard an even mildly distinctive dialect; one called it "whining," though it's hard to say what he meant by this. Finally, there is documentary evidence that even in the eighteenth century New England was already dropping its R's; thus "liberty" is misspelled "libety," as it is pronounced in New England today. This is not to say, however, that *all* the distinctive features of New England phonetics were present two hundred years ago. The "Brahmin" or "broad" A of "keep off the grahss" pretty certainly comes from nineteenth-century upper-class imitation of upper-class British English (for the same reason, it is used by some upper-class Southerners), while the "Boston A" of "change at Paak Street" may have come over with the Irish.

The "dese, dose and dems" of Metropolitan New York unquestionably came from non-English-speaking immigrants. From 1850 on, a majority of the newcomers landed in New York, and a lot of them stayed there: between 1870 and 1920, a majority of the city's population, or nearly so, was foreign-born or born of immigrant parents. (Even in 1930, signs on the New York subway dealing with penalties for smoking, spitting and other offenses were often printed in six languages: English, German, Italian, Yiddish, Chinese and Russian.) And except for the Irish, none of these immigrants had either of the TH sounds, /th/ or /dh/, in their native phonetic repertory, and would therefore have substituted the nearest equivalents, /t/ and /d/. The "New York diphthong" of "Toity-toid Street," however, remains a linguistic mystery. Though often credited to the Jews, it seems to have appeared in New York speech before this group was present in numbers, and moreover is also found in parts of the Gulf Coast where Jews have always been scarce, yet where a political speaker can quite naturally refer to "mah woythy opponent."

Southern American English, finally, must surely owe many of its distinctive features to the "invisible" part of its population, the blacks, who as late as 1950 made up an absolute majority in large areas of the South (in population, not on the voting rolls). There is abundant historical evidence that during the eighteenth and much of the nineteenth century most southern blacks—in particular, plantation field hands—spoke a dialect distinctively different from any white dialect, educated or otherwise. There is equally convincing evidence that on the plantations black and white children played together (other white kids were several miles off); often certain black kids were specifically designated as "play children." Under these circumstances, it is inconceivable that black speech habits would not have influenced white ones, especially in phonetics, which as we've noted are shaped in early childhood and are the aspect of language most resistant to later change. *They are also the most distinctive feature of Southern American.* A similar process operated in the West Indies, though somewhat differently, because of the larger proportion of blacks (up to 90 percent on many islands): to this day, both black and white children have the same regional accent—which is not at all like any regional British accent.

Some critics have rejected the notion that blacks could have influenced Southern white speech, often with high indignation. Cleanth Brooks of Yale, for example, says that Southern English is distinctive merely because the region "must have" been settled from England's West Country. Maybe it "must have," but neither Brooks not anyone else has ever offered any evidence that it was. Brooks gives a number of supposed parallels between Southern American and West Country dialects, and indeed British dialects are diverse enough so that if you pick your examples carefully, you can plausibly root almost any group of American settlers anywhere in England. But the most conspicuous feature of West Country speech—the consonant shift of "Did 'e zee the vox?"—finds not an echo on this side of the Atlantic.

The Southern speech region fits the region of plantation agriculture almost like the proverbial glove—a region whose population differed from that of the rest of the South in only one significant respect: lots of blacks. These were obviously linguistically influenced by the whites, since they did after all learn English; to suppose that the influence operated in only one direction is to take a remarkably one-sided—or bigoted—view of human nature.

There has been little work done on American class dialects. For example, in a recent standard text on American dialects, only two of fifty chapters deal with class dialects; a few others touch on the subject peripherally. One of the two, however, includes some interesting observations on these dialects in New York City: middle-class people tend to be more phonetically "correct"—as in pronouncing their R's—than either the rich or the poor. I'd guess this is not uncommon in other parts of the country. In language, manners or morals, the upper classes have always "known" that whatever they did was "correct," while the lower classes usually didn't give a damn—and the middle classes, poor devils, worried.

This same text, fairly representative of the Establishment viewpoint in American dialectology, says almost nothing about what is unquestionably the most interesting class dialect in this country, both in its own distinctive features and its contribution to American speech generally: Black English.

Before going into what Black English is, we must be clear on what it is not. It is not the dialect spoken by all American blacks: an educated black growing up in a mixed, middle-class neighborhood will speak the middle-class English of that neighborhood. It may not even be spoken today by a majority of American blacks. In its "purest" form, it appears to be the dialect of black children, living in segregated conditions, between the ages of (roughly) four and eight. Thereafter, it is subject to "age grading": contact with "white English" in school and (later) at work gradually alters the dialect in the direction of that spoken in the wider community, though it will likely retain traces of its origin, especially in conversations among blacks. There are no surveys on how widely Black English is spoken or understood; J. L. Dillard, one expert on the subject, estimates that 80 percent of American blacks use it. I think this is way too high, unless it refers to people who have spoken it *at some time during their lives;* Dillard himself discusses the phenomenon of "age grading" mentioned above.

Phonetically, today's Black English shows little difference from blue-collar Southern white English, though this was not always true. Its vocabulary, too, is not terribly distinctive, apart from relatively transient slang terms, some of which have passed into white English. The syntax of Black English, however, has some very distinctive features, notably its use of verbs. For one thing, it has dispensed with many of the few verb inflections still found in other dialects of English (themselves, as we know, the sparse survivors of a much larger collection). "He run" replaces "he runs," and "he go" may replace "he went," though only if the context shows that the action took place in the past. The verb "to be" is omitted in certain constructions, such as "he (is) sick."

Perhaps the most striking feature of Black English verbs is their emphasis on "aspect" rather than tense. In virtually all other varieties of English, whatever verb form is used *must* indicate the time of the action—past, present or future; it may or may not indicate the kind (aspect) of action—whether it is complete or incomplete, single or repeated. In Black English, the emphasis is reversed: the verb form shows aspect, while time (tense) is often inferred from the context, as in the example "he go" above.

Forms like "he go" imply a single, completed action; thus "he go to de sto' " may mean "he went to the store" (yesterday) or "he will go to the store" (tomorrow). "He goin' to de sto'," by contrast, implies continuing action—"he is on his way to the store," or "he was on his way to the store (when) . . . " Finally, "he be goin' to de sto' " implies repeated or habitual action, meaning "he used to go to the store" (every day) or "he goes to the store" (every Saturday) or even, conceivably, "he will go to the store" (any time you ask him). This subtle difference in meaning shows up in the classic ghetto put-down "You makin' sense, but you don't *be* makin' sense"—literally, "You're making sense now, but you don't usually make sense" or, more loosely, "You're making sense—for a change." (Note that these interpretations are approximate: Black English has never been "standardized," and moreover is often influenced to some degree by white English. Thus the precise shade of meaning conveyed by a given verb form often depends on the speaker and the situation, not just the form itself.)

As for the origins of Black English, we can dismiss without discussion the theory once put forward by certain "scholars" that its phonetic peculiarities are due to the blacks' thick lips, and its other features to their innate stupidity. We can dismiss almost as quickly the claim of a few black scholars, echoed by some muddle-headed white liberals, that the dialect is a "mutilated," "corrupt" variety of English that is part of the blacks' legacy from slavery, and hence an appropriate focus for black anger and white guilt. Black English certainly originated during slavery (where else?), but it is no more corrupt or mutilated than any other dialect of English: it can say anything its speakers feel like saying, and say it, not infrequently, with considerable color and wit, as in the "You makin' sense" quotation above. The worst you can say of it is that its vocabulary is rather small, and inevitably so: the slaves who were its first speakers led very limited lives, with little or no access to books, while its present speakers, young schoolchildren, seldom have large vocabularies, whatever their color. Those blacks who speak, or once spoke, Black English do so for the same reason that other blacks speak other English dialects: they learned it. The question is why they learned this particular dialect and not some other.

The only credible reason is either that the whites from whom the slaves originally learned English did not speak Standard English (at least to the slaves), or that the blacks failed to learn "proper" English for the same reason that almost anyone has difficulty learning a foreign language: the influence of the linguistic habits they had already formed in their African homeland, a process technically called "interference." Or both.

The blacks of West Africa, as we've already noted, spoke at least a dozen different tongues. Moreover, the slavers made a policy of mixing blacks from different tribes, since they had learned the hard way that when slaves could communicate among themselves they often expressed their dislike of enslavement quite violently. Yet the slavers did need some rudimentary way of communicating with their "goods" during the months these were being collected in the great barracoons at Whydah, Fernando Po and other ports along the Slave Coast, and, later on, aboard ship. For this purpose they used a "trade language" or "lingua franca."

The first of the slave-trade languages was Pidjin Portuguese, since West African commerce was initially a Portuguese monopoly. With the growing English maritime supremacy of the eighteenth century, however, this was largely replaced by Maritime or Pidjin English, employing a radically simplified syntax and a very limited vocabulary, adequate for bargaining and ordering slaves about, but not much else. (More on this remarkable language later.) This, then, was the slaves' first contact with English; further contacts with Pidjin English came on the plantations, where at least some slaveowners habitually used it to communicate with newly arrived slaves. Moreover, it served as a medium of communication among the polyglot slaves themselves—rudimentary, certainly, but for that very reason much more easily mastered than any of the many native tongues they spoke.

Pidjin English was certainly not the only kind of English the slaves heard: some, at least, would have heard the more or less educated "colonial" English of their masters, as well as the less educated dialects of their white overseers. But whatever variety of English was their model, they would have learned it as any adult learns a foreign tongue: with modifications reflecting the phonetics, syntax and vocabulary of their native languages.

Pidjin English of some sort served well enough at the beginning, but was inadequate for the next generation of blacks. Their native tongues were largely lost, since they were useless for communicating with most of their fellows, who had different native tongues, let alone with their masters. The new language had to be expanded to serve the manifold functions of any language—not just communication with "massa" (which, by the way, may be a blend of English "master" and West African *masa*, chief) but making love, making dinner, telling stories, gossiping and even discussing the newfound Christian religion, which most slaveowners considered it their duty to impose on their slaves. (As it turned out, at least some slaves got more from Christianity than their masters had reckoned on: there is a good deal of subversive talk in the Bible about people liberating themselves from slavery, smiting the oppressor and so on.) By 1850 or earlier, the Pidjin or Pidjin-like English of African-born slaves had evolved into "Plantation Creole"—a creole language being a pidjin that has "grown up": become the native tongue of some community, and expanded and changed accordingly.

We can get a fair notion of Plantation Creole from the "Uncle Remus" stories of Joel Chandler Harris, published in the 1870s and '80s. The stories themselves (though Chandler didn't say so) are African animal fables with a slightly Americanized cast of characters (there is, for example, no African equivalent of "Bre'r B'ar," the bear). The dialect seems authentic, though probably somewhat modified for literary purposes: we know that Chandler had an excellent ear from his use of two different versions of Plantation Creole, a relatively late type for Uncle Remus himself, and a somewhat heavier dialect for "Daddy Jack"—who, significantly, is described as having been born in Africa.

Something like the Plantation Creole of 1850 is still spoken by blacks along the swampy South Carolina–Georgia coast and especially on the Sea Islands that fringe it: the dialect is called Gullah (the word may be from the Gola tribe of West Africa or from Ngola—Angola). The region's population was heavily black even before the Civil War, and almost totally so after it: most of the Sea Islands were occupied early on by Union forces, the plantation system was destroyed and most of the whites fled. Since the region was isolated to boot, its language, like other isolated tongues, changed little.

Phonetically, Gullah sounds less like other Southern U.S. dialects, black or white, than like uneducated West Indian English (blacks have always heavily outnumbered whites in the English-speaking islands), and both sound not unlike the English spoken by many educated Africans in such West African countries as Nigeria. All three, then, must reflect "interference"—directly in West Africa, where those who learn English learn it in school, and indirectly in West Indian and Gullah, where earlier phonetic patterns have been preserved by isolation and/or black preponderance. Thus there is every reason to believe that similar phonetic patterns were found in the Plantation Creole of a century and a half ago.

The most interesting feature of Gullah, however, is its vocabulary, which according to the black scholar Lorenzo D. Turner includes, or included, more than five thousand terms borrowed from various West African tongues. Most of these are personal names or nicknames, such as *Angku* (boy born on Saturday), *Betsibi* (mischievous) and the like. But others are used in conversation, like *bong* (tooth), *dafa* (fat) and *gulu* (pig), as well as words like "gumbo" and "goober" that have entered general American English. Significantly, a sizable number of African words are not used in conversation, but only in traditional songs and stories. Again, one may reasonably suppose that these Africanisms were much more widespread among blacks at an earlier period.

Elsewhere in the South—and also in the North, as more and more blacks migrated there during the twentieth century—Plantation Creole lost many of its distinctive features. Some survived, but mainly in the speech of elderly people born in slavery, for obvious reasons, and among black children, for reasons not so obvious. We now know that children acquire many of their language habits from their peers rather than their parents—in part, automatically, and in part, no doubt, from the near-universal desire to be one of the gang. In effect, Black English was (and is) passed from six- and seven-year-olds to four- and five-year olds, who in another year or two would pass it on to a new crop of little kids. The special languages and subcultures of children can be extraordinarily per-sistent—witness such "languages" as Igpay Atinlay (Pig Latin), which most white Americans know or once knew, but which few acquired from adults.

So far as I know, nobody has yet undertaken the arduous task of relating the *syntactic* peculiarities of Black English to those of the West African languages. Worth noting, however, is that verbs in many of these languages stress aspect rather than tense, like Black English verbs.

Black English, as noted earlier, brought a number of African words into the American vocabulary during the eighteenth and nineteenth centuries, and the flow by no means ceased with the end of slavery. A surprising number "surfaced" from 1900 on, mainly through the worlds of popular music and drugs, where blacks and whites have long mingled most freely. Another influx came from protest movements of the 1960s, in which—for a while—there was a good deal of interracial mingling. Jazz, America's outstanding contribution to popular music, of course originated among blacks, and the word itself is from a West African term meaning "lively, energetic" (it has also been used to refer to an equally energetic but much more intimate activity). "Boogie-woogie" is apparently an elaboration of *bogi*, dance; "hip" is from *hipi*, to be aware; and a *hipikat* is an aware person. ("Hip" was borrowed by many whites as "hep"; when used to blacks as a supposed demonstration of white linguistic sophistication—"I'm hep"—it might draw the ironic reply "I'm hip you're hep.") If you've got the jitters, you're *jitaw* (frightened), while a *jitaw-baga* is literally a frightened person, hence one moving in an agitated manner—a jitterbug.

Another kind of bug comes from *bugu*, annoy—"Quit buggin' me, man"—which may also have contributed to the ancestry of "humbug" (which in West Indian English means "annoy"). Yet another kind of bug may derive, via sailors in the slave trade, from *baga-baga*, insect. (The varied meanings of these similar West African words of course reflects their source in different tongues.) To "bad-mouth" someone or "be with it" or "do one's own thing" may be loan translations of African phrases with the same meaning—and if you dig all of this, then you *degu* (understand) it.

For all their phonetic and semantic plausibility, however, it isn't clear how these apparent Africanisms got from there to here. There is no evidence that any of them appeared in Black English before 1900 (often, much later)—that is, fifty to a hundred years after the last African-speaking blacks arrived in the U.S. We don't, for example, find them in the Uncle Remus stories, or in the later writings of such black authors as the late Zora Neal Hurston (who wrote extensively on back-country blacks), or even in Gullah, with its thousand or more African terms. However, it may well be that once scholars start looking, they will find earlier written traces of these words, as they eventually did with "O.K." A good place to start might be the Black English of the New Orleans area circa 1900, where jazz was born, and the earlier Black Creole French of the same region, which could well have provided an additional channel for African words to infiltrate into Black English.

American linguistic snobbery is less marked and systematized than that of Great Britain: there is no American equivalent of "Public School English." Provided someone uses educated syntax ("good English"), looks reasonably prosperous, and has a white skin, most Americans will accept him or her as a social equal. Except in parts of the South, we are too diverse and mobile a people for "gentlemanly" ancestry (real or assumed) to count for much, and so much the better for us.

Australia, home of still another regional variety of English, was discovered by Europeans early in the seventeenth century, when Dutch merchantmen, using the powerful westerly winds of the "roaring 40s" (40° –50° south longitude) for a quick passage to the spice-rich East Indies, sighted—and sometimes bumped into—a large landmass. However, neither merchants nor anyone else found anything there to attract them until 1788, when the British, no longer able to ship their undesirables to America, set up a prison colony at Botany Bay, near modern Sydney. As late as 1830, the total European population was still under 100,000, but with the discovery of gold in the 1850s, the population leaped and by 1880 was numbered in the millions.

Australian English has inevitably borrowed from the native tongues to describe the unique flora and fauna of the continent—more than sixty words altogether. (New Zealand, with its own distinctive plants and animals, has similarly borrowed from aboriginal Maori.) Other "Australianisms," like earlier "Americanisms," amount to redefinitions of standard English words: forest is "bush," a landowner is a "squatter," and the vast, semiarid pasturelands that make up much of Australia's habitable area are the "outback," beyond which lies the "never-never," a desert inhabited by almost nobody but aboriginal "Blackfellows."

Phonetically, Australian can be most accurately described as an outgrowth of Cockney; at any rate, it sounds more like that dialect than like any other variety of English. The "Cockney diphthong" is omnipresent: an old story tells of the schoolboy who, asked to define "bison," replied, "A plyce where you bythe your fyce." And the Cockney "obtrusive R" is even more obtrusive in "Strine," the blue-collar variety of Australian, so that "I can hardly live without you" comes out as "Iker nardly liver thout you." Distinctively Australian, however, is a tendency to run syllables and words together, so that "Australian" comes out "Strine," "How much is it?" as "Emma chisit?" and "head of the hit parade" as "heather hip ride." Educated Australians, though they joke about "Strine" among themselves, complain that outsiders exaggerate the peculiarities of Australian speech. I daresay they do—but not much. I once had the experience of flying to England aboard a budget flight originating in Sydney. En route, I had a pleasant chat with a couple of English ladies, who were returning from a visit to Australia, but the Strines on board defeated me. Clearly they were speaking a kind of English—but not clearly enough for me to make much sense of it.

Next to England, Australia is the most linguistically snobbish country in the English-speaking world—but in reverse. It was initially settled by convicts, many of them poachers and petty thieves whose main crime was being poor, and later by famine refugees from Ireland, trade-union and Irish nationalist agitators "on the run" and similar hard cases, who not only didn't "know their place" but had an ingrained dislike of upper-class manners and speech. The average blue-collar or white-collar Australian is likely to regard even educated Australian speech as somewhat affected, and educated British English as positively effeminate: "You can't tell whether he's a Pom [Englishman] or a poof." ("Pom" or "Pommy," the standard Australian term for an Englishman, is of unknown origin. One theory, no more implausible than any other, derives it from "pomegranate," referring to the ruddy complexions of just-arrived English unused to the powerful Australian sun.)

This impatience with linguistic proprieties is also reflected in a predilection for strong language, notably the "Australian adjective"—originally, of course, English. Some of the flavor can be gotten from a set of verses known to most only as "The Australian Poem," concerning the efforts of a "stockman" (rancher) to ride a "brumby" (unbroken horse) across a creek—in Australia, as in the U.S., a stream. I give the final verse:

> Said he "This nag must bloody swim
> The same for me as bloody him";
> The creek was deep, and bloody floody.
> And e're they reached the bloody bank
> The bloody nag beneath him sank,
> The stockman's face a bloody study,
> Ejaculating "Bloody! Bloody!"

Nowadays, what with four-letter words and all (which Strines also use with considerable abandon), this is pretty mild stuff, but to Pommies of forty years ago the adjective was almost as outrageous as when Eliza Doolittle first enunciated it on the London stage circa 1900. And even to some Australians: in one of Kylie Tennant's novels, a "sundowner" (tramp, migrant worker) is berated for "foul language" when he uses it in front of a squatter's wife. His response, in honest bewilderment: "What bloody foul language?"

Of all the versions of our native tongue spoken around the world, easily the strangest is Pidjin English. Once spoken from the West African coast along the Gulf of Guinea to the Straits of Malacca, and from the West Indies to the South Pacific, it is still current today as a lingua franca in West Africa, the wilder parts of Australia, and especially in Papua–New Guinea, though varying considerably from one place to another. Whether the different varieties of Pidjin can even be considered English is arguable. Their words are about 80 percent English, but are numbered in the hundreds rather than the tens of thousands of other English dialects. Their phonetic repertory is a good deal smaller than that of other varieties of English, and their syntax, though English in several important respects (notably, in reliance on word order), is distinctly un-English in others. About the best one can say is that whatever pigeonhole (no pun intended) one chooses to put Pidjin English in, it is a lot closer to English than to any other tongue.

"Pidjin" supposedly derives from a Chinese approximation of "business," and though the phonetics of this etymology are rather dubious, it was certainly as "business"—trade—English that Pidjin got its start. As we've already noted, it originated on the coast of West Africa, where British seamen used it to communicate with the polyglot natives; this began around 1600. During the next three centuries it was carried around the world by the expanding British merchant navy; at the same time, it moved into North America and the Caribbean as a medium for communication between slaves and slaveowners, between settlers and North American natives, and finally, closing the circle, between American settlers and gold-seekers and Chinese immigrants in the Far West, the latter having learned it along the China coast. Its creolized descendants include West Indian English, Plantation Creole, Black English and the Hawaiian creole known as "da kine."

Generalizing about Pidgin English is difficult, because during its lengthy travels it picked up words, and phonetic and syntactic practices, from the various native groups who used it. Broadly speaking, however, it amounts to an exceedingly stripped-down version of English. Instead of more than a dozen vowels, it usually has no more than five (/ah/, /eh/, /ee/, /o/, /oo/), and has also lost up to half a dozen consonants. These include /th/ and its "softer" relative, /dh/, replaced by /t/ (occasionally, /s/) and /d/ respectively, and often /f/, /v/ and /sh/ replaced by /p/, /b/ and /s/. Thus "three" becomes *trifela*, "mouth" becomes *maus*, and "this" becomes *disfela* or *dispela*. (The suffix *-fela*—"fellow"—is normally added to demonstrative pronouns, numerals and certain other kinds of words). Likewise "heavy" and "finish" may become *hebi* and *pinis*. (Significantly, we find many of the same phonetic changes in Plantation Creole; thus the old servant Jupiter in Poe's "The Gold Bug" says "heaby" and "dis.")

Though Pidgin English syntax relies mainly on word order, it also employs its own distinctive ways of showing meaning. The most consistent of these—it seems to occur in all known varieties of Pidgin—is the so-called "transitivizer": a suffix, variously rendered as *-em*, *-im* or *-um* (from "him"), attached to verbs that take an object. Thus *tok* means, as in English, both "speak" and "speech," but *tokim* means "speak to." Sometimes the transitivizer modifies meaning as well: *fait* sounds like and means "fight," but *faitim* means "hit, beat."

A more localized syntactic practice is found in Melanesian Pidgin, spoken in Papua–New Guinea and adjacent islands: the use of two different equivalents for English "we/us." *Mifela* or *mipela* ("me-fellow") means "we/us but not you," while *yumi* ("you-me") means "we/us including you." This distinction between the exclusive and nonexclusive "we" is taken over from the native Melanesian tongues.

The vocabulary of Pidgin English is, as we've noted, tiny compared with that of other English dialects: usually less than a thousand words. However, it can deploy those words in hundreds of compounds to express many additional concepts. Thus *haus* (house) and *moni* (money) are joined into *haus-moni* (bank). In Chinese Pidjin, *joss* is "God" (ultimately, from Portuguese *deos*), whence *joss-pidjen* ("God-business"—religion), *joss-house* and *joss-pidjen-man*, both meaning exactly what you would expect. According to one possibly fanciful account, "bishop" was rendered by *"topside-piecee-heaven-pidjen-man."*

Another way of compounding, especially common in Melanesian Pidjin, employs the preposition *bilong* ("belong"), meaning "of," "for," "pertaining to" and so on. (Most other prepositions are combined into *long*—"along"). Thus "mustache" is *gras bilong maus* ("grass belong mouth"), "foundation" is *ars bilong haus* (*ars* can mean not merely "arse" but "bottom," "base" and even "cause") and "ashes" is *shit bilong faia* (fire)—a precise and graphic if, to some people, shocking metaphor for the waste a fire leaves behind.

The unself-conscious use of "bad" words in Pidjin to express ordinary meanings reflects the uninhibited vocabularies of the British sailors who first devised it. Thus *bagarap* ("bugger up") is found in such statements as *Leg bilong mi e bagarap*, "My leg is injured," while *bagarimap*, with the transitivizer inserted, means "ruin, destroy" (*E bagarimap haus bilong mi*). Other bits of maritime vocabulary are *haisimap* ("hoist 'im up"—lift) and *plantim* ("plant 'im"—bury).

With the aid of these and many other compounds, Pidjin English can say a surprising number of things; even the Bible has been translated into it. For example, *Bipo, bipo, God e stat long mekim kamap heben na graun* ("In the beginning, God created heaven and earth"), and *Papa bilong mipela, i stap antap, naim bilong yu i tambu* ("taboo") ("Our father who art . . ."). And, in the somewhat different Australian Pidjin, *Big Name watchem sheepy-sheep, watchem blackfella. No more belly-cry fella hab* ("The Lord is my shepherd; I shall not want"). Not the King James Version, exactly, but it gets the point across.

Pidjin English has made its own contribution to the general English vocabulary. "Pickaninny," like "joss," came originally from Portuguese (*pequenino*, "tiny one"); though considered patronizing in England and America, it remains a neutral term in West African Pidjin, where it has even begotten an adjective, *pickin* (small). Another Portuguese Pidjin English term is "savvy" (from *save*, know), originally a verb ("You savvy what I'm saying?") but now more often a noun, meaning "know-how." ("He's got plenty of savvy"). The much larger English component of Pidjin has contributed "take a look-see," "no can do" and "long time no see," as well as the classic "No tickee, no shirtee!" Also Pidjin are such clichés of Hollywood "Indian" dialogue as "heap big chief" and "me scalpum paleface" (note the transitivizer)—which, like nearly all stereotypes, are grounded in fact. Whether or not any Native American actually used these particular expressions, many of them unquestionably used Pidjin to communicate with the palefaces—because that was the language the palefaces used to communicate with them. "No-see-ums," a common U.S. dialect term for various species of almost invisible stinging gnats, almost certainly originated in this "Frontier Pidjin," and "firewater" (whiskey) and "paleface" may come from the same source.

In most parts of the world, Pidjin English ultimately became creolized, as in the West Indies and the U.S. South. A later example is the version of English widely spoken in Hawaii (and understood, I am told, by practically everyone who has lived in the islands for any length of time). This is known as "da Hawaii kine talk," or simply "da kine"; it developed as a lingua franca among the tens of thousands of contract laborers shipped into the islands in the decades before and after 1900 to work in the cane and pineapple fields. These included Chinese, Koreans, Japanese, Filipinos, Portuguese, Puerto Ricans and native Hawaiians, and da kine has borrowed words from most of them (Chinese has contributed very few, because its phonetics, in which the pitch of a vowel can radically alter the meaning of a word, differ too radically from those of English or the other languages). Whether via da kine or directly, a number of native Hawaiian words have infiltrated into the general vocabulary of Hawaiian English; these include *pau* (/pow/—finished; exhausted) and two invaluable directional terms, *makai* (toward the sea) and *mauka* (toward the mountains) —almost any place in the islands being located in one or the other direction. A common weather forecast in the local papers—and a source of some confusion to *haole* (Caucasian) tourists—is "Mostly sunny, but with a few mauka showers in the afternoon."

Pidjin English has been described as "racist" and "a relic of imperialism," and there is a measure of truth to both statements. It reflects the assumption among English-speaking sailors and traders that the simple, childlike natives they dealt with could not be expected to understand ordinary English, and therefore required a sort of baby-talk version of it. (It was naturally taken for granted that the natives would learn English, not the reverse.) But in another sense, Pidjin was a practical answer to a practical problem: how to establish communication with, and sometimes among, peoples speaking dozens or even hundreds of different tongues, which no individual could have mastered in several lifetimes. In vocabulary and syntax, it is English stripped down to a few essential words and syntactic rules, and therefore quickly learnable by almost anyone who needed to use it.

It is for this practical reason that Pidjin has survived where it has: it makes communication possible. This is notably the case in Papua–New Guinea, whose natives speak well over a thousand different tongues—by some accounts, half the total number of languages in the world. Often tribes on opposite sides of a river cannot communicate with one another except by sign language—or in Pidjin. By a historical irony, therefore, this admitted relic of imperialism has become an absolutely essential ingredient in enabling the former Territory of Papua–New Guinea to achieve self-government: debates in the local legislature are conducted in Motu (most widely spoken of the native languages), Standard English and Pidjin, now given the more respectable title "Neo-Melanesian." (A similar historical irony operates in India, where a much more conventional dialect of English serves as a medium of official communication among ethnic groups that don't care to learn one another's tongues.)

Not surprisingly, the vocabulary of "Neo-Melanesian" is expanding: from some seven hundred words in 1920 to perhaps fifteen hundred now. If this process of creolization continues, we may in another couple of generations see this strange offspring of our native tongue emerge as a full-fledged language.

Stori bilong Pidjin Inglis e pinis.

II. NOT EVERYBODY'S ENGLISH

Some Remarkable Vocabularies

❧

> *My two mince pies are full of tears,*
> *My raspberry tart is jelly;*
> *My daisies I bullocked for two pig's ears*
> *To warm my Auntie Nellie.*

—COCKNEY LAMENT, C. 1920

Slang . . . the most powerful of all the stimulants that keep language alive and growing . . .

—H. L. MENCKEN

REGIONAL and class dialects do not exhaust the infinite variety of English. Within each dialect is a bewildering mishmash of jargons, argots and lingoes: specialized vocabularies used by one or more occupational, avocational or, in some cases, ethnic groups. Some of these are limited to small and specialized occupations; others extend over several groups (who may also speak rather different dialects); still others may be used by, or at least are familiar to, most people in a sizable region or entire country —in which case we may call the words in question "slang."

For example, when a New York City police officer mentions his "rabbi," he doesn't mean his spiritual adviser but rather his unofficial sponsor and protector, at headquarters or City Hall—who, like a real rabbi, is thought to have influence with higher powers. Similarly, a mugger will talk of "doing time," not "serving a sentence," and his lawyer will say "capias," not "court order to pick up a fugitive criminal." And since the cop, the crook and the mouthpiece all have business with one another, their lingoes will include some of the same terms: all three, for instance, know that a "stand-up guy" is a criminal who stands up for his associates; he doesn't fink to the cops when picked up in hopes of drawing a lighter sentence or copping a plea (being allowed to plead guilty to a lesser offense).

Yet the fuzz, the gonif and the shyster will each of them speak his or her "own" variety of Metropolitan New York dialect: the lawyer, a more or less educated version (more when he's talking to a judge, less when

he's talking to his mugger-client); the mugger probably a very uneducated version; and the cop, who has finished high school and perhaps
college, something in between. Note, moreover, that the lingoes we've
been talking about involve merely the "working" vocabularies of these
three people; after hours, they may well use quite different ones: the
lawyer, the jargon of tennis; the cop, that of bowling (or perhaps both
may use that of golf); and the mugger, that of drug addicts.

In short, the words we use depend not just on where we live and grew
up, or how much education we had, but on what we do for a living, what
we do after work, and whom we happen to be talking to. It's all English
—but not everybody's English.

The specialized vocabularies of different groups develop for several
reasons. The first is simple convenience: terms like "rabbi" and "capias"
are verbal shorthand for fairly complicated concepts. Similarly, it is a lot
quicker for a cannery worker to say "corn-snitcher" than "man who cuts
bad places out of corn ears," or an oil-field worker to say "Christmas
tree" rather than "collection of valves installed on top of the well." These
terms and many others, both specialized and general, reflect the operations of "Zipf's Law," an apparently fundamental principle of linguistics
formulated by G. K. Zipf, a professor of "psycholinguistics": the more
often a given word or expression is used (whether by the population
generally or some specialized group) the more likely it is to be ab-
breviated or (what amounts to the same thing) replaced by a shorter
equivalent. Zipf's Law turns the college student's "political science" into
"poly-sci," the stock-speculator's "option to buy a stock at a specified
price" into "call," and so on.

The ultimate in abbreviation is the acronym, formed from the initial
letters (sometimes, several letters) of the words in a phrase. Thus, "Inter-
Continental Ballistic Missile" becomes ICBM, the U.S. Navy's Commander IN Chief, PACific, becomes CINCPAC. If the acronym can be pronounced, so much the better; some of these have passed into the
language to become ordinary English words, as did "RAdio Detection
And Ranging." If the acronym forms an existing word that "fits," still
better: thus the 1972 Republican "Committee to Re-Elect the President"
was acronymed (by Democrats) as CREEP—which turned out to fit that
body's activities all too appropriately.

Acronyms are common in the jargons of governmental, corporate and
military bureaucrats, all of whom favor mouth-filling terms and titles. (In
the military, the need for rapid communication also plays a part.) In other
trades and professions, acronyms are less common: their jargons are

made up mostly of standard English expressions, or abbreviations of them, that have acquired a specialized meaning.

Just how specialized jargons can be is often startling to the outsider. Lawyers, as we've noted, have a jargon; corporation lawyers, a more specialized jargon; and corporation lawyers involved in "takeovers" of one firm by another, a jargon more specialized still. To this elite corpus of jurists, an aggressive takeover bid is a "bear hug," while a more casual one is a "teddy-bear pat." If the "target company" fails to respond to a bear hug, it is an "iron maiden," whose officers will begin putting together a "Pearl Harbor file" of facts, figures and legal schemes to keep the bear from the door. Legal maneuvers actually taken, however, are "shark repellent." If the repellent doesn't keep the sharks at bay, however, the target may still be saved by a "white knight" or "Prince Charming"—another corporation with a better offer.

Likewise, members of the New York State Legislature faced with a controversial bill will "hang loose" (refuse to commit themselves) as long as possible before "going into the tank" (openly supporting it). A "motherhood bill" (one as popular with the voters as motherhood) poses no problems, but in other cases a "marginal" (legislator elected by a narrow margin) will pray that his party leaders will "let him off the hook" (advise him that he needn't go on record for it because enough votes are already in the tank). An old quip around the New York State capitol asks, "Why are there gaps between the signatures on the Declaration of Independence?" Answer: "Because of all the guys who were let off the hook."

But convenience in dealing with technicalities, though an important reason for the development of specialized lingoes, is by no means the only one. Another is symbolic solidarity: a way of demonstrating that you're part of the tribe. It is not convenience, for example, that leads a cop to refer to a criminal as a "perpetrator" or a "perp," and an arrest as a "collar"; rather, in using these terms to his fellows he is demonstrating that he's one of the gang, not an outsider.

The flip side of solidarity within the tribe is "mystification"—symbolic exclusion—of those outside the tribe. Often this involves nothing more complicated than the pleasure of saying, in effect, "I know something you don't." Thus a clique of third-graders who, talking Igpay Atinlay, mutter amid giggles that "Oeyjay Ownbray inksstay" are asserting their superiority over Joey Brown, and anyone else that hasn't aughtcay onyay.

A common fallacy about jargon—especially criminal jargon—is that it is intended to deceive, rather than simply exclude, outsiders. Occasionally it may do so, but a more likely result would be to alert the outsider that something was fishy. A prospective victim of a con game who happened to overhear his new "friends" discussing how to rope a mark for the wire might or might not know that "the wire" was a particular kind of "big con" operation, but he would have to be a mighty lop-eared (stupid) mark not to be knocked (scared off) by such curious terms. A cop overhearing such a conversation would be even more certainly alerted, since the police are almost as familiar with criminal jargon as the crooks themselves.

Sometimes, however, unobtrusive deception goes with the territory, as with bureaucratic jargon, one of whose aims is often to say nothing while appearing to say something. In other cases, it's hard to be sure whether the jargon users are trying to deceive others or themselves—that is, to blunt their own awareness of what they're up to. For example, the chilling Nazi phrase, "final solution" was little (if at all) used in public, but rather *among the Nazis themselves,* who even as they organized the logistics of mass murder shied away from calling it by its proper name. The Soviet KGB refers to murder as "a wet operation" (either an oblique reference to blood or a rather grisly play on "liquidation"), and their CIA counterparts have proved equally inventive, bureaucratically euphemizing homicide as "termination with extreme prejudice." During the Vietnam War, the phrase was used often enough to bring Zipf's Law into play, producing the acronym TWEP, so that "counterinsurgency experts" could chat coolly about "TWEPping" someone. In the same way, more conventional types of criminals speak of "hitting" or "wasting" or "offing" or "whacking-out" a victim, not killing him.

Last but far from least among the motives for devising jargons and lingoes is—play. Children enjoy playing with words almost as soon as they can use them with any facility, and few of us lose that enjoyment as adults. At least two remarkable English lingoes seem to have been invented mainly for the fun of it, and even in the workaday world of trade jargons not a few terms derive from exaggeration, understatement, puns and other forms of what the users, at least, consider humor. Often these terms supply a concise commentary on the trade, its working conditions, customers and the like.

Terms in trade jargons (like slang words generally) tend to be transient; thus I cannot certify which of those I am about to cite are still current. But if they aren't, they have almost certainly been replaced by others no less colorful.

In the bookselling trade, an "interior decorator" is a dealer specializing in bound sets of books—presumably bought for show, not use. Likewise, when a bartender calls his cheapest whiskey "the cop's bottle" he is giving a thumbnail sketch of his relationship to the man on the beat. And a union member who describes a union official as a "pork-chopper" leaves us in no doubt on how he thinks the man views the organization: as simply a meal ticket or (to use an obsolete slang term) a pie card—which in the 1920s meant both a meal ticket and a pork-chopper.

Workers who are producing or selling junk know it; in the furniture trade, a piece made of "Nova Scotia mahogany" in "Russian Renaissance" style is one manufactured from cheap, stained pine carved—sloppily—in a rush. Hotel workers call a super-deluxe establishment, its lobby paneled in marble, a "quarry," while its ornately uniformed doorman is an "admiral." Interestingly, few trades, at least in America, have coined special terms for the boss, which might suggest a deficiency in "class consciousness." But consciousness is in there pitching when describing a boss's stooge: to longshoremen he is a "termite," to cannery workers a "ball rubber," and to Jewish retail clerks a "T.L." (from Yiddish *tuchus lekker*—ass licker).

Often enough, however, workers' wordplay is no social statement but merely a way of making a dull or tough job more bearable, or a frightening one less terrifying. Oil workers call the gook that accumulates at the bottom of a tank "B.S." (sometimes "translated" as "basic sediment"); a dry hole is a "duster" (that's all you get out of it); and a trucker who hauls nitroglycerine is "dead-in-a-hurry." Safeblowers call nitroglycerine itself "soup" (it can be obtained by gently—*very* gently—simmering dynamite in a pan of water). In a distillery, top-grade whiskey is "angel teat" (the sort of delectable potion you would expect from such an exhalted source); the lowest grade is "bug juice." The construction worker calls a massive 12 × 12 beam a "toothpick," which he may trim with his "George Washington" (hatchet). And a trucker hauling an empty trailer says he's got "a load of post holes."

Peculiarly prolific in such wordplay are workers at lunch counters, perhaps because they often work under pressure, which can stimulate the mind even as it fatigues the body. In any case, the customer's order can undergo a remarkable metamorphosis when relayed to the cook: frankfurters turn into "Coney Island bloodhounds" (hot *dogs*, sold there by the millions every summer); corned beef becomes "Irish turkey," and ham, potatoes and cabbage are "Noah's boy with Murphy carrying a wreath." Lively alliteration produced "dough well done with cow to cover" (bread and butter) and "clean up the kitchen" (hash). As many Americans know, a cup of coffee translates as "draw one" (also used of a glass of beer), whence "draw one in the dark" (black coffee) and "a pair of drawers" (two cups).

Terms like these seldom get beyond the workplaces of the people who coin them. Others, however, originating in more glamorous fields, have supplied English with some of its best metaphors. Probably the very first of these "glamour" occupations was that of the sailor—in actual fact, generally ill paid and dangerous, but to landlubbers, flavored with the romance of far-off lands and exotic merchandise. From sailors' jargon we have the "bitter end" to which we may pursue something—literally, the end of a rope fastened to the heavy bitts in a ship's bow; when you reach the bitter end you are at the end of your rope. A ship that sailed too close to the wind might find itself suddenly "taken aback," with the wind forcing it backward rather than forward.

Seaman making the long passage to India around the Cape of Good Hope often found themselves "in the doldrums"—the belt of light, shifting winds near the Equator in which a ship could drift, its sails "backing and filling," for days on end. If this went on long enough, the ship's cook would have to "scrape the bottom of the barrel" for a little half-rotten salt meat. And sailors who complained too energetically about the food might feel the dreaded cat-o'-nine-tails—administered on deck, since belowdecks there was "not enough room to swing a cat."

Railroading, as we saw earlier, has contributed some of its specialized jargon to general English, and more recently the aviators have given us "on the beam," "flying blind," "go into a tailspin" and "bail out" (of a dangerous situation). "Show biz," even more glamorous, has contributed "backstage," and "behind the scenes," "ad-lib," "ham" and "heavy" (a literal or figurative villain), along with "deadpan," "double take" and "pratfall." Now obsolete, alas, is that wonderful term for a complimentary ticket, "Annie Oakley," whose punched-out hole (for tax purposes) might have been shot out by that famous markswoman. Motion-picture and broadcasting jargon, on the other hand, has contributed relatively little to vivid English, though numbers of its terms have passed into the general vocabulary in their literal senses. One relative newcomer from this field, however, is worth noting: the "scenario" of military and political planners—which often has about as much relation to reality as its Hollywood prototype.

One of the most curious, and evanescent, Anglo-American trade jargons was "cablese." It flourished from shortly before 1900, when overseas cabling of news stories began to be commonplace, to around 1950, when cables were replaced by the cheaper teletype and radiotelephone.

Cable charges were high—something like a dollar a word—and correspondents were under some pressure to cram as much information into as few words as possible; this they did by extensively prefixing, suffixing and otherwise manipulating ordinary English words.

When I was a newspaper "cub" in 1940, a good deal of my work involved "translating" documents such as

CHAMBERLAIN PREFLYING LONDONWARD POSTPARIS CONFERENCE CUMDALADIER OPINED NAZI TROOP MOVEMENTS NORWAYWARD UNTHREATENING ADALLIES SAYING QUOTE HITLERS MISSED BUS UNQUOTE

In print, this would appear as "Prime Minister Chamberlain, just prior to boarding a plane for London following his conference here with Premier Daladier, expressed the opinion that Nazi troop movements toward Norway posed no serious threat to the Allies. 'Hitler,' he declared, 'has missed the bus.' " Nineteen words have expanded to forty-one.

Newspapermen are inveterate storytellers, and some of their best yarns involve cables. Thus Evelyn Waugh, covering the 1935 Italian invasion of Ethiopia for a London daily, received a cable from his boss, who had heard that an English nurse had been killed in an Italian air raid on a hospital: SEND TWO HUNDRED WORDS UPBLOWN NURSE. Waugh, unable to turn up any evidence that any English nurse had been killed, wired back NURSE UNUPBLOWN. Another tale has also been ascribed to Waugh, as well as to various other correspondents known for not mincing words. The journalist in question, having neglected to file any copy for some two weeks, received the cabled warning UNWORK UNJOB. He replied, almost as concisely, JOB UPSHOVE ARSEWISE. Cablese contributed "quote" and "unquote" to the English vocabulary, along with a few semitechnical terms like "update."

Of all the trades and professions, easily the champion, both at coining words and in its contributions to the general vocabulary, is crime. Like aviation and show business, it has glamour, and as such has been a staple of English literature for some four centuries. Among the most successful examples of Elizabethan "pop" prose were Robert Greene's pamphlets on "coney catching" (swindling "coneys" or marks); later parallels include the eighteenth-century *Beggar's Opera* (which begot the twentieth-century *Threepenny Opera*), and novels like *Tom Jones,* many of whose characters were, as Raymond Chandler later noted, only a jump or two ahead of the cops.

The reasons behind our long fascination with crime are (to borrow another phrase from Chandler) work for more patient minds than mine, but whatever the reasons, popular interest in criminals and their jargon has left numerous traces in the modern English vocabulary.

Crime of some sort has probably existed as long as people. Criminal jargon, however, evolves not from individual malefactors but from a more or less permanent class of professional crooks. In England, such a class apparently developed around 1500. Its first recruits may have been soldiers left unemployed after the Wars of the Roses, plus the wandering gypsies who, arriving in England around 1450, quickly won a reputation for knavery summed up by the slang term "gyp." ("Gypsy" itself reflects the myth that these people came from Egypt; in fact, the Rom, as they call themselves, originated in northern India, and their language, Romany, is akin to Hindi.) The ranks of crime were further swelled by the progress of English capitalism ("It hath made . . . of the common sort, rank beggars"): tenants and farm workers displaced from "enclosed" lands and compelled to beg or steal for a living.

By 1550 this motley crew had evolved its own quite elaborate jargon, called cant. Most of its terms were ordinary English words given extraordinary and esoteric meanings; others were borrowings from Low Dutch and Romany, and still others were nonsensical inventions. Some early examples are listed in a 1563 pamphlet by one Thomas Harman, which after recounting the depredations of the "vagabondes" gives a brief glossary of "the leud, lousy language of these lewtering luskes and lasy lorrels" (loitering loafers and lazy rogues). Among the esoteric "English" terms he cites are "mint" (gold), "stamps" (legs) and "couch a hogshead" (lie down and sleep). From Romany, apparently, come "ken," house, whence such compounds as "boozing ken" (alehouse), and the suffix "-mans" ("state of being" or "thing"), whence "darkmans" (night) and "ruffmans" (woods, bushes). The Low Dutch contributions have already been mentioned in an earlier chapter; many were acquired simply in the way of trade, but many of the lowest may well have reached English through cant; *luk* is believed to have originated as a gambler's term. Nonsense terms include "yaram" (milk) and "nosegent" (nun).

Most of Harman's "leud, lousy" terms are long obsolete (though some of the "-mans" words remained in criminal use well into the nineteenth century). At least two, however, have passed into more or less standard, if not necessarily elegant, English: "drawers" (originally, hose, drawn on over the legs) and "prat" (buttocks)—whence, of course, the vaudevillian's "pratfall." The verb "booze" may have been reintroduced into English through this channel; at any rate, there is no record of it between its first appearance in 1300 and Harman's citation nearly three centuries later. Another cant term borrowed at about the same time is "pal" (from Romany *phral,* brother). And, coincidence or not, the name of Shakespeare's sinister, dark-skinned aborigine, Caliban, is remarkably like Romany *kaliben,* blackness, which might well have been a cant term in the dramatist's day.

Another, much larger compendium of cant appeared in 1698, when an anonymous writer, "B.E.," published *A New Dictionary of the Terms Ancient and Modern of the Canting Crew.* It includes such still-current terms as "crony," "fence" (receiver of stolen goods), "duds" (clothes), "sock" (beat) and "clap" (venereal disease).

The passage of cant words into the general vocabulary has been going on ever since; some recent examples include "slam(mer)" (jail), "scam" (deceptive or crooked scheme) and "hit" (destroy, figuratively or literally), whence the political "hit man" and the pressure group's "hit list." Not to belabor the point, whatever the "criminal classes" have done in, and to, the English-speaking world, they have contributed notably to the English vocabulary.

Authentic modern cant is much rarer in literature than is crime itself: few writers have much firsthand contact with criminals. Moreover, by the time a cant term reaches the ears of outsiders, the clannish crooks will likely have evolved a more "private" replacement: a lingo is no fun if everybody knows it. Dashiell Hammett, however, was a private detective for years before he began writing, and his novels and especially his short stories are both vivid and authentic in their use of U.S. cant of the period from 1910 to 1925. Hammett, like some of his contemporary crime writers, enjoyed using his knowledge of cant to throw a linguistic curve past his rather straitlaced editors. Thus when he referred to Wilmer, the undersized killer of *The Maltese Falcon,* as a "gunsel," both editors and public took it to mean "gunman." In fact, it was a hobo-crook term (ultimately from German or Yiddish *gansel,* gosling) meaning an inexperienced youth, but more specifically, one accompanying an older man as a sexual partner. When Sam Spade told Gutman, "the fat man," to "keep that gunsel away from me," he was being a lot nastier than most of the book's readers ever realized.

Hammett's modern counterpart in the authentic use of cant, and almost his literary equal, is George V. Higgins, a former assistant U.S. attorney and still a practicing lawyer, with extensive firsthand knowledge of the activities and lingo of the Eddie Coyles and Digger Doughertys of New England crime. Writing fifty years after Hammett, however, Higgins has no need for devious devices like "gunsel": his characters employ four-, five-, seven- and ten-letter words in appalling profusion.

Hammett and Higgins have no true British equivalents in the field of crime fiction, though one gets bits and pieces of authentic cant in some of the works of the late Margery Allingham, who was interested enough in language to get it right. Other modern crime writers, both British and American, may or may not use cant with literary skill, but seldom do so with real authenticity. Raymond Chandler, Hammett's successor as master of the literate "private eye" novel, unabashedly invented much of his characters' "criminal slang," as John Le Carré made up the elaborate espionage jargon of George Smiley and his people. Other, less inventive writers simply borrow from their colleagues: not long ago I read a highly touted cops-and-robbers book set in Atlanta; most of its slang was indistinguishable from that spoken by Higgins' authentic Boston hoods, which I doubt exceedingly is true in real life.

One of the most fascinating English lingoes, which has contributed heavily to British criminal argot, is Cockney rhyming slang. Rhyme is a common and perhaps universal ingredient in wordplay, as witness such common American expressions as "hot shot," "culture vulture," "legal eagle" and "wheeler dealer." These phrases, however, are composed of words that mean what they say: thus the legal eagle is as preeminent among lawyers as is the eagle among birds—and is also, one suspects, something of a predator; the wheeler-dealer is a hard-driving contriver of financial deals, and so on. Cockney rhyming slang is quite different: typically, the literal meaning of its terms has no connection with their slang significance. For some examples, we can do no better than explicate the verse that opened this chapter:

> *My two mince pies (eyes) are full of tears,*
> *My raspberry tart (heart) is jelly;*

This looks simple enough—but wait:

> *My daisies I bullocked for two pig's ears (beers)*

Here "daisies" is short for "daisy roots" (boots) and "bullocked" for "bullock-horned" (pawned). I won't bother to translate the last line:

To warm my Auntie Nellie.

Cockney rhyming slang, then, begins with a phrase that rhymes with a given word, invented (usually) quite arbitrarily, though there are exceptions like "trouble and strife" (wife) and "I'm so frisky" (whiskey). But once the phrase has become current in the community, it may be "Zipfed" by dropping the rhyming element, thereby making the expression completely unintelligible to the uninitiated. In this way were created such common Cockney expressions as "Use yer loaf!" (loaf of bread—head) and "Let's 'ave a butcher's" (butcher's hook—look).

The wholly arbitrary character of most rhyming-slang terms suggests that a prime element in its creation was mystification of outsiders, and this indeed was the view of the late Julian Franklyn, who compiled a dictionary of more than fifteen hundred rhyming-slang expressions, though only a minority of these were or are in use at any given time. He traced the lingo to the 1830s, when Cockneys and Irish worked together as "navvies" ("navigation laborers") in the construction of canals and, later, railways. Initially, he believed, it was the Cockneys' way of one-upping the Irish, as by remarking darkly that so-and-so needed a new I'm afloat (coat), or inviting a fellow worker to share a cup of split pea (tea). Before long, however, the Irish caught on and began giving as good as they got, threatening the Cockney with a fist in the salmon and trout (which rhymes with "mouth" in Irish dialect) or intimating that his mother was a Rory O'More.

It may have been at this point that the Cockneys, to stay one-up on their Celtic confreres, began abbreviating. Or perhaps it occurred later, when the collapse of the railway boom pushed thousands of unemployed navvies into criminal or semicriminal pursuits. Certainly the slang was quickly taken into the cant of the British underworld, which, like most things British, centers in "The Smoke" (London). Abbreviation would then have aided the tea leaves (thieves), Johnny Ronces (ponces—pimps) and other babbling brooks (crooks) in further mystifying the grasshoppers (coppers), though the latter soon picked up the lingo, as of course they always do.

But rhyming slang also spread quite rapidly to the general working-class population of the London area, and moreover continued to evolve new terms—a sure mark of a living "language." The Cockneys certainly enjoyed mystifying outsiders who wandered into their neighborhoods, especially "toffs" (gentlemen); moreover, the lingo was a convenient way of euphemizing: one could, without being grossly offensive, vocally admire a young woman's Bristols (Bristol Cities), or announce that one was leaving the room to take a tomtit. And to tell somebody you didn't give a Friar Tuck for his opinions was less combative than its cruder equivalent. Yet I myself feel certain that the main reason rhyming slang survived and grew was simple *joie de vivre:* in London's grimy East End, as in similar areas throughout the world, yer takes yer fun where yer finds it.

A sizable number of Cockneys migrated to Australia—some of them under compulsion—and carried the new lingo with them; its adoption there, in my view, clinches the case for Australian English as fundamentally Cockney, whatever subsequent modifications it has undergone. At any rate, the Aussies were soon coining their own terms like "Maggie Moores" or "Maggies" (women's drawers), "charming mottle" (bottle) and "Port Melbourne Pier" (ear).

The last stage in the odyssey of rhyming slang occurred when numbers of Australians—many of them "ticket-of-leave" men (parolees) and similar rough customers—migrated to San Francisco, where their rhyming slang quickly became naturalized into the local cant, and American crooks began coining their own expressions like "rattle and jar" (car), "here and there" (chair) and the like. Hammett's writings show that it was well entrenched in the area by 1910 or earlier; from other evidence it was still used in the 1940s. Meanwhile, it had worked its way east, where it eventually encountered other rhyming terms that had reached the U.S. directly from England and Ireland. However, it never seems to have caught on widely among crooks east of the Rockies; thus we find few examples in the 1930s writings of Damon Runyon, chronicler of New York's petty and not-so-petty crooks. Two turn up in the remark of one of his characters to a young woman who claims to be engaged—the contemptuous "I don't see no Simple Simon (diamon') on your lean and linger!" Today, it is extinct, or all but, even in California.

Why rhyming slang should have died out in the U.S. is unclear. One likely reason was the growing domination of American crime by people whose native tongues were not English: you have to grow up with a language to play around with it skillfully. But the lingo remains alive in London, Sydney and the British underworld. It has also, surprisingly, made a few contributions to the vocabulary of general colloquial English. "Twist and twirl" (girl), though now obsolete, got into one of e. e. cummings' poems, while in England respectable people may call a man or woman a "berk" (figuratively, "fool"), though its literal meaning—which rhymes with "Berkshire Hunt"—is highly improper. Both English and Americans refer quite unself-consciously to giving someone "the raspberry" (in England it may mean no more than a mild reproof), which in American has even begotten a verb, "razz." Its more literal meaning, the rude noise also known as a Bronx cheer, takes us back to its rhyming original, "raspberry tart." (This expression, as noted earlier, could also mean "heart"; such dual or even triple meanings are not uncommon in rhyming slang.) And the "brass tacks" we are always urging people to get down to rhymes with "facts" in many English and American dialects.

Rhyming slang did not exhaust the Cockneys' linguistic exuberance: they also invented "back slang," whose reversed spelling produced such terms as "ecilop" (pronounced "slop") and "yob" (nowadays, usually a *delinquent* boy). They also borrowed words from an earlier lingo, Parlyaree, used especially by theatrical folk and "showmen" who ran concessions at local fairs (U.S. carnivals). Parlyaree terms were mostly borrowed from Italian immigrants; examples include "donah," woman (Italian *donna*); "omee," man (*uomo*); "madza," half (*mezzo*); and "scarper," run away (*scappare*, escape, with the Cockney "intrusive R.").

Another remarkable lingo, hardly less striking than rhyming slang, originated at almost the opposite pole, both socially and geographically, from the bustling East End of London: the small town of Booneville in the backwoods of northern California. "Boontling" (a telescoping of "Booneville lingo") was invented around 1890, but nobody knows by whom, or why. What seems clear is that it somehow caught the imagination of the community as a game at which any number could play—though it also served to mystify residents of neighboring communities, many of whom regarded the "Boonts" as ignorant yokels.

Boontling's vocabulary of over a thousand words came from many sources. The Spanish of an earlier generation of Californians contributed "breggo," sheep (from *borego*, yearling lamb) and "layche," milk (*leche*). From the local Pomo Indians came "boshe," hunt deer (from *bishe*, deer), which in turn begot the "bosher" (deer hunter) with his "boshe barl" (barrel—deer rifle). "Chiggle," eat, is an English dialect term meaning "chew," while the old verb "harp" (as in Polonius' "Still harping on my daughter!"') meant "talk."

Most Boontling terms, however, were invented, not borrowed. They are of three types: "telescoped" phrases from ordinary English; metaphors; and references to (usually) local personalities and happenings. Of the first type is "boarp," boar-pig, whence the somewhat derogatory "boarch," male Chinese. "Nonch," bad, inferior, blends "non" with "much," whence "nonch harpin," bad (dirty) talk. A dog was a "haireem" ("hairy mouth"—the Boonts favored animals of the shaggy-muzzled Airedale persuasion), and a "boshe haireem," naturally, a hound used in deer hunting.

Metaphors include "milky" (foggy), "bullrusher" (illegitimate child, "found in the bullrushes" like Moses) and "mink" (girl with expensive tastes). Expressions like "charlie ball" (embarrass) recall names of local personalities, in this case an ultra-shy Indian; from Joe McGrinsey, a formidable fighter, came "joe mack" (defeat at fisticuffs), while the nonch harpins enshrine the name of a local madam, Madge, meaning "whore" (one could go "madgin" at a "madge house"). The liveliest of the nonch terms is "burlapin" (fornicating)—according to local legend, from an incident when a boy, peering into the back room of a local store, spied the owner and a customer thus engaged on a pile of sacks; he charged into the street crying, "They're burlapin in there!"

Boontling, I think, amounts to a much enlarged "family lingo." Most families have their own modest store of private expressions—words mispronounced or misused by the children, or recalling bits of family history, that survive for a generation or two and then vanish. The isolated Boonts, inevitably much intermarried, were comparable to an oversize "extended family."

Like many extended families, this one disintegrated as auto travel became more common, taking Boonts elsewhere and bringing in numbers of outsiders. By the 1960s, though Booneville was still on the map, Boontling was harped only by a minority of mostly elderly people. Harpin was fun—but as one of them remarked rather sadly to a reporter, "Who's left to harp to?"

As we've seen, jargons, lingoes and cants have enlarged and enriched the English vocabulary—not least, in the area called slang, the most colorful and perhaps the most curious aspect of language. It is curious, among other reasons, because nobody is certain where the term came from (it seems to be akin to Norwegian *slengeord,* offensive language), and especially because, though most people use it, there is no accepted definition of just what it is. Various authorities stress its transience, its metaphorical vividness and humorous exaggeration, and its use in extremely informal situations—all of which qualities apply to some but not all slang expressions, and none of which sharply distinguish slang from more conventional categories of English.

Most slang terms are unquestionably transient, used for a few decades (sometimes only a few years) and then either dropped or, much less often, upgraded into the general vocabulary. Yet "bones" was a slang term for dice in Chaucer's day, and remained so until a generation or so ago; it would probably be current today if dice were still made of bone instead of plastic. "Clap" was low slang in the sixteenth century and is still so considered today, though probably more people know and use it than its respectable equivalent, "gonorrhea," and so with scores of other terms.

Likewise, much slang is unquestionably lively and colorful, and is invented and used for that reason: thus "light colonel" puns on "Lt. Colonel" to intimate that the rank carries less "weight" than a full or "chicken" colonel (from his U.S. insignia, an eagle). "Plumber" is a vivid metaphor for someone assigned to stop political "leaks," and "ants in the pants" (now Zipfed to "antsy,") graphically expresses the state of an irritable or restless person, as "climbing the wall" does that of a hysterical one. Yet not all slang is colorful—nor, for that matter, is standard English without colorful and often exaggerated metaphors of its own, many of which we've discussed earlier. A blockhead doesn't literally have a block of wood for a head—he just acts that way; breakbone (dengue) fever doesn't literally break your bones—it just feels that way. Informality is perhaps the most reliable hallmark of slang, yet here, too, there are confusing exceptions. The "four-letter words" are surely used only on the most informal occasions, yet most authorities classify them as Standard English. (To compound the confusion, some experts call them Standard when used literally—"You want to bleep?"—but slang when used figuratively—"Go bleep yourself!")

More interesting than the almost unanswerable question of what slang is is where it comes from. H. L. Mencken, a 22-karat intellectual snob, claimed that it originates in "a very small group" in the population, in which he included campus wits and "smart" writers. "The folk," he declaimed, "create nothing." Yet it is precisely "the folk" that create jargons and lingoes, which are the seedbeds of a great deal of slang— meaning that Mencken's remarks tell us more about his politics (which ended up slightly to the left of the Ku Klux Klan) than about slang. There weren't many smart writers or campus wits swilling far and near (beer) in London's East End in the 1850s, or burlapin around Booneville in the 1900s.

Campus wits have contributed to slang, as did the Cambridge "cronies" who coined that term from Greek *chronios,* long-standing; so have "smart" young men of fashion, like those who "Zipfed" Latin *mobile vulgus* (fickle crowd) into "mob." But more often slang arises among some low-life gang of navvies, sailors, soldiers, thieves or actors (considered pretty low even a century ago), whose contributions to the language begin as jargon or lingo, are taken up by hip individuals in other occupations, and eventually catch the fancy of the general public. Just so, the seedy hangers-on of the boxing ring—perhaps with some help from "smart" writers for the sports pages—gave us "knockout," "punch-drunk" and "saved by the bell."

Yet an enormous proportion of slang arises by what amounts to linguistic spontaneous generation, through the operations of Zipf's Law; witness "photo"(graph), "dipso"(maniac), "ad"(vertisement) and thousands of others. Who would say "high-fidelity radio-phonograph" when he could say "hi-fi," or "coin-operated automatic phonograph" when she could say "juke box"? There is no way in the world to ascertain who first coined these terms and their innumerable Zipfed relatives—and no reason in the world to suppose that the coinage was the work of any one person.

To the Menckens of this world, "the folk" is, by definition, neither imaginative nor creative, qualities that are the exclusive property of "smart" people. Yet when one examines the actual contributions of such people to slang, it turns out to be minor. *The Dictionary of American Slang* does, indeed, include numbers of alleged "slang" terms credited to such media figures of the 1930s, '40s and '50s as the columnists Walter Winchell, Lee Mortimer and Robert Ruark. Most of these, however, never got beyond the columns of the papers that printed them, and nearly all of them are as unfamiliar today as the names of their coiners will be to many readers of this book. The same goes for the coinages of their modern "smart" equivalents—disk jockeys and talk-show hosts—for whom trendy language is as much a professional necessity as trendy clothes and a trendy haircut—and has to be restyled almost as frequently. In the world of today's mass media, words—up-to-the-minute expressions for this, that or the other—have become marketable commodities. But like many other modern commodities, they suffer from built-in obsolescence.

Having said this, I must add that the rate of attrition in slang has always been high. Perhaps one term in ten eventually makes it into ordinary colloquial or even formal English, as did "mob," "crony" and, more recently, "phony"; another will remain current for generations or even centuries, always around yet never quite respectable, like "clap." The other 80 percent or so will sooner or later vanish into linguistic limbo: in their flaming youth they were the cat's pajamas and the bee's knees, but it was twenty-three skidoo and thirty for them.

The stream of slang is not unlike the Mississippi to which Noah Webster compared American English: full of all sorts of junk, perennially overflowing its banks, yet leaving behind a sediment that enriches the language, giving us such terms, once disreputable but now simply vivid, as "bogus," "bamboozle," "cave in," and hundreds of others—including many of the "slang" terms cited earlier, which for all their base origins have become current coin in cultivated speech and writing. Slang, said Mencken—and here we must give him full credit for cogency—is the most important of the processes by which language renews and replenishes itself. It is also, even in its unrefined state, a linguistic condiment. Like any condiment, it should be used in moderation—but stirred in judiciously, it can make the difference between a merely nutritious dish and a tasty one.

Perhaps the most omnipresent jargon in modern society is that of the bureaucrat. I have left it for last because it differs in almost every respect from those we have previously surveyed. It is seldom innovative (and never for the better); it uses (more often, abuses) terms taken overwhelmingly from Standard English; and it employs them in the most oppressively formal (or would-be formal) style. The bureaucrat, whether employed in government, the military or (in that fine bureaucratic phrase) the private sector, may in his personal life enjoy a good joke or even invent one, but once behind his desk his face freezes. Only people whose humor capability is totally inoperative could, with straight faces, emit such statements as "Before prioritizing this project, the cost-benefit ratio should be finalized by the agency" (translation: before we go ahead with this, we'd better make sure it's worth what it will cost). Or "As I review the growing constraints of the new year, I have to conclude with the greatest of regrets that we simply are not in a position to direct any funds from the established priorities for this purpose" (translation: Sorry, but they've given us less money this year than last, and what there is has already been spoken for by people who were ahead of you in line).

One could multiply the examples endlessly from the *Federal Register*, the fine print of insurance contracts, or the correspondence files of our great public utilities, and one can have a good deal of fun—in a rather perverse way—savoring the barbarities perpetrated on our native tongue by the usually anonymous authors. But merely poking fun, or viewing with alarm, is pretty superficial: the really important question is *why* bureau-

cratic prose so often fits the pungent term (coined by the Texas congressman Maury Maverick) "gobbledygook."

One cannot understand the bureaucrat, including his distinctive and
infuriating jargon, without understanding a fundamental law of all organizations, public or private, bureaucratic or otherwise: they do what they
are presently designed to do—which is not necessarily what they were set
up to do, or "supposed" to do. The "design" of any organization—the
regulations and customs under which its members operate—involves a
system of rewards and punishments, whereby people are encouraged to
do certain things and discouraged from doing certain others. These
arrangements are sometimes called "feedback"—a term originally borrowed from engineers' jargon.

Organizations (or parts of organizations) become bureaucratized when
feedback becomes divorced from "output"—the product or service that
the organization is supposed to be producing or providing. This split can
come about in a number of ways. Sometimes output is impossible to
measure with precision, if at all. For example, personnel departments in
large corporations deal in, among other things, "employee morale"—
hard to define and even harder to measure; the Pentagon, one of the
world's largest bureaucracies, deals in "national security," an even more
elusive kind of output. Clearly, if nobody can be sure just what the
organization is supposed to be doing, let alone how well it's doing it, then
even less can one be sure how well or how badly individual members are
doing *their* jobs—and reward or punish them appropriately.

In other cases, the organization's output is measurable enough, but the
connection between it and individual performance is obscure—or, sometimes, deliberately obscured. In any school system, for example, it is
possible to measure with considerable precision how well the students in
any grade can read and write; it is much harder to say who or what is
responsible for the skills they have—or have not—acquired: is it the
teachers, the texts, the "educational methods," the administrators, the
"home environment," or perhaps all of these? In such a situation, we can
be sure of only one thing, human nature being what it is: individuals
inside the organization will labor to shift the responsibility somewhere
else—preferably to someone or something outside it, but if not, than to
somebody else within it. Passing the buck—also known, and most appropriately, as "the old army game"—becomes easier, and therefore commoner, the larger and more complex the organization becomes.

In this sort of situation, where what you do and how well you do it have
little to do with what you get, the organization increasingly generates its

own, largely artificial criteria for judging the performance of its members; these can usually be summed up as following "regulations," or company or agency "policy." At lower levels this translates as "keep a low profile," "don't make waves," "follow orders" and "CYA" (Cover Your Ass) an acronym coined by our military bureaucrats.

For these purposes, bureaucratic jargon makes a good deal of sense— from the bureaucrat's point of view. In most kinds of writing, saying what you mean in clear, simple language is a plus; for the bureaucrat, it may well be a minus: a clear "yes" or "no" will please some people, be they bureaucratic superiors or outsiders, but will very likely displease others. A concise, unambiguous statement can get you in trouble; one that is wrapped up in verbiage and blurred by half a dozen qualifications won't: no matter how many people complain that you said thus-and-so, you can always reply, truthfully, that you really said something else.

Thus, from one standpoint, bureaucratic jargon is merely a special case of jargon in general, with mystification as its prime ingredient. But bureaucratic mystification, unlike that of other jargons, faces a special problem: it should not seem to be what it is. An oil-field roustabout or broadcast technician doesn't give a damn if outsiders find his occupational jargon bewildering—in fact he prefers it that way. But the bureaucrat—especially if he deals with the public—needs to *appear* responsive, while actually saying as little as possible. Unfortunately, very few people outside the highly-paid advertising and public relations industries have the considerable literary skills needed to say nothing well; the bureaucrat, therefore, says nothing badly.

If bureaucratese were no more than this—an elaborate kind of evasive action enabling its users to continue drawing pay for performing their ill-defined duties—it would perhaps be merely a tolerable nuisance, part of the price we pay for living in a complex and highly structured society. In some bureaucracies, however, mere evasion becomes active concealment, and bureaucratese a verbal smokescreen designed to hide activities that will not bear public scrutiny.

Thus the CIA's bland phrase, "clandestine activities" (doubtless paralleled in the jargons of other secret services) covers everything from spreading "black propaganda"—in plain English, lies—to bribery, blackmail and murder. The Pentagon's much-sought "first-strike capability" (again surely paralleled in other tongues) means the ability to start a nuclear war and get away with it—a "scenario" as phony as it is horrifying. The ultimate bureaucratic euphemisms are such terms as "final solution," "wet operation" and "termination with extreme prejudice"—the last, significantly, borrowed from corporate bureaucracies in which "termination" is a euphemism for "firing"; these, as we've already noted, serve to insulate the bureaucrat himself from the moral implications of his own actions.

All this is bad enough. Even worse is the infiltration of these and similar euphemisms into the general vocabulary—because it encourages all the rest of us to embrace the bureaucrat's moral neutralism, to "think about the unthinkable" with equanimity. At this point, bureaucratese has become much more than an irritant: it is a linguistic poison that can pervert public discussion and judgement on matters of—literally—life and death.

As we've seen in this chapter, jargons and lingoes—even the jargon of the organizational time-server—can be amusing as well as instructive. But jargon that fosters muddled thinking and moral insensitivity about the gravest public issues is a very bad joke: we could die laughing.

12. FROM HERE ON IN

English Today and Tomorrow

Ѣ

No one who is interested in the subject of language can have failed to be struck with the prevalence of complaints about the corruption which is overtaking our own speech. Reference to it turns up not infrequently in books; discussion of it forms the staple of articles contributed to magazines, and of numerous letters written to newspapers. . . .

There seems to have been in every period of the past, as there is now, a distinct apprehension in the minds of very many worthy persons that the English tongue is always in the condition approaching collapse. . . . These foretellers of calamity we have always had with us; it is in every way possible that we shall always have them.

—Thomas R. Lounsbury (1908)

As Lounsbury, a distinguished American grammarian, shrewdly conjectured nearly eighty years ago, we indeed still have with us very many worthy persons who prophesy the imminent decline and fall of English. In books, magazines and letters to the editor—and these days on radio and TV talk shows—they are, as he noted, "always pointing to the past with pride," conjuring up some golden age when "the language was spoken and written with the greatest purity." And they are still viewing with grave or sometimes shrill alarm the "corruptions of all kinds" which, Lounsbury noted dryly, "are not merely stealing in, they are pouring in with all the violence of a tidal wave."

Since English, despite being in a "condition approaching collapse" eighty years ago, hasn't collapsed yet, surviving the corruptions of the Edwardian era even as it survived earlier corruptions deplored by, among others, Ben Jonson and Swift, it is tempting to dismiss our modern prophets of linguistic disaster as merely the Calamity Janes which, like the Biblical poor, we have always with us. Such, indeed, is the view of not a few experts in linguistics, who not only deny that English is being corrupted but declare that the very notion of linguistic corruption is meaningless. They describe the viewers-with-alarm as "prescriptive"—in their terms, a linguistic no-no; their opponents, in turn, denounce them as "permissive," which is of course even more of a no-no.

Since that the controversy shows no signs of abating, it seems worth-
while to examine the views of both sides and try to discover which of them
(if either) makes sense. This is the more true in that the dispute between
"prescriptive" and "permissive" experts is linked to some very real and
important questions about English—notably, how dictionaries should be
compiled, and how English should be taught.

One thing—about the only thing—both parties to the dispute agree on
is that the English language is changing, a fact that will come as no
surprise whatever to readers of this book. The point at issue is whether
these changes, or any of them, should be viewed as "corruption" or
simply as facts to be noted: are they or are they not "bad English"; is
there, in fact, any such thing as bad English?

Some leading members of the "permissive" school say categorically
that there is not. Thus Prof. Robert A. Hall, in his popular paperback
Linguistics and Your Language, declares flatly that "there is no such thing
as good and bad (or correct and incorrect, grammatical and ungrammatical, right and wrong) in language." In fairness to Hall, when he gets down
to discussing these points at length he becomes rather less categorical,
but categorical or not, he said it, and what he said is worth discussing to
make some basic points.

Consider the following sentences:

1. Hall doesn't give a damn about grammar.
2. Hall don't give a damn about grammar.
3. About grammar Hall a damn don't give.

The first of these would be used naturally by tens of millions of
English-speaking people, and would be understood by just about anybody who knows the language. The second would be used just as naturally by other tens of millions, and would be understood as widely. The
third, however, would not be used by any native speaker of English, and
most of us would puzzle a bit before grasping what the speaker was trying to tell us. Sentences (1) and (2) are both grammatical English—(1)
is "Standard," (2) is "nonstandard"—but (3) is not grammatical English.

To hammer home the point: English, like every other language, has a
grammar: a set of arbitrary conventions specifying the sounds and combinations of sounds that can be used to make words; which of those sounds
and combinations are meaningful words, and what they mean; and how
words can be combined to form meaningful sentences. As we've seen,
these conventions vary considerably from one part of the English-speaking world to another, and from one occupational or social group to

another. But there are limits to the variations, and any "English" utterance that falls outside those limits—as sentence (3) clearly does—is, by definition, ungrammatical.

In addition to being ungrammatical English, the sentence is also bad English, which is not necessarily the same thing, though Hall seems to imply that it is. To understand the distinction, we must examine—or reexamine—a concept that few of the experts, "prescriptive" or "permissive," devote much attention to: communication.

Most of us talk to ourselves occasionally, and some of us jot down notes or scribble in diaries strictly for our own information. But these activities account for only a tiny fraction (probably less than 1 percent) of our use of language; the rest of the time, we normally speak or write in the expectation, or at least the hope, that somebody will hear or read us and comprehend what we're trying to say.

We now have at least one meaningful standard for distinguishing good from bad English: when we communicate clearly, we are using good English; when we communicate unclearly, we are using bad English. Moreover—and this is a key point—while ungrammatical English is likely to be bad (unclear) English, as sentence (3) above certainly is, the reverse is not true: grammatical English is not necessarily clear English.

Consider some examples. The first is from a recent article on the early history of Edenton, North Carolina: "Located at a considerable distance from the coast, Edenton's commercial importance was unrivaled within the colony." Now in a formal (some would say nit-picking) sense, this sentence is ungrammatical, since as written "located" refers to "commercial importance," whereas it was obviously intended to refer to "Edenton." Yet merely correcting this error, so that the passage reads "Located at a considerable distance from the coast, Edenton possessed a commercial importance unrivaled within the colony," leaves untouched the sentence's real weakness: its structure implies that there was some relationship between Edenton's location and its commercial importance, yet neither the sentence nor its context gives us a clue to what that relationship was. Indeed the context makes things even murkier: the author has already told us that Edenton was located *on* the coast—was in fact a leading colonial seaport. Conceivably he was trying to say that Edenton was located far from the open sea, which it was, but what (if anything) that had to do with its commercial importance is something you have to guess. And if you have to guess, it's bad English.

A second example comes from a recent book on international terrorism: "But his sex life would be loudly revealed when he turned up a phonograph to recordings of gunfire and martial music." The sentence is arguably grammatical, though "turned up recordings . . . on a phonograph" would perhaps read better. But no matter how you phrase it, it makes no sense; one can only speculate on various things the author *might* have meant. That is, she was using bad English.

A third example takes us back to Professor Hall, who immediately after assuring us that there is no such thing as bad English declares that "there is no such thing as 'written language.' " The sentence is simple, incontestably grammatical, and hopelessly unclear. You can't read it literally; the fact that you're reading it defines it as written language. Hall may have been trying to say that there is nothing distinctive about written, as opposed to spoken, language (which I believe is false, for reasons I'll explain later), or that spoken language is much more important than written language (which is at least arguable), or something else entirely. His sentence is bad English, not because it is ungrammatical (it isn't) or because it's nonsense (though I think it is) but because it fails to make clear precisely what kind of nonsense (or sense) it is.

Our definition of clear English as good English needs to be qualified in one important respect: some authors (along with some politicians, businessmen and ordinary people) deliberately aim at linguistic confusion. Thus, returning to our writer on international terrorism, we read, "There is no firm evidence that Fidel Castro ever entrusted Feltrinelli [an Italian terrorist] with direct responsibility for delicate political missions." Now this sentence is grammatical, seems to be clear, and is undoubtedly true as far as it goes: since the author detests Castro, had any "firm evidence" existed she'd certainly have told us about it. Yet read more carefully, the sentence is ambiguous, since it implies that *less than firm* evidence exists, or that Feltrinelli was entrusted with *indirect* responsibility—in short, that something sinister was going on. The author manages this rhetorical fast-shuffle quite skillfully—nobody can call her an outright liar. From the standpoint of what she intended to communicate, then, her English is excellent, though one can't say as much for her honesty.

Having established at least a foundation for evaluating English usage, let's look at some of the changes in usage and meaning that the "prescriptive" experts deplore. The first thing that must be said about them is that many of them aren't changes at all: reputable writers have been "misusing" certain words now in question for generations or even centuries. Thus Edwin R. Newman, a widely read writer on words, considers the use of "rhetoric" in the sense of exaggerated, empty language to be incorrect; if he is right, then it's been used incorrectly for more than three centuries by (among others) Milton, Cowper and Swinburne. Equally venerable are such "errors" as "aggravate" (annoy), which dates from 1611. The late Theodore Bernstein, for many years chief of the *New York Times* copy desk, described the usage as, if not incorrect, at least "inept," from which we would have to conclude that Richardson, Austen and Thackeray were inept writers. Bernstein also objected to "critique" as a verb ("Let's critique the performance"), though English writers have used it in this sense since 1751.

Fifty-odd years ago, and for years thereafter, much ink and emotion were devoted to denouncing the verb "contact"—formed, of course, from the noun of the same name, as English-speaking people have been forming new verbs for centuries. You may therefore be surprised (as I certainly was) to find in the OED that the "new" formation dates from 1836 ("the spark and the gunpowder contacted"), while its modern, transitive sense ("Mr. Dickey contacted every family") dates from 1929. Yet more than forty years later, the panel of "usage experts" who advised the editors of *The American Heritage Dictionary* voted the verb unacceptable in formal usage, by a margin of two to one. Just what they meant by "formal usage" is unclear. It would, perhaps, be startling to hear a preacher exhort his flock to "contact Jesus," but I personally find it hard to imagine any other situation, formal or otherwise, in which the verb would be out of place. Except, perhaps, in addressing a usage panel.

Note that in none of these cases does the matter of unclarity arise. Thus whether one uses "aggravate" to mean "annoy" ("The doctor's manner aggravated the patient") or in its other sense of "make worse" ("The doctor's treatment aggravated the patient's condition"), the context will make clear which is meant: the first can refer only to people; the second, only to situations. (The use of "aggravate" to mean "annoy" is unquestionably seen by many educated people as evidence of ignorance or "poor breeding," a problem discussed below.)

Ambiguity does arise in the case of "unique," whose original meaning was "one of a kind." On this ground, many experts object to such usages as "very unique"; a thing, after all, either is or isn't one of a kind. Or, as the OED gravely puts it, "The usage in the comparative and superlative, and with adv[erb]s, as *absolutely, quite, totally, thoroughly* etc. has been objected to as tautological." But then, in one of those bits of deadpan scholarly humor that makes the OED such a delight to read, it cites "thoroughly unique" (1809), "absolutely unique" (1866) and even "uniquest" (1885); Conan Doyle used "very unique" only a few years later.

"Unique," in short, no longer has an absolutely unique meaning: for well over a century it has been used in the weakened sense of "unusual." Nor is there anything unique (in either sense) about this semantic shift: a dozen once-powerful English adjectives have similarly shrunk into triviality. We speak of a "terrible cold" or a "horrible bore," though few if any colds are terrifying and bores generally induce slumber, not horror. Similarly devalued are "tremendous" (originally, "making one tremble"), "awful" ("awe-inspiring") and so on. One is reminded of the old tale of the Hollywood executive who, asked how business was, replied, "It's fantastic, it's sensational, it's spectacular—but it's picking up."

But the very ambiguity attached to "unique" means that we need to be careful in using it: if we really mean "one of a kind," then it requires an adverb like "absolutely" or "literally," otherwise some readers will take it to mean simply "unusual." In the latter sense, it is probably best avoided; English has plenty of synonyms.

In contrast with these much-deplored but far from new "innovations" is a genuinely new usage, that of "hopefully." Once an adverb signifying "in a hopeful manner"—one could pray, or invest money, or court a lady hopefully—it is now widely used to mean "it is to be hoped that." Comments on this usage in *The Harper Dictionary of Contemporary Usage* include "barbaric," "horrible," "damnable" and "makes me physically ill." People with less delicate stomachs may note that the word, in accordance with Zipf's Law, makes for more concise discourse, saying in three syllables what would otherwise take six. It is also by no means the first English adverb to be transformed into a shorthand introductory phrase. Conceivably ("it is conceivable that") the experts don't know this, or possibly ("it is possible that") they don't care. Admittedly, these usages are not precisely parallel to the "damnable" use of "hopefully"—and I personally couldn't care less. The usage is concise and absolutely clear; if it bends the rules of English syntax a bit, as English-speaking people have been doing for centuries—so what?

A remarkable aspect of these disputes is the amount of emotion they can stir up—witness the heated adjectives quoted in the preceding paragraph. Other representative comments on allegedly corrupt expressions include "barbaric patois," "Horrors!" and "Vile," with "sloppy" and "illiterate" almost routine. Such emotions reached something of a peak with the publication, about thirty years ago, of *Webster's Third International Dictionary* ("Webster III" for short), which brought on a head-to-head confrontation between the "permissive" and "prescriptive" schools. The latter accused the book's editors of (naturally) "permissiveness," "degrading the language" and conducting "a sack of the uttermost citadel and sanctuary" of English. More substantive grounds for criticism included the elimination of over 200,000 words that had appeared in the book's predecessor, "Webster II," which one critic called "verbicide"; its alleged listing of transitory expressions as standard English; its virtual obliteration of distinctions between levels of usage ("colloquial," "erroneous" and so on); and its failure to distinguish between words often confused (e.g., semimonthly/bimonthly, forceful/forcible, depreciate/deprecate). The book's editor-in-chief, Dr. Phillip B. Gove, showed no remorse for these crimes: a dictionary, he declared, "should have no traffic with . . . artificial notions of correctness or superiority. It should be descriptive, not prescriptive."

This last was the real heart of the controversy, of course. Before discussing it, however, let's consider briefly some of the peripheral criticisms. First, the dictionary's deletion of 200,000-plus words (all those not used since 1755) was doubtless a simple commercial decision, aimed at holding down the size and price of the volume. The publisher's description of the abridged work as "unabridged" may perhaps be faulted as deceptive labeling, but the deleted words have not been run through some literary crematorium: they are still in English literature and, for those seeking their meaning, still in the OED.

Equally trivial, I think, is the dictionary's alleged inclusion of "transient" expressions. It would be interesting to check back and see how many of these words are in use today, thirty years later, but hardly worth the trouble. If they've dropped out of use, the fact that they're "in Webster" won't resurrect them (and would it matter anyway?); if, on the other hand, they are still current, then the more credit to Gove and his associates for having the prescience to include them.

Turning now to Gove's "descriptive, not prescriptive" approach, I myself would describe it as right in principle, but wrong in execution. He was certainly on target in saying, in effect, that a dictionary must be guided by usage: that whatever words may have meant in the past, what they mean today is what people use them to mean. Meanings and usages change, and to insist that they haven't or demand that they shouldn't are, in Samuel Johnson's phrase, "the undertakings of pride, unwilling to measure its desires by its strength."

But if I cannot quarrel with Webster III for being descriptive, I can and do quarrel with it for not being descriptive enough. Changes in meaning and usage are facts and must be recorded as such. But change, while it is still underway—that is, when two different meanings are both current

—can, as we've seen, become a source of ambiguity, and that too is a fact that readers should be alerted to. The problem is far from new: in Chaucer's day *wyf* could mean either "woman" (its original sense) or "wife." Should we then refer to his outspoken matron as "The Woman of Bath" (she was every inch a woman) or "The Wife of Bath" (she was that too —five times)? Here you can take your pick, since nobody knows precisely which meaning the poet intended. But modern ambiguities such as those of "unique," "disinterested" ("uninterested" vs. "impartial") and scores of other words should have some sort of "Go Slow" sign attached, to alert the reader.

Were I constructing a dictionary, I would go further and recommend ways of avoiding such ambiguities, as I did in discussing "unique" earlier on. In some cases, indeed, I would have no hesitation in recommending that the words be avoided entirely, as with those unholy twins "semimonthly" (twice a month) and "bimonthly" (every two months), which are virtually guaranteed to confuse the reader—in fact I wasn't sure myself which was which until I looked them up just now.

Finally, if some social group considers a particular usage "incorrect" or "substandard," that too is a fact that belongs in any truly descriptive dictionary, and to reject such considerations as "artificial" (i.e., the product of social convention), as Gove does, is plain silly: name one thing about language that is *not* the product of social convention! Here, as in so many other ways, the OED points the way: hundreds of its entries include such notations as "sometimes considered incorrect" or "considered a solecism" or "objected to by grammarians." Such notations are not "prescriptive": they don't order the reader to shun a given word or usage. Rather, they say in effect, "Many writers have used the word in this way, but some people object; if you use it, be prepared for criticism." What could be more reasonable?

Clear communication of meaning is the most fundamental criterion of "good English"—but communication extends beyond simple meaning, be it never so clear. The words we use, and how we use them, can communicate not simply our ideas and feelings, but the kinds of people we are, in others' eyes if not our own. Consider, for example, "lay" and "lie." Millions of people naturally say "I was laying on the bed," while millions of others just as naturally say "I was lying on the bed," and in neither case will anyone be in any doubt as to what the speaker was doing. But it is also true that not a few people, hearing the first sentence with its blue-collar syntax, will deduce that the speaker is poorly educated and/or stupid. One may censure such people as snobs or "elitists," but

they exist, and communication with them must take their personal characteristics, snobbish or not, into account.

No dictionary, and no panel of experts either, can have the last word
on English usage: that will be said only when—and if—English ceases to
be a living tongue, as happened with Sumerian, Egyptian and Hittite.
Equally, not even the most scholarly and comprehensive dictionary can
convert the enormous, disorderly and mutable vocabulary of English into
something neat, rational and unambiguous. On the contrary: a dictionary
that claims to be comprehensively descriptive must recognize these features of English, and suggest how we can prevent them from hindering
or blurring communication with our fellows.

In my considered judgment this sort of sober, rational approach is
likely to do far more for the preservation of "good English" than the
overheated, sometimes hysterical denunciations of "prescriptive" critics.
Indeed, the very violence of their comments suggests that something
more than the English language is at stake: a power struggle between
these Swiftian authorities and the "permissive" linguists and lexicographers. Another major source of this rhetorical overkill is plain personal
prejudice. That is, certain words and expressions are violently rejected
by the purists, not because they are "bad English" in any definable sense,
but because the purists violently dislike the kinds of people who use or
are believed to use such expressions. For example, Leo Rosten heatedly
characterizes "meaningful" (as in "meaningful relationship") as "student
cant of the 1960s. Baloney!" Since the word actually dates from the
1850s, Rosten's indignation tells us more about his feelings for 1960s
students than about good usage.

Particularly irritating to some critics are words or usages supposedly
deriving from the world of commerce, for which these authorities have
as rooted a contempt as did any Victorian aristocrat for people "in trade."
The long argument over the verb "contact" almost certainly sprang from
its use by businessmen and salesmen who, since they frequently had to
get into contact with suppliers and customers, Zipfed four words into one.
Similarly, Barry Bingham, Sr., a member of the Harper usage panel,
denounces the verb "gifted" ("he was gifted with a vivid imagination")
as "vulgar advertising jargon. NO, NO, NO," and Joseph Alsop demands
that the verb "craft" (as in "crafting a foreign policy") be "banished from
the English language" because it "had its provenance in trade, in the
mercantile world of advertisers." Yes, m'lord, certainly, m'lord.

This transmutation of personal dislike into stylistic principle surfaced
in many comments on the so-called "Watergate English" used by Richard

Nixon and his honchos. Many writers and critics had a profound—and, as it turned out, thoroughly justified—dislike of Nixon, which they transferred from the man to his language. Thus Edwin S. Newman professed to be appalled at the "poverty of expression" allegedly revealed in the Watergate tapes, in which he included such presidential expressions as "kicking butts," "can of worms," "playing hardball" and the like. Yet surely the last thing one can say of such expressions is that they are impoverished or colorless; on the contrary, they are lively and vivid.

William and Mary Morris, editors of the Harper usage dictionary, were similarly distressed by such specimens of Watergate English ("horrible examples of language torn asunder") as "stroke" (soothe, cajole), "plumber" and "launder" (i.e., money). Personally, I find "stroke" a fine metaphor, perhaps because I have been soothing and cajoling cats in this manner for years. Equally, "plumber" is an almost inevitable word for someone assigned to plug political leaks, and "launder" is surely the perfect term for manipulating dirty money to eliminate ring-around-the-bankroll. I'll go further: though the Morrises believe (or hope) that these expressions will soon perish from the earth, I'll bet them any reasonable sum that "launder," at least, will still be around twenty years from now. It is clear, vivid and concise, and the phenomenon it describes promises, alas, to be with us for a long time.

Don't misunderstand me: I yield to no one in my detestation of Richard Nixon, but the fact that he had a bad character doesn't mean that he used bad English. In private, on the famous tapes, he demonstrated that he could be, if not "perfectly clear," then certainly too clear for his own good, and if in public he and his associates frequently employed obfuscation and prevarication, they did so for the same reason other people do: the clear, unvarnished truth would have been embarrassing if not downright incriminating. My objection to Nixon and his merry men, then, is not that they corrupted the English tongue but that they corrupted the processes of government, seeking to replace the limited powers specified by our Constitution with the unlimited power of "executive privilege."

English, in fact, is *not* being "corrupted," or at any rate no more than at most times in its long history. Yet for all that, one aspect of English is in serious trouble: the one most of us (despite Prof. Hall) continue to call written English. Increasingly large numbers of people who speak English can't read it, and many who can read it can't write it. They can, to be sure, put down words on paper and often spell them correctly, but they cannot select and organize their words to convey clearly what they want to say.

I don't propose to present a mass of statistics, since the basic facts aren't in dispute. Rudolf Flesch, author of *Why Johnny Can't Read,* has estimated that in 1981, a quarter of the U.S. population was illiterate— literally: they couldn't read the label on a can of soup or a bottle of medicine. Another third, he believes, was semiliterate, meaning that they could read the labels but not much else. These figures, which add up to more than half the nation, may be over-pessimistic, but even if we cut them in half they'd still be appalling—and incidentally nearly six times the "official" figure supplied by such bodies as the U.S. Office of Education. Flesch believes that in Canada the situation is not much better.

A common explanation for this depressing situation, peddled both by professional educationists and professional right-wing agitators, is television and (of course) "permissiveness." Chronologically, this won't wash. Mass illiteracy in the U.S. began to develop around 1930, expanded during the 1940s, and was well entrenched by the time Flesch published his book in 1955, when TV was still in its infancy and the "permissive" '60s and '70s were still to come.

The real culprit was a radical change in how children were taught to read: the introduction during the 1920s of the so-called "see and say" method. That is, young kids were no longer taught to spell out the sounds of syllables and words ("A-D, ad-; M-I, mi-; admi-" and so on) but to recognize the word "as a unit." Phonetics—learning to relate sounds to letters—was introduced only in the higher grades, if at all. This "progressive" innovation turned the clock of literacy back more than three thousand years, to hieroglyphics.

Egyptian hieroglyphics, like other early writing systems such as cuneiform, relied heavily on symbols—thousands of them—representing whole words, *which had to be memorized individually.* The result was that what we'd call primary education—reading, writing and simple arithmetic— required some twelve years of schooling. (In today's China, with a similar writing system, literacy still comes slowly, since even fairly simple texts embody several thousand different characters.) The invention of the alphabet, some time before 1000 B.C., amounted to an educational revolution: it was designed to represent sounds, not words, and did so, moreover, with only a couple of dozen different symbols. It was not a perfect system then and is not one today, especially in English, in which the number of sounds considerably outnumbers the available symbols. But it is still far more easily learned than any other system of writing.

The story of how alphabetic phonetics was replaced by the back-to-hieroglyphics method is a long and complicated piece of social history of which we can examine only the high spots. To begin with, see-and-say didn't arise completely out of thin air: it was based on a long-known scientific fact, that when *adults* read they aren't aware of individual letters or sounds but perceive words (often, groups of words) as units. From this single fact, however, educationists and educational psychologists reached an altogether unscientific conclusion: since we want kids to learn to read as adults do, let's teach them to perceive words as adults do—as units. Which, as a piece of reasoning, made about as much sense as saying that the way to teach kids roller skating is to start before they can walk.

Commendably, the educationists and psychologists wanted to teach reading "scientifically"; unfortunately, they hadn't a clue as to how to go about it, since the psychology of the time threw little if any light on how children learn reading or anything else. From the 1920s on, in fact, studies of learning involved mainly animals, not children, thanks to the influence of the school of psychology called behaviorism, which idolized "controlled" laboratory studies of the sort that can be done on rats but not on kids. Even the minority of psychologists who studied "verbal learning" did so, as psychologist Eleanor J. Gibson dryly remarked much later, "by means of experiments with nonsense syllables and the like—that is, materials carefully divested of useful information."

The other—perhaps the major—force behind the adoption of see-and-say was the textbook industry, for which a radical change in teaching methods opened up an enormous market for new series of readers, new teaching guides for instructors, and new texts for teachers' training schools. The publishers wanted to make money, the educationists wanted to be "scientific," and between them they made see-and-say virtually universal in American schools.

The character of the new see-and-say readers, consciously or not, reflected the tenets of behaviorist psychology, which dealt in "objectively observable" behavior. To the behaviorists, learning as such (as of a new action by an animal) was not objectively observable. What was observable was whether, and how often, the action was spontaneously repeated; animals were induced to do this by "reinforcing" (rewarding) them when they performed the desired action, until eventually the reinforcement was no longer required. Thus repetition became both the means of changing behavior and the measure of whether it had changed.

Following the same line of reasoning, the educationists downgraded *comprehension* of written material—hard to define and even harder to measure—and latched on to something that *could* be measured: the number of words to which a child was exposed. Enter "vocabulary limitation," whereby children were introduced to only a few new words at a time (the working rule was about one per page of text).

On the face of it, deliberately *minimizing* the number of words that children were allowed to read sounds like a recipe for noneducation. In context, it made a certain amount of sense. When children were being taught phonetically that C-A-T spells "cat," then learning "bat," "fat," "hat" and so on was not very difficult. But when it became a matter of teaching them to recognize each word individually, without making the phonetic connection between them, introducing new words a few at a time was not illogical. The professorial scribes of ancient Egypt did much the same thing.

With vocabulary limitation and repetition as parents, the character of their offspring—the new generation of elementary readers—is not hard to deduce: few words, repeated interminably, and never mind if they don't say much. Look, look, look! See Dick run. See Jane run. See Spot run. See Dick and Jane learn to read like Spot.

By 1960, the consequences of see-and-say were all too visible: according to the writer Lincoln Barnett, American *fourth*-grade readers had a vocabulary of only eighteen hundred words—less than that of Russian *first*-grade readers! (Soviet *fourth*-graders were reading ten thousand different words.) The actual situation, indeed, was worse than these figures indicated; not a few American schoolchildren failed to master even the limited number of words they were allowed to see. A major reason is that readers of the Dick-and-Jane type were almost as carefully "divested of useful information" as the nonsense syllables that the educational psychologists had been studying. Kids who had already been exposed to meaningful, interesting books at home were probably little affected by this, but those for whom these dreary little volumes were their first experience with the printed word must often have concluded that learning to read was a waste of time. On the evidence before them, they were absolutely right.

One might think that while all this was going on, somebody would have taken the trouble to check on how the new method was panning out: was it actually teaching kids to read better than had the old phonetic method? Amazingly, few such tests were ever carried out, and even fewer were conducted under anything approaching scientific conditions. Of this last group, says Flesch, *every one* showed clearly that *phonetics* yielded better educational results! Later, during the early 1960s, Eleanor Gibson and her associates at Cornell did carry out some "controlled" experiments on how people learn to read words, rather than nonsense syllables; not surprisingly, they found that learning to sound out the letters first markedly speeded up learning.

By this time, however, see-and-say had so dug itself into the educational system that dislodging it would have required dynamite. The textbook publishers were committed to it; so were the teachers colleges; so were the teachers themselves. Reintroducing phonetics would have made every elementary reader in the country, and every textbook on how to teach reading, obsolete; it would also have involved retraining an entire generation of teachers and professors of education. The result is that today, over twenty-five years after Flesch exposed see-and-say, and over fifteen years after Gibson published her study, the back-to-hieroglyphics method sails serenely on: Flesch estimates that it is still used in about four out of five public schools, though (thank God for small favors) it is now "supplemented" by phonetics in most of these.

Dick and Jane are, indeed, dead, but their replacements are no less mind-deadening, as witness one recent primer: "Come, Mark, come. Come here, Mark, come and jump." Mark's reply: "Here I come, Janet. Here I come. Jump, jump, jump." Ask a stupid question . . .

Kids who don't learn to read evidently won't learn to write either. But a sizable number who, despite the worst efforts of Dick, Jane and their educational and corporate sponsors, have learned to make sense of printed letters are still unable to put their own ideas down on paper with any ease or clarity. We've already looked at some recent examples of bad writing; here are some worse ones, culled from various publications:

- A college freshman: "It's obvious, in our modern world of today, their's a lot of impreciseness in expressing thoughts we have."
- A candidate for an M.A. at a large Midwestern university: "If you know the problems, the children are difficult to evaluate with."
- A doctor: "Symptomatology relative to impending or incipient onset of illness generally manifests itself initially via a marked chill, followed by a rapid rise of temperature to the 103 degree–105 degree range is characteristically observed."
- A teacher (!) writing to a parent: "Scott is dropping in his studies he acts as if he don't Care. Scott want pass in his assignment at all, he had a poem to learn and he fell tu do it."
- A writer in *The New Yorker:* "If he were trying to pull himself together by hanging on to Esther's sanity, and she knew that and parlayed it, there would be some dynamics and edges." (This was from a book review—not the magazine's "How's That Again?" department.)

The reasons why so many American high school and even college graduates write so abominably are numerous and complicated. There is no one group that can be saddled with most of the blame, like the educationists and their allies in psychology and publishing in the case of reading. Educationists have certainly done their share, but so have various well-meaning but muddle-headed experts on linguistics, incompetent teachers and the unions that protect their jobs, tight-fisted school boards and taxpayers, shortsighted college admissions officers, and the designers and marketers of "aptitude tests." Unhappily, there is plenty of blame to go round.

The linguistics experts referred to above are typified by Prof. Hall, who assures us that there is no such thing as "written language." Of course there is the thing that he calls "writing," but this, he assures us, is "much less important" than speech. Hall wrote in 1950, but his views were echoed a quarter century later by the writer Peter Farb, who described writing as an "imperfect communication, a pale reflection of the speech it is supposed to substitute for."

All of this is mostly quite true, and utterly beside the point. The issue is not whether written communication is perfect or imperfect, or whether it reflects speech palely or vividly, and certainly not whether it is or is not as "important" as speech. Writing, as even Hall concedes, *is* of major importance in modern industrialized societies, and not because it is "supposed to" substitute for speech. In certain situations writing *does* substitute for speech, and for precisely the reason it was invented some five thousand years ago: it can do things speech can't do.

If you want to get information to somebody three thousand miles away, you either pay the toll charges—and take your chances on a bad connection—or write a letter. If you want to put information in permanent form, so that you or others can refer to it a month or a year or a century from now, you either talk into a tape recorder (if you have one), producing a record that is very cumbersome to refer to, or write it down. In addition, writing is the quickest method yet devised of transferring information from one human brain to another (assuming, of course, that writer and reader both know their business): even without speed-reading, most of us can absorb information from a printed page in less than a third the time we'd need to absorb it by ear.

Another major "expert" contribution to creeping illiteracy is summed up in Hall's declaration that "there is no such thing as good and bad in language." As elaborated later in his book, this seems to mean that people should not be made to feel inferior or self-conscious because they speak an uneducated or "nonstandard" dialect, as the majority of English-speaking people do. Who could disagree? Unfortunately, a number of other experts have elaborated this humane sentiment into a philosophy of education.

Their view was summed up in 1974 by a statement of policy adopted, after bitter debate, by the Conference on College Composition of the National Council of Teachers of English. Under the title "Students' Rights to Their Own Language," it declared that "linguistic snobbery" has throughout our history been "tacitly encouraged by a slavish reliance on rules" (try figuring out what *that* means!). The consequences, it continued, went "far beyond the realm of language. People from different language and ethnic backgrounds were denied social privileges, legal rights and economic opportunities, and their inability to manipulate [*sic*] the dialect used by the privileged group was used as an excuse for this denial."

Now it is a historical truism that many immigrants, and not a few other Americans, have faced discrimination. But history also shows that the main reason was their own poverty and powerlessness, and other people's ethnic or racial prejudice; the kind of English they spoke, or whether they spoke it at all, had little if anything to do with the matter. Irish immigrants, nearly all of whom spoke English, were early targets of discrimination; so were their children, even those who learned to "manipulate" American upper-class dialects. Immigrant Jews, whose English was almost invariably accented, were discriminated against, but so were their children, speaking English from birth, who prior to World War II were admitted to most private colleges only in small numbers, and were flatly excluded from some jobs and "restricted" neighborhoods. And American blacks still face widespread discrimination, whether their English is Black English or Ivy League. Indeed there have been periods in our history when an educated black, speaking Standard English, was considered an "uppity nigger" requiring special treatment; readers who know their *Huckleberry Finn* will recall Old Finn's drunken rage at encountering a well-dressed, well-spoken black "college p'fessor" who could "talk all kinds of languages and knowed everything."

Dialects, as we have seen, have long been involved in social snobbery, but to conclude from this that all dialects are equally "good" is a non sequitur. Before reaching this conclusion, we must ask: good for what? To which the obvious answer is: good for communication. And by that criterion, some dialects are unquestionably better than others, in certain situations. If you're a trucker talking to your good buddies at a bar or truck-stop, you'll communicate best in your native blue-collar English; if you're a black kid rapping with your soul brothers, you'll do best with Black English; and so with face-to-face communication in any group of people speaking the same dialect.

But when we are communicating with "outsiders," and especially if we are communicating in writing, we will almost certainly do best with colloquial Standard English. The reasons are not very obscure. To begin with, though most English speakers *speak* some nonstandard dialect, they almost certainly *understand* the educated speech of their region and, if they're literate, written Standard English. (The latter, in fact, is acceptable currency almost anywhere in the English-speaking world.) The overwhelming majority of English-language publications—newspapers, magazines and books—are written, apart from some dialogue passages, in Standard English. The directions and manuals that come with medicines, many foodstuffs, and the innumerable gadgets that enrich or complicate our lives are in Standard English. And the governmental and corporate bureaucrats that most of us have to correspond with from time to time deal in Standard, if often heavily jargonized, English.

In short, Standard English is "better" than other dialects because—and only because—with it we can give information to and get information from many, many more sources than with any other dialect. Students unquestionably have a right to use their own "language" (i.e., dialect), and in fact most of them continue to use it at home and around the neighborhood. But they also have an equal right to learn to read and write the only "language" that can serve them beyond the boundaries of their own neighborhood or occupational or ethnic group.

The final contribution of misapplied expertise to creeping illiteracy is what I call the "Now We Are Six" illusion. Psychologists generally agree that normal children master the phonetics and syntax of their native tongue (i.e., dialect), except for a few minor details, during their first six years, though their vocabularies continue to expand for years or decades thereafter. But to leave matters there ignores a basic fact noted by Ben Jonson in the early seventeenth century: "To speake, and to speake well, are two things." Granting that nearly all kids of six or seven can "speake" their native dialect grammatically, this doesn't mean they can "speake well"; as we noted earlier, grammatical English is not necessarily clear English, or—even less—eloquent English.

Moreover, the "minor" points that the six-year-old has not mastered, though minor enough in speech, are not so minor in writing: because we use writing in situations where speech will not serve, it makes demands on us that speech does not. When we are talking face to face, or even phone to phone, misunderstandings can be dealt with and corrected immediately. In writing, if we don't make ourselves clear, there is no easy way—often no way at all—to set matters right. In short, if to speak and to speak well are two things, to write well is yet another thing, whose essential quality was summed up by the Roman orator Cicero some two thousand years ago: the aim of writing is not simply to be understood, but to make it impossible to be *mis*understood. The skills involved in doing this, unlike the skills involved in speaking one's native dialect, are seldom if ever acquired automatically: they must be taught. And if, as is transparently the case, large numbers of American kids fail to acquire those skills, they are clearly being taught badly, or not at all. Let's look at some of the reasons why.

Obviously, children can be taught the skills of writing only by people who, at a minimum, have themselves mastered those skills: who can write clear, coherent English. In fact, many grade-school and high-school teachers can't; some say 20 percent, some say more. One would think that such incompetents should be identified, given a fair chance to improve their writing skills and, if they can't or won't do so, be invited to exercise their illiteracy in some other career.

Of course, nobody denies that teachers ought to be competent, in writing or whatever else they need to know. But proposals to actually test that competence have run into heavy flak from teachers' organizations. The American Federation of Teachers objects to such tests for "experienced" teachers; its main competitor in organizing teachers, the National Educational Association, rejects the idea of competence testing in toto. Both organizations point out that many other things, apart from teachers, determine whether kids will or won't learn to write: overcrowded classes, ill-conceived texts and methods (as with reading), home environment, and so on, all of which is perfectly true. But the fact that teachers don't have the *sole* responsibility clearly doesn't mean that they don't have *any* responsibility for what their students learn—or that they shouldn't be encouraged or (if necessary) compelled to face up to that responsibility.

The teachers' organizations, as the bottom line of their argument, point out that passing tests doesn't prove competency, and of course it doesn't. But as the president of the Mobile, Alabama, Board of Education remarked not long ago, even if you can't prove a teacher is competent, "you certainly can prove he's incompetent." A teacher who can write English competently may or may not be able to teach it competently, but one who can't write it certainly can't teach it.

Teachers and their unions have every right to defend what they conceive to be their interests—but so, after all, do the rest of us. And one of our interests surely involves recognizing that what teachers do in the classroom has *some* connection with what their students learn, or don't learn. Having recognized that connection, we can examine it, define it and set up a further connection between teachers' performance in the classroom and whether they get promoted or fired. Most of us, unless we happen to be professional bureaucrats of some sort, take it for granted that if we do a good job we'll be rewarded in some way, and if we don't we won't, and may even be punished. I find it hard to see why teachers should not be subject to the same rules as the rest of us.

The same kind of feedback can and should be applied to the teachers' bosses—principals, boards of education, and the administrative bureaucracies that surround them: rewards if the school or school system they run is doing a good job, punishment if it isn't. But this, in turn, will require some fundamental rethinking on how we measure school performance.

Until quite recently, when some cities and states began introducing "competency" exams that actually test whether students can read and write, the main and sometimes the only measurement of a school's effectiveness was how well its students did on the Scholastic Aptitude Test (SAT). Yet the SAT *did not and does not test students' writing skills.* What its "verbal" section tests is reading ability and vocabulary; you can get a perfect score without writing one English sentence. The Educational Testing Service, the powerful, self-perpetuating bureaucracy that designs and administers the SAT, does, indeed, give an optional "Test of Standard Written English," yet even this test, despite its name, involves no actual writing. Instead, it asks the student to spot mistakes in passages written by others, which, according to ETS, gives a good idea of the student's own writing ability. Many outside experts disagree.

If the SAT doesn't test writing skills, the reason is simple: money. Its tests are composed of what psychologists call "objective" questions—true-or-false, or multiple-choice. Such tests can be scored cheaply, by machine; "essay" questions, which require written answers, can only be scored by people. Objective tests are, to be sure, considered more reliable than essay tests, meaning that they measure whatever they measure more accurately. But this claim, though true, evades the central issue: does the test measure what needs to be measured? Objective tests can measure whether someone understands the meaning of a passage they have read—though even here some people question how well they measure it. They cannot measure whether someone can write a passage that will be clear to a reader. A passenger in a car may be able to say very precisely whether, and in what ways, the driver is skillful or unskillful, but the only way to measure the passenger's own driving skills is to put him or her behind the wheel.

The SAT's failure to measure writing skills was and is bad enough in itself; in addition, however, it exerted the most pernicious kind of feedback on our schools. As Prof. Thomas C. Wheeler, of the City University of New York, explained it recently, "Until the 1950s, students wrote essays in schools because they were expected to write essays on college entrance exams. . . . When the SAT became dominant, secondary schools asked for less writing. Urged on by test manufacturers, high schools began to use objective tests both to prepare their students [to take the SAT] and for their own examinations." Thus, thanks in large part to the SAT, the objective of primary and secondary education was radically redefined without anyone's quite realizing it. Even fifty years earlier, that objective was, at a bare minimum, to teach children to read and write; the new aim was to teach them to pass tests.

The redefinition was accelerated by the fact that teaching kids to pass tests, like the tests themselves, is cheap. Teaching writing is more expensive than not teaching it, basically because the only way anybody learns writing is by writing. That is, they don't learn by memorizing grammatical rules (did anyone ever learn to drive simply by memorizing the rules for operating a car?). But writing is only half the learning process; the other half is provided by teachers who have not only the ability but also the time to read what their students have written, correct mistakes, and discuss these with the students. And no teacher, unless he or she is willing to work sixty or seventy hours a week, can do these things for a class of forty or fifty students. Writing can be taught effectively only in relatively small classes, which of course means hiring more teachers, which means spending more money. Which is something that taxpayers—including some parents—dislike doing.

But in education or anything else, there's no such thing as a free lunch. If we believe that literacy is important for the proper functioning of our society—and I doubt that many people believe otherwise—we've got to be prepared to pay what it costs. If we don't care to pay the price, then we will end up paying a different price: a society whose members are increasingly unable to communicate on paper.

One of the most curious aspects of creeping illiteracy is how it crept up on American society almost unnoticed, even by the colleges that had to deal with its products. By the 1960s, certainly, college teachers were becoming aware that increasing numbers of incoming freshmen could not write intelligible English—yet there was no widespread outcry against the aptitude tests that had, in effect, certified these students as ready for college.

There doesn't seem to be any neat answer as to why. I strongly suspect, though I can't prove, that one reason was the old commercial maxim that the customer is always right. By the 1960s, the "baby boom" that began in 1946, plus growing national affluence, had markedly increased the number of potential "customers" for a college education, whose admission would raise both the number and the remuneration of college teachers and administrators. The temptation to accept the masses of new customers, by (in effect) lowering admission standards, was powerful— too powerful, alas, for many colleges to resist.

Another factor involved in lowering standards—though it is hard to say to what extent it was cause or effect—was a redefinition of the goals of writing: to achieve "authenticity," "originality" and "self-expression." The new objective was eloquently, if something less than clearly, set down by the writer Jack Kerouac, who aimed to "get it all down without modified restraints and all hung-up on like literary inhibitions and grammatical errors." Of course, nobody expects a novelist to be an educational philosopher; unfortunately Kerouac's views were echoed by a sizable number of educators who, in the words of one of them, disdained "formal learning" in favor of "the true exercise of self-expression."

Now there is no point whatever (aside from, possibly, a psychotherapeutic one) in putting words on paper unless they say something to the reader. And it is precisely the "modified restraints" and "hangups" of syntax and sentence structure that enable us not just to "express" our thoughts and feelings, but to communicate them clearly to others. The basic syntax that all of us learn automatically does, indeed, enable us to make ourselves understood, after a fashion. But it is only mastery of the subtleties of syntax that makes it impossible for us to be misunderstood —and these we seldom learn unless someone teaches them to us.

I am referring, of course, to *English* syntax. I make this seemingly self-evident point because to some quite eminent educators it seems not self-evident: for several years they have been urging that students be taught to handle English syntax by—learning Latin. The reason, in the words of one of them, is that Latin, unlike English, has ways of indicating "unmistakably" the grammatical relationships between words. Yet if English did *not* have ways of indicating syntactic relationships unmistakably, neither this distinguished scholar nor anyone else could put together an unambiguous statement in English. Also a fact, as we've noted earlier, is that English syntax differs radically from Latin syntax, since it depends primarily on word order rather than inflection. Thus to suggest that learning how Caesar and Cicero constructed Latin sentences will teach children how to construct English sentences makes about as much sense as saying that the best way to learn carpentry is to study plumbing.

Teaching children to understand English syntax is essential, but no less essential is maintaining a sense of proportion about it: if our standard is clear communication, then some syntactic principles are a lot more important than others. Some "principles," indeed, neither contribute anything to communication nor conform to actual Anglo-American usage; one example is the "unsplittable infinitive" mentioned earlier—a principle borrowed, significantly, from Latin. Other rules, though they contribute nothing to clarity, do reflect "good" educated usage; knowing them is equivalent to knowing which fork to use: important in dealing with people for whom using the right fork, or its linguistic equivalent, is important. And some rules are of central importance because violating them can do anything from momentarily distracting the reader's attention ("A person is bound to resent it when your house is robbed") to inducing total confusion ("The microscope has an uncertain origin lost in improbable legends of the Middle Ages which, if true, could have been the ancestor of the first magnifying glass").

Finally, and most important, let us never forget that good syntax isn't necessarily good sense. A sentence may be acceptable to the most compulsive grammatical nit-picker, yet may still be cumbersome, or muddy, or willfully misleading.

The "prescriptive versus permissive" controversy and the "children have a right to their own language" principle have recently helped to heat up two widespread educational arguments, concerning Black English and bilingual education.

Black English is, of course, only a special case of dialectical English in general, and it raises the same basic question as any other dialect: if our schools aim to teach kids how to communicate clearly in spoken and written English, which of the many varieties of English should they teach? The question almost answers itself.

As regards Black English, there is no point whatever in teaching black kids to speak it: if it's spoken in their community, then they already speak it fluently by the time they get to school. What they need to learn in school is the Standard, colloquial "white-collar" English of their region, which will enable them to function outside their own segregated neighborhoods when they grow up, and which, more immediately, is the essential foundation for learning to read and write Standard English.

But teaching Standard English to any kids speaking a nonstandard dialect requires both some sophistication about dialects (which many teachers lack) and some plain human sensitivity. A good way *not* to do it is to downgrade the kids' own natural speech as "bad English." A much more sensible approach was recently described by a white teacher in a predominantly black Chicago school: instead of "correcting" the speech of his students, he tells them they're going to learn another language (which is almost true). And, he says, it works: no longer do they resent him for trying to make them talk "honky English."

Dialectical sophistication and sensitivity can also avoid such tragicomedies as that of a black child in Philadelphia who, not so many years ago, was classed as retarded because she "couldn't tell the difference between a pen and a pin." Her real "problem" was that, like her Southern parents and millions of other Southerners, black and white, she pronounced "pen" like "pin." Similarly, a white girl who had moved from New York City to San Francisco was diagnosed as having a "speech defect" because she "couldn't pronounce R"—for example, she said /teech-uh/, like most New Yorkers, instead of /teech-ur/, like most Californians. These may perhaps be extreme cases, but the need for schools to recognize and respect dialectical differences is both real and important. Children who "talk funny"—i.e., use a different dialect from their schoolmates—are almost routinely given a hard time by their peers, as my wife discovered long ago when her family moved from Liverpool to the Bronx; the last thing they need is additional flak from their teachers.

In this sense, black kids or any others have a "right" to their own language—and will in any case exercise that right among themselves, whether or not anyone gives them permission. But this right in no sense negates an equally important right: to receive from their schools whatever tools they will need to function outside the narrow boundaries of their own neighborhood or ethnic group. And of these tools, the ability to speak, read and write Standard English is surely the most basic.

The controversy over bilingual education developed following a recent court decision that it is unfair to "teach" children in a language they don't understand, which seems obvious enough. Less obvious is the further ruling, by some courts, that the best way to solve this problem is to teach the children in their native tongue. The dispute has been further complicated by the demand of some Hispanic leaders (Hispanics are the main group involved) that a "bilingual" education should also include classes in Spanish grammar, composition, literature and culture—all of them given in Spanish.

Whatever the value of such studies to Hispanic (or, for that matter, non-Hispanic) children, however, they have nothing to do with the basic job our schools must do: training children to function in a society that, for the foreseeable future, will use English for nearly all purposes. Which is to say that Hispanic kids, or any others whose native tongues are not English, need first of all to learn to speak English. Since they obviously won't learn it at home, or in most cases from kids in their own neighborhoods, the only place they will learn it is in school. And the longer that learning is delayed—by teaching them in their native tongues—the harder it will be.

The solution, as I see it, is not to try to teach the children *in* English, but rather to devote the entire first half year or year of school to intensive instruction in speaking English. There is, in fact, a proven method for doing this fast: the intensive or "total immersion" technique, in which people are put into a totally English-speaking environment for several hours a day. By this method, most adult foreigners can learn to speak and understand English quite fluently in a matter of months; with kids, who learn languages much quicker, it should go even faster.

English has survived the perennial pseudo-threat of linguistic "corruption"; it will survive the very real threat of creeping illiteracy and misconceived "bilingualism," provided we are willing to give the problem the thought, effort and money it deserves. More problematic at this writing is whether English, and especially the great literature of which it has been the vehicle, can survive a more insidious danger: current threats to limited government, that other great heritage from our past which we are obligated to pass on to the future. As we've seen, our language and literature and our basic philosophy of government developed in parallel:

if English-speaking people have been writing well for over four centuries, the reason is not simply that they wrote in English but that they had a lot to write about—and could write it, generally speaking, with relatively little interference from government or anyone else.

I see the current threat to limited government as threefold. First is the attempt to impose, or reimpose, secrecy covering increasingly broad areas of governmental activity. Second is the rise of what might be called para-government: private bodies that in many areas of our society exercise governmental power in all but name. The third, and most immediately dangerous, is the attempt to introduce censorship, involving the removal of books from schools and libraries and, in some cases, their physical destruction.

Concerning secrecy in government, one need make little more than the obvious comment: secret government sooner or later becomes oppressive government. Eternal vigilance will always be the price of liberty, and we cannot be vigilant if we are forbidden to see what government is up to, or to report and comment on what we see.

No less threatening is the expansion of para-government: the great conglomerates and multinational corporations that already dominate our economic life and, to an increasing and frightening extent, our political life as well. Most of us don't think of these bodies as "government," yet they exercise powers that many ancient tyrannies would have envied. Within rather wide limits they determine, or exert a preponderant influence on, what we can buy and for how much, what sort of books are published, what sort of broadcasts are aired, what sorts of jobs we can work at, and what sort of environment we and our children will live in. They can also determine, with no limits whatever, where we can work and often whether we can work at all: a mega-corporation can shift its operations from one city, or even continent, to another without either due process of law or consent of the governed—those whose livelihoods are abolished by such actions.

Any useful discussion of the problem of para-government, and of how the principle of limited government can be applied to it, would take us far beyond the proper bounds of this book. But we should at any rate recognize that the problem exists: that these groups *are* government, in fact if not in law, and, like any government, must have limits placed on their power if we are to continue to enjoy life, liberty and the pursuit of happiness.

The third threat, censorship, is one that I as a writer naturally find specially ominous. But I find it no less ominous as a reader, viewer and citizen. If censorship were important only to writers and "the media" it would hardly be worth the average citizen's attention; what makes it of supreme importance is that without freedom to write, publish and broadcast for people like me—the tiny fraction of the population that ever gets on the presses or on the air—there is no freedom to read, hear and view for anybody.

The current drive for censorship is widely portrayed as a crusade for morality—meaning, of course, the brand of morality endorsed by the crusaders themselves. But when we look at its actions rather than its claims, it turns out to go far beyond morality as most of us conceive the term. Its ideological hit list includes Darwinian evolution, meaning a large chunk of modern biological and geological science, and an equally large chunk of Anglo-American literature. Authors whose books have been banned, and sometimes burned, include Bernard Malamud, Kurt Vonnegut, Philip Roth, Richard Brautigan, Joseph Heller, Alexander Solzhenitsyn, Eric Fromm, Alice Childress, Claude Brown, Richard Wright, Ernest Hemingway and Aldous Huxley—along with such immoral works as *The Grapes of Wrath, The Merchant of Venice, Huckleberry Finn* and *The American Heritage Dictionary*.

The case of *Huckleberry Finn* is particularly distressing because pressure to ban it comes from some blacks, who have been persuaded that the book is anti-black (one black leader has called it "racist trash" which "implies that blacks can't be trusted and are not human"). Leaving aside the fact that the book, saving only its farcical conclusion, is one of the finest novels ever written in America, the truth is that far from being racist it is one of the most powerful antiracist, antislavery statements ever written. Jim, the book's only important black character, emerges as one of the few decent human beings in a cast composed largely of (white) drunkards, killers, yokels and swindlers, and—by no means incidentally —becomes far more of a father to Huck than the boy's own vicious (and racist) father ever was. Beyond that, there is hardly a chapter in the book in which Twain does not work in some oblique dig at the slave system, and at the dehumanized view of blacks that made it possible.

Some commentators, while conceding all this, claim that it is too subtle for teenagers to take in. I don't believe it. I was about twelve when I first read the book, and clearly remember noting how Twain, while seeming to say one thing, was in fact saying the opposite—that (for example) when Huck grumbles, "You just can't teach a nigger to argue," his real complaint is that Jim has just outargued him. I doubt that any teenager, black or white, is incapable of grasping this sort of thing, assuming the book is intelligently presented. *Huckleberry Finn* belongs in every school library, not simply because it is a "classic," but because of what it says about racism and the slavery that begot it.

Specific cases aside, the trouble with censorship, like the trouble with political killing, is: where do you stop? If we are to ban *Huckleberry Finn* for being anti-black (which it isn't), then with equal logic we should ban some writings of the black poet and playwright Amiri Baraka, for being anti-white (which in my judgment they are). If, as some feminists have been urging, pornography should be banned for degrading women, which much of it does, then by all means let us ban any writings by feminists that degrade men, which some of them do. If *The American Heritage Dictionary* is too dirty to be allowed in the hands of schoolchildren, because it contains words that every schoolchild knows, then so is *Romeo and Juliet,* because its teenagers make dirty jokes of the kind that every teenager makes.

The great stream of English literature rivals the Mississippi in its size and power; to demand that every eddy and backwater in it be to everyone's taste is to demand the impossible. If that indeed is what we want our literature to be, then we will find ourselves settling for a puny, deodorized, filtered rivulet: books that few people will care to read and even fewer to write.

Our native tongue is unique in the original sense of that overused word: the most marvelous communicative instrument yet devised by the human race. Its vocabulary has drawn on a score of tongues: ancestral Indo-European, transmuted in sound and sense across eight thousand years; the aboriginal Baltic speech that I have called Folkish; the Vulgar Latin of Roman traders and legionaries and the learned Latin of monks and scholars. Listen to its cadences and you can hear the voices of Danish pirates and their peasant descendants; of Norman knights and courtiers who came to conquer but were themselves linguistically conquered; of shrewd Dutch merchants and hardy, bawdy Dutch sailors; of Italian poets, painters and musicians; of Arab traders and alchemists; of Spanish commanders, conquistadors and cowboys. And behind the voices are the faces: copper-hued Native Americans, blacks kidnapped into bondage, liquid-eyed Indian rajahs and craftsmen, narrow-eyed Malay pirates and merchants of Cathay. Poets and playwrights have enriched English with their taffeta phrases, scientists and physicians with their strange jargons, craftsmen and crooks with their lively lingoes, and common folk of all sorts with homely metaphor and rude humor.

From century to century the great river of English has flowed on, fed by all these streams, and itself an inexhaustible source of song and story, of comedy and tragedy, of histories, sermons, orations and manifestos and of mere polite—or impolite—conversation. As it enriched the lives of past generations, so it will continue to enrich the lives of our children and their children's children—provided we take care that they learn how to understand and appreciate it.

And provided they remain free to use it.

NOTES ON SOURCES AND SUGGESTIONS
FOR FURTHER READING

THE notes that follow include all the important sources I have used in writing this book, keyed to the indicated pages. I have not, obviously, tried to give a source for all statements in the text; some are what might be called common knowledge, and others are based on my own very miscellaneous reading over the years, representing my own distillation and interpretation of this material. While I naturally consider these interpretations valid, some specialists in particular areas of language or history may well take a different view. To them I would point out, first, that even scholars differ in their interpretations and, second, that anyone seeking to summarize broad historical trends in a few sentences or paragraphs cannot help oversimplifying.

For the more important sources, I have added brief comments for the guidance of readers disposed to delve further into the engrossing subject of their native tongue.

GENERAL SOURCES

Dictionaries
On the history and usage of English words, *The Oxford English Dictionary* (OED), unabridged, is of course in a class by itself, and belongs in the library of anyone seriously interested in the English tongue. Its one drawback is that its photographically reduced version can be consulted only with the aid of a magnifying glass (one is supplied with it), while the more legible "standard" edition is much more expensive and much more bulky.

On etymology, I have relied almost entirely on *The American Heritage Dictionary* (AHD) and *The Oxford Dictionary of English Etymology* (OEtD). Each has strengths and weaknesses, but these complement each other rather neatly. AHD traces every word back to its earliest source, known or conjectured—usually to specific Indo-European roots—but in some cases tries too hard (for examples, see the note on page 51.) OEtD, by contrast, does *not* systematically give Indo-European roots; its strength is in listing cognates for English words in other Germanic, and Romance, tongues. Sometimes, I think, it doesn't try hard enough, describing as "of obscure origin" words for which AHD gives plausible Indo-European etymologies. However, it provides a valuable fringe benefit by listing the main meanings (including obsolete ones) of its words, together with the centuries in which these appeared, thereby providing a handy thumbnail guide to semantic changes, though the OED remains the definitive source in this area.

I have made occasional use of Eric Partridge's etymological dictionary, *Origins* (Macmillan, 1977). For the general reader, this book has the advantage of listing words by "families" —i.e., each entry includes all words descended from a single ancestor, thereby pointing up many fascinating and unexpected relationships between apparently unrelated words. Its etymologies are usually sound, though Partridge occasionally presents probability as fact and once in a while indulges in outright fantasy—which, however, sometimes hits closer to the mark than do the professional lexicographers (e.g., see "horse" in the Index of Words). Partridge remained to the end of his life an amateur—in both senses—of words, and *Origins*, like his other works, reflects his love and enjoyment of his subject, an enjoyment which only the dullest reader can fail to share.

History of English
My main source has been Albert C. Baugh's *A History of the English Language*, 2nd ed. (Appleton-Century-Crofts, 1957). This is a textbook, and therefore goes into some matters at what many readers will find rather wearisome length and also waffles on some controversial issues. But it is full of valuable and interesting facts (many of which I did not have space for), presented clearly if not always gracefully. Other interesting material will be found in Lincoln Barnett's lively *The Treasure of Our Tongue* (New American Library, 1967), which touches on some of the areas covered in this book, though at times from a rather different viewpoint. Another useful source is W.F. Bolton, ed., *The English Language*, Vol. 1 (Cambridge University Press, 1966), a collection of essays published between 1490 and 1839. The second volume, edited by Bolton and D. Crystal and published in 1969, brings the story up to the present. John Moore's delightful *You English Words* (Dell, 1965) is both useful and "required reading."

Linguistics
A useful if sometimes oversimplified introduction to the general field of linguistics is Robert A. Hall, Jr., *Linguistics and Your Language* (Doubleday, 1960), though one ought to be aware of Hall's personal biases, some of which I discuss in Chapter 12. The best single book on linguistics for the general reader is still Margaret Schlauch's intelligent and literate *The Gift of Tongues* (Modern Age, 1942). Its first chapter, dealing with phonetics, is not easy, since it involves learning the International Phonetic Alphabet, but is worth the trouble as an essential introduction to the fascinating material that follows. Schlauch includes some interesting material on the history of English.

History—General
For guidance on broad historical trends, and sometimes on specifics, I am heavily indebted to Colin McEvedy's invaluable *Penguin Atlas of Ancient History* (1967) and its companion volumes on medieval and modern (up to 1815) history (1961 and 1972); these are cited as McEvedy: *Ancient*, McEvedy: *Medieval* and McEvedy: *Modern*. I have also made some use of *The Times Atlas of World History* (Hammond, 1979). For other historical information, and on some linguistic questions, I have relied on *The Columbia Encyclopedia*.

Page 2: The Auden–MacNeice quotation is from their "Letter to Iceland."

1. THE IMPORTANCE OF SPEAKING ENGLISH

Page 3: The lines from Kipling are in his *Debits and Credits;* those from Thomas are from his poem "You English Words," quoted in Moore, who took the title of his book from the poem.

On the current ubiquity of English, see, *e.g.*, "English, English Everywhere," *Newsweek*, Nov. 15, 1982.

"Lingua franca" means any language used as a medium of communication between groups speaking several different languages; the term comes from the name of the "trade language" (also called Sabir) used in the Mediterranean during the Middle Ages—basically, a dialect of some Romance tongue (Old Italian and/or Old Spanish) with heavy borrowings from Greek and Arabic. The term is often confused with "pidgin language" (see Chapter 10), but though all pidgin languages are lingua francas, not all lingua francas are pidgins— e.g., Vulgar Latin in the Western Roman Empire (see Ch. 5), French in eighteenth- and nineteenth-century diplomacy and English in a number of areas today. The term itself, literally "tongue of the Franks," may be a loan translation from Arabic, in which "Frank" *(ferengh)* still means any European.

Page 4: On the worldwide spread of English and its infiltration into other languages, see Barnett. For recent developments in *franglais*, see "Franglais Work Has the French in Tizzy Again," *The New York Times*, June 7, 1981. The story describes a new dictionary of Anglicisms in French which, in contrast with Etièmble's alleged 5,000 English terms borrowed since World War II, lists only 2,620 borrowed *since the twelfth century,* of which only about 1,500 are still current. As a reviewer in *Le Monde* dryly commented, "We are a long way from [Etièmble's] apocalyptic visions of a language invaded by another." On English infiltrations into German, see "Anglicisms Irk German Purists," *The New York Times,* Dec. 3, 1966.

Page 8: On language as communication vs. language as "self-expression," see Ch. 12.

Page 10: My phonetic spellings are makeshifts; they will be intelligible only to English speakers, and even so may sometimes be ambiguous. To render all English sounds accurately would have involved introducing readers to the International Phonetic Alphabet or some similar system, which would have raised more problems than it solved.

Page 12: My classification of methods for showing syntactic relationships into "inflection," "addition" and "position" is inevitably oversimplified. Professional grammarians have dug far more deeply into English syntax than I have tried to do, and the deeper they dig, the less comprehensible and more controversial their conclusions become.

Page 14: The analysis of "Jabberwocky" is expanded and elaborated from that of Prof. William G. Moulton, quoted in Barnett.

Page 21: Assimilations of foreign words by the British armed forces are taken from Eric Partridge's *Dictionary of Slang and Unconventional English* (see notes to Ch. 11); the process is sometimes called "Hobson-Jobson," defined in the same work.

Page 22: English dialects are discussed at length in Ch. 10.

Page 24: The etymology of "indri," improbable as it sounds, is from OEtD.

2. THE COMMON SOURCE

By far the best sources for the general reader on Indo-European and the Indo-Europeans are Calvert Watkins' two essays in AHD, and the "Index of Indo-European Roots," "Table of Indo-European Sound Correspondences" and "Chart of the Indo-European Languages" in the same work. (Watkins, I should note, does not agree with the "Danubian" theory of the Indo-European homeland, which he believes was more likely in the northern foothills of the Caucasus.) Other useful information can be culled from George Cardona et al., eds., *Indo-European and Indo-Europeans* (U. of Pennsylvania, 1970), and R.A. Crossland and Ann Birchall, eds., *Bronze Age Migrations in the Aegean* (Noyes, 1974). Both these books, however, were written by and for specialists, and most other readers will find them heavy going.

Page 25: The quotation from Brown is from his famous essay "Urn Burial"; that from Jones is given in full on page three and is quoted in Watkins' first essay in AHD.

On the limitations of the primitive human vocal tract, see my "What Caused the Sudden Rise of Modern Man?" in the collaborative volume *Mysteries of the Past* (American Heritage, 1977).

Pages 30f: On techniques for reconstructing Indo-European words, see Watkins' second essay in AHD.

Page 34: For evidence of early regional differentiation in Latin, see Anson Piper, "From Latin to Spanish," *Berkshire Review,* Autumn 1965.

Pages 37f: Gimbutas' Kurganian theory is set forth in her paper (Ch. 9) in Cardona et al., and in another paper in Crossland and Birchall.

Page 38: On the spread of farming in Europe, see McEvedy: *Ancient,* and especially H. T. Waterbolk, "Food Production in Ancient Europe," *Science,* Dec. 6, 1968. (Refinements in dating methods since 1968 make it necessary to move back Waterbolk's dates by about a thousand years, except for his latest ones, in his Fig. 7, which must be moved back about seven hundred years.)

Page 39: On the distribution of river names in Europe, see W. C. Renfrew's paper in Part Three of Crossland and Birchall.

Page 40: On the post–Ice Age "depopulation" of Central Europe, see Waterbolk.

Page 41: Renfrew's equation of the expansion of farming societies from the Danube with the spread of Indo-European is from his previously cited paper; McEvedy: *Ancient* takes the same view.

Hittite documents, especially those dealing with religious rituals, contain words and

sometimes whole passages in a language known to us as Hattic. It is not well understood, but sufficiently so to make clear that it is not Indo-European, as Hittite itself unquestionably is. Dead languages not infrequently survive in religious ceremonies—e.g., Latin and Coptic.
Page 42: On the Iberians, see the article on them in *Columbia;* on apparent North African traits in Celtic grammar, see "Celtic Languages" in *Columbia.*

The non-Indo-European "tribal" names were culled from AHD.
Page 43: The ancient Egyptian words cited are drawn from the vocabulary in Alan Gardner, *Egyptian Grammar* (Aris & Phillips, England, 1978). On resemblances between Indo-European and Finno-Ugric, see the second note to page 48.

3. THE FIRST CONQUEST

Unfortunately there are no materials on Common Germanic (at least in English) that are of much use to the general reader, and even the few specialized studies available devote much more attention to phonetics and syntax than to vocabulary, which is the main focus of this chapter. My "vocabulary" of Common Germanic comes mostly from a careful reading of OEtD, with additional examples from AHD and a few from miscellaneous sources.
Page 45: The quotation from Parkman is from his *Pioneers of France in the New World;* that from Johnson is from Boswell's *Life of Johnson.* I include both because while I've tried to imbue myself with "the life and spirit of the [Germanic] times," I wouldn't want to mislead readers into supposing that I can prove everything I've said.
Page 46: The phonetic changes summarized in Grimm's Law are from the "Table of Indo-European Sound Correspondences" in AHD, but are in any case a linguistic truism. My reasons for stating that the changes occurred in the order given are technical and not very important; the essential point is that they occurred, not how or when.
Page 48: On Danubian settlement in loess areas, see Waterbolk; for an account of excavations in such a settlement, see Sarunas Milisauskas, "Olzanica: An Early Farming Village in Poland," *Archaeology,* Jan. 1976.

On Finnish borrowings from Common Germanic and its ancestors, see the interesting little pamphlet *The Finnish Language* (Helsinki, 1971), obtainable from the Finnish Consulate General in New York; other examples have been culled from OEtD. The transformation of the Indo-European aspirates $/b^h/$, $/d^h/$ and $/g^h/$ into Finnish /p/, /t/ and /k/ is my own deduction, though some scholar has probably anticipated me.
Page 49: On the Ertbölle and TRB cultures, see Waterbolk, op.cit.
Page 51: On the geographical distribution of the whooper swan and other maritime birds see Bertel Braun, *The Hamlyn Guide to Birds of Britain and Europe* (Hamlyn, London, 1970). AHD sees Indo-European *eti- as a possible source of "eider." However, no species of this duck comes south of the Baltic, meaning that the original Indo-Europeans could hardly have seen, or named, them. AHD also suggest Indo-European *al-, brown, as a possible root of "auk," but in fact these birds are conspicuously black-and-white. For these reasons, I strongly favor an exotic origin for both terms.
Page 52: The quotations from Tacitus here and later are from his "Germania," most easily available in *Agricola and the Germania* (Penguin, 1971). The actual quotations are, however from a different translation.

On changing climates in Europe, see my *Climate, Man and History* (Norton, 1970).
Page 53: The transformation of *wantuz into the quite different "gauntlet" resulted from its passage into English via Old French, some dialects of which assimilated initial /w/ in borrowings from Germanic tongues into /gw/, spelled GU. Compare modern French *guerre* with its English synonym and cognate, "war," borrowed from the *Norman* French dialect, in which this phonetic change did not occur.
Page 55: On the arrival of bread wheat in Europe, see "Wheat" in *Columbia.*
Page 56: On *stofa* and *stof-bæth* see *The Student's Dictionary of Anglo-Saxon,* cited in the next chapter.
Page 59: On the development of the wheel and its diffusion to northern Europe, see Stuart Piggott, "The Beginnings of Wheeled Transport," *Scientific American,* July 1968.

Page 61: On the spread of ironworking in Europe and its impact on Celtic and Germanic societies, see McEvedy: *Ancient* and Ralph M. Rowlett, "The Iron Age North of the Alps," *Science,* July 12, 1968.

Page 62: On Celtic and Germanic expansion, see McEvedy: *Ancient.*

Page 67: The conventional source of "beer" and its Germanic cognates (e.g., in OEtD) is Church Latin. However, this would imply a relatively late borrowing into several Germanic languages independently, for which reason an earlier borrowing, from soldiers' Latin, seems to me more plausible.

4. THE SECOND CONQUEST

Page 70: The Field Quotation is from his "Good-by—God Bless You"; the Dunne quotation is from his famous "Mr. Dooley" sketch on the Anglo-Saxon alliance and Anglo-Saxon supremacy—ideas that were much in vogue around 1900 among such "Anglo-Saxons" as Theodore Roosevelt.

On the computer analysis of word frequency, see Henry Kucera's essay in AHD; on the preponderance in modern English of words derived from Old English, see Watkins' first essay in AHD.

Page 72: Arthur's legendary Camelot has been placed in half a dozen locations in southern England, John Morris, in *The Age of Arthur* (Scribner's, 1973)—a fascinating if exhaustive study that is my main source on historical developments before and during the English conquest—makes clear that there was a historical prototype for the mythical Arthur, and hence presumably one for Camelot. His location of it in Camulodunum seems plausible on both linguistic and strategic grounds: as he points out, the town lay near the point of the British "wedge" separating the two English settlement areas and would thereby have enabled Arthur's forces to move quickly against a threat from either.

Page 77: My account of Old English, including its spelling, is based mainly on Baugh, on Henry Sweet's *The Student's Dictionary of Anglo-Saxon* (Oxford, 1896; it is still in print) and on *Sweet's Anglo-Saxon Primer,* 9th ed. (Oxford, 1953). Other useful material is in Barnett and Schlauch.

The symbol *þ* survived in English documents for centuries, eventually becoming confused with Y, whence the "ye" (the) in "Ye Olde Englishe Tea Shoppe" and similar establishments.

Page 79: The Old English passage concerning Pharaoh's daughter is from Schlauch.

Page 80: The Old English Lord's Prayer is from Barnett.

Page 82: Note that the borrowed Roman-British term *castra* survives in English with both initial /k/ (e.g., Brancaster) and initial /ch/ (e.g., Dorchester). This is part of the evidence indicating that the latter sound developed in English after its speakers arrived in Britain.

Page 85: The lines from *Beowulf* are quoted in Barnett.

The cited Old English borrowings and loan translations from Latin are mostly from Baugh, with some additions from Barnett and Schlauch.

Page 88: Vin is the Norse term for "wine," corresponding to Old English *win;* the phonetic shift of Germanic initial /w/ to /v/ is characteristic of Old Norse and the modern Scandinavian tongues descended from it.

Page 90: On Norse town names in England, see Baugh, and Gösta Bergman, *A Short History of the Swedish Language* (Swedish Institute for Cultural Relations with Foreign Countries, Stockholm, 1973).

Page 91: On Norse loan words in English, see Baugh.

Page 92: The influence of the Danish (and later French) migrations into England on the simplification of Old English syntax is my own deduction. It is based mainly on common sense, and on analogy with vulgar Latin and the Greek *koine* (see Ch. 5): the latter were both widely spoken by peoples whose native tongues were not Latin or Greek, and both possessed much-simplified inflectional systems as compared with those of Classical Latin and Greek. See also the account of the loss of English "strong" (i.e., irregular) verbs in Joshua Whatmough, "Natural Selection in Language," *Scientific American,* April 1952; note especially the precipitous fall in the number of such verbs between 1100 and 1200 (i.e., following the linguistic assimilation of the Danes) and the almost equally precipitous fall between

1300 and 1400 (following the assimilation of the French-speaking English). I should add here that Whatmough himself does not note these factors; his own theories of linguistic change are rather abstract.

5. THE THIRD CONQUEST

My main source for the historical background and events of the Norman Conquest is David Howarth's intelligent and readable *1066: The Year of the Conquest* (Viking, 1977). For its linguistic effects my main source is Baugh.

Page 95: The Kipling quotation is from *Puck of Pook's Hill.*

Page 96: Exotic words in the Latin vocabulary are culled from AHD and OEtD.

Page 98: Many of the examples of Latin prefix + verb compounds are taken from Schlauch's entertaining discussion of them.

Page 100: Gaulish or probably Gaulish words borrowed into Vulgar Latin considerably outnumber the few examples I have given, since I have ignored those that passed into French but not into English—e.g., *alauda,* lark, which became the *gentil alouette* that many of us sang about in school or camp.

Page 101: Though for simplicity I have called the dialect that entered England at the Conquest Norman French, it is by no means certain (as Baugh notes) that all the invaders spoke this dialect, and absolutely certain that many later French immigrants did not. Borrowings from other French dialects are especially conspicuous in words originally taken from Germanic and beginning with /w/, which in Norman French remained unchanged (e.g., *werre,* war) but in most other French dialects was assimilated to /gw/ (e.g., *g(u)antelet,* gauntlet—see note to page 53). In some cases both French forms were borrowed at different times, giving us such doublets as "warden" and "guard," "warranty" and "guarantee."

Page 105: The "Great Charter" that John signed is, of course, Magna Carta, its Latin title.

Page 106: On bilingualism in England, see Baugh.

Page 107: "The two nations have become so mixed . . ." this and later quotations, on the decline of French, are from Baugh, whose extensive discussion of the subject is worth reading at length.

Page 113: On the simplification of English syntax, see note to page 92).

6. THE FIRST FLOWERING

Page 117: The Emerson quotation is from his *Parnassus;* that from Shakespeare is from *Romeo and Juliet.*

Page 121: For more on Arabic star names, see the Appendix to my *The Summer Stargazer* (Penguin, 1981).

Most of the examples of the "triple" vocabulary of English are from Baugh.

Page 122: On the general historical background of the fourteenth century, see Barbara Tuchman, *A Distant Mirror* (Knopf, 1978), and McEvedy; *Medieval.*

Page 123: There are no reliable figures on the casualties of the Black death; most estimates range from 40 percent to 50 percent of the total European population. Historically, this toll has been surpassed only by that of the Native Americans following their contact with Europeans: they may have lost as much as 80 percent of their population, mostly to imported diseases such as smallpox. See Fernand Braudel, *The Structures of Everyday Life* (Harper and Row, 1981), Ch. 1.

Page 124: On the general literary background of the fourteenth century, see Boris Ford, ed., *The Age of Chaucer* (Penguin, 1969); of particular interest are its many examples of Middle English poetry, notably *The Wicche, the Bagge and the Bisshop* (The Witch, the Bag and the Bishop), by Robert Mannyng of Bourne.

Page 125: I have borrowed the device of indicating "pronounced" E's in Middle English by *ë* from John Gardner, *The Life and Times of Chaucer* (Knopf, 1977), my basic source along with Ford, for the poet's life, times and poetry; it is required reading for anyone interested in Chaucer.

Page 127: "The smiler with the knife . . ." This and subsequent "translations" of Chaucer were made by me from the original text. All inevitably resemble other translations, in some cases perhaps word for word. When people are tackling the same problem—in this case translating a given Middle English passage into modern English rhymed couplets—they sometimes come up with identical solutions.

Page 131: For the benefit of any devout Catholics who may read this book, I should emphasize that in describing clerical abuses of the time—which are a matter of history (see, e.g., Tuchman)—I am not attacking (or defending) Catholic theology, or the moral doctrines of Christianity generally, many of which I find admirable. The anticlericalism we find in Chaucer and elsewhere sprang, in fact, precisely from the radical contrast between the moral preachings of the Church and the immoral practices of its higher officials.

Page 132: The precise point of Chaucer's jibe at the Clerk, hard to convey in a modern English couplet, is that for all his philosophy he had not found the legendary "Philosopher's Stone" that could turn base metal into gold.

Page 137: My main source on family names is Basil Cottle, *The Penguin Dictionary of Surnames* (1967).

Page 143: On modern Welsh personal surnames, see Gary Jennings, *Personalities of Language* (Gollancz, London, 1967), an intriguing account of some linguistic byways.

Page 144: The European equivalents of "Johnson" and "John Smith" are from Jennings.

Page 145: The "aureate" lines from Dunbar are quoted in Baugh.

Page 146: "In southern English was it drawn" is translated from the original in Baugh, as is the quotation from John Trevisa.

Page 148: Caxton's preface is given in full in Bolton (see General Sources).

7. "THE VERIE HEIGHT"

For general historical background, see S. T. Bindoff, *Tudor England* (Penguin, 1950), and McEvedy: *Modern;* for literary background, as well as much valuable social background, see Boris Ford, ed., *The Age of Shakespeare* (Penguin, 1969).

Page 150: The Mulcaster quotation is extracted from a much lengthier discussion in Bolton; the Shakespeare line is from *The Tempest.*

On urbanization and population growth in England, see McEvedy: *Modern.*

Page 152: On inflation in Spain, see ibid.

"has made of yeomen and artificers, gentlemen . . ." and the other quotations on page 153 are from Ford.

Page 153: The growth of higher education is documented in Ford. Specifically, nearly half the House of Commons had such education in 1584 "and more again subsequently," as against only a third in 1563. On literacy generally, McEvedy estimates a rate of 50 percent among adult males in Protestant northern Europe in 1715; the figure was probably reached rather earlier in England.

The Great Vowel Shift is described, in much more detail, in Baugh.

Page 154: On Latin and Romance borrowings, see Baugh, Schlauch and Barnett.

Page 158: "Avocado." Note that in modern Spanish this has been replaced by *aguacate,* a reborrowing from native *ahuacatl.*

Page 159: On "Low Dutch" borrowings, see Baugh and Schlauch; other examples are taken from OEtD and Partridge's *Origins.*

Page 160: On "bugger": Latin *Bulgarus* acquired the secondary meaning of "heretic," since many Bulgarians were regarded as such. It passed into French, as *bougre,* heretic, and picked up the additional meaning of "sodomite" (heretics in religion or politics were and are often accused of unspeakable sexual practices), which passed into Dutch and English. Subsequently, it was softened to mean "fellow, chap" in both England and France, with "a good old bugger" paralleled by *un bon bougre.* The etymology of *kunte* and its English derivative has never been satisfactorily explained. My own view is that it and its Chaucerian equivalent, *queynte,* both derive from some unattested Germanic word probably akin to **kwenon,* woman. See Partridge's *Origins.*

The material on sixteenth-century borrowings and coinages, and contemporary reactions to them, is mostly from Baugh; see also Schlauch. For a witty commentary on over-Latinate *modern* diction, see Moore. Mulcaster's discussion of the current (1582) state of English, cited in the first note to this chapter, is worth reading in full, despite its occasional syntactic difficulty.

Pages 164f: The quotations on the expanding use of English by scholars are from Baugh.

On the development of "pop" literature and the rise of the professional writer, see Ford. The volume notes that not all pop literature was of low quality; some was produced by men of considerable education. However, such authors were seldom if ever *professional* writers —i.e., they got their living from other sources.

Page 166: "Select and choose out words of vehemence . . ." is quoted in Ford.

Page 167: The discussion of Shakespeare's sensitivity to the rhythmic possibilities of English is entirely my own, though some industrious scholar may have anticipated me; the same goes for my account of Shakespeare as a political writer.

Page 171: On sexual references and humor in Shakespeare, see Eric Partridge, *Shakespeare's Bawdy* (E. P. Dutton, 1960).

Page 174: On the bowdlerization of the Bible, see Moore.

"I take this present period of our English tung . . ." is quoted in Baugh.

8. A SEARCH FOR ORDER

Page 175: The quotations from Swift and Johnson are immediately from Baugh; the documents from which they are extracted are given in full in Bolton (see General Sources).

"Learned in all things, wise in none" is Kipling's characterization of James I.

Page 176: On Richard Cromwell, see "Queen Dick" in Partridge's *Dictionary of Slang and Unconventional English.*

Page 177: The Butler quotation is from his *Hudibras.*

"That whatsoever king may reign . . ." is from an anonymous eighteenth-century ballad.

On attempts to rationalize English spelling, see Baugh.

Page 181: "I am often put to a stand . . ." is quoted in Baugh.

Pages 182f: Swift's proposal for an English academy is in Bolton, which also includes Daniel Defoe's similar proposal. Swift's proposal was couched as a letter to the Earl of Oxford.

Page 183: Oldmixon's attack on Swift and Sheridan's on the idea of an academy are quoted in Baugh.

Page 184: Johnson's preface is given in full in Bolton.

Page 185: On Johnson's dictionary, see both Baugh and Moore.

Page 186: "It's me": Note that French, despite its Latin ancestry, parallels the non-Latin, "incorrect" English "It's me" with *C'est moi.*

The Churchill quotation is from Moore; I have been unable to track down the Thurber quotation, if indeed it is his. Whoever said it, it's good sense.

Hazlitt on misconceived Latinity in English grammar: see his essay in Bolton.

Page 191: The eighteenth-century "generation gap" over coffee drinking is reflected in J.S. Bach's *Coffee Cantata.*

Page 192: The precise native original of *kangooroo* has never been traced; the spelling is Cook's.

Some recent examples of "Third World" imperialism are Indonesia's annexation of Western New Guinea (West Irian) and Timor, Pakistan's attempt to subjugate Bangladesh, and the perennial Iranian and Iraqi suppression of their Kurdish citizens.

Page 194: German contributions to mineralogical terms reflect German preeminence in mining technology during the late Middle Ages; the first text on the subject was written in 1556 by the German Georg Bauer (Georgius Agricola).

Page 195: The slang sense of "screw," which burst into the public prints through the Watergate tapes, is merely the latest disreputable incarnation of a word with distinctly dubious antecedents. It derives ultimately from two similar Latin words, *scrofa*, sow, screw (presumably because a screw thread curls like a pig's tail), and *scrobis*, ditch, vagina, whence the Vulgar Latin sense, female (inside) screw.

Page 197: The original Italian saying, which I have translated rather freely, is *Se non è vero, è ben trovato.*

9. ONLY IN AMERICA

Main sources for this chapter are Baugh, Barnett and J. L. Dillard's lively *All-American English* (Random House, 1975). This last is not, despite its subtitle, "A History of the English Language in America," but rather an examination of some neglected aspects of that history. It would be a more useful, if perhaps less lively, book had Dillard devoted more attention to his subject and less to polemicizing against his academic opponents. His etymologies, too, are not infallible: thus he derives the square-dance call "Dozy dozy" (more often, "do-si-do") from a French or Spanish phrase meaning "two by two"; in fact, it comes from French *dos à dos*, back to back (it calls the partners to circle one another in this fashion). Another invaluable source is H.L. Mencken, *The American Language* (Mencken: *AL*), which with its two equally massive supplements (Mencken: *Supp. I* and Mencken: *Supp. II*) constitutes a mine of invaluable information about almost every aspect of American speech. As in most mines, however, the precious metal is surrounded by much dross; the work is poorly organized, repetitious and far too long, fascinating to browse through but very difficult to read.

Page 198: The line from Dunne is quoted in Mencken: *AL;* Shaw's epigram is quoted in Mencken: *Supp. I.*

The verse from Daniel is quoted in Barnett, who took from it the title of his book.

Page 200: On the influence of the American environment, especially its varied climates, on American pragmatism, see my *Climate, Man and History* (Norton, 1970).

Jefferson's remarks are quoted in Barnett.

Page 201: AHD derives "flicker" from the bird's supposed "flickering" flight. Whoever dreamed this up had obviously never seen or heard the creature.

Page 202: On the probable Native American etymology of "Yankee," see Dillard, *All-American English.*

Page 203: On *schouw*, note that Dutch SCH is pronounced /sk/, not /sh/ as in German.

Page 204: On Africanisms in American English, see David Dalby's essay in Thomas Kochman, ed., *Rappin' and Stylin' Out* (U. of Illinois, 1972); also Dillard, *All-American English* and his later *Black English* (Random House, 1972).

Page 206: "fell first upon their own knees . . ." is from the American writer William Maxwell Evarts, though it has been ascribed to many others (see *Bartlett's Familiar Quotations,* 14th ed.).

Pages 208–209: The famous "firebell in the night" quotation is from one of Jefferson's letters; "I tremble for my country" is from his *Notes on the State of Virginia.*

Page 209: The anonymous proposal for an American academy is quoted in Baugh.

Page 210: The material on Webster is from Baugh and Mencken: *AL.*

Page 214: The peccary, an animal unknown to most Americans, inhabits the wilder parts of the Southwest; it is our only native pig.

Dillard and some others derive "buckaroo" from the Pidjin English (ultimately African) *buckra*, white man, but the semantic shift from that sense to "cowboy" seems to me unlikely. Derivation from *vaquero* (whose initial V is very close to /b/) involves no semantic shift whatever.

Page 217: My association of "bucket shop" with "watered stock" is very much a minority view, but seems to me at least as plausible as the "standard" (e.g., AHD) derivation, from places where whiskey was allegedly sold by the bucket. Beer was certainly sold by the bucket before Prohibition—but *whiskey?*

A "limited"—now almost obsolete with the decline of long-distance passenger trains—was an express that stopped at only a limited number of places. The word became incorporated into (or perhaps was extracted from) the names of various deluxe trains such as the Twentieth Century Limited between New York and Chicago and the Overland Limited between Chicago and San Francisco.

"Roorback" appears without qualification in many American dictionaries, but in my judgment is effectively obsolete; I have never seen it used without an explanation of its meaning.

Page 218: On the national origins of immigrants to the U.S., see *The Times Atlas of World History.*

"Song fest" has begotten a few, generally jocular, compounds—e.g., "talk fest."
Page 222: The various denunciations of American English are all quoted in Baugh, Mencken: *AL* or both.
Page 223: "We have no distinct class of literati . . ." is quoted in Baugh.
Page 224: On speeches made by or credited to Davy Crockett, see Bernard Botkin, *A Treasury of American Folklore* (Bantam, 1981).

The dialogue between Webster and Hall is quoted in Mencken, as are the remaining comments on American vs. British English, except where specifically noted.
Pages 225–226: Kenneth Hudson's and Anthony Burgess' fantasies on American syntax are quoted in Jim Quinn's delightful *American Tongue and Cheek* (Pantheon, 1980).
Page 226: The syntactic eccentricities of "Timestyle" were not limited to premodification; another favorite gambit was inverted word order, along the lines of "Convicted of income-tax evasion last week was Chicago gang-boss Al Capone." This device was brilliantly parodied by Wolcott Gibbs in *The New Yorker*, as "Backward ran sentences until reeled the mind."

10. OUR INFINITE VARIETY

My main sources for this chapter are Baugh (though his treatment of modern dialects is rather summary) and Dillard's two books already cited. For a contrasting, more "establishment" view of American dialects, see Juanita V. Williamson and Virginia M. Burke, eds., *A Various Language* (Holt, Rinehart & Winston, 1971). These sources have been supplemented by my own reading of various English authors, and my own ear in various parts of North America.
Page 228: The line from Shakespeare is from *Antony and Cleopatra;* Shaw's remark is quoted in Mencken: *AL.*
Page 229: Kurath's quotation on "folk speech" is from his article "The American Languages," *Scientific American,* Jan. 1950. His approach to dialectology is exemplified at length in his *A Word Geography of the Eastern United States* (U. of Michigan, 1949).

The Kentucky study referred to is that of Lawrence M. Davis, in Part 4 of Williamson and Burke.
Page 230: On the confusing and contradictory picture presented by vocabulary isoglosses, see those in Kurath's *A Word Geography;* for the similar confusion in British isoglosses, see those in W. Nelson Francis' paper in Part 2 of Williamson and Burke; note that of his seven isogloss maps, only two resemble one another.

The resistance of phonetic habits to change, as contrasted with the much greater fluidity of vocabulary, has surely been documented, but is for me a matter of common observation. For example, my father's speech showed marked traces of his Virginia upbringing until his death, though he had not lived in the South for nearly fifty years. I myself have *never* lived in the South, yet retain a few Southern speech habits picked up from my parents before I left home in 1942 (e.g., I tend to say /greezy/ rather than /greesy/).
Page 232: Differential migration as the source of dialectical differences in Old English is impossible to prove, but no one has come up with a better explanation.

On Middle English dialects, see Baugh; for those deeply interested in the subject, he includes an appendix giving actual samples of the six dialects, with comments on their differences.
Page 233: "firty-free fevvers . . ." is from Eric Partridge *A Dictionary of Catch Phrases* (Stein & Day, 1979).
Page 234: On the antiquity of the Southern English shifts of /f/ to /v/ and /s/ to /z/, see Baugh.

For an interesting sample of contemporary, though archaic, rural East Midland (specifically, Suffolk) dialect, see "The Cook's Tale" in Ronald Blythe, *Akenfield* (Dell, 1969).
Page 235: On the distinctive vocabulary of Scotland, much of it now archaic or obsolete, see *The Old Scots Tongue* (Lang Syne Publishers, Newtongrange, Midlothian), an undated modern reprint of a dictionary compiled in 1857.
Page 236: The characterization of Burns as a "proven fornicator" is, of course, his own, though the verses from which it is taken do not appear in most collections of his works. See *The Merry Muse* (Luxor Press, London, 1966).

Page 236–237: The examples of Gaelic influences on the syntax of Irish English are quoted by Dillard in the notes to ch. 3 of his *All-American English.* The absence of Gaelic equivalents to "yes" and "no" was drawn to my attention by Mervyn Jones.

Page 237: On Murray's self-consciousness about his Scots accent, see the biography by his granddaughter, K. M. Murray, *Caught in the Web of Words* (Yale, 1977); it is well worth reading in its own right.

Page 237: The Puttenham quotation is from Baugh.

Page 238: On "U" and "non-U," see Nancy Mitford, ed., *Noblesse Oblige* (Harper, 1956).

On linguistic homogenization in English public schools, see, e.g., Kipling's *Stalky and Co.,* one of whose protagonists had been "carefully kicked" out of his Irish dialect by his two chums.

Page 238–239: On "character" rather than "intellect" as the aim of public-school education, see Mark Girouard, *The Return to Camelot* (Yale, 1981).

Page 239: Worth noting is that "gentlemanly" education was until quite recently limited to English gentle*men.* Cambridge University, for example, admitted a few women beginning before World War I—but did not give them degrees until after World War II.

Page 239: On the revival of chivalry, see Girouard,—a fascinating, well-documented and lavishly illustrated piece of social history worth anyone's time.

Page 240: On the number and boundaries of U.S. dialects, compare Kurath's *Word Geography* with Baugh. I have followed the latter because his divisions are based on phonetics rather than vocabulary, which for reasons given in the text seems to me a more solid foundation for defining dialects.

The regional terms for "dragonfly" are from Kurath; those for an "Italian" ("hero," etc.) sandwich, from " 'Discombobulating' Twists in the Way Americans Talk," *Boston Globe,* Sept. 29, 1980.

Page 241: My account of the phonetic differences among American dialects is based on Baugh, on some facts culled from Part 5 of Williamson and Burke, and a good deal of personal observation. None of the scholarly sources discusses "vowel reversal," a term which so far as I know is my own invention; I can personally testify to its existence in both Cape Cod and New York City.

Page 243: Some Canadians, who like to stress their cultural differences from the U.S., may object to my characterization of Canadian English as essentially General American, but facts are facts. The phonetics of Canadian speech obviously tell us nothing about the quality of what its speakers have to say.

On the dialect of "Bawlamer," see "He Talks Bawlamerese, Duddney?" *The New York Times,* Sept. 21, 1980. Russell Baker's phrase book for "Yurpeans" appeared in his *New York Times* column of June 12, 1966.

Page 244: For the traditional, differential migration theory of American dialect origins, see Part 2 of Williamson and Burke, especially Kurath's contribution. He and his disciples consistently refer to "southern" England, meaning the southern half of that country—a term that is linguistically meaningless. Actual studies of the dialect-area origins of seventeenth-century colonists (quoted in Baugh) show, for New England, 69 percent London and East Midland, 32 percent Southern; for Virginia, 56 percent London (only), 27 percent Southern, 16 percent West Midland and Northern. Heavy concentrations of both groups in London and Bristol, England's two major ports, suggest that many of the individuals in question merely *sailed* from these towns, with their actual origins uncertain. Note also that the origins of a large proportion of both groups (two-fifths in New England, half in Virginia) cannot be traced at all.

The contemporary accounts of the homogeneity of colonial American speech are quoted from Dillard, *All-American English.*

Pages 246–247: For historical documentation of the influence of black speech on Southern (white) dialect, see both of Dillard's books. Cleanth Brooks' "West Country" theory is set forth in Part 2 of Williamson and Burke; in fact (see note to page 244 above) *none* of the traceable Virginia immigrants came from that area.

Page 247: The "recent standard text" is Williamson and Burke. On class dialects in New York City, see William Labov's paper in Part 6 of that volume.

Page 248: My main source on Black English is Dillard. A contrasting view is that of Williamson, in Part 5 of Williamson and Burke. She appears to be arguing that "Black English" is merely Southern American English spoken by black people, and gives copious examples showing that some (but by no means all) syntactic features of Black English are also widely found among Southern whites. This fact, however, tells us nothing about where these forms originated—i.e., whether the blacks learned them from whites or vice versa.

The powerful influence of "age grading" in erasing many of the distinctive features of Black English is something I have myself noted in eavesdropping on conversations between adult blue-collar Blacks in New York City: their phonetics are almost invariably more or less Southern American, but their syntax differs little from white blue-collar syntax of the metropolitan region.

Page 256: The influence of Pidjin or "Maritime" English on both Black English and American English generally is discussed extensively by Dillard in both his books; they are well worth reading, though I think he rides this particular hobbyhorse a bit too hard.

Page 251: On Harris' accuracy as a recorder of black dialect, see Dillard, *Black English,* and Sumner Ives' second paper in Part 3 of Williamson and Burke. Ives describes "Daddy Jack's" dialect as Gullah; Dillard argues more persuasively that it, like Gullah, represents an earlier form of Plantation Creole.

Page 251: On the phonetic resemblances between Gullah and West Indian English, I have the word of Prof. Dillard (personal communication) and Lorenzo D. Turner (see next note); on those between West Indian and West African English, I have the evidence of my own ears.

Lorenzo D. Turner's findings are described in his *Africanisms in the Gullah Dialect* (U. of Chicago, 1949); an abridged version, plus some rather technical material on Gullah phonetics, is given in his article in Part 2 of Williamson and Burke. How far the dialect he described has survived thirty years of "development" in the Sea Islands I don't know.

Page 252: On the importance of verb aspect in some West African tongues, see Schlauch.

The Africanisms listed are from Dalby's essay cited earlier (see note to page 204). "I'm hip you're hep" is quoted in Dillard, *Black English.*

Page 253: On Louisiana Creole French as an additional channel for introducing Africanisms into English, note the "Compair Bouki" Louisiana folk tales in Botkin. "Compair" is French *compère,* phonetically rendered, equivalent to the "Br'er" in Uncle Remus' Br'er Rabbit; "Bouki" is African, and means "hyena."

The "definitive" source on Australian English is Sidney J. Baker, *The Australian Language;* a more lighthearted treatment will be found in *Let Stalk Strine* and *Nose Tone Unturned* by "Afferbeck Lauder" (Alistair Morrison), published by Ure Smith (Sydney), 1962 and 1966. Baker doesn't think much of the Australian-as-modified-Cockney theory, but offers no plausible alternative.

Page 254: "A plyce where you bythe your fyce" is from Mervyn Jones; the other examples of Strine are from "Lauder's" two books.

"You can't tell whether he's a Pom or a poof " is from Baker.

Page 255: The verse from "The Australian Poem" is adapted from Moore (see General Sources); it exists in several versions.

Pages 255–256: On Pidjin English, see Robert A. Hall, Jr., "Pidjin Languages,": *Scientific American,* Feb. 1959, and Dillard, *All-American English.* Note that Hall uses a phonetic spelling, giving the vowels their "Continental" values, /ah/, /eh/, /ee/, /o/, /oo/. Thus Pidjin *said* is not pronounced like "said" but blends /ah/ and /ee/ to sound much like its English original, "side." It means roughly "place where," as in *haussaid,* "house-side," at the house. These spellings are now "standard" in, e.g., Papua–New Guinea, but can confuse English speakers because they obscure the English origins of the Pidjin terms. Thus when I recently observed the sign AIR NIUGINI over a ticket counter in the Honolulu airport, it took me a few moments to realize that it meant AIR NEW GUINEA.

Page 257: "Topside-piecee-heaven-pidjin-man" is quoted by Schlauch from the nineteenth-century American critic and humorist Charles Leland, but sounds a bit too good to be true. The other examples of Pidjin are mostly from Hall.

The first two Biblical quotations in (Melanesian) Pidjin were supplied me by David Park; the one in Australian Pidjin is from Baker.

Page 258: On "Frontier Pidjin," see Dillard, *All-American English.*

On "da kine," see Elizabeth Ball Carr, *Da Kine Talk* (U. Press of Hawaii, 1972). She notes that around 1900, only a little over 5 percent of the population spoke English by birth, making a lingua franca absolutely essential.

The incorporation of Hawaiian words into "Standard" Hawaiian English (on which see also Schlauch) was, I suspect, partly inspired by the desire of "old hands" to impress newcomers, and later by a conscious effort to preserve an exotic atmosphere for tourists. The weather forecast is from a recent issue of the *Honolulu Advertiser.*

11. NOT EVERYBODY'S ENGLISH

As a general source on slang, see Eric Partridge, *Slang Today and Yesterday*, 4th ed., (Routledge & Kegan Paul, England, 1970). Mencken *(AL* and *Supp. II)* discusses both slang and jargon extensively, though many of his examples are inevitably dated. Among dictionaries, the definitive work on English (including Australian, Canadian and some South African) slang, jargon and cant is Partridge's *Dictionary of Slang and Unconventional English* (DSUE), 7th ed. (Macmillan, 1970). Unfortunately there is no comparable work on American unconventional English: Harold Wentworth and Stuart B. Flexner's *Dictionary of American Slang* (DAS), 2nd ed., (T.Y. Collier, 1975) is, for reasons largely beyond the authors' control incomplete, loaded with ephemeral nonce words, and sometimes plain wrong (e.g., its definition of "dark meat" as "black in roulette" is based on a misreading of a passage in Raymond Chandler); it also contains almost no etymologies. I understand that it has been taken over by a new publisher and will be extensively revised; I await the results with interest. My terminology for specialized vocabularies follows Partridge: "jargon" = occupational or trade vocabulary; "cant" = criminal jargon. I use "lingo" as a generic term for all special vocabularies, including local ones *(e.g.,* Boontling).

Page 260: The verse heading this chapter is from the late Gerald Kersh's hilarious novel *Fowler's End;* it is "translated" later in the chapter. The Mencken quotation is from *AL.*

The police, legal and criminal jargon is from my own reading.

Page 261: "Corn-snitcher" and "Christmas tree" are from Mencken: *Supp. II;* the latter, at least, was current a few years ago and may still be.

Page 262: The lawyers' "takeover" jargon is from an internal memo circulated in a large New York law firm where my daughter happened to be working a few years ago.

The jargon of the New York State legislature was described in "A 'Must List' That 'Will Fly' for Legislative Cliche Lovers," *The New York Times*, June 7, 1976.

Pages 262f: On jargon as supposed deception, see e.g. Mencken: *AL* and the next reference. The confidence-game terms are from David Maurer's *The Big Con* (Bobbs-Merrill, 1940), a fascinating account of a criminal subculture—though one occasionally has the feeling that Maurer's criminal informants were, well, conning him.

Pages 264f: The jargon terms cited are mostly from Mencken: *Supp. II;* as noted, they may or may not be still current today. Some of the lunch-counter terms are from Schlauch.

Page 267: The two remarks by Raymond Chandler are from his brilliant essay "The Simple Art of Murder," collected in his book of the same name (Ballantine, 1977).

The citations from Harman and "B.E." are given in Mencken: *AL;* they also appear individually in DSUE. On Caliban/*kaliben*, see Jean-Paul Clébert, *The Gypsies* (Penguin, 1967).

Page 269: An example of Chandler's invented slang is the verb "juice," bribe; more authentic terms are the verb "grease" (i.e., make things run smoothly) and the noun "ice" (the payoff money that keeps things cool).

Pages 270f: The definitive source on Cockney rhyming slang is the late Julian Franklyn's *A Dictionary of Rhyming Slang*, 2nd ed. (Routledge & Kegan Paul, England, 1961), which includes a lively essay on the origin and spread of this remarkable lingo. Unfortunately, his information on Australian and U.S. rhyming slang was based on sources that seem to me less than reliable: Sidney J. Baker of Australia and Prof. David W. Maurer of the University of Louisville. Baker frankly dislikes rhyming slang, and therefore, as Franklyn notes, would presumably not "irritate himself by going far to seek it." Maurer and Baker report a number of terms, supposedly current on the U.S. West Coast in 1944, that I suspect were made up on the spot by their all too cooperative "informants," since they reflect English or Aus-

tralian, but not American, word usage. Thus "ship in sail" (pint of ale) is suspect, first, because ale is little drunk in this country, and, second, because while it and beer are consumed in the U.S. by the can, bottle, glass, stein, schooner, seidel or keg, I have never seen, heard or read of either being dispensed by the pint. Suspect for similar reasons are "bread and jam" (tram) and several other "U.S." terms. In the U.S. or anywhere else, rhyming slang makes no sense unless it rhymes with a word in the user's native vocabulary.
Page 270: Readers unfamiliar with British slang should be advised that neither "The Smoke" nor "toff" is *rhyming* slang; for their origins see DSUE.
Page 271: The evidence for Pacific Coast use of rhyming slang as late as the 1940s is that of Maurer and Baker, reported in *American Speech*, Oct. 1944; as I've suggested, it should be taken with a grain or two of salt. My evidence for the extinction of rhyming slang in the U.S. is its absence from any fictional or factual account of criminal life I have read in the past thirty years, including Maurer's *The Big Con* and the linguistically authentic crime fiction of George V. Higgins.
Page 272: On back slang and Parlyaree, see DSUE.
  The definitive source on Boontling is Charles C. Adams, *Boontling: An American Lingo* (U. of Texas, 1971); the book, especially its vocabulary, is well worth looking into.
Page 273: For divergent definitions of slang, compare Partridge's essay in Bolton and Crystal (see General Sources), Flexner's introduction to DAS, and especially Norman Hoss' "Guide to the Dictionary" in AHD and the dictionary's own definition—two by no means identical definitions in the same volume.
Pages 273–274: On "Standard" vs. "slang" classification of four-letter words, see, e.g., "fuck" in DAS.
Page 274: The Mencken quotation is from *AL.*
Page 276: For definitions of "cat's pajamas" etc., see DAS.
  Though denunciations and horrible examples of bureaucratic jargon abound in the popular press, I have been unable to turn up any serious discussion of its origins. My treatment of the subject is therefore "my own invention," though I may for all I know have been anticipated on some points by others.

12. FROM HERE ON IN

For varying approaches to English usage, see Wilson Follett, *Modern American Usage* (Hill & Wang, 1966), and William and Mary Morris, *The Harper Dictionary of American Usage* (Harper & Row, 1975), both highly "prescriptive"; Bergen and Cornelia Evans, *A Dictionary of Contemporary American Usage* (Random House, 1957), which is either "permissive" or sensible, depending on your point of view); and also Morris Bishop's stimulating essay "Good Usage, Bad Usage and Usage" in AHD. A lively and at times hilarious dissection of the "prescriptive" approach is Jim Quinn's *American Tongue and Cheek* (See note to page 225), though I think he occasionally overstates. I would also criticize him for ignoring the fact that clarity, even more than precedent, is central to good usage (see note to page 284 below).
Page 280: The quotations from Lounsbury are taken from Quinn.
Page 281: The Hall quotation is from *Linguistics and Your Language* (see General Sources).
Pages 283–284: The examples of "bad" usage cited by Newman and Bernstein are taken from Quinn, as are the facts refuting them.
Page 284: The discussion of "unique" is based partly on Quinn; he does not, however, go into its ambiguity.
Page 285: The "heated adjectives" cited are mostly quoted from Quinn and (on Webster III) from Barnett, whose own views on that dictionary were almost equally heated.
Page 286: The Johnson passage was previously quoted in Ch. 8; see note to page 184.
Page 288: The quotations from Rosten et al. are taken from Quinn.
  "crafting a foreign policy" is from a recent (1982) editorial in *The New York Times.*
Page 290: On illiteracy in the U.S., see Flesch's *Why Johnny Can't Read* (Harper & Row, 1955), and *Why Johnny Still Can't Read* (Harper & Row, 1981). On illiteracy in Canada, see Mary Johnson, *Programmed Illiteracy* (Clarity Books, Winnipeg, 1970).
  The account of "see and say" is mainly based on Flesch, 1955. For a discussion of

hieroglyphic and other early writing systems, see my *The Birth of Writing* (Time Inc., 1975). The analogy between hieroglyphics and see-and-say, by the way, is my own, though I later discovered that Flesch had anticipated me.

Page 291: For a fuller account of the behaviorist approach to learning, see my *God or Beast: Evolution and Human Nature* (Norton, 1974).

The quotation from Gibson is from her article "Learning to Read," *Science*, May 21, 1965.

Page 293: The dialogue between Dick and Jane's successors, Mark and Janet, was quoted in Fred M. Hechinger's column, "About Education," *The New York Times*, June 29, 1982. Further up-to-date information on deficiencies in the teaching of reading are given in his column of Dec. 8, 1981.

For these and other examples of contemporary horrible writing, see, e.g., Susan Jacoby, "The End of a Dream: Illiteracy Invades the Middle Class," *The New York Times*, Dec. 7, 1978; "Why Johnny Can't Write," *Newsweek*, Dec. 8, 1975; and "Help! Teacher Can't Teach," *Time*, June 16, 1980.

Page 294: The Peter Farb quotation is from his *Word Play* (Knopf, 1974).

Page 295: The statement on "Students' Rights to Their Own Language" was quoted in the *Newsweek* article previously cited.

Page 296: The Ben Jonson quotation is from his essay in Bolton (see General Sources).

Page 297: On incompetence among American teachers, and competency testing, see the *Time* article previously cited.

Page 298: On the SAT and its proprietor, the Educational Testing Service, see Thomas C. Wheeler, *The Great American Writing Block* (Viking, 1979), and Ed Kiersh, "Testing Is the Name, Power Is the Game," *Village Voice*, Jan. 15, 1979.

Page 300: The emphasis on "authenticity" etc. in writing is discussed in Barnett, from which the Kerouac quotation and the following one are taken.

Page 301: Latin vs. English syntax: "unmistakably" is from a 1982 letter from Jacques Barzun to *The New York Times*, but he is only one of many clinging to this ancient fallacy (see Ch. 9).

Page 302: The cited incidents of dialectical ignorance are both recounted in Williamson and Burke.

Page 305: The examples of authors and books that various groups have banned or tried to ban are from Colin Campbell, "Book Banning in America," *The New York Times Book Review*, Dec. 20, 1981, and M. L. Stein, "Book-Ban Moves That Go Unreported," *Boston Globe*, June 4, 1982.

INDEX OF WORDS, PHRASES AND PROPER NAMES

This section lists all words, phrases, and family and place names discussed in the text, excluding only those not in the current general vocabularies of U.S. and/or British English. Jargon and cant (criminal) terms, discussed extensively in Chapter 11, are *not* included unless they have passed into general use, nor are regional terms, discussed in Chapter 10.

All words are indexed by their *modern* spelling, whether or not this appears in the text. Where the text includes only an obsolete spelling (often that of the language from which the word was borrowed), the modern spelling is given *first*, in parentheses, followed by the text spelling in italics—e.g., (wine) *uinam*. Words or word-roots that are "reconstructed" (not attested in written documents) are indicated by an asterisk—e.g., (keel) **kelaz*. Family names are indicated by (f), place names and other geographical terms, by (p).

snob, 195
(snoop) *snoep*, 203
snow, 34
sock (hit), 268
sodomite, 18
solace, 111
soldiers, 110
sole (fish), 111
solitary, 119
soluble, 16
solution, 98
sombrero, 214
song fest, 218
Soper (f), 141
Sophocles, 31
soubrette, 190
sound, 236
(soup) *soupe*, 111
spaceman, 31
spaghetti, 220
(spaniel) *spaynel*, 111
spear, 52
Speare (f), 142
speculation, 154
Spicer (f), 141
(spice) *espice*, 111
spill, 47
spin, 33
(spinach) *isfinaj*, 120
spirit, 112
splice, 159
(split) *splitten*, 159
spoil, 47
spoils system, 216
spoke (of a wheel), 60
sponge, 87
(spook) *spooke*, 203
(spool) *spole*, 159
spoor, 192
sport, 5
(spur) *spuron*, 60
squash (vegetable), 202, 220
St. Croix (p), 202
St. John (p), 202
St. Lawrence (p), 202
St. Louis (p), 213
stable (horses), 111
stake a claim, 216
(stallion) *staloun*, 111
(stampede) *estampida*, 214
(starboard) *stiurbordaz*, 52
star, 47
starve, 92
steam, 195
Steamboat Springs (p), 215
Steele (f), 141
(steering) *stiuringe*, 52

stellar, 47
(steppe) *step'*, 191
stern (ship), 52
stirrup, 60
stockfish, 111, 159
stone, 33
(stool) *stole*, 111
[stoop (porch)] *stoep*, 203
stories, 110
stove, 56
stream, 51
street, 66
strike, 217
strikebreaker, 217
strike it rich, 216
striped bass, 201
stripteaser, 31
stroke (cajole), 289
stucco, 156
sturgeon, 51, 101, 111
(subject) *subget*, 110
subjugated, 96
substance, 112
succotash, 19, 202, 220
suede, 18, 190
sugar, 19; *sugre*, 111; *sukkar*, 120, 193
summary, 119
(summer) *sumaraz*, 67
(Sunday) *sunnondagaz*, 68
superman, 118
superhuman, 118
(surgeon) *surgien*, 112
surpass, 4
Susquehanna (p), 19, 202
Sussex (p), 76
swan, 51
Swann (f), 142
sweatshop, 216
Swedes, 43
swine, 32; *swin*, 105
switch (railroad), 217
(sword) *swerda*, 61
Syracuse (p), 215

Taber (f), 142
(table) *tabula*, 100, 110
(taboo) *tabu*, 192
(tabor) *tabour*, 111
(tackle) *takel*, 159
taco, 221
take a look-see, 257
taken aback, 265
tallow, 53
tamale, 221
[tank (all senses)] *tankh*, 193–4
Tanner (f), 140

tanning, 100
tape-recorder, 31
tar, 52
[tart (pastry)] *tarte*, 111
Taverner (f), 140
(tea) *t'e*, 191
teak, 19, 193
teat, 101
telegraph, 216
telephone, 216
telescope, 31, 99
temptation, 110
ten, 46
Tennessee (p), 212
tequila, 214, 221
termination, 279
termination with extreme prejudice, 278
terrible, 112, 285
(testimony) *testimonie*, 110, 119
textile, 31
Thames (p), 206
Thatcher (f), 141
the old army game, 277
their, 92
them, 92
thesaurus, 5
they, 92
Thompson (f), 138
thread, 33
three, 46
thug, 193
(Thursday) *Thor*, 68
(thyme) *thym*, 111
tick (bedding), 66
tie (RR), 217
tile, 66
tin, 60
(tobacco) *tabaco*, 157
(toboggan) *tobakan*, 213
Toller (f), 142
toll (*e.g.*, highway), 66
(tomahawk) *tamahak* (p), 202
(tomato) *tomatl*, 158
Tombstone (p), 215
tone, 111
(tongs) *tanguz*, 61
tonic, 156
tool, 57
(tor) *torr*, 82
tortilla, 221
towel, 56
town, 62
(tragedy) *tragedie*, 112
(traitor) *traitour*, 110
transfusion, 98

SUBJECT INDEX